From Piety to Professionalism—
And Back?

From Piety to Professionalism—
And Back?

Transformations of Organized Religious Virtuosity

Patricia Wittberg

LEXINGTON BOOKS

A division of
ROWMAN & LITTLEFIELD PUBLISHERS, INC.
Lanham • Boulder • New York • Toronto • Oxford

LEXINGTON BOOKS

A division of Rowman & Littlefield Publishers, Inc.
A wholly owned subsidiary of The Rowman & Littlefield Publishing Group, Inc.
4501 Forbes Boulevard, Suite 200
Lanham, MD 20706

PO Box 317
Oxford
OX2 9RU, UK

British Library Cataloguing in Publication Information Available

Library of Congress Cataloging-in-Publication Data

Wittberg, Patricia, 1947–
 From piety to professionalism and back? : transformations of organized religious
virtuosity / Patricia Wittberg.
     p. cm.
 Includes bibliographical references and index.
 ISBN-13: 978-0-7391-1377-6 (cloth : alk. paper)
 ISBN-10: 0-7391-1377-1 (cloth : alk. paper)
 ISBN-13: 978-0-7391-1378-3 (pbk. : alk. paper)
 ISBN-10: 0-7391-1378-X (pbk. : alk. paper)
 1. Women in charitable work—United States. 2. Monastic and religious life of
women—United States. 3. Women in the professions—United States. 4. Group
identity—United States. 5. Religious institutions—United States. I. Title.
HV541.W57 2006
261'.1—dc22   2005029565

Printed in the United States of America

♾™ The paper used in this publication meets the minimum requirements of American
National Standard for Information Sciences—Permanence of Paper for Printed Library
Materials, ANSI/NISO Z39.48–1992.

For Sisters, Deaconesses, and Mission Society members everywhere

Contents

Tables

Acknowledgments

This book has been "in process" for almost eight years—since the spring of 1998, in fact. During this time, I have benefitted from the help of more people than can possibly be mentioned here. Without their assistance, I could never have completed this work.

My gratitude goes, first of all, to the Indiana University Center on Philanthropy, the Baltimore Regional Community of the Sisters of Mercy, and the Sisters of Charity of Cincinnati, who provided funding for my research. I hope that, upon reading the finished product, they will consider their money well-spent.

Sister Mary Aquin O'Neill, RSM, first alerted me to the similarities in the experiences of Catholic religious orders and Protestant Women's Missionary Societies, and provided me with my initial contacts within the United Methodist Church. Numerous individuals, including Barbara Campbell, Ruth Daugherty, Carolyn Marshall, and Mary Ruth Nickels, directed me to other Methodist deaconesses and the leadership of the United Methodist Women. These leaders—Joyce Sohl, Sarah Shingler, and Rita Gaither-Gant—and the leaders of the various Catholic religious orders—Sister Catherine Madigan, DC, Sister Jolise May, PHJC, Sister Mary Ellen Murphy, SC, Sister Rosalind Picot, RSM, and Sister Barbara Wheeley, RSM—kindly agreed to encourage their members to participate in the interviews. Jeannette Byrd, Sybil Dodson, Sister Particia Smith, RSM, Sister Paulette Williams, RSM, and Sister Jane Vogt, SC, facilitated arrangements at the various interview sites.

Several long-suffering persons read the entire manuscript in draft form and alerted me to numerous errors. As a result, this book is much better than it otherwise would have been. I owe a profound debt of gratitude to Sister Mary Stephen Brueggeman, PHJC, Barbara Campbell, Ruth Daugherty, Sister Jolise May, PHJC, Albert Meyer, Arlene Merritt, and Melanie Morey for their insights and feedback. Sister Mary Aquin O'Neill, RSM, and Sister Doris Gottemoeller, RSM, also provided valuable insights at various stages of the research. Here in the Sociology Department, Velma Graves and Whitney Hendress provided indispensible assistance in readying the manuscript for publication. Any remaining errors, of course are mine alone.

Acknowledgments

Finally, although they cannot be mentioned by name, I wish to thank the participants in the 36 focus groups and the 30 individual interviews. Their honesty, good humor, dedication, and obvious spiritual depth profoundly touched me and all those—my research assistants, the tape transcribers, and the students coding the transcripts—who came into contact with them, directly or indirectly. It is my deepest wish that the reader of this book will also come to value activist religious virtuosity through their words.

Patricia Wittberg, SC
Indianapolis
November 30, 2005

PART I

HISTORICAL AND THEORETICAL

OVERVIEW

Introduction

A Statement of the Problem

The involvement of churches and church groups in a wide variety of educational, health care, and social service organizations has been a taken-for-granted fact of life in North America and in Western Europe for several centuries. The Catholic sister in a hospital or classroom, the intrepid Protestant missionary in an Appalachian "holler" school or a Chinese clinic, and the Protestant deaconess in an inner-city mission or soup kitchen were staples of film and fiction, as well as an integral part of childhood memory for the lay men and women who had attended these schools, collected funds for visiting missionaries, and daydreamed of performing similar feats themselves one day. Most probably assumed that the involvement of church groups in such organizational activities was natural and normative.[1]

It is not. While most, if not all, religious traditions require their individual adherents to perform private acts of charity, for a religious group to construct and operate formal *organizations* which are specifically dedicated to education, health care, or social service has been far less common. Only within the last four or five centuries for Catholics—and the last two centuries for Protestants—has it been a common practice to create formal church groups for the express purpose of operating schools, hospitals, orphanages, and the like. Similar activities in Eastern Christianity, Buddhism, and Islam are more recent still.

And this period of active organizational involvement may already be ending, at least in Western Europe and North America. Many religious colleges and hospitals—where few if any Catholic nuns or Protestant deaconesses remain on staff—have loosened or severed their ties to their parent denominations. The bureaucratic regulations associated with public funding insure that those organizations which nominally remain under denominational control increasingly resemble their secular counterparts. Despite the desire of government authorities to channel more public monies through church social services, the actual willingness and ability of churches to operate such organizations in today's society is problematic.[2]

What are the implications of this change? The impact on the schools, hospitals,

3

and social agencies is fairly clear: increasing isomorphic pressures to conform to secular models. A lively debate exists over whether religious organizations will be able to resist this pressure. But what effects will their withdrawal have on the denominations that once sponsored these organizations? Even more specifically, what will be the impact on the denominational groups—Catholic religious orders, Protestant deaconesses, mission societies—that had been expressly created to administer, staff, and finance them?

Historical Background

The Novel Idea of This-Worldly Religious Virtuosity

At least since Max Weber's seminal work on the subject, social scientists have known that, while a division between mass and virtuoso religiosity occurs in many faith traditions,[3] the actual form and content of religious virtuosity manifests itself in widely varied ways.[4] Virtuoso practice may be a temporary life cycle stage for every adherent in one religious tradition, but a lifelong commitment for a small spiritual elite in another. In some traditions, only males may follow the higher spiritual path; in others, most of the virtuosi may be women. Some virtuosi are expected to live as solitary hermits or wandering pilgrims; others may reside together in stable monastic communities. In one religion, the virtuosi may serve as revered teacher-gurus to the spiritually immature; in another, they may avoid all contact with the outside world. If an organized religion possesses a formally-established priestly hierarchy, the virtuosi may be expected to be members of it—or they may be rigorously excluded. Some religions contain two or more versions of virtuoso spirituality, coexisting in varying degrees of harmony or mutual suspicion.[5]

Whatever their particular practices or lifestyles, religious virtuosi in most faith traditions have usually focused on attaining, or helping others to attain, some form of inner spiritual perfection. Instead of being expected to nurse the sick, care for the poor, or teach orphans—or even to grow the food for their own sustenance— "an essential feature of all virtuoso leadership [was] its complete separation . . . from direct labor and economic employment."[6] In fact, religious virtuosi in many traditions, from medieval Franciscans to Theravada Buddhist monks, were bound to mendicancy. Giving alms to one of these "professional poor" was considered more spiritually meritorious than giving alms to the merely materially poor.[7] While many early monastic orders did perform large-scale social services within their walls—conducting a monastic school, for example, or caring for the aged and the sick—they had *not* originally been established for this purpose. Similarly, the mendicant orders of the thirteenth and fourteenth centuries were geared primarily to saving the souls of others. Only as a "by-product" of this evangelization interest did they concern themselves with performing other charitable practices.[8]

The Protestant Reformation challenged the validity of this type of religious virtuosity. The Reformers argued that Catholicism's religious orders were useless and parasitic. This was especially true, they felt, of the women's orders:

> Protestantism attacked the spirituality most associated with women, denying the redemptive value of prayer and sacrifice. The mystical power nuns derived from reception of the Eucharist was scorned. Processions and chanting, the extrasacramental liturgies that accumulated indulgences, came under attack. . . . Thus the monastic life, based on the idea of saving souls . . . through prayer and self-mortification became a futile exercise.[9]

According to Weber, a key characteristic of Protestantism was its demand that all Christians work out their salvation "*solely* through the ethical quality of [their] conduct in this world. . . . Rationally raised to a vocation, everyday conduct becomes the locus for proving one's state of grace."[10] Protestant women were told that their true vocation was to be wives and mothers, raising and educating the next generation of Christians within the confines of their families. Their husbands were to seek holiness through diligent work at their trades and through personal study of the Scriptures, assisted by the teachings of their pastor in his Sunday sermons. All men and women were called equally to holiness within their everyday lives; the very idea of a separate and superior virtuoso state was vehemently rejected.

This rejection of a separate virtuoso path had an unanticipated side effect: it inhibited the development of organized service efforts by the churches in Protestant countries. In so far as the poor, the sick, or the uneducated were to be assisted in their need, it was considered to be the responsibility of the Christian common-wealth, and not of monastic virtuosi, to provide schools, hospitals, and social services for them.[11] As one historian has noted: "By the beginning of the modern period, congregations in the state churches of Europe had relinquished most social-welfare responsibilities to the state and had limited *diakonia* mainly to an expression of individual Christian piety."[12]

Only limited expressions of organized service survived within Protestantism. In some denominations, each individual congregation's pastor—aided, perhaps, by a locally-selected deacon or deaconess—was to see to any needs which arose among his own flock.[13] This tactic was especially favored by congregationally-organized denominations attempting to revive the primitive, non-institutional lifestyle of the apostolic era. Such groups were deeply suspicious of any attempts to establish human organizations within the church for addressing the needs of the poor, and preferred that each separate local congregation take care of its own members.[14]

In response to the challenge of the Reformers, some sixteenth century Catholics also began to question the value of the traditional, spiritually-focused religious virtuosity which had been prevalent during the Middle Ages. Rather than discard the concept altogether, however, men and women such as Ignatius of

Loyola, Vincent de Paul, and Angela Merici created a *new* form of religious virtuosity within Catholicism, one which incorporated many of the welfare policies advocated by Catholic Humanists and Protestants.[15] Their "apostolic" orders[16] enshrined active service—teaching, nursing, caring for the poor—on an equal plane with spiritual exercises.[17] Indeed, the desire personally to tend the poor, sick, and uneducated was characteristic of these new orders—in sharp contrast to the mendicant friars of the thirteenth and fourteenth centuries, who had preferred to encourage their lay listeners to meet these needs on a private basis.[18] And, whereas Catholic laity in the late medieval period had established religious fraternities primarily for mutual benefit or to organize festivals, Counter-Reformation Catholics developed lay confraternities devoted to charitable work among the sick and poor.[19]

The religious tension between the two poles of active service and personal spiritual growth, which had always existed in Catholic religious virtuosity to some extent, was felt much more acutely in these new apostolic orders.[20] As late as the nineteenth century, there was a strong tendency within both the Church hierarchy and the orders themselves to see the purely contemplative life as the superior—and active service as the inferior—spiritual path. And in Eastern Christian traditions, religious orders continued their traditional emphasis on inner-focused virtuosity:

> Traditionally in Orthodoxy there have never been separate religious orders dedicated to particular apostolic works, whether of teaching, nursing, social care, or evangelism. In principle, the Orthodox monastery is not particularly concerned with any of these things. It is concerned to celebrate the liturgy and provide a place in which the men and women who join them can work out their salvation with fear and trembling. Many insist that that is still the work of a monastery and that to do anything else is to distract them from their primary role and lead to corruption.[21]

Religious traditions that deny the value of a separate, inner-oriented form of religious virtuosity, as the Protestant reformers did, are relatively rare.[22] For a religion to develop an alternate form of virtuosity centered on external service in the larger society, as Catholicism did after the Reformation, is also unusual. For several hundred years, however, Catholicism's hybrid form of religious virtuosity proved a useful social invention for church officials wishing to address the social dislocations of an industrializing Europe. During the nineteenth century, therefore, the number of the new active orders grew exponentially: from six orders to 35 in Ireland between 1800 and 1900; from 31 to 175 in England and Wales between 1857 and 1937. In France, four hundred new active orders for women were founded between 1800 and 1888.[23] The percentage of religious orders that continued to follow the traditional, contemplative, version of Catholic religious virtuosity steadily declined: while still a majority of the orders in 1800, such groups comprised only 11 percent by 1917.

By the nineteenth century, even Protestants, despite their initial reluctance to embrace something that resembled Catholic religious orders, had begun to recognize the need for organized groups of men and (especially) of women to perform the Church's missionary and charitable services. As a Protestant clergyman in the U.S. wrote in 1903:

> In the seventeenth and the first half of the eighteenth century, the public appearance of women in Christian work is scarcely known, and perhaps in no period of church history was the co-operation of women less sought. At the beginning of the Reformation the cloisters were closed, the only remaining opportunity for the exercise of Christian benevolence by women being thus cut off.[24]

Several Protestant denominations thus began to channel lay virtuoso enthusiasm into social service in an organized way. In Germany, for example, the Inner Light Mission Movement attempted to catalyze a concerted effort within Lutheranism that would unite all the denomination's separate organizations and charities into a single, Church-sponsored home mission organization, the better to respond to the spiritual and social needs of society.[25] German Protestants also combined to send 521 ordained missionaries to Asia, Africa, Latin America, and the West Indies by 1890; England sent 1,002 in the same period. On the home mission front, English churches also began mobilizing their members to conduct "Sunday Schools," in order to inculcate literacy, cleanliness, and religion in child factory workers. By 1811, 500,000 children attended these schools.[26] English Anglicans went so far as to revive religious orders within the official Church structure: by 1900, there were over 2,000 Anglican sisters serving in schools, hospitals, and orphanages throughout Great Britain.

Similar pressures were felt in the United States, as the original Protestant ideology of a Christian Commonwealth abated. As early as the eighteenth century, "Puritan leaders like Cotton Mather were urging their congregations to establish the Kingdom of God on earth through the voluntary action of congregations and reform societies rather than through the instruments of government—which they could no longer control."[27] The British Sunday School Movement was imported to New York in 1816; by 1828, Movement activists estimated that 345,000 children, or one-seventh of all school-aged children in the United States, attended a Sunday School. By mid-century, the role of the Sunday School teacher had expanded to include visiting the families of her pupils: an early form of social work. In the early nineteenth century, Protestant women also began to organize benevolent and missionary societies in cities from Boston to Charleston. The first such group was formed in Boston in 1802 by Baptist women; Presbyterian women established a similar society in Pennsylvania in 1812 and in Charleston in 1814. By 1835, there were 680 such associations in the United States.[28] In subsequent decades, these women busied themselves in distributing tracts, collecting pennies for orphanages and trade schools, and serving as "friendly visitors" to uplift the poor.[29] Throughout the early nineteenth century, Protestant women established hundreds of urban missions in the burgeoning cities of the United States.

The Civil War caused a brief hiatus in this missionary activity; afterwards, a new wave of women's missionary societies arose in the United States. "Unlike prewar aid societies that organized for a specific project and then disbanded, . . . the postwar societies became a permanent fixture in the late nineteenth century Evangelical Church."[30] As one historian of the period noted: "The standard cluster of women's benevolent organizations in any given white Protestant church included at least one mission society, a cent or mite society, an education society, and a Dorcas society for relief of the poor."[31] In many parts of the country, such societies were the only available organizational outlet for women's talents.

By 1882, there were at least sixteen women's home and foreign mission societies in the United States, which had raised almost six million dollars and sent out 694 single female missionaries.[32] In the South, Baptist women alone raised $75,000 between 1874 and 1884. So many societies were founded or consolidated between 1870 and 1880 that the executive of one such Presbyterian group labeled this period the "Church Women's Decade."[33] By 1900, the societies were supporting 856 single female missionaries, 359 missionary wives, 96 doctors, and numerous educational and health care institutions. The Presbyterian Bureau of Home Missions raised over $500,000 in a single year in 1905. Overall, the women of the mission societies raised over $42 million between 1860 and 1911 to support the foreign missions.[34]

By 1915, there were 40 denominational mission societies in the United States, containing over three million members, and supporting over 9,000 foreign missionaries. Another seven had been formed in Canada.[35] One author calls these mission societies "the largest of the great nineteenth century women's movements, and perhaps the largest nineteenth century religious movement in America."[36] By the turn of the twentieth century, the women's missionary societies formed almost the entire service arm of U.S. Protestant denominations.

Between the sixteenth and the nineteenth centuries, therefore, a distinct form of religious virtuosity achieved hegemony in Western Christianity, both in its Protestant and its Catholic versions. In this new form, the active provision of needed services was given equal, if not greater, weight over prayer and personal spiritual growth. And these services were not merely financed by the churches. They were also staffed and administered by denominational groups of women which had been established expressly for this purpose. More than 600 new religious orders were founded in Catholicism worldwide between 1800 and 1900, almost all of which were devoted to teaching, nursing, or social work.[37] Many Protestant denominations in Europe and the United States revived the office of deaconess at this time. By 1884, there were sixty Deaconess Houses in Germany, France, Switzerland, and Scandinavia, housing over 6,000 deaconesses. Within the United States, the northern branch of the Methodist Church commissioned its first deaconesses in 1888; the southern branch did so in 1903. By 1904, Methodist deaconesses numbered 450, and counted 906 by 1936.[38] There were 85 Methodist

Deaconess homes in the United States by the early twentieth century, and 110 world-wide.[39] Orders of deaconesses were also established in the Episcopal and German Reformed churches, and the Congregationalists, Baptists, and Presbyterians were considering similar programs. In Canada, Methodists began to commission deaconesses in 1893; Presbyterians did so in 1909. The total number of deaconesses in North America never matched the number in Europe, however, possibly because they had to compete with the various women's missionary societies for members.[40] Also, the requirement that deaconesses remain single was a deterrent, since the overwhelming majority of mission society members were married.

The missionaries' schools and clinics had the additional effect of spreading the concept of active religious virtuosity world-wide. By the mid-twentieth century, the novel idea that providing a concrete service could be an appropriate task for religious virtuosi was spreading to Hinduism, Buddhism, and Eastern Christianity.[41] In more recent decades, organized Islamic societies often provide the only social and educational services available to the poor in many Middle Eastern countries.

Service Institutions as a Component of Religious Virtuosity

After the mid-nineteenth century, the unique service focus of religious virtuosity in Western Christianity developed a second distinctive characteristic: increasingly, this service was dispensed, not by individuals on a one-to-one basis, but through large-scale institutions. The active orders in sixteenth century Catholicism and the early Protestant pastors and deacons had conducted their works of charity primarily on a personalized basis, visiting the sick in their own homes, conducting small parish catechism schools, sheltering orphans within the convent itself, and generally providing assistance as the need arose.[42] The early Ursulines, Daughters of Charity, and Jesuits did not reside in monasteries, but lived singly or in small groups among the people they served.

By the seventeenth century, however, European Catholics had come to believe that "[t]he informal, haphazard charity of monasteries, parishes and individuals was no longer adequate for the numbers of poor that filled the cities."[43] Increasingly, Catholic charitable works in Europe took on an institutional character, and religious orders began to be founded for the express purpose of running these institutions.[44] This view was imported to the U.S. and Australia by Catholic immigrants in the nineteenth and early twentieth centuries:

> Given their limited financial resources, institution-building seemed to them the most efficient way to assist the poor. . . . An imposing array of orphanages, hospitals, schools, and social agencies, most of them staffed by orders of nuns, had become the hallmark of Catholic philanthropy by 1890.[45]

By 1900, Catholic sisters ran 3,811 parochial schools, 633 girls' academies, 645 orphanages, and at least 500 hospitals in the United States.[46] The Sisters of Mercy also operated an employment service for immigrant women in New York City, which placed almost 17,000 women in "respectable situations" between 1849 and 1864. In England and Wales, the sisters operated over 100 orphanages, 18 industrial schools, 14 hospitals, and at least 25 homes for the aged. The public recognition gained through these institutions was a valuable "first-line defense" against Evangelical criticism that Catholic and Anglican religious orders were parasites on society.

Spurred on by a sense of "acute rivalry" with the Catholic orders, European and American Protestants began to realize the importance of establishing their own church-sponsored institutions.[47] As one Methodist woman complained in 1872:

> When will the women of America awake to a sense of their responsibility? And what great soul, filled with love to God and man, shall open the way and prepare the means whereby we may be enabled to compete successfully with our Sisters of Rome, not only as general charity women, educators, and succorers of the unfortunate, but especially as nurses of the sick—a department of such great good to soul and body, yet so long monopolized by the daughters of Rome? . . . If so much is accomplished by the desultory labors of Protestant women, how much greater success would crown concerted action![48]

Similar fears were voiced in England and Wales.

Protestant-sponsored social service and health care institutions thus began to proliferate in Europe, Australia, and North America. By the mid-nineteenth century in Germany, the Lutheran deaconess Motherhouse at Kaiserswerth "conducted a thriving and multifaceted enterprise consisting of a hospital, an orphanage, a nursery school, and a hostel for former female prisoners, facilities which administered nearly 150 nurses in the field and where some 300 teachers had been trained."[49]   In the United States, competing denominations and denominational groups established a plethora of hospitals, clinics, old age homes, orphanages, academies, settlement houses, rooming houses, and other less likely endeavors. Seventh-day Adventists created "a vast network of publishing facilities, an international system of hospitals, and the second largest parochial school system in the world," together with an assortment of vegetarian restaurants and health food companies. Through their institutions, the Adventists thus created "an alternate social system meeting the needs of Adventists from cradle to grave."[50] Even church-run savings banks could fulfill a Christian purpose: converting the poor to the exercise of prudence and thrift. By the late twentieth century, it was impossible even to imagine the denominations without the panoply of institutions they had founded.[51]

These institutions, and the denominations or denominational groups that staffed, funded, and administered them, have thus been intimately intertwined throughout their history. The relationship has been a complex and multifaceted one, resulting from the rich variety of formal and informal arrangements in the different denominations. Some institutions were directly established by the parent denomination; others were set up and operated under the aegis of an denominational subgroup—a Catholic religious order, for example, or a Protestant women's missionary society. Some of these groups owned, administered, staffed, and financed "their" institutions with no assistance at all from the larger denomination.[52] In other cases, a group might administer and staff an institution that was owned and financed by the larger denomination, or, alternatively, might own and fund an organization that was staffed by outside professionals.[53] In Europe, the state or local municipality usually owned the hospitals in which the nuns and deaconesses worked.[54]

Furthermore, the relationship has been a constantly evolving one. As their schools, hospitals and social service agencies grew, the role of the sponsoring group often changed from *providing* the services themselves, to *supervising* others who provided them, and, finally, to *controlling,* through their presence on the boards of directors, those who administered the provision of the services.[55] As the institutions expanded and professionalized, the committed virtuoso workers—nuns, deaconesses, home missionaries—were increasingly outnumbered by officially credentialed lay professionals.[56] Institutions that had once been owned by a religious group became separately incorporated under lay boards. Denominational hospitals or colleges merged with former competitors—both with religious and secular nonprofits as well as with public and for-profit institutions.

Many studies have documented these changes from the institutions' perspective.[57] Critics have fretted that the attenuation of denominational ties has reached the point where formerly denominational institutions can no longer be considered religiously distinctive.[58] Much research has been conducted to explore the possible implications—both for the institutions themselves and for the larger society—of the institutions' loss of their religious identity.[59] The institutions themselves have rearranged their administrative hierarchies to incorporate "Mission Effectiveness" departments, in an attempt to define and retain what it is that makes their operations uniquely Catholic, Baptist, Methodist, or Lutheran.

But similar attention has not been paid to the implications for denominations and denominational groups of losing their institutional identities. It is probable, however, that religious sponsors have been at least as profoundly changed by loosening their ties to their sponsored schools, hospitals, and social agencies, as the institutions themselves have been changed by their absence. Yet, in study after study, the importance of schools or hospitals for the sponsoring denomination, religious order, or missionary society has been duly noted at the outset and then ignored in the subsequent discussion.[60]

The present book is intended to redress this omission. Its main argument is that the attenuation or dissolution of their institutional ties has affected denominations —and especially specific denominational subgroups such as Catholic religious orders, Protestant deaconesses, or women's missionary societies—in profoundly important ways: shifting or obliterating their recruitment bases, eroding their power both in society and in the larger denomination, altering the backgrounds and expectations of their leaders, and often causing fundamental transformations in the very identity and culture of the groups themselves. It is beyond the scope of this book to say whether such changes are desirable or deplorable, inevitable or contingent. But their depth and extent are such as to merit closer examination.

Organizational Theories: Review and Application

The theoretical lens which will be used to examine this topic is that of organizational sociology. In previous decades, organizational theories were rarely applied to churches.[61] Since the early 1990s, however, several researchers have begun to investigate the factions and insurgencies, the adaptation and co-optation, the career ladders and labor markets within churches, using the insights and methodologies gained from research on their secular counterparts.[62] Still, none of these previous works directly address the impact on the churches of losing their sponsored institutions. The present work will draw on two theoretical schools within the sociology of organizations, neo-institutionalism and theories of organizational culture, to address this issue.

Theories of Organizational Culture

A recent school of organizational theory sees every organization as permeated by a distinct culture and identity, which expresses itself in rituals (of passage, of integration, of conflict resolution), in symbols (including dress and office decor), and in the sagas, stories, myths, and jokes that are told and retold among members.[63] These cultural elements serve as a "tool kit" with which the members of an organization construct "strategies of action."[64] The cultural elements in its "tool kit" thus determine the choices and activities of the organization. But, on a more profound level, the choices and actions of the organization also shape the values and beliefs of its members, and their conception of its very identity.[65] In a reciprocal process, therefore, the organization's choices and activities, its values and beliefs, shape and re-shape each other.

Initial writings on organizational culture tended to focus more on its value components. From this perspective, it was the *values* of an organization, both expressed and latent, that shaped and were shaped by the activities of its members. More recently, however, writers have begun to focus more on the *cognitive* components of organizational culture: on the members' unquestioned assumptions about the basic identity of the organization they inhabit, the benign or malign character of its larger environment, the challenges it currently faces, how urgent its problems are, and how amenable they are to solution.[66] Some organizations may possess a single uniform culture, but it is more likely that different administrative or work units within an organization will each possess a different and often competing subculture.[67] Over time, in fact, organizations tend to drift toward "hybrid" cultural identities, whose component parts may be unrelated or even contradictory.

Still other organizations may not possess a coherent cultural identity at all. Their members "do not agree on clear boundaries, cannot identify shared solutions, and do not reconcile contradictory beliefs and multiple identities. . . . The members contend they belong to a culture. They share a common orientation and overriding purpose, face similar problems, and have comparable experiences." But each member interprets and enacts these commonalities so differently "as to make what is shared seem vacuously abstract."[68] Moreover, these interpretations are in constant flux. It therefore becomes hard for members to agree on exactly what the purpose of the organization is, or how it should go about achieving its purpose if it has one.[69] This state of organizational ambiguity differs from mere uncertainty in that it cannot be remedied simply by amassing more facts. Indeed, additional information may actually make the ambiguity more acute.[70]

The most commonly postulated roots of organizational cultures are internal to the organization: the personality and vision of the founder and first members, the *esprit de corps* developed by common activities in the initial years, and "homosocial recruiting" whereby new recruits are hired because of their similarity to the current members.[71] Researchers who emphasize the cognitive components of organizational culture also note that the vocabulary developed during the first year of an organization's existence continues to interpret its identity to subsequent members. Once this initial "sensemaking" is done, it is extremely resistant to change.[72]

The concepts and hypotheses of organizational culture theories would thus lead the researcher to investigate the effects of this early cultural "imprinting" upon the identity of religious orders, denominational missionary societies, and deaconess groups.[73] While many of these groups could cite official theological or scriptural bases for their initial identities, their early years were also shaped by the schools, hospitals, and social work agencies which they had been founded to staff and maintain. Each group's identity and *raison d'etre*, therefore, were strongly influenced by these institutions, and their service in them attracted the kinds of new members who believed in and perpetuated this identity. Subcultures within a group often arose, based on the type of services provided in its institutions. Internal leadership ladders reflected corresponding institutional administrative ladders, with consequent impacts on the cognitive culture of the group's leaders.

Neo-Institutional Theories

In addition to the cultural impact of an organization's initial "imprinting" and its early history, however, one must also consider the influence of its surrounding environment. This has been less commonly done. Previous organizational culture theorists, when they considered external environments at all, tended to focus primarily on the national "feeder cultures," which provide all of an organization's members with the beliefs, values, and ideas prevalent in their country.[74] But the other organizations in its environment—its "organizational field"—are equally influential in shaping of an organization's culture. For the most part, however, research on these organizational fields has been conducted, not by culture theorists, but by a second theoretical school: that of Neo-Institutionalism.[75] According to neo-institutional theory, a hospital's organizational field would include other hospitals, insurance companies, physicians' and nurses' associations, pharmaceutical companies, training schools, governmental oversight agencies, and the like; a college's would include accrediting agencies, professional associations, "feeder" high schools, foundations, equipment suppliers, and, of course, competing colleges. The organizational field for a denominational group such as a religious order or a Protestant women's missionary society would include other, similar groups (other religious orders, other orders of deaconesses, women's missionary societies in other denominations), as well as denominational officials, charitable donors within and outside the denomination, and the educational and service organizations to which the group was originally tied. Organizational fields intersect and diverge: a religious order is merely one component (along with the other, secular, elements listed above) of its hospital's organizational field; the hospital, in turn, is only one component of the order's field. The strength and salience of the field ties may increase or decrease over time—and not necessarily in tandem with each other. A denomination or a religious group may become a less important element of its college's organizational field, but the reverse may not be the case.

The accumulated expectations of the other actors in an organizational field "institutionalize" the field, making it difficult for a single organization within the field to deviate in any significant way.[76] Pressures for institutional conformity arise from several sources. "Coercive pressures" develop from government mandates, tax laws, or the requirements of accrediting agencies. "Normative pressures" are embodied in the training courses and expectations of the professional schools which provide the organization's workers, and in the cultures of the foundations which provide its funds. And "mimetic pressures" arise in times of uncertainty, when each organization tends to model itself, consciously or unconsciously, on what its competitors are doing.[77] Over time, the combined effect of these pressures is "institutional isomorphism": a hospital, a college, or a social agency tends increasingly to resemble all of the other hospitals, colleges, or social agencies—religious or secular—in its organizational field.[78] A religious order or a missionary society may likewise experience isomorphic pressures to imitate the practices of other orders/societies.[79]

What happens when one component of an organizational field experiences isomorphic changes and other components do not, or when two components change in mutually incompatible ways? This difficulty may be especially likely to arise if, for example, religious colleges or hospitals begin to mimic the standards and practices of their secular counterparts while their religious sponsors model themselves on other orders or mission societies. The competing expectations in the resulting field environments may place contradictory demands on the component organizations. Such organizations may then experience "disagreement and confusion regarding core vision and mission, high uncertainty levels within subcultures, clinging to 'traditions' that thwart innovation, and low morale at key organizational levels."[80] In short, they are likely to exist in that state of cultural ambiguity and fragmentation studied by organizational culture theorists.

In some cases, an organizational paralysis may develop from such competing environmental pressures, resulting in an inability to make any decisions at all. "An organization that makes no decisions is a non-organization; it is disorganized. It neither takes binding actions nor makes compelling reasons."[81] In other unstable environments, "organized anarchies" may arise. Organizations then become "a collection of choices looking for problems, issues and feelings looking for decisions-in-process through which they can be mediated, and solutions looking for questions."[82] Members of organizational anarchies view sustained commitment to any one course of action as something to be avoided.

"Because they generate so many commitments and justifications, anarchies should make more sense to members than they do to observers."[83] But the outside observers are the ones who may be needed to funnel necessary resources—including new members—to the anarchic organization. To keep from alienating these outside observers while preserving their autonomy of action, organizations may actively *cultivate* institutional ambiguity: "Mission vagueness permits managers and trustees to alter behavior in response to changing financial constraints while—at least arguably—continuing pursuit of the same goals."[84]

Changes in institutional fields, therefore, may lead to fragmentation and paralysis—or to adaptation and change—in the cultures of component organizations. The very identity of an organization may change when its institutional field changes.[85] However, organizational culture researchers have "been very slow to acknowledge environmental influences such as these organizational fields."[86] And the work of neo-institutional researchers and organizational ecologists, who *do* consider these influences, has remained largely separate from culture research, even though their descriptions of institutionally-embedded routines and structures appear quite similar to several of the definitions of organizational culture advanced by researchers in the former tradition.[87]

Theories of Secularization

The combined insights of Neo-Institutional and Organizational Culture theories for this book's topic also have implications for a third body of literature: the studies of secularization within the sociology of religion. The "inevitable" decline and marginalization of religion in the face of an ascendant secular society was taken for granted by sociologists from the early nineteenth to the mid-twentieth centuries. "Rationalization" theorists claimed that, on an individual level, modern men and women were less religious in both their beliefs and practices; societal-level "differentiation" explanations postulated an increasingly thorough removal of religious influences from education, the economy, and the state.[88] Recent researchers, however, have contended that such assumptions are exaggerated and premature, if not actually false.[89] On one hand, critics have noted that there has been little or no decline in individual religiosity: the average person is as religious —or irreligious—in belief and practice as s/he was in the so-called "golden ages" of twelfth century Catholic Europe or seventeenth century Puritan New England.[90] On the societal level, still other authors have postulated a postmodern "deprivatization" of religions seeking to reclaim authority in the public sphere.[91]

But both the micro and macro theories of secularization—or their more recent "desecularization" counterparts—have been less frequently applied to the intermediate levels of society.[92] Several of the weaknesses[93] of secularization theory —its over-abstraction, its lack of attention to human agency or other specific causal mechanisms—could be remedied by applying the insights of Neo-Institutionalism (coercive, normative, and mimetic pressures on religious organizations), or of Organizational Culture theory. To the extent that differentiation processes are leaching religion from schools, hospitals, social service agencies and the like, some degree of isomorphic pressure is probably responsible. And the privatization of religion and personal belief may well be a response of church members—especially virtuoso members of religious orders or mission societies—to the attenuation of a meaningful religious culture in these organizations, as well as to the lack of an operant connecting tie between sponsor and institution.

Research Focus

In examining the impact of organizational withdrawal on denominations and denominational groups, therefore, this book will also be attempting a previously neglected synthesis of two schools of organizational sociology—organizational culture and neo-institutionalism—with secularization and desecularization theories in the sociology of religion. How might these bodies of research apply to the shifting relationship between denominations or denominational groups, on the one hand, and the schools, hospitals, or welfare agencies they once operated? The first chapter of this book will briefly review the history of religious institutional sponsorship from its beginnings until 1960, focusing primarily on the cognitive and cultural value components which prompted churches and church groups to expend such a prodigious amount of time, energy, and money in establishing and nurturing so many of these organizations.

Part II will summarize historical findings on the *impacts* which these organizations had on their sponsoring denomination, religious congregation, order of deaconesses, or missionary society in the decades prior to 1960. In what way(s), if at all, did being connected with these organizations affect a denomination's or a religious group's identity and/or its articulation of its essential Christian mission? How clear was this identity/mission to its members? To outsiders? To denominational officials? Did organizational sponsorship unite a denominational sponsor, or fracture it into organization-based subcultures? These questions will be addressed in Chapter 2. What was the impact of the sponsoring group's organizational connections on the number and background of new members it was able to recruit? What was the impact on the number and background of the denominational and local church leaders? Chapter 3 will consider these issues. And Chapter 4 will ask how organizational sponsorship affected the power and role of the denomination within the larger society and of the denominational group within the denomination.

In Part III, Chapter 5 will briefly review the factors behind the withdrawal of religious sponsors after 1960, concentrating primarily on the ways that organizational sponsorship became ideologically or organizationally problematic both for the sponsors and for the institutions. In the language of secularization theory, the institutions "no longer need[ed] or [were] interested in maintaining a sacred cosmos or a public religious world view."[94] In the language of organizational theory, both the institutions and their religious sponsors were impacted by profound changes in the larger, national culture and in the respective organizational fields in which they were each imbedded. The isomorphic changes in their institutions might in turn affect the culture of the sponsoring religious group, privatizing its religious focus and changing its very definition of religious virtuosity.[95]

Chapter 6 will outline the limited anecdotal and case study evidence for these impacts, both on the sponsoring religious group and on the larger denomination. This preliminary evidence has shown that, as a result of the loss of their institutions, religious sponsors have experienced a loss or alteration of their common identity, a lessened appreciation of the religious value of Christian organizational activities, a reduced ability to attract new members, and a constricted scope for action on the part of the group's leadership. For religious groups of women, there is also some indication that their power *vis à vis* the larger denomination has changed. Chapter 6 will also briefly review the alternative forms of "sponsorship" that religious groups have developed with their institutions.

Part IV will be devoted to exploring the impact of institutional loss in greater detail. In 1999 and 2000, I conducted 36 focus groups and numerous individual interviews with the members of three Catholic religious orders, one Protestant women's mission society, and an order of Protestant deaconesses.[96] This section of the book summarizes the patterns revealed in these interviews. Chapters 7 and 8 will explore the ways declining institutional sponsorship has affected the identity and basic goals of each order or society, both directly and through their lessened common activities. Chapter 9 will describe the development of an internal culture that devalues institutional maintenance in favor of alternative activities, together with some of the unexpected effects that institutional withdrawal has had on the employment opportunities for Catholic sisters and Protestant deaconesses. Chapter 10 will examine the competing ties of professional and religious commitments for these women, together with their loss of mentoring and leadership development opportunities. Chapter 11 will chart the impacts on the women's power in their respective denominations. Finally, Chapter 12 will reflect on the implications of institutional loss on the changing definitions of religious virtuosity and secularization in Western Christianity.

The world of the Reformation led to the creation of a unique type of Christian religious virtuosity, one that gave a spiritual meaning to organized service activities. Inspired by this virtuoso ideology, first Catholic and later Protestant women formed orders and societies expressly dedicated to the foundation, support, and operation of religious schools, hospitals, and social agencies of all sorts. As Christianity completes nearly half a millennium since the Reformation, however, the link forged between its traditional educational, health care, and social service organizations, on the one hand, and its theologies of holiness and spiritual progress on the other, are rapidly dissolving. The result will have profound implications for the denominations, for the virtuoso groups, and for society as a whole.

Notes

1. One could argue, looking at the present "Charitable Choice" initiatives, that many government officials still believe this, although some churches have their doubts. See Chaves (1999), Campbell (2002), and Pipes and Ebaugh (2002).

2. See Chaves (2004:75-93) and Pipes and Ebaugh (2002) for a discussion of this issue.

3. According to Max Weber (1958:287-88), all religions contain a majority of average, or "mass," adherents, together with a minority of "virtuosi" who are particularly interested in or able to attain valued religious states. These virtuosi may or may not be the officially-designated leaders of the religion. See also Silber (1995:1-2).

4. In previous works, I have outlined these differences in greater depth: see Wittberg (1994:14-22; 1996:19-31).

5. See Sharot (2001:81-89, 156-201) for examples of this in Taoism and Buddhism.

6. Turner (1991:89). See also Weber (1958:289).

7. Henderson (1994) and Riis (1997:130) both make this point for the Catholic mendicant orders of fourteenth through sixteenth century Europe. See Gutschow (2004:110-15) for the merit of giving to Buddhist nuns and monks.

8. Grell (1997:49).

9. McNamara (1996:419-20).

10. Weber (1958:291).

11. See Smylie (1986:212), Soly (1997:89), and Grell and Cunningham (1997:3-4) for this arrangement in Geneva and the Calvinist states of the sixteenth century. See Lindberg

(1986:179) and Cnaan et al. (1999:99) for a similar statement about early German Lutherans. Mitchison (2002) makes a similar point for nineteenth century Scotland. More recently, the governing body of the Jehovah's Witnesses stated that "it was not the function of the Society to operate hospitals and clinics, just as it was not its function to run police and fire departments" (Cumberland, 1986:472).

12. Lindberg (1986:190).

13. See Klaassen (1986:276) for this arrangement among the Mennonites; Vanderpool (1986) and Cnaan et al. (1999:112) among the eighteenth and early nineteenth century Methodists and Anglicans; Grell (1997:50) and Grell and Cunningham (1997:9) for the seventeenth century Calvinists.

14. According to Alexander Campbell, the founder of the Disciples of Christ: "The early Christian churches were not fractured into missionary societies, bible societies, education societies; nor did they dream of organizing such a world. . . . They knew nothing of the hobbies of modern times. In their church capacity alone they moved." (Quoted in Harrell 1986:383).

15. Grell (1997:48).

16. Strictly speaking, many of these active groups were not religious "orders," since "orders," especially for women, were required by Rome to be cloistered contemplatives. The official term for the new active women's groups, therefore, was not "orders" but rather "congregations" or "societies of the apostolic life." However, since the term "congregation" is more usually applied to local church congregations, I will rarely use it here to refer to the Catholic religious groups. Also, strictly speaking, "nuns" are members of cloistered, contemplative "orders," while "sisters" are members of active, apostolic "congregations." In this work, however, I will follow the colloquial practice of using the two terms interchangeably.

17. Indeed, according to Rapley (2001:15), apostolic service was the *primary* objective of some of these groups, displacing even prayer.

18. Henderson (1999:58). As Coser noted: "While the pre-eminent objective of the monastic community [was] care for the salvation and perfection of the souls of its own members, the prime task of the Jesuit, though not unmindful of his own soul, [was] the care and perfection of the souls of others" (Coser 1974:120).

19. Grell and Cunningham (1999:5), Pullan (1999:22), and Jones (1999:228) all make this point.

20. Silber (1995:204-5) makes this point. See Wittberg (1996:64) for documentation of the assertion in the following sentence.

21. Stebbing (2001:227).

22. In addition to Protestantism, one might also place Sunni Islam and rabbinic Judaism in this category: "Separate and supererogatory piety, such as is represented in other religions by monasticism, played no role in rabbinic Judaism. Jews could not escape from the world to find God; they met him in their daily lives. They saw their task to be sanctifying the world as given, not leaving it to find a higher way" (Cohn 1987:92. See also Dorff 1986:9). Sharot (2001:202-9) notes, however, that, while *official* Islam and Judaism admitted of no division between virtuoso and mass paths to salvation, both venerated saints in their popular versions and among sectarian groups such as the Hasidim and Sufis. One might also argue that to be a Jew in the predominantly Christian environment of Europe required *all* Jews to take a virtuoso or sectarian oppositional stance. Prior to the destruction of the temple and the dispersal of the Jewish people, Judaism did have virtuosi: the brotherhoods of the prophets and the Essenes, for example. And in modern Israel, the ultra-

Orthodox communities may serve a similar virtuoso function. Similarly, the ultra-orthodox Islamist graduates of the madrasas may be an example of rising religious virtuosity in contemporary Islam.

23. See Clear (1987:35) for the Irish figures, Walsh (2002:1, 63) for the English figures, Langlois (1984:152, 308, 520, 545) for France. Similar growth can be calculated for Poland (Bukowczyk 1988:24-25), Quebec (Denault 1975:42-43), and the United States (Finke and Stark 1992:135; Ewens 1981:101; 1989b:18; Dolan 1985:220, 356). See Walsh (2002:18, 21) for the figures on the decline of contemplative orders in the following sentence.

24. Golder (1903:171). See also Miller (1985:32-33).

25. Lindberg (1986:189). See Field (1974:36) for the figures on German and English missionaries in the following sentence.

26. Van Liere (1991:28). This was not a new idea. As early as 1592, the Protestant clergy of Antwerp had begun Sunday schools to educate children in religion and basic literacy. By 1620, these schools had 3,200 pupils aged seven to fifteen (Soly 1997:101). The first English Charity Schools were established in 1698 to teach poor children to read the Bible and catechism. By 1715, 25,000 English children attended these schools in their local parish churches (Cnaan et al. 1999:100). For the figures on the Anglican religious orders in the next sentence, see Dunstan (2003).

27. Hammack (1998:38). See Miller (1985:144, 147, 158), and Boyd and Brackenridge (1983:176) for the information on the Sunday School Movement in the U.S.

28. Plus 923 men's associations, for a total of 1,603 (Beaver 1968:37).

29. See Miller (1985:113-14), Boyd and Brackenridge (1983:7-8), and Beaver (1968:35-43) for information on the activities of these groups.   Most of these early women's societies, while religious in inspiration, were unconnected with any particular denomination, in order to escape the control of the clergy (Ginzberg 1990:60; Miller 1985:84-86; Rosenberg 1971).

30. Friedman (1985:111).

31. Lebsock (1998:240). See Friedman (1985:113) for the assertion in the following sentence.

32. Brereton and Klein (1979:306). These included the Women's Board of Missions (Congregational, 1868), the Women's Foreign Missionary Society (Methodist Episcopal, 1869), the Woman's Foreign Missionary Societies of the Presbyterian Church, U.S.A. (1870), the Woman's Auxiliary (Protestant Episcopal, 1871), the Woman's Baptist Foreign Missionary Society (1873), the Woman's Parent Mite Missionary Society of the African Methodist Episcopal Church (1874), the Christian Women's Board of Missions (Disciples, 1874), the Woman's Board of Foreign Missions of the Reformed Church in America (1875), the Woman's Missionary Association of the United Brethren of Christ (1875), the Woman's American Baptist Home Missionary Society (1877), the Woman's Executive Committee for Home Missions (Presbyterian, 1878), the Woman's Board of Foreign Missions (Methodist Episcopal Church, South, 1878), the Woman's Missionary Society of the Evangelical Lutheran Church (1879), the Congregational Women's Home Missionary Association (1880), the Woman's Board of Foreign Missions of the Cumberland Presbyterian Church (1880), the Woman's Home Missionary Society (Methodist Episcopal, 1884), the Woman's Missionary Union (Auxiliary to the Southern Baptist Convention, 1888), and the Woman's Auxiliary, Presbyterian Church in the U.S. (1912). See Brereton and Klein (1979:305-6), Beaver (1968:98), and McDowell (1982:7-9).

33. Boyd and Brackenridge (1983:15). See Pearson (1990:137) for the 1900 figures.

See Friedman (1985:116) for the amount of money raised by Southern Baptist women; Boyd and Brackenridge (1983:49) for the Presbyterians.

34. Figures reported in Mobley (2003:169).

35. See Hill (1985:1, 3) for these figures. See Beaver (1968:86) for the Canadian figures. Note that this was *in addition to* the 2,406 missionaries sent overseas by the denominations' male-run, official, mission boards (Field 1974:38, 378 ftn. 12).

36. Hill (1985:23).

37. Cada et al. (1979:39). In France alone, there were at least 100,000 women in the new orders (Faure 2002:313). Fewer than 5 percent of the new groups were contemplative monastic ones, in contrast to earlier periods, when *all* the women's orders were monastic (Walsh 2002:18, 21).

38. Nelson (2001:137), Dougherty (1997:38-55), and McDowell (1982:64-65) report these figures.

39. Golder (1903:334). See Boyd and Brackenridge (1983) and Stebner (2003:58) for the information in the following sentences.

40. Golder (1903:306-7) argues that the existence of these mission societies is the reason why more American women did not become deaconesses; Brereton and Klein (1979:311) and Meeker (1969:96) come to a similar conclusion. Boyd and Brackenridge (1983:111-112) also attribute the relatively slow growth of the deaconess programs to Protestant fears of something which looked too "Catholic," and to questions about the apostolic basis for such an office. Also, the idea of deaconesses was not as attractive to middle-class Presbyterian women, due to the minimal educational opportunities in the program and to its identification with "tedious" works such as nursing. Missionary societies did, however, actively encourage young women to become deaconesses, and often paid for their training.

41. See Bartholomeusz (1994:148, 223) and Arai (1999:145) for the spread of activist religious virtuosity to Buddhism, Sundar (2001:273) for Hinduism, Stebbing (2001:227-28) for Romanian Orthodoxy, and van Doorn-Harder (1995:44, 78, 81, 114) for Coptic Christianity. According to Gutschow (2004:249), the adoption of an activist from of religious virtuosity has been recommended for Tibetan Buddhism by no less an authority than the Dalai Lama himself. She quotes a 1996 memorandum which states: "H.H. The Dalai Lama has repeatedly said that the time for monks and nuns to sit in the monasteries and pray is over. We should become trained as doctors, lawyers, and nurses to serve society, taking as our example the social activities of Christian monks and nuns."

42. Grell and Cunningham (1997:9-11).

43. Ranft (1998:118).

44. According to Hehir (1995:20), "The Catholic Church is institutional by instinct and by nature." Hogan (1996:146) notes that many Catholic religious orders, especially those founded since 1800, "have been founded to meet specific apostolic needs and have more of a charism of foundation" that stresses responding to the particular needs of a specific setting, rather than a particular variety of religious virtuosity unique to a given founder.

45. Oates (1999:15). See McGrath (1998:84) for the development of Catholic social service institutions in Australia at this time.

46. Evans (1981:103) and Finke and Stark (1992:134) report these figures for the U.S.; Walsh (2004:107; 2002:18, 175) for England. See Diner (1983:135) for the employment centers of the Sisters of Mercy. The Sisters operated similar agencies in other cities. Dunstan (2003:339-40) makes the observation about the public recognition of the sisters' valuable services.

47. Prelinger (1986a:216) notes this rivalry for nineteenth century England; Arrizabalaga (1999:170) for sixteenth century Spain. Colin Jones (1999:218) states that, in Counter-Reformation France, "there were few stronger stimulants to Catholic Charity . . . than the presence within the same locality of a Protestant community. Neither Protestant nor Catholic elites wanted their poorer brethren attracted into the opposing camp by the lure of more or better-attuned charitable provisions, and so an emulative process of bidding and counter-bidding occurred between the two sides." Keller (1981:253) cites a similar fear by Methodist women's missionary societies in the nineteenth century United States, when they were faced with the fact that over 500 Catholic nuns were evangelizing more women in India than the Methodist missionaries were. Miller (1985:184) notes that nineteenth century Presbyterians founded "female seminaries" largely in response to the perceived threat of the Catholic academies for young women which were operated by the nuns. Walsh (2002:31) and John T. Smith (1998:17, 67) note a similar Catholic-Protestant competition in England and Wales during the nineteenth and early twentieth centuries. In addition to this inter-denominational competition, the home and foreign mission societies in a single denomination often competed with each other (Boyd and Brackenridge 1983:56).

48. Susan M.D. Fry, quoted by Golder (1903:305, 309). See John T. Smith (1998:17, 67) for England and Wales.

49. Prelinger (1986a:215). See Diner (1983:131-33) for an extensive list of the Catholic institutions in the United States. See Dougherty (1981:213) for social work institutions operated by the Methodist deaconesses.

50. Vance (1999:66). See also Numbers and Larsen (1986:459) for the Seventh-day Adventist endeavors in health foods. See Schwartz (2000:46) for church-run savings banks.

51. Bontrager (1997:341) makes this point for Mennonite institutions, Vance (1999:61) for the Seventh-day Adventists.

52. This arrangement was typical of the hospitals and colleges run by Catholic religious orders in the United States during the nineteenth and early twentieth centuries.

53. The former situation would describe Catholic sisters in parish-owned elementary schools in the United States and Australia, and Protestant deaconesses in early twentieth century denominational hospitals. The latter situations would describe the early twentieth century mission works funded by Protestant Home Mission Societies and, more recently, that of Catholic sisters "sponsoring" the hospitals and colleges they no longer staff or own. See below, Chapter 6.

54. See Dross (2002:87) and Ramsey (2002:283) for examples.

55. An entire literature cites this transformation as evidence of one type of secularization in modern society. See Casanova (1994) and Chaves (1994).

56. According to Rabe (1974:63), this occurred in Protestant foreign mission societies as early as 1916.

57. Among them, see the works of Schier and Russett (2002), Dovre (2002), Daigler (2000), Gallin (2000, 1999, 1996), Hughes (1999), Shea (1999), Leahy (1997, 1991), Gleason (1995, 1967), Morey (1995), Sloan (1994), Annarelli (1987), Brewer (1987), Fitzgerald (1984), and Hassenger (1967) for denominational higher education. See Morey (2001), Nelson (2001), Risse (1999), Kaufmann (1995), Conroy (1989), Maher (1989), and Starr (1982) for health care. See Vanderwoerd (2004), Cleary (2001), Coleman (2001), Anderson (2000), Schwartz (2000), Dolan (1998), Brown and McKeown (1997), and Oates (1995) for social service institutions.

58. Making this argument are Holtschneider and Morey (2000a, 2000b, 2003), Burtchaell (1998), Marsden (1997, 1994), and Cunniggim (1994) for denominational

colleges and universities; Risse (1999:542), Fennell and Alexander (1993:93), Clarke and Estes (1992:961), Gottemoeller (1991), Marmor et al. (1987:222-34), Hollingsworth and Hollingsworth (1986), and Lindberg (1986:195-6), for health care; and Chaves (2004:67), Coleman (2000:3), and Oates (1995:90, 171-172) for social services.

59. The authors listed in the previous two footnotes explore the implications for the institutions themselves; secularization theorists such as Casanova (1994) and Chaves (1994) explore the implications for the larger society.

60. For example, Conroy (1989:151) pointed out that, as the ratio of nursing sisters to lay nurses declined in Catholic hospitals, the sponsoring religious orders "had to re-examine their basic assumptions: were their members primarily labor or management? And, if the latter, how did their management functions relate to their traditional ministry of caring for the sick?" Stoltzfus (1992:26) approvingly cites Methodist F. Thomas Trotter to the effect that "if the Church divests itself of all institutional forms of expressing its mission, its own sense of mission will be profoundly altered." And Gallin (1996:4-5) stresses how vital Catholic colleges were to their sponsoring religious orders' self-identity and recruitment efforts. But neither Conroy nor Trotter gave any indication of how the churches or the orders changed in response to changes in their institutions. And both Stoltzfus and Gallin devoted the rest of their books to describing the impact of religious attenuation on the colleges and *not* on the religious sponsor. Similarly, Daigler (2000:106) notes that "just as a college can demonstrate the values of the [Sisters of Mercy] in its policies and programs, so can the Mercy community reflect the values inherent in the intellectual ministry of those members who work in higher education." Daigler then cites a source as having explored the influence of colleges on religious orders "in detail," but gives no specific page numbers. Holtschneider and Morey (2000a; 2000b) explore, almost exclusively, how having fewer vowed religious affects the colleges and universities these orders sponsored, but they give little or no attention to how the loss of the colleges affects the sponsoring orders. The study's critics (Cernera 2000; Hayes 2000; Hellwig 2000; Mackin 2000; O'Hare 2000; Reinhart 2000; Vale 2000) also fail to address this issue. The only studies to explore the impact of colleges on religious sponsors are Puzon (1996a) and Meyer (2000, 1974).

61. Harrison (1959), of course, is an obvious exception.

62. See, for example, Baggett (2001), Demerath et al., eds. (1998), Chaves (1997), and Lehman (1993) and Ammerman (1990).

63. See Weick (1995:127-131), Trice and Beyer (1993:87-109), Martin (1992:46), Riley (1991:220), and Albert and Whetten (1985). Culture also includes the stories that people *don't* tell, the taboo topics they studiously avoid (Martin, 1992:139; Riley, 1991:220).

64. Swidler (1986:273).

65. As Weick (1995:183) puts it: "People act in order to think"—that is, their actions help determine their beliefs and values. See also Caronna (1999).

66. Weick (1995:24-43). See also Sackman (1991). Alvesson (2002:158) also includes the idea of cognitive frames borrowed from the larger environment: e.g., what a "boss" is.

67. See Fligstein (1987, 1990), Kanter (1977), and Martin (1992:85-90) for examples. See Albert and Whetten (1985:276-77) for organizational drift toward hybrid cultures.

68. Meyerson (1991:132). See also Schein (1991b:245). See Martin (2002:107) for flux and change in members' interpretations and enactments of organizational culture.

69. Feldman (1991:147-52). See also Martin (1992:134, 142-57).

70. Feldman (1991:146).

71. See Schein (1991a:14).

72. Weick (1995:85, 124-127). See also March and Simon (1958).

73. Dunstan (2003:335) makes this point with regard to the nineteenth century Anglican sisterhoods.

74. The role of national culture is covered at length in Trice and Beyer (1993:46-52, 310-11, 331-53), and in Martin (1992:111-12).

75. See Martin (2002:164-67) for a recent exception.

76. This is as true of denominations and church groups as it is of the institutions they sponsor. Finke (2004:24) lists churches' efforts "to mimic and conform to peer institutions" as a primary factor preventing the development of innovations. Dunstan (2003:349) notes that Anglican religious orders resisted change primarily because "whatever is deeply ingrained as the basis of 'success' and growth in one era"—the sisters' institutions—"is hard to dislodge in the next." See also Trice and Beyer (1993:304-5).

77. See DiMaggio and Powell (1983:150-52) and Swartz (1994; 1998:324) for examples.

78. DiMaggio and Powell (1983:149). Vance (1999:69) notes this process for the Seventh-day Adventist organizations.

79. Finke (2004) gives examples of this for mainline Protestant denominations.

80. Mohan (1993:135). Bartunek (1984:364) describes an example of this in a Catholic religious order.

81. Weick (1995:159). See also Martin (1992:143).

82. Olsen (1976:84).

83. Weick (1995:161).

84. Weisbrod (1998a:290).

85. Albert and Whetten (1985:276-77).

86. Martin (1992:113). See also Caronna (1999).

87. Zucker (1987:446-47) and Weick (1995:49-55) both make this point.

88. See Casanova (1994:34, 211-14).

89. See Smith (2003:5-12), Casanova (1994:11-39), and Turner (1991:135-46) for a review of this literature. See Yamane (1997), in turn, for a rebuttal of secularization critics.

90. Stark and Finke (2000:57-79), Finke and Stark (1992:22-53), and Martin (1969:113) summarize these critiques.

91. The term is Casanova's (1994). See also Regnerus and Smith (1998) and Kepel (1994).

92. Smith (2003:81, footnote 12) makes this point.

93. These weaknesses are listed in Smith (2003:14-17).

94. Casanova (1994:37).

95. According to Casanova (1994:34, 211-214), societal secularization consists precisely in the removal of functions such as education, the economy, or the state from the religious sphere and the "marginalization" of religion to the privatized sphere of one's personal and subjective quest. If such a shift of focus is occurring in religious groups such as Catholic orders or Protestant mission societies, this would be a further manifestation of such secularization.

96. See Appendix A for a detailed description of these religious groups and the interview format.

Chapter 1

Religious Institutions:
A Historical and Ideological Survey

As the previous introduction has argued, the religious virtuosity of Christian denominations in Western Europe and North America during the nineteenth and twentieth centuries—especially for women virtuosi—was primarily expressed through founding, staffing, and administering specific organizations to educate youth, tend the sick, and provide assistance to the needy. Expending the Church's financial resources, as well as the time and talents of its most committed members, in these organizationally-focused endeavors was relatively unusual in the history of Christianity, and required the development of specific ideological formulations to justify it. The present chapter will first briefly review the history of these organizations, and will then explore the rationales articulated for their support.

The Rise of Religious Organizations

Educational Institutions

In Europe prior to 1800, elementary education for the children of the lower classes was considered a charitable and religious work, and not a state responsibility. In Protestant countries, local congregations established free schools for the poor, in which the pastor or a seminarian taught the children. The Prussian state ceded control over education to the Lutheran Church throughout the 1600s and most of the 1700s; the Anglican Church claimed similar authority in England.[1] Pastors were also appointed by the state to inspect the schools, an office they held in Germany until 1787. In Catholic countries, the newly-formed religious teaching orders undertook the responsibility for instructing the poor.[2]

Not until the mid-nineteenth century was it commonly accepted that universal, free elementary education was a state responsibility. In most countries, however, even the state schools included instruction in religion and the Bible, and the pupils were led in common daily prayer and the singing of hymns.[3] A survey of English elementary schools between 1858 and 1861 found that, while only 80 percent of them taught writing and arithmetic, 100 percent of them taught religion. Likewise, priests and nuns continued to teach in the French public schools throughout the nineteenth century; the sisters comprised 49 percent of all female teachers in the French girls' schools in the 1840s, and 60 percent in 1872.[4] Not until the early 1900s were the orders formally barred from teaching in the French public schools. In many countries, parallel systems of denominational and secular schools were established; in England's Roman Catholic Diocese of Salford, for example, there were 1,066 parochial schools by 1900.[5] In England and Wales, the Methodists operated 912 schools in the late nineteenth century, with over 131,000 pupils attending. Initially the religious schools received no state support or supervision, but this situation was reversed in England in 1902 and in France in 1951. In the mid-1950s, 20 percent of French elementary students and 40 percent of French secondary students attended Catholic schools.[6]

State-provided public education did not exist in most parts of the United States during the eighteenth and early nineteenth centuries, and so many denominations undertook this task. The Sunday School Movement has already been mentioned as one example of the involvement of churches in education. In addition to their Sunday Schools, however, some denominations also constructed their own regular school systems. In the late 1700's, Bishop Francis Asbury urged all Methodist congregations to erect a school "in the vicinity of every church."[7] During the early nineteenth century, the Presbyterian General Assembly also encouraged its local churches and synods to establish and administer parochial schools for young children. The Presbyterians also established several "Female Academies" for older girls.[8] Once the public school system was begun, however, most Protestant denominations stopped sponsoring their own elementary schools.

Catholic immigrants to the United States brought with them from Europe the expectation that elementary schooling was the province of the religious orders, as well as a suspicion, among many national groups, of the state's schools. These suspicions were reinforced by the overtly Protestant character of the U.S. public school system.[9] In addition, the religious orders themselves were forced to find remunerative work once they arrived in the United States, since the American government did not subsidize them as European governments had done. The women's orders typically established residential academies for wealthy—invariably Protestant—girls, and used the money they earned from these endeavors to operate "free schools" for the Catholic poor. The first of these academies was opened in 1727 by the Ursuline sisters in New Orleans. By 1810, various orders of sisters ran ten such academies throughout the United States; by 1852 they operated more than one hundred.[10] Most provided a "finishing school" type of education, designed primarily to fit young, middle-class women for a good marriage.

During this same period, the Catholic men's orders established a number of six-year "colleges" for boys along the European model, often enrolling students as young as ten years of age. Since the colleges' curriculum was largely classical and theological, they attracted a much smaller student population than the sisters' academies did; pupils rarely completed the full six-year course. Both the male and female orders owned their schools, and comprised the entire staff.

As the Catholic population of the United States grew after mid-century, local parishes also began to establish elementary schools for the children of their parishioners. In 1884, the Plenary Council of U.S. Bishops in Baltimore mandated that *all* parishes do so, stating that "[n]o parish is complete till it has schools adequate to the needs of its children, and the pastor and people of such a parish should feel that they have not accomplished their entire duty until the want is supplied."[11] By 1900, some 63 percent of the nation's Catholic parishes had built these elementary schools, and 50 percent of all Catholic school children were enrolled in them. A few parishes were beginning to offer high school classes as well. Some of the religious orders' academies and colleges also adopted the standard four-year high school curriculum and began admitting mostly students from the new Catholic middle class. Meanwhile, the sisters found that their free schools were often stigmatized as "schools for the poor," and so they either closed them or merged them with the parish schools.

Unlike the sisters' academies and free schools, the parochial elementary and high schools were owned by the local parish, or by the bishop of the diocese acting as corporation sole. The parishes contracted with religious orders of women to teach the younger pupils and girls, and with orders of men to teach the older boys. The orders usually received small stipends from the parishes for the teaching sisters' living expenses.[12] The male orders, who found their private high schools more lucrative, soon withdrew from teaching in the parish grade schools, and the sisters assumed instruction of all of the pupils there.

With the exception of the Seventh-day Adventists and some of the German-speaking Lutheran groups, most Protestant denominations in the United States and Great Britain did not continue supporting their own elementary schools, once the public school system was in place.[13] By the end of the nineteenth century, however, it was becoming obvious that some of the nation's poorest children were being neglected by the public educational system. The newly-founded women's home missionary societies therefore began to establish vocational classes for these disenfranchised groups as early as the 1880s, and their informal efforts rapidly crystallized into full-fledged schools. By 1940, for example, the Woman's Home Missionary Society of the Methodist Episcopal Church owned and supported nine grade schools, nine high schools, two junior colleges, and one four-year college. Four of these schools served White Appalachian children; ten served Blacks in the southern states; two served Spanish and Mexican children, and one each served Native Americans, Puerto Ricans, and "problem girls."[14] Bennett College for

Women in Greensboro, North Carolina, was established in 1926 as a four-year college by the Society in order to educate African American women. By 1940, it enrolled 356 students. Two co-educational junior colleges, in Mississippi and North Carolina, were also established by the same Society. Among the southern Methodists, the Women's Missionary Council established a high school for mountain children in London, Kentucky. This later became a normal school and finally a junior college. The Council also co-operated with the Christian (or "Colored," as they were then called) Methodist Episcopal churches to establish Paine College in Augusta, Georgia.[15] In other denominations, the Presbyterian home mission societies supported 22 teachers in 110 schools by 1888, where they instructed Native Americans, Mexicans, African American former slaves, and Southern Whites. In 1892—less than a decade after its founding—the American Baptist Home Mission Society supported thirteen schools of higher education for Southern Blacks, enrolling 5,167 men and women. One, the Atlanta Baptist Female Seminary, later became Spelman College. Most of these "colleges," however, were also forced to offer grade school- and high school-level remedial work, since previous educational opportunities for African Americans in the South had been poor. Many had only tenuous financial connections with their parent denominations and were dependent on special fund drives for their support rather than regular budget allotments. Today, there are still 42 church-related senior colleges serving African American students.[16]

In addition to colleges for underserved populations, both Catholics and Protestants in the United States established a wide range of religious colleges for the young men—and a smaller number for the young women—within their own ranks. The exact mode of the colleges' religious sponsorship varied from denomination. Most (93 percent) of the Catholic colleges and universities were founded and operated by Catholic religious orders.[17] As such, they have remained completely separate both from the diocese in which they are located and from Vatican authorities.

> Catholic colleges and universities have always been more independent from church authorities in their governance, finance, and intellectual initiatives than any of the [Protestant] traditions, including even the Congregationalists. Only fourteen of these schools are now sponsored by bishops or local dioceses, and the presence of representatives on the governing boards is minimal. Direct contributions [to the colleges] from Catholic parishes or dioceses are mostly unheard-of.[18]

Until recently, the Catholic hierarchy also made no attempts to ensure the doctrinal orthodoxy or Catholicity of these colleges, assuming that this responsibility was secure in the orders' hands.[19]

Most mainline Protestant denominations, on the other hand, tended to found, fund, and administer their colleges more directly. The typical pattern for the men's colleges connected to the Episcopalian, Congregational, Presbyterian, Baptist, and Lutheran churches was for a group of ministers or local ecclesiastical authorities to establish a seminary for training future clergy in theology and the classical languages. These institutions later began to educate lay students as well.[20] Methodist colleges, on the other hand, were typically established by church authorities or laymen primarily to educate Methodist *laity* in good moral behavior.[21] In all Protestant denominations, however, the founding denomination directly supplied its colleges and academies with operating funds and safeguarded the orthodoxy of their curricula. In most denominations, the majority of the faculty and staff were either ordained ministers or active laymen from the same religious tradition.[22] As with the Catholic colleges, their presence was considered sufficient to ensure the religious identity of the institution.

As the men's colleges were usually founded as seminaries for prospective clergy, many of the women's colleges often evolved from missionary training schools. The first Protestant missionary training school for women was established in Chicago in 1885. In 1910, there were 25 denominational and ten interdenominational missionary training schools open to women in the United States and Canada; by 1916, this number had increased to sixty.[23] Most of these schools eventually closed or were merged with the male seminaries, but some—the Methodist Episcopal deaconess training schools in Washington, Kansas City, and San Francisco, for example—operated until the early 1930s, when training was centralized in the National Training School (later National College) in Kansas City. A Methodist training school for women foreign missionaries, Scarritt Bible and Training School, likewise became a co-educational senior college and graduate school after its relocation to Nashville, Tennessee, in the early 1920s.[24] In a similar fashion, many Catholic women's orders established "Normal Schools" to train their own novices as teachers, and later upgraded these institutions to two- or four-year colleges open to lay students.

Other women's colleges, Catholic and Protestant, evolved from secondary-level academies by gradually adding college classes to their curricula.[25] The Presbyterians had established 25 such academies by the 1860's, many of which later became colleges. Catholic orders of nuns began to upgrade their academies to the postsecondary level in the late 1880s, and, by 1910, the nuns owned and ran thirteen women's colleges. This increased to nineteen by 1915, and to 74 by 1930. Most of the sisters' colleges were small, geographically remote, less likely to be accredited, and financially precarious.[26] Still, by 1967, women's religious orders had founded 223 colleges in the United States, enrolling approximately 25 percent of the 446,459 students attending Catholic colleges and universities at the time.[27] Subsequent mergers reduced the number to 117 by 1994—still more than half of the 230 U.S. Catholic institutions of higher education. By 2000, Catholic colleges and universities enrolled almost 20 percent of the students in private, degree-granting institutions.

Denominational initiatives have thus been an important causal factor in determining the landscape of American higher education. Of the more than 1,300 accredited private colleges and universities in the United States, 44 (including

Harvard, Yale and Dartmouth) trace their origins to the early Congregationalists, 64 to the Presbyterians, 87 to the Methodists, 50 to the Southern Baptists, and 16 to the American Baptists.[28] Even today, over 800 institutions of higher education retain some religious affiliation, as Table 1.1 shows. This involvement in their schools, colleges, and universities would have profound effects on the orders of Catholic sisters and Protestant deaconesses that staffed them, as well as on the denomination as a whole.

Health Care Institutions

Religious involvement in health care has also had a long tradition. Healing the sick had been a key responsibility of monks in early medieval Europe, even though health care was not the purpose for which the monasteries had originally been founded. By the late Middle Ages, however, new monasteries were established specifically for the purpose of caring for the sick. "The first monasteries with a special nursing vocation were attached to the hospitals under the Knights of St. John and the Ladies of Mary Magdalene, respectively, in Jerusalem after the first crusade."[29] The first non-monastic nursing order was a community of Augustinian canonesses who founded and operated the Hotel Dieu in Paris at about the same time. Additional male nursing orders were founded in the sixteenth and seventeenth centuries. The Fatebenfratelli founded or administered over one hundred hospitals in Catholic European countries. The Hospitallers of St. John of God had founded several hospitals in Spain by 1570; in the early 1600's they had spread to Italy and the Americas. The Daughters of Charity, founded in 1638, nursed in more than 200 French hospitals by 1700. In Quebec, Augustinian sisters had founded a hospital as early as 1639, in order to nurse Native American smallpox victims.[30]

Protestants also began making organized arrangements for health care. By the seventeenth century, most Protestant congregations in Holland had permanently-appointed, paid visitors to the sick, who helped these unfortunates draw up their wills, offered them spiritual advice, and arranged to hire nurses for them.[31] In the nineteenth century, the Deaconesses at Kaiserswerth, Germany, chose nursing as their first occupation at least partially because of its long-established identification as a holy work.

Nowhere, however, did religious involvement in health care reach the level that it did among Catholics in the United States: one writer calls the U.S. Catholic Church "unique within the Universal Church for its maintenance of a Church-related system of health services."[32] Of all hospital beds in the United States in the mid-1920's, 60 percent were in Catholic hospitals. Overall, 70 percent of American hospitals in 1929 were private—largely Catholic—while only 12 percent of European hospitals were. This percentage remained unchanged until the 1970s.[33] Almost all of the Catholic hospitals in the United States were originally founded and owned by male or female religious orders, and not by the dioceses themselves.

Table 1.1. U.S. Religious Colleges and Universities, 2005

Catholic	220
United Methodist	108
Presbyterian (USA)	65
Assn. of Advanced Rabbinical and Talmudic Schools	56
Southern Baptist	55
Lutheran (ELCA)	36*
Churches of Christ	21
Episcopal	19
Christian Church/Disciples of Christ	17
American Baptist	16
Christian Church/Churches of Christ	16
Assemblies of God	14
Friends	14
Seventh-day Adventist	14
Lutheran (Missouri Synod)	12
Mennonite	11
Nazarene	10
Church of God	8
African American Episcopal	5
Reformed Church in America	5
Free Methodist Church	5
Wesleyan Church	5
Other**	96
Total	828

Table assembled by Dr. Bob Andringa, president of the Council for Christian Colleges sand Universities, 321 Eighth Street, NE, Washington, DC 20002. A listing of 722 institutions by religious affiliation can be found in the *2005 Higher Education Directory* by Higher Education Publications, Inc., Falls Church, VA.

* Includes 8 self-standing seminaries.
** Estimated from 20+ other denominations/organizations with 4 or fewer accredited campuses.

For Catholic religious orders of women in the United States, nursing had as long a history as education did. In addition to teaching in their academy, the New Orleans Ursulines did home nursing as early as 1728, and by 1734 they had founded the first Catholic hospital in the country.[34] An infirmary established in Baltimore in 1823 had seven Sisters of Charity on staff; four women from the same religious order started Mullanphy Hospital in St. Louis in 1828. By 1861, seventeen different orders of nuns were staffing a total of thirty hospitals, and their services were in high demand during the Civil War. As the New York City commissioners stated in their letter to Secretary of War Stanton concerning the staffing of a proposed army hospital in Central Park, "We want the nurses of this hospital to be the Sisters of Charity, the most faithful nurses in the world. Their tenderness, their knowledge, and the religious conviction of duty render them by far the best nurses around the sick bed which have ever been found on earth."[35] Some 20 percent of all army nurses during the Civil War were Catholic sisters—a total of 617 women from 21 different orders.[36]

After 1865, the sisters continued to establish hospitals in response to acute needs, and they were often asked to take over financially-strapped public hospitals as well.[37] Few other groups were doing so; as late as 1873, there were only 178 hospitals of any sort in the entire United States, and about a third of these were mental institutions.[38] Between 1886 and 1966, however, 59 different communities of sisters founded over 300 hospitals in the United States. The sisters also established nursing schools—403 of them by 1931—and had devised a rudimentary health insurance system as early as the 1880s.[39] As with their academies and colleges, the sisters, not the larger church, owned and financed their hospitals. Although most were separately incorporated, their governing boards were composed entirely of sisters, and the nuns continued to fill all of the administrative positions.

With the exception of some immigrant groups, few other American denominations or individual church members were involved in building hospitals prior to the 1860s.[40] After modern medical discoveries such as anesthesia and antiseptic practices, however, hospitals began to be seen, not as warehouses for the chronically ill or dying poor, but as places that might actually cure people. Once hospitals showed some prospect of being a help rather than a hindrance to health, many denominations began to establish them, both in the United States and in missionary territories. The first Methodist Hospital, Seney Methodist Episcopal Hospital in Brooklyn, was opened in 1882. A Baptist layman in St. Louis, Dr. W. G. Mayfield, established the Missouri Baptist Sanitorium in 1890; Northern Baptists began Samaritan Hospital in Philadelphia in 1892. The Tabernacle Baptist Church in Atlanta opened an infirmary in 1903 that later became Georgia Baptist Hospital.[41]

In addition to the hospitals' value in curing the sick, Protestant missionaries considered them essential adjuncts in their evangelization efforts. By the late 1800s, the superiority of Western medicine had become evident—and attractive—to the Asians and Africans whom the missionaries hoped to convert. As early as 1876, therefore, missionaries had established sixteen hospitals and dispensaries in China, where they treated some 41,000 patients. Thirteen years later, they operated 61 hospitals and 44 dispensaries, treating almost 350,000 Chinese patients.[42] To prepare women missionaries to serve in these institutions, training hospitals and nursing schools were needed in the sending countries. The first Methodist training hospital in the United States, Sibley Hospital in Washington, DC, was begun in 1894 to educate deaconesses and missionaries studying in that denomination's missionary training school.[43] These training hospitals quickly became respected health care institutions in their own right.

Deaconesses were heavily involved in these health care institutions, more so than in other works. In the 1930s, Methodist deaconesses "managed and supervised thirty hospitals, nine children's homes, four old age homes, and five homes for business women."[44] Of the 26 hospitals founded by the Methodist Episcopal Church between 1888 and 1903, all but two employed deaconesses.

Both in Europe and in America, however, the deaconesses had much less authority within their hospitals than the Catholic sisters had. To begin with, they did not own these institutions, nor, for the most part, did they serve on their governing boards. Pastors or wealthy laymen administered and funded the Methodist and Lutheran hospitals, served on their boards of directors, and contracted with the deaconesses for their services. The public religious character of the hospitals thus rested primarily on the sponsorship of these board members and the clergy: "In fact, the 1895 Annual Report of the German Hospital does not mention the deaconesses until page twenty-nine, and then only for one paragraph. The public face of the hospital de-emphasized the role and importance of the deaconesses, and focused instead on the largesse of [the board president] and the board's prestige."[45]

In subsequent decades, the number of religious hospitals continued to grow. By 1923 there were 75 Methodist hospitals—second in number only to the Lutheran hospitals among U.S. Protestant groups. In 1965, the American Baptists ran eight hospitals and 68 homes for the aged; eleven of the 34 state conventions of the Southern Baptists owned and operated approximately fifty medical facilities. By the mid-twentieth century, the Seventh-day Adventists operated a world-wide network that included 167 hospitals and sanitoria, 246 clinics, 47 schools of nursing, and a medical school. Within North America alone, Adventist Health System contained 53 hospitals and 28 nursing homes, making it one of the largest health care systems on the continent.[46] Catholic religious orders operated 950 hospitals and 376 homes for the aged in 1965. Connected to these institutions were medical schools, dispensaries, and even world-renowned research institutions such as the Mayo Clinic.[47]

Social Work Institutions

Social services, too, have long been seen as a proper role for churches and church groups. As early as the twelfth century, Augustinian canonesses ran hospices for travelers, asylums for the poor, shelters for widows, and orphanages.[48] In subsequent centuries, numerous new Catholic orders were founded specifically to do these types of work.

By the end of the seventeenth century, at least one poorhouse stood in every French town with over 5,000 people. They were all run by new orders of religious

women: Sisters of Providence, Filles de la Sagesse, Paulines of Trequier, Soeurs
Chretiennes de Nevers, Soeurs Hospitalieres de St. Alexis de Limoges, Soeurs
Hopitalieres de St. Joseph du Puy, Sisters of St. Thomas de Villeneuve. . . .
However they operated, they could never keep apace of the demand for service.[49]

In England and Wales, Catholic sisters ran 39 orphanages by 1879, together with
industrial schools, Magdalene asylums, and homes for the aged. In Ireland, too,
religious orders were essential in the operation of Catholic social services for the
poor. In Germany, the Kaiserswerth Deaconesses engaged in an extensive prison
visitation ministry and ran orphanages in addition to their hospital work.[50]

Protestant women in the United States also became involved in organized
social service activities. Their role as "protectors of the moral life of the nation"
made them the logical choice—in their own eyes at least—to operate and control
the various efforts to reform moral conduct.[51] Presbyterian women in Philadelphia
raised the funds to open an orphanage and school in 1815, modeled on a similar
institution which had been established in New York City in 1806. By 1820, the
Philadelphia orphanage was caring for ninety children. After the Civil War, the
newly-established denominational mission societies founded settlement houses in
the burgeoning urban slums, modeling their efforts on the first settlement house
established in London by a clergyman earlier in the century. Black Baptist women
established a settlement house in Washington, DC, in 1913; its soup kitchen fed
1,200 in the winter months two years later.[52] The mission societies also owned and
supported community centers, homes for employed single women, orphanages, day
care centers, and settlement houses for new immigrants.[53]

Trained cadres of deaconesses and missionaries were needed to staff the social
service agencies which the mission societies had established. The missionary
training schools therefore began to offer courses in sociology in the early twentieth
century, which often developed into full-fledged social work programs.[54]

As the numbers of local church mission societies and of the separate
organizations they sponsored grew, it was felt necessary to create larger structures
to co-ordinate them. The Charity Organization Society Movement promoted the
idea of "Scientific Charity"—the theory that modern social problems were too
complex to be dealt with by untrained volunteers:

> The COS Movement was a response to the rapid growth of relief-giving agencies,
> the lack of co-ordination among them, and the absence of any guiding principles
> for decision-making about people in need. The relief situation was perceived to
> be excessive and chaotic. The COS leaders sought to replace the existing system
> of charity with one rational system that stressed investigation, co-ordination, and
> personal service.[55]

In 1916, the Methodist Woman's Home Mission Society created its Bureau for
Children's Homes to co-ordinate support for the group's many orphanages. In
denomination after denomination, oversight boards run by credentialed profession-

als were created in order to supervise the workers at home and foreign mission sites.[56]

Catholic sisters began social work in the United Stated by informally caring for the orphans whose parents had died in the sisters' hospitals. Other early targets for service were unwed mothers and abandoned infants. The New York Sisters of Charity established a foundling hospital in 1869. Between 1870 and 1930, 35 infant and maternity hospitals were founded by the sisters to care for unwed mothers and their babies.[57] In 1919, the various branches of the Sisters and Daughters of Charity cared for 10,653 children in their maternity hospitals and orphanages. The plight of impoverished Catholic immigrant women inspired the sisters to initiate other endeavors as well: day care centers, rooming houses, Catholic probation offices, "Magdalen" houses, schools for the retarded, employment bureaus, and homes for the aged. Catholic sisters were also among the first to become involved in settlement house work. As a result of their efforts, and "because of the fairly rigid gender division which defined nuns' work as that which involved women, the services available to women exceeded those available to men."[58]

After the Civil War, many of the sisters' small, parish-based social service efforts were consolidated into larger institutions, since institution-building seemed a more efficient way to stretch their limited funds to assist the poor. This was in contrast to the "friendly visitor" approach taken by benevolent Protestants, which "demanded relatively more money than labor."[59] Unlike their hospitals and schools, however, many Catholic social service institutions did not remain under the sisters' control. Diocesan officials had been influenced by the Charity Organization Society Movement's belief that social problems were too complex to be dealt with by untrained volunteers, and the haphazard allocation of alms to various charitable works was deemed inefficient. By the early twentieth century, therefore, many Catholic social agencies were funded and overseen by governing boards of businessmen, with lay, credentialed social workers to supervise the nuns' efforts.[60] Lay social workers looked down on the sisters as "old fashioned," "out of touch," and "too easily hoodwinked" by the undeserving poor.[61] They argued that religious orders were preoccupied with institutional charity and had neither the energy nor the personnel to engage in this new work.

Since fewer than 5 percent of the sisters worked in social services, their orders had little incentive for, or tradition of, professionally educating them in this field.[62] Often, it was assumed that no training at all was needed for sisters working in orphanages or settlement houses—in contrast to those working in schools and hospitals. As a result, the least capable new recruits were often assigned to this task.

Throughout the nineteenth and early twentieth centuries, therefore, Catholics and Protestants established a wide range of educational, health care, and social service institutions, and also developed organized groups of religious virtuosi—primarily women—specifically to staff, fund, and administer these institutions. While the relationship between the religious sponsors and their institutions varied by denomination and type of institution, these links were always profoundly influential, both for the sponsor and for the institution. Foremost among these influences was the development of a specific organizational culture and ideology that gave religious value and meaning to institutional service. The next section will outline the beliefs and values of this ideology in greater detail.

Ideologies Supporting Institutional Involvement

Educational Ideologies

For both Catholics and Protestants in Europe, the provision of formal schooling for the masses had had a primarily religious purpose at least since the Reformation. Both Luther and Calvin urged free education for all children, in the local vernacular language, so that they would be able to read and study the Bible. As Luther said to the rulers of German towns and cities:

> If the magistrates may compel their able-bodied subjects to carry a pike and musket and do military service, there is much more reason for them compelling their subjects to send their children to school. For there is a far worse war to be waged with the devil, who employs himself secretly in injuring towns and states through the neglect of education.[63]

For John Wesley, religion and education were inseparable; he wrote that "if the Methodists were not a reading people, the work of grace would die out in a generation."[64]

If Protestants valued mass education to develop a scripturally-literate population, Counter-Reformation Catholicism used it to insulate the populace against the Reformers' efforts.[65] Both Catholics and Protestants were also threatened by the political and social dislocations of early industrial Europe and saw religious education as a way to combat their deleterious effects.[66] In seventeenth century France:

> Early religious reformers started with the premise that the world was hopelessly corrupt. They despaired of the morality of adults and argued that the best way to safeguard the future was to remove children from their influence. . . . [Convent boarding schools] provided the young with "a pedagogical 'other place' that was purified and sterilized." The walls that enclosed this "other place" served a double purpose: they kept out the evil influences of the world, and they allowed the space within to be continually monitored. . . In the minds of religious pedagogues, the work of the [convent boarding school] was the work of salvation.[67]

Similarly, the nineteenth century Prussian emperor Frederick William II blamed "irreligious pseudo-education" for the social disruptions of 1848. And the English Methodist educator J. H. Rigg noted in 1873:

> Banish the Bible and the Gospel from the schools and the only foundation left on which the teacher can attempt to ground the authority of his moral injunctions, is his own word and assurance. . . . Either there will be no discipline in the school, or there will be only the discipline of fear. . . . The reign of barbaric force will return to our schools.[68]

Catholic immigrants to the United States and Australia had similar ideas. As early as 1829, the First Provincial Council of Bishops, held in Baltimore, held it "absolutely necessary that schools be established in which the young may be taught the principles of faith and morality, while being instructed in letters."[69] Education that neglected religion and morality was considered fundamentally flawed. In fact, for Catholics, the primary goal of education was the salvation of the students' souls; academic knowledge was secondary. As late as the 1940s, one could find Catholic educators arguing that

> to the religious teacher, every child is a study, a charge, a responsibility, a sacred personality possessed of the dignity of an adopted child of God, redeemed by Christ, called to membership in His Church, and destined in soul and body to eternal life, to be therefore respected and loved, benefitted morally, mentally, physically, and assisted along the path to heaven. Not to be neglected, *but only in secondary place,* are efforts to educate the child for society, each in the measure of her abilities.[70]

To nineteenth century U.S. Catholics, public schools were dangerous to salvation—initially because of their heavily Protestant bias, and later because of their basically secular, a-religious character, which weakened children's attachment to spiritual things. In fact, the entire American society was spiritually dangerous, as Philadelphia's Cardinal Denis Doherty maintained in 1923:

> A parochial school is a necessity, especially in this country where our children breathe in the atmosphere of heresy, unbelief and sometimes irreligion. On the street, in the factories, in the mills, in the mines—everywhere—false doctrines are propagated. . . . Priests and parents are bound to provide a religious education for their children.[71]

In England and Australia, as well, both Catholic and Methodist clergy saw parish schools as "playing a crucial role in stemming the falling away or 'leakage' of the faith among the next generation."[72]

Most U.S. Protestant denominations, on the other hand, did not share this feeling of being threatened by modern culture.[73] American Protestants *were*, however, threatened by the specter of Catholic proselytization in the Midwest.

"The principles of American democracy," Catharine Beecher felt, were identical with the teachings of Protestant Christianity, and both would be lost if the pernicious influence of Catholic sisters' academies in the new states of Ohio, Indiana, Illinois, Michigan, and Missouri was not checked.[74] Evangelical women, therefore, competed with the orders of nuns in founding female academies throughout the early nineteenth century.[75]

In addition to its value in stemming a perceived Catholic onslaught, education was held by Protestants to be an essential part of their own faith development. All believers needed to be literate in order to read the Bible, preferably in the original biblical languages.[76] The scholar's gown became the accepted attire for Protestant preachers—their education was what qualified them to preach. In the post-millennial theology of the mid-nineteenth century, education was an essential prelude to the promised second coming of Christ. As late as 1927, the president of the Methodist Woman's Home Mission Society was able to assert:

> Any plan for the creation of a better world to live in, as peace instead of war, the spirit of co-operation between employees and workers, more of beauty and enduring felicity in sex relations, and the growth of the ideas of brotherhood, is not feasible unless children are educated to meet the requirements of the plan. To the Christian mind, no education fits the individual for living in this better world for which we are striving which does not put Jesus Christ and his teaching at the center of the program.[77]

Women's education, especially, was important in forming virtuous mothers who would lead their families, and ultimately the entire nation, to Christ.[78]

The Protestant vision of the essential religious purpose of education was most pronounced in the case of colleges—which, unlike elementary and secondary schools, Protestants *did* establish and sponsor in large numbers. A primary purpose of the early colleges was to prepare men (and, less often, women) for the ministry or for evangelization work. Most of these institutions were begun, as the sponsors of Davidson College put it in 1845, "for securing the means of Education to young men within our bounds of hopeful talents and piety, preparatory to the Gospel ministry."[79] Similarly, the goal of Mt. Holyoke Female Seminary at its founding in 1837 was "to cultivate the missionary spirit among its pupils; the feeling that they should live for God and do something as teachers, or in such other ways as Providence may direct."[80] The goal of Calvin College was "to bring all human life and culture under God's sovereignty. All truth is God's truth." Spelman College's motto was "Our Whole School for Christ," and a large proportion of its students converted to evangelical Christianity while there.

The colleges' sponsoring denominations articulated similar sentiments. An 1873 Baptist policy statement held that

> The establishment of schools of higher education is an indispensable supplement of all evangelical work. Every period of successful evangelical activity, from the

Christian era down, has blossomed into such schools, and these schools have been the conservators of all achievements gained, and the essential preparation for all further and greater conquests. . . . OUR EDUCATIONAL CENTRES ARE OUR CENTRES OF INFLUENCE AND POWER. . . . With the general advance of education in the country, educated minds pass to the higher spheres of control in every department of life, and any denomination of Christians which fails to push forward its educational in an even ratio with its evangelical work, will sink more and more to inferiority, and ought to sink.[81]

Similarly, Presbyterians felt that the main goal of a college education was to save the nation from godless learning.[82] The central purpose of nineteenth century colleges was thus to promote and facilitate the development of Christian civilization through the education of learned Christian gentlemen.[83]

The development of some of their denominational colleges into modern research universities did not lessen mainline Protestants' identification of higher education as a religious work. In fact, such universities were seen as additional evidence of the progress of civilization and the coming of the Kingdom of God on earth, and it was expected that they would implant the cause of Protestant Christianity at the very center of the commanding values, ideas, and aspirations of the American people.[84]

The founding goals of Catholic colleges and universities mirrored and extended the reasons which the bishops had advanced for the Church's primary and secondary educational system. As with their other schools, the primary purpose of Catholic higher education was to save students' souls by building up their characters, shielded from the corrupting influences of the larger society. In fact, according to Philadelphia's Cardinal Doherty, Catholic colleges were even more necessary than Catholic grade schools, because young adults in secular or Protestant colleges were exposed to more dangerous theories.[85] As the founders of Georgetown University wrote in 1789:

> Persuaded that irreligion and immorality in a youth portend the most fatal evils to subsequent periods of life, and threaten to disturb the peace, and corrupt the manners of society at large, the directors of this institution openly profess that they have nothing so much at heart as to implant virtue and destroy in their pupils the seeds of vice. Happy is the attainment of this sublime object, and they would consider their success in this alone as an ample reward for their incessant endeavors.[86]

Or, as an early president of Villanova College put it in 1842:

> In educating the mind a woeful mistake is committed. Too much attention is lavished on the Intellect whilst little or no attention is paid to the Will, the faculty of the Soul the most closely connected with both the temporal and eternal interests of man. In other words, the head is educated, the heart is neglected.[87]

According to the documents of the Jesuits' 25th General Congress in 1906:

> In drawing up these ordinations, it is proper to take account in the first place, of the end which the Society proposes to itself in its colleges. This end is not only to develop all the faculties of our students by good methods of teaching, but to educate them in faith and piety, to build up their character, to accustom them to self-control, and to help them acquire habits of virtue.[88]

The primary goal of Catholic higher education, as of Catholic elementary and secondary education, was thus the preservation and development of the students' Catholic faith; academic scholarship was merely a means to that end.

Other religious reasons were also advanced for Catholic colleges. One was to prepare their students to serve the church and the larger community. The first men's colleges were founded, as the Protestant colleges had been, primarily to serve as seminaries.[89] In the early twentieth century, Bishops also pressured sisters to found or expand women's colleges within their dioceses because they wanted them to produce "real Catholic" lay teachers for the burgeoning Catholic school system.[90] As a result, some dioceses contained as many as five or six small, struggling women's colleges—a situation which, many critics felt, hampered the ability of these institutions to achieve even educational adequacy.[91] Still another reason, especially in the early to mid-twentieth century, was the desire to develop a specifically modern Catholic culture and disseminate it to the larger society: "Catholic educators aspired to convey to their students an 'integral Catholic culture,' and ultimately to convert the larger world to that culture."[92] As late as the 1950s, Gallin notes, "Catholic colleges saw their mission as one of fortifying Catholic culture, magnifying and developing the tradition which was their heritage."[93]

Catholic church officials felt so strongly the necessity of religious schooling for the preservation of students' faith that they fought to require it of all Catholics. According to a decree of the 1884 Plenary Council of Bishops,

> We not only exhort Catholic parents with paternal affection, but we *command* them with all the authority in our power, to procure a truly Christian education for their dear offspring, given them by God, reborn to Christ in baptism and destined for heaven: and further, to defend and secure all of them from the dangers of secular education during the whole term of their infancy and childhood, and, finally, to send them to Catholic, and especially parochial schools.[94]

Catholic high school principals and guidance counselors often refused to write letters of recommendation for any of their graduates who intended to apply to non-Catholic colleges or universities; a few even refused to send student transcripts to such institutions. As recently as 1960, the archbishop of St. Louis required Catholics in his diocese to obtain his explicit written permission before sending their children to a non-Catholic college.

Religious schools, therefore, were considered essential in many, if not most, of the variants of western Christianity.[95] In an era when many denominations believed themselves to be the sole repositories of the truths necessary for personal salvation or the perfection of society, schools served essential religious purposes.[96] Minority or immigrant faiths, such as Catholicism, Lutheranism, or Seventh-day Adventism, valued separate schools as a way of preserving their distinctive identity in the face of a hostile or indifferent Anglo-Protestant culture. Catholics and Mennonites also saw their colleges as prophetic witnesses to the larger society. And such schools needed teachers and administrators—preferably dedicated virtuosi committed to furthering the faith through their institutional service. The home and foreign missionary societies, the deaconesses, the Catholic religious orders—all were founded, at least in part, in order to provide these virtuosi for these schools.

Health Care Ideologies

"From their earliest origins," Starr states, "hospitals had been primarily religious and charitable institutions for tending the sick, rather than medical institutions for their cure."[97] In medieval Europe, the sick were often housed in monasteries, where they were assisted in cleansing their souls through confession and prayer in preparation for death. Hospitals were "sacred places," and were often constructed like cathedrals with a floor plan in the form of a cross, with four wards radiating from a central altar where Mass was celebrated daily. Wealthy donors to the monastic hospitals believed that their contributions earned "merit" in heaven. Donors were also entitled to share in the heavenly benefits gained by the prayers of the sick, who were considered temporary monks and closer to God by virtue of their suffering.[98] Facilitating the proper monastic observance by the patients and their caregivers was considered more important than the provision of professional health care.

The religious ideology of the medieval hospitals was delegitimated by the Protestant Reformation:

> For Protestants, a new relationship to both God and the community stood at the center of a profound change in charitable assistance. Divine Providence, not the quest for indulgences, was the path toward salvation, with an emphasis on individual faith and grace, not priestly mediation. Gone was the need for inmates' prayers on behalf of hospital patrons that had driven so many donations to charitable institutions before the Reformation. Gone also was the charitable institution as an instrument of salvation. In addition, living within a Christian community assumed that individuals had a right to charitable assistance together with obligations to contribute and assist others. Thus Protestant countries in Europe tried to organize local or national systems of relief financed by subscriptions or taxes.[99]

Protestant ideas of self-improvement made it incumbent on individual workers to safeguard their health. But, if they did become ill, it was not necessarily the responsibility of churches to assist in their physical cure. *Spiritual* curing, of course, was another matter. The burgeoning urban slums were breeding grounds of diseases such as cholera and typhus, and the prevailing Protestant doctrine was that such illnesses were caused by the sinful lives of the inhabitants, thus necessitating their conversion and penance.[100]

Even after the Reformation, however, European Catholicism continued to teach that caring for the sick was a spiritually meritorious activity. Work among incurable patients was especially efficacious as "an ascetic exercise and a means to mortify the senses."[101] However, the Post-Reformation Catholic hierarchy realized that the medieval system of attaching hospitals to monasteries had been subject to inefficiency and abuse.

> As a result of the Tridentine reforms, the Catholic Church reorganized religious hospitals and closed small, poorly endowed institutions. . . . In their place, privately endowed, large general hospitals or shelters, often run by local confraternities, were designed to bring together diverse groups of needy people. These included orphans, chronic sufferers, mentally ill individuals, and the elderly. . . . In the eyes of the Catholic Church, the distinction between worthy and unworthy poor remained blurred. They were all sinners who should be saved. Indeed, spiritual salvation remained the primary objective of hospitalization, and religious ceremonies continued to be central to hospital life, leading to tensions with medical caregivers.[102]

Caring for and curing the sick were also a valuable conversion strategy; as a seventeenth century French handbook for priests put it, "it is certain that by cure of the body one can as often cure souls as with sermons and good advice."[103]

Catholic immigrants brought this tradition with them when they came to the United States in the nineteenth century. In fact, as late as the 1950s, "Catholic hospitals prided themselves on being institutions where the patients' spiritual and social needs were recognized. . . . Where nuns worked, a more solemn atmosphere prevailed: 'virtue works wonders which technical aids and medical skills alone are powerless to accomplish.'"[104] Or, as the head of the Catholic Hospital Association stated in 1940: "The Catholic institution towers here on earth, but its purposes are in heaven."

Immigrant Catholics had additional reasons for founding hospitals. One was to preserve the faith of Catholic patients:

> The fear of Protestant proselytization exerted a decisive influence, even as late as 1865. In the minds of German Catholics, it was "a fact, universally known and felt, that the sick and infirm of the Congregation of the church of the Most Holy Redeemer were not satisfactorily well-cared-for in the public hospitals, not only on account of their language but still more on account of their religion since in these institutions they were surrounded by Infidels, Apostates, and even around

enemies of religion, circumstances which rendered those institutions anything but desirable for a Catholic who wished to prepare for eternity.[105]

Care in a Catholic hospital would insure that one received the sacraments as death neared. Hospitals also protected the cultural identity of non-English speaking Catholics, and served as an avenue of upward mobility for Catholic doctors. Finally, the positive impression made on Protestant soldiers by the sisters who nursed in the Civil War encouraged Catholics to regard their hospitals as evangelization tools, drawing non-Catholic patients to the true faith.[106]

Other minority faiths had similar reasons for founding hospitals in the United States. Mennonites began to establish hospitals to serve their own communities in 1900, and greatly expanded the number of these institutions after 1919 to serve injured soldiers. After World War II, Mennonites founded a series of mental hospitals as well—a response to the appalling conditions they had observed during their alternative service assignments in that conflict. Adventist hospitals were initially opened to care for ill Adventists in an atmosphere compatible with their distinctive beliefs about diet and Sabbath observance. Ellen White, however, also considered them to be a means of improving the church's image by breaking down anti-Adventist prejudice and opening the way for evangelization. Later, the Adventist hospital system also provided career paths for Adventist doctors, nurses, and other health care professionals. Similar reasons underlay the foundation of Jewish hospitals.[107]

Mainline U.S. Protestants had not, at first, considered the founding and staffing of hospitals to be an appropriate activity for the Church. As the science of medicine advanced, however, mainline Protestants began to see hospitals and clinics as a participation in the healing ministry of Christ.[108] Protestants also recognized the evangelization value of religious hospitals; the unsaved were considered most vulnerable to evangelical persuasion when they were sick.[109] Many felt that it was necessary to relieve the physical sufferings of the underserved and marginalized poor before their true "soul healing" could begin. As the Southwide Baptist Hospital Commission declared, "a Baptist hospital exists to bring men into a saving relationship with God through Jesus Christ by means of direct personal witness as occasion presents, and by a positive Christian interpretation of the experiences of disease, disability and death."[110] Finally, as has already been mentioned, denominational hospitals were indispensable training grounds for deaconess and missionary nurses.[111]

If religious motives supported the foundation and maintenance of denominational hospitals, they were even more salient in the training and practice of nurses. Initially, in the Middle Ages, service to the sick was a penitential exercise practiced by the monks and nuns, or—for the most menial work—by lay brothers, lay sisters, and servants. The latter groups were not officially recognized as members of the religious order, but they were expected to serve the sick in a spirit of monastic penance.[112] In the later nursing orders, however, nursing was afforded a spiritual value of its own. One fourteenth century nursing order, the Grey Sisters,

clearly thought their apostolic work was of equal spiritual value to their prayer
life, for they were excused from the Office if their work demanded their presence
elsewhere. Indeed, if a superior noticed that a woman preferred the contemplative
life to the active life, the superior was to force the woman back to her nursing
duties.[113]

A seventeenth century group, the Daughters of Charity, stated in their first rule that
the sisters' primary reason for nursing was to honor and serve Christ, who was
present in the sickest and most unfortunate of the patients.[114]

Catholic sisters in North America inherited this spiritual view of nursing: they
were religious caregivers first and nurses second. In the predominantly Protestant
and anti-Catholic environment of the United States, nursing was also an invaluable
way to wrest souls of dying heretics and lapsed Catholics from the grip of Satan.
This was an "evangelizing opportunity that belonged to them alone, and, as such,
the sisters were able to participate in 'man's work' of saving souls without
overstepping their place."[115]

As Mother Saint Pierre boasted to [her order's mother house in] Lyons in 1884:
"In the hospital we did good work with souls this year. I think that's why the
devil torments us so much in our works; he is losing some fine fish under the roof
of the Incarnate Word. We have had several conversions; baptism has regenerated
many a good thief who has gone straight to heaven after having received the grace
of reconciliation."[116]

One superior refused an offer of paid hospital work for her sisters until she could
be assured that it would offer them the opportunity to save the souls of lapsed
Catholic railroad workers. "No division was seen between devoted and attentive
nursing and evangelical work. It was actually *through* good nursing that hearts
were opened to God and souls on the way to hell were rescued."[117] Additionally,
as has already been mentioned, the sisters were extremely conscious of the role of
their nursing efforts in lessening anti-Catholic prejudice.

The religious dimension of nursing also inspired the Protestant deaconesses in
both Germany and the United States. The German Methodist deaconesses
considered nursing to be the ideal form of Christian social service. Spiritual
motivations were thus essential:

"Under no circumstance shall a young woman enter the hospital for the sole
purpose of only receiving the Nurse training, and then serve 'on her own'" . . .
Lack of the "necessary spiritual gifts" in an applicant constituted "a divine barrier
which closes the door of entrance" to the office of deaconess nurse.[118]

The Nurses Training School at Sibley Hospital required all probationers to have
taken "at least one year of Bible work" before entering the program.

Until the late nineteenth century, therefore, nursing remained idealized as a
religious, ascetical practice best suited to religious virtuosi, rather than as a

profession. Most people held hired lay nurses in very low esteem: "Poor working conditions, low pay, and lack of training were the three most notable deficiencies."[119] Lay nurses were often ill-educated and unmotivated; many were addicted to alcohol or narcotics, or were accused of lax moral behavior. Despite Florence Nightingale's attempts to reform the occupation after the model of the Catholic Sisters of Charity and the Deaconesses at Kaiserswerth, the nursing practices in most hospitals left much to be desired. The sisters and deaconesses were thus encouraged to offer their more spiritual training as a model to form lay students. "Much of the increased professionalization of nursing as a respectable career for women resulted from the high standards and rigorous discipline set in place by women's religious communities in the first half of the [nineteenth] century."[120] The first nursing schools had been limited to Catholic sisters or Protestant missionaries, but they soon began to accept lay students as well. Later, some nursing schools were founded by the home mission societies to train underprivileged and minority women as nurses.[121]

The nursing school faculties were especially diligent in attempting to inculcate religious motives in both the sisters/deaconesses and the lay students. "Emphasis on Christian principles and obedience to the Sisters in charge made this training somewhat akin to a novitiate."[122] The first Catholic nursing textbook, published in 1893, stated that nurses should be "activated by the holiest motives which religion inspires, to devote their lives to the alleviation of suffering humanity for Christ's sake."[123] Even secular nursing schools attempted to instill a mix of religious ideals, domestic practices, and military discipline in their students.

Like teaching, therefore, nursing was—even for those who were *not* sisters, deaconesses, or missionaries—a profoundly religious vocation.[124] In caring for the sick, the sisters were, quite literally, caring for the suffering Christ. They were also wresting souls, at the last possible moment, from the grip of the devil, and witnessing to heretics the superiority of their holy faith. Deaconess and missionary nurses likewise were converting souls to Christ through their ministrations, and their curing activities were in imitation of Jesus, the Great Physician. Hospitals, as the locales and training grounds for these holy activities, were themselves sacred places.

Social Work Ideologies

Throughout the Middle Ages, Catholics had viewed the poor and sick alike as unfortunate sinners, to be cared for in generalized hospitals which housed a mixed population of orphans, mental patients, the acute and chronically ill, and the elderly. Medieval Catholics focused on the spiritual benefits which donors would receive by giving alms to the poor, and "demonstrated little concern for whether the charity really benefitted the recipients."[125]

The poor were the keepers of the gates of heaven, where they awaited the coming of those who had practiced the Christian love of fellow men and women. The poor had earned their eternal happiness by accepting their lot with patience and by working hard, since work was a religious duty, a way to worship God. The rich, for their part, could only earn their place in heaven by carrying out good works, which in concrete terms meant that they had to give alms.[126]

As late as the eighteenth and nineteenth centuries, Catholics in Europe continued to view almsgiving as a religious duty, and as less meritorious if given to an agency rather than *personally* to the poor. Catholic priests and bishops during the Counter-Reformation also feared the sins that resulted from poverty: prostitution, incest from sleeping several to a bed, and theft, for example. Social services were deemed essential in stemming such evils.

Protestants, on the other hand, were concerned with differentiating between those worthy and those unworthy of assistance. "A new view of poverty emerged [after the Reformation] . . . homeless people and strangers, as well as drifters, vagrants and beggars, were identified with social unrest and crime."[127] Poverty was caused by sin, and the poor were in need of active attempts to discipline and reform their lives. The conversion and reform of the sinful poor would help to bring about the second coming of Christ and the promised millennium.[128] As the annual report of the American Board of Commissioners stated in 1834:

It is not only practical for multitudes to unite in the great purpose of evangelizing the world; but such a union is absolutely necessary, in order to bring about this great event in the shortest time. All the power and influence of the whole Christian world must be put in requisition, during the course of those beneficent labors which will precede the millennium.[129]

The first sociology professor at Scarritt College in Kansas City noted that "Jesus came to establish a new world order" of righteousness and brotherhood.[130] Social work would be instrumental in bringing this new world to its millennial fruition.

Social work activities in the nineteenth century United States were the special province of Protestant churchwomen:

Nineteenth century middle class women, freed from certain household labors by prosperity and emboldened by the religious impulse of the age, acted on the social definition of female virtue by establishing private missions, charities and benevolent societies whose efforts went beyond the informal assistance that had previously sustained communities for centuries.[131]

The immigrants in the new industrial cities were a particular focus of the women's efforts. It was imperative that these new arrivals be "Christianized," or they would "corrupt our people and destroy our own beloved institutions and substitute for our religion that of heathenism."[132] The archetype was a woman who visited indigent families "bearing food and clothing in one hand and a Bible in the other."

However, the women realized that, while their primary goal was spiritual reformation, "unless immediate relief is given to the suffering, the words of counsel and consolation fall coldly on the ear; they will not suffice to clothe the naked nor satisfy the cravings of hunger; we can only hope to render the mind susceptible of advice and consolation by relieving the body from its pressing wants."[133]

In addition to reforming the morals of the poor, Protestant reformers also attempted to save Catholic children from a "Popish" religion that they considered synonymous with poverty and intemperance.[134] It was precisely these "child saving" efforts, of course, that Catholics objected to. Nuns' efforts to preserve Catholic children from Protestant influence were "the single most important strain of charitable work through the rest of the nineteenth century."[135] By the end of the century, the Catholic hierarchy also worried that adults as well as children would succumb to Protestant proselytization, or that the temptations of the city would harm their immortal souls.

Conclusion

For the sisters, the deaconesses, and the members of the mission societies, therefore, building a panoply of religious schools, hospitals, orphanages, settlement houses, and other institutions was a holy work that would effect the salvation of the entire world.[136] If the masses were not saved, if the millennium did not come, it would be their fault and responsibility:

> How many women might die unsaved or unbaptized if the money isn't there to witness to them? How many women in prison for theft, prostitution, or murder will not hear the gospel because of scarce resources? How many Chinese, Indian, or Moroccan women will persist in believing "false doctrines" rather than following Christ because they never had access to a Bible? We cannot do it all, the leaders imply; we are doing all we can; you must give more, more, more to God through us.[137]

If the world was to become Christianized, as Christ had commanded, then the schools, hospitals, and social agencies established by the churchwomen were the indispensable agents of that Christianization.

Staffing and administering these holy institutions were the primary reasons for the very existence of the nineteenth century religious orders of nuns and the deaconesses. Securing financial support for these institutions was the defining activity of scores of Protestant missionary societies. Their combined efforts had profound and beneficial effects on the larger society of the nineteenth and early twentieth centuries. But founding, funding, staffing, and administering a set of religious schools, hospitals, or social welfare agencies had other effects: effects on the sponsoring groups themselves. The following chapters will outline these, both for the virtuoso groups involved and for the larger denominations as well.

Notes

1. See Mulhern (1959:528, 534) for England, Muller (1987:16) for Germany. See Cleary (2001:21) for a similar arrangement in Australia.

2. See Quartararo (1995:24) and Rapley (1990:149; 2001:218-34) for this arrangement in France.

3. See Mulhern (1958:526, 535) for this arrangement in Prussia and England. Beyerlein (2003:163-66) reports similar religious practices in nineteenth-century American public schools.

4. Quartararo (1995:41). This was because the nuns' stipends were low or virtually nonexistent; lay teachers would have had to be paid a salary (Quartararo 1995:73). The male teachers in the French boys' schools, in contrast, were 93 percent lay (Quartararo 1995:41).

5. See Walsh (2002:36) and John T. Smith (1998:237) for this information.

6. Mulhern (1958:548).

7. Cook (2002:249). See Miller (1985:26) for information on Presbyterian parochial schools.

8. These included Edgeworth Ladies Seminary in Pittsburgh (1825), Ipswich Female Seminary in Massachusetts (1828), Steubenville Female Seminary (1829), Mt. Holyoke Female Seminary (1837), and Hanover (Indiana) Female Academy (1835). See Miller (1985:25, 178-82). Several of these—Scotia Seminary in Concord, North Carolina (1867), and Atlanta Baptist Female Seminary (1881)—were for African American girls (DeBare 2004:112, 121). See Miller (1985:103) for the withdrawal of most Protestant denominations from elementary education after the development of the public school system.

9. Noll (2002:81). See also Beyerlein (2003).

10. Coburn and Smith (1999:161, 179), Brown (1949:156), and Kenneally (1990:56) provide these figures. A similar pattern occurred in Australia; see Cleary (2001:38).

11. Quoted in Oates (1980:146-47). See Oates (1999:36) for the figures in the following sentence. Similarly, the Australian and New Zealand bishops, meeting in 1885, adopted a policy of "schools before churches." Local parishes were required to construct a Catholic primary school even before constructing the church building, although in some areas the same structure was used for both purposes (Cleary 2001:38).

12. For the women, especially, these stipends were extremely small to non-existent: for sisters in the late nineteenth century, they averaged between $150 and $200 per sister per year. This was not enough for the sisters to live on, let alone fund the education of the novices, the care of the aged sisters, and the maintenance of the sisters' motherhouse. Furthermore, pastors often reneged on their contracts and refused to pay the sisters at all, forcing them to support themselves by giving music lessons outside of class (Logan, 1978:297). The stipends rose only slowly and did not keep pace with inflation: while the cost of living rose 43.7 percent between 1909 and 1921, the sisters' stipends rose only 24.9 percent (Oates 1985:192). Similarly, salaries paid to unmarried women missionaries by many Protestant denominations were lower than the salaries paid to unmarried men (Boyd and Brackenridge 1983:169).

13. John T. Smith (1998:67). See Lawson and Carden (1983) and Vance (1999:69) for the Seventh-day Adventists' schools. The first Adventist school was founded in 1872. By 1997, the Adventists operated 4,522 primary schools and 900 secondary schools (Vance 1999:67).

14. Meeker (1969:112).

15. See Meeker (1969:176-177) and Tatum (1960:225) for information regarding the

Society's colleges. See McDowell (1982:12) for schools sponsored by the Southern branch of the Methodist Church. See Boyd and Brackenridge (1983:40) for the Presbyterians, and see Higgenbotham (1993:24) and DeBare (2004:112, 121) for the American Baptists.

16. Cook (2002:255). Eleven of these are, or were, related to the United Methodist Church: Bennett College (Greensboro, NC), Bethune-Cookman College (Daytona Beach, FL), Claflin College (Orangeburg, SC), Clarke Atlanta University, Dillard University (New Orleans), Huston-Tillotson College (Austin, TX), Meharry Medical School (Nashville, TN), Paine College (Augusta, GA), Philander Smith College (Little Rock, AR), Rust College (Holly Springs, MS), and Wiley College (Marshall, TX).

17. Burtchaell (1998:562). The most heavily involved orders are the Jesuits, with 28 colleges and universities, and the Sisters of Mercy, with 19. See Gleason (2003) for a bibliographic survey of research on Catholic colleges and universities.

18. Burtchaell (1998:562-3).

19. Recently, the Vatican has ordered local bishops to exercise more administrative oversight over these colleges, especially with regard to their theology departments. Observers question whether this will be possible. See Tripole (2000) for an overview of this issue.

20. Burtchaell (1998:259, 261, 465, 518) outlines this history for several denominations.

21. The first such college was Cokesbury College in Abingdon, Maryland, established as one of the first acts of the 1784 Christmas Conference, which also established the Methodist Church in America (Elliott et al. 1976:13).

22. Lambert et al. (2002:144) note that "clergy and laypersons, both male and female, filled vital roles as faculty and administrators in [the Nazarene universities]: to a large extent, they *were* the universities."

23. See Hill (1985:127), Brereton and Klein (1979:309), and Boyd and Brackenridge (1983:177-78) for this information.

24. National College closed in 1964, and its records were transferred to Scarritt College. The Scarritt Bible and Training School had been founded in Kansas City in 1892 to train young women for foreign missionary service. It was expanded after 1902 to include deaconess training. After moving to Nashville in the early 1920s, it became a co-educational senior college and graduate school (Barbara Campbell, private communication). See Brereton (1981:197) and Tatum (1960:303-317) for a history of Scarritt College.

25. See Oates (1987), Madden (1991:339-346), Anthony (1997:34), and Noonan (1997:150) for examples of this process among Catholics; Miller (1985:184) for Presbyterians. See Stewart (1994:380-81) for the statistics on the number of Catholic women's colleges in 1915 and 1930.

26. Oates (1987:viii) notes that the average enrollment of the Catholic women's colleges during this period was less than 300, and that only one in five were accredited.

27. See Brereton and Klein (1979:313) for Protestant women's colleges; see Leahy (1991, chapter 3) for women's colleges run by Catholic religious orders. Morey (1995:3-5) and Gleason (1997:81) provide the 1994 figures on Catholic colleges. See Pettit (2004) for the 2000 figures.

28. These figures were compiled from Burtchaell (1998). See also Parsonage (1978:292) for a list of church-related colleges in 1975, and Elliott et al. (1976:35-143) for a comprehensive list of Methodist colleges.

29. McNamara (1996:253). See Maher (1989:33) for information on the Augustinian canonesses.

30. See Henderson (1999:76) for the Fatenbenfratelli. See Arrizabalaga (1999:166) for the Hospitallers of St. John of God, Jones (1999:232) for the Daughters of Charity, and Maher (1989:33) for the Quebec Augustinian Sisters. Other European groups included the Alexian Brothers (1330), who cared for plague victims, and the Third Order Franciscan Hospitallers, or "Grey Sisters," (1388), who had some 100 separate houses in France and Germany by 1500. See Kauffman (1995:14-15), McNamara (1996:254), and Ranft (1998:101).

31. Grell and Cunningham (1997:9).

32. Weber (2003:vii).

33. See Jones (2003:3) O'Neill (1989:67) and Risse (1999:473) for these figures. By the end of the twentieth century, however, the proportion of hospital beds that were in Catholic hospitals had fallen drastically, due to the expansion of public, for-profit, and other non-profit hospitals. Still, Catholics operated 637 hospitals and 122 home health care agencies in the United States at the end of the century—17 percent of all of the hospitals in the country (Weber 2003:16).

34. Thompson (1996:iii). See Maher (1989:33-34) for the information in the following sentences.

35. Quoted in Farren (1996:14). Similar opinions on the superiority of nursing sisters were current in Australia (Cleary 2001:45).

36. See Kauffman (1995:83), Maher (1989:70) and Farren (1996:3). In comparison, there were only 70 Catholic priests serving as army chaplains.

37. Coburn and Smith (1999:191). Nelson (2001:38-42) states that the three main reasons the nuns founded hospitals were: 1) pestilence, 2) lack of a hospital in an area, and 3) medical education. See Farren (1996:20-26) and Risse (1999:578) for examples.

38. O'Neill (1989:71).

39. See Wall (2002:22) and Nelson (2001:48) for the statistics on the number of hospitals the sisters founded. See Amos et al. (1993:2) for the number of nursing schools. See Nelson (2001:118) and Farren (1996:137-9) for a description of the sisters' insurance activities. By 1965, the number of nursing schools had fallen to 337, and it dropped precipitously after that (O'Connell 1986:136).

40. One exception was Sarah Doremus, who founded the New York City Women's Hospital in the early nineteenth century to care for poor women with gynecological problems (Van Liere 1991:22). And, beginning in the 1850's, the Seventh-day Adventists began to build or acquire hospitals; by 1900 they owned fourteen (Vance 1999:58).

41. See Vanderpool (1986:339) for the Methodists, Weber (1986:306-7) for the Baptists.

42. Barr (1972:91). The Disciples of Christ sponsored four hospitals in the Belgian Congo, three in the Philippines, and one in Tibet (Harrell 1986:389).

43. See Harrell (1986:388) and Meeker (1969:271) for a discussion of Sibley Hospital.

44. Dougherty (1997:207). See Golder (1903:334) for the figures in the following sentence.

45. Nelson (2001:139).

46. Vance (1999:68).

47. See Vanderpool (1986:339) for the Methodist hospitals; Weber (1986:306-307) for the Baptists; Vance (1999:68) and Numbers and Larson (1986:452, 459) for the Adventists; and O'Connell (1986:136) and Risse (1999:411) for the Catholics. In Australia, religious orders currently sponsor 50 hospitals and 54 nursing homes (Cleary 2001:107).

48. McNamara (1996:205).

49. McNamara (1996:485). See McNamara (1996:459ff), Maher (1989:32), and Ranft (1998:118) for other examples. See Walsh (2002:45, 175) for the information on Catholic social institutions in England and Wales.

50. See Luddy (2001:15) for social work and Irish nuns; see Nelson (2001:135) for the Deaconesses. See Cleary (2001:30) for social work by Australian sisters.

51. Wall (2002:24). See Miller (1985:13) for the Presbyterian orphanage in Philadelphia.

52. Higgenbotham (1993:177). See Cnaan et al. (1999:38) for further examples.

53. See Meeker (1969:179-263) and Tatum (1960, chapter 10) for social agencies sponsored by the Methodist mission societies; see Rosenberg (1971:127-120) for the agencies sponsored by the Episcopal mission societies.

54. Brereton (1981:187-189).

55. Popple and Reid (1999:10). See also Cnaan et al. (1999).

56. Rabe (1974:63). This is an early example of "secularization" of religious institutions in the U.S.—the replacement of religious authorities by professionals. See Chaves (1994).

57. See Farren (1996:82,106), and Brown and McKeown (1997:86-87, 90) for the statistics in this paragraph. See Anderson (2000) and Diner (1983:131) for the sisters' other social service activities.

58. Diner (1983:132).

59. Oates (1999:15). See Cleary (2001:42) for a similar rationale for Australian institutions.

60. Brown and McKeown (1997:52-61, 86). See also Oates (1995:73), and Moylan (1993:93). See Weber (2003:13) for a description of the professionalization of Catholic social services in the Los Angeles diocese.

61. Coburn and Smith (1999:212) and Moloney (2002:47,49) document these beliefs.

62 Brown and McKeown (1997:88) and Coburn and Smith (1999:212) both make this point.

63. Quoted in Beck (1965:64). See also Mulhern (1959:525). Similarly, the "Old Deluder Law" of the Massachusetts Bay Colony Puritans cited the need for universal education to enable children to read the Scriptures.

64. John T. Smith (1998:1) See also Elliott et al. (1976:14). Note, however, that not all churchmen were equally enthusiastic about education: Smith (1998:2) also reports a prevailing belief that too much education would render the poor dissatisfied with their God-given lot in life.

65. Mahoney (2002:36).

66. See McNamara (1996:620) for this belief among Catholics; Prelinger (1986b:221) and Nelson (2001:135) for Protestants.

67. Rapley (2001:234-5). See also Rapley (2001:233) and McNamara (1996:468) for the development of a Catholic ideology that advocated educating women: changing the women who nurtured the world in order to change the world. See Mulhern (1959:529) for Frederick William II of Prussia, following sentence.

68. Quoted in John T. Smith (1998:103).

69. Quoted in Morey (1995:71). Similarly, the 1869 Provincial Council of Australian bishops saw the primary purpose of education as providing a pervasively religious atmosphere that "would act upon the child's whole character of mind and heart." (Cleary 2001:25).

70. Brown (1949:527), italics added. See also Pfau (1934:28), Annarelli (1987:30),

Brewer (1987:11), Murphy (1988:246), and Ververka (1988:39), who also make this point.
    71. Quoted in Walch (1995:8). See also Kunkel (1988:68), who makes a similar point.
Smith (1998:17, 20) notes a similar fear among English Methodists.
    72. Quoted in Walsh (2002:110). See Cleary (2001:27) for Australian bishops.
    73. There were a few exceptions to this. German Lutheran immigrants wished to
preserve their culture and language from submersion in an English-speaking environment,
and Seventh-day Adventists wished to preserve their distinctive way of life. Both groups
also founded separate systems of religious schools.
    74. Hill (1985:40). See also Huehls (2004:54).
    75. See Hill (1985:42); Coburn and Smith (1999:162); Mahoney (2002:29) and
Marsden (1994:83-84) for accounts of this rivalry.
    76. Marsden (1994:37). See Thomas, Peck, and DeHaan (2003:358) for the influence
of post-millennial theology on education.
    77. Quoted in Meeker (1969:70). See also Phillips (1974:101). If the world was to
become Christian, early Methodist social activists thought, America must lead them to the
truth—which meant that Americans themselves had to be thoroughly evangelized
(McDowell 1982:71).
    78. See Miller (1985: 25, 187, 196) and McDowell (1982:37) for this belief among
Presbyterians and Methodists, respectively. Rapley (2001:233) makes a similar point for
Catholics.
    79. Quoted in Burtchaell (1998:820).
    80. Mary Lyon, founder. Quoted in Hill (1985:42). See Hughes (1999:85) for the
quote in the following sentence, and Higgenbotham (1993:34) for Spelman College's motto.
    81. Quoted in Burtchaell (1998:396). Emphasis in the original.
    82. Carpenter (2002:193). See also Longfield and Marsden (1992:102).
    83. Roberts and Turner (2000:20). See also Thomas, Peck, and DeHaan (2003:358).
    84. Cherry (1995:ix, 2). See also Sloan (1994:22), Marsden (1994:37).
    85. Contosta (1995:87).
    86. Quoted in O'Connell (2002:67-68).
    87. Fr. John P. O'Dwyer. Quoted in Contosta (1995:31).
    88. Quoted in Shea (1999:203). See also Ververka (1988:39), Annarelli (1987:30),
Brewer (1987:11), Murphy (1988:246), Morey (1995:121) and Shea (1999:212).
    89. John Carroll, the first American bishop, stated that the main reason for founding
Georgetown College was the recruitment and formation of priests (Heft 2003:36).
    90. Leahy (1997:52). See also Morey (1995:179) and Daigler (2000:203-209).
    91. See, for example Leahy (1997:50) and Oates (1987:vii), who make this criticism.
    92. Gleason (1995:90). This may have been due to the "Americanist" controversy: in
1899, Pope Leo XIII had condemned the notion that Catholicism could ever conform to
American ideals of liberty and individual autonomy. As a result, Catholic colleges may have
focused more on developing their own Catholic culture rather than integrating their students
into the intellectual life of the larger American society (See Noll 2002:81).
    93. Gallin (1999:112). See also Gallin (2000:10) and Leahy (1997:54).
    94. Quoted in Morey (1995:72). See Leahy (1997:52) and Gallin (2000:23) for the
information in the following sentences.
    95. See Lambert et al. (2002:145) for Nazarene ideologies of education; Vance
(1999:63, 67) for Seventh-day Adventist ideologies; Carpenter (2002:182) for Presbyterian
ideologies; and Keim (2002:270-273) for Mennonite ideologies. Benne (2002:98) notes,
however, that not all denominational traditions have been equally committed to valuing

higher education.

96. Marsden (1994:83) makes this argument. See Hughes (1999:85-90) for colleges as a prophetic witness.

97. Starr (1982:145). See Risse (1999:85, 104) and Kauffman (1995:10) for the information on the housing of the sick in monasteries. See Palmer (1999:89-90) and Dinges (1999:249) for the information on hospitals as sacred places.

98. Risse (1999: 108,123, 151, 193) and Kauffman (1995:106) make this observation. As late as the late 1700s, French Catholics who donated money to hospitals or visited the sick were granted indulgences.

99. Risse (1999:216-217).

100. Kauffman (1995) discusses this belief in chapter 3 of his book.

101. Pullan (1999:23).

102. Risse (1999:218-219). See also Pullan (1999:29).

103. Quoted in Jones (1999:224).

104. Risse (1999:514). See Kauffman (1995:224) for the quote in the following sentence.

105. Quoted by Dolan (1998:197). See also McNamara (1996:624).

106. See Risse (1999:468), Coburn and Smith (1999:195), and Kauffman (1995:71) for ethnic tensions that resulted in the founding of separate hospitals for (e.g.) Irish and German Catholics. See Starr (1982:174) and Wall (2002:32) for accounts of the struggles of Catholic sisters to keep their hospitals open to all doctors. See Risse (1999:523) and McNamara (1996:624) for the use of hospitals as evangelization tools.

107. See Numbers and Larson (1986:453, 461) for the ideology underlying Adventist hospitals; Dorff (1986:19) for the Jewish hospitals. See Klaassen (1986:279) for the reasons for founding Mennonite hospitals.

108. Meeker (1969:271). For example see Coburn and Smith (1999:191) on Florence Nightingale.

109. See Weber (1986:300-301, 306) and Hill (1985:129). See Dougherty (1997:94) for prerequisites to soul healing.

110. Quoted in Weber (1986:306).

111. Quoted in Dougherty (1997:125). See also Meeker (1969:271).

112. See Kauffman (1995:154) for the religious motives for nursing. See Kauffman (1995:22), McNamara (1996:255), and Risse (1999:107, 141, 143-52) for the religious status of lay brothers and lay sisters.

113. Ranft (1998:101).

114. Maher (1989:38, 120). Many of the nursing communities' Rules quoted Matthew 25:34-40, "As long as you did it for one of the least of these..." See Maher (1989:101), Kauffman (1995:22), and McNamara (1996:255).

115. Nelson (2001:109). See also McNamara (1996:624, 627).

116. Quoted in Nelson (2001:104). Deathbed conversions were the basic goal; the sisters considered their nursing efforts a failure otherwise, even if the patient was healed in body (Nelson 2001:108).

117. Nelson (2001:113). See Nelson (2001:104) for the anecdote in the previous sentence.

118. Resolution of the 1904 German Central Annual Conference Deaconess Board, quoted by Dougherty (1997:54). See also Dougherty (1997:135) for the quotation from the Training School at Sibley Hospital.

119. Risse (1999:368).

120. Walsh (2002:14).

121. Brewster Hospital in Jacksonville, established by the Methodist Women's Home Missionary Society, was one of these. See Meeker (1969:278-80).

122. Risse (1999:519). See also Coburn and Smith (1999:200) and Kauffman (1995:158). See Cleary (2001:48, 148) for similar religious underpinnings of nurses' training in Australia.

123. Quoted in Kauffman (1995:159).

124. McNamara (1996:625-6), Kauffman (1995:154-58), Risse (1999:369, 371), and Coburn and Smith (1999:191) all make this point.

125. Kouri (1997:177). Many pious foundations were established in the late Middle Ages by wealthy donors to distribute money to the poor in return for a Mass being said for the soul of the founder (Riis 1997:132).

126. Soly (1997:98). Cnaan et al. (1999:101) note that the Russian Orthodox church, too, saw poverty as a fact of life and God's will for the poor. See Stolberg (2002:117) for the superior merit of almsgiving personally to the poor.

127. Risse (1999:216-17). See also McNamara (1996:477-478), Soly (1997:89),and Schwartz (2000:8). See Gijswijt-Hofstra (2002) and Dross (2002) for the idea that poverty was caused by sin.

128. Schwartz (2000:85). See also Field (1974:28) and Phillips (1974:93).

129. Quoted in Boyd and Brackenridge (1983:241). See also Edwards and Gifford (2003:3). Edwards (2003:37, 40) notes that these beliefs were also influenced by "newer Social Darwinist views of the evolution of human history."

130. McDowell (1982:23).

131. Stadum (1999:31). See also Ginzberg (1990) and Gifford (2003).

132. Eleventh Annual Report of the women's Parsonage and Home Mission Society, 1896. Quoted in McDowell (1982:65). See Stadum (1999:31) for the quotation in the following sentence.

133. Mrs. J.P. Webb, Secretary of the Wasnington, DC, Female Union Benevolent Society of the Presbyterian Church. Quoted in Miller (1985:104).

134. Coburn and Smith (1999:205). See also Rosenberg (1971:5-8, 23).

135. Coburn and Smith (1999:205). See also McNamara (1996:624), Oates (1999:15), and Anderson (2000:69,71) for the worries of the hierarchy.

136. A point made by Wendy Edwards (2003:40) in her study of the writings of Josiah Strong, and by R.A.R. Edwards (2003:152).

137. Quoted in Griffith (1997:164). See Keller (1981:253), McDowell (1982:29), and Miller (1985:122), who also make this point.

PART II

IMPACTS OF INSTITUTIONS

As many historians and social scientists have noted, the dominant presence of religious virtuosi serving as founders, administrators, and staff exerted a profound influence on the early years of their colleges, hospitals, and social service agencies.[1] The religious order or mission society was often the parent corporation that owned the institutions' facilities, chose their original sites, and drew up plans for their subsequent expansion. The majority of the Catholic institutions' staffs—or at least of their administrators—were sisters, whose lifestyle set the pattern for the institutions' day-to-day operations.[2] The institutions' boards of trustees, too, were composed of sisters or mission society members. The sisters or deaconesses, in their distinctive garb, were a visible sign of the institutions' religious character, relieving the larger denomination of immediate responsibility to ensure this identity.[3] In some cases, the boundaries between the institution and the religious sponsor were so blurred that the institutions "operated more like a family enterprise than an impersonal corporation."[4]

But the influence was also reciprocated. The following chapters will argue that religious institutions shaped the basic identity of the sponsoring denominations and denominational groups, affected their recruitment of new members, served as focal points of internal division, and provided resources that sisters, deaconesses, and mission societies could use to increase their power, both in the denomination as a whole and in the larger society.

Chapter 2

Organizational Identity

The first and most obvious impact of religious institutions was in shaping the very identity of the sponsoring groups. According to organizational culture theorists, "corporate or organizational identity concerns those features of the organization that members perceive as ostensibly *central, enduring,* and *distinctive in character* that contribute to how they define the organization and their identification with it."[5] Corporate identity can have both a private, internal aspect (how the members perceive the organization), and a public, external one (how outsiders view the organization). Public identity can be further subdivided into a "construed external image"—how the members think outsiders perceive the organization—and a "desired or communicated image"—the one they want outsiders to have.[6] Some writers claim that the larger the gap between an organization's public and private identities, the less healthy the organization is.

All organizational identities, whether public or private, must meet the three basic criteria implied in the definition given above. They must define both what is *central* or most important about the organization and what is unique or *distinctive* about it. The organization's identity must also be perceived as *enduring* continuously since its beginning, without any significant or fundamental change. This latter characteristic can be more problematic, and will be explored in this chapter.

While it is true that organizations' identities are fundamentally shaped by the circumstances of their founding, it is *not* true that these identities remain unchanged in subsequent decades. Most, if not all, organizations experience an "identity drift," as they gradually assume a hybrid of two or more distinct, and sometimes incompatible, identities.[7] There are several reasons for this identity drift: 1) the organization's surrounding environment often grows more complex and exerts pressure on it to adapt, 2) it is difficult for an organization to jettison old identities to which some of its members are still attached, and 3) it is relatively easy for organizations to add on new identities, either by default or by being successful at their first one.

But the organizations rarely notice how their identities have changed:

> [T]he identity of an organization during the growth phase of its life cycle exists
> often only in latent form. It is taken for granted and lies submerged under the
> press of the day-to-day problems of managing growth. Under these conditions
> organizations often begin to play roles and take on orientations different from
> those originally envisioned by their founders. But this transformation process
> often occurs so unobtrusively and at such a slow pace that it is not fully
> recognized until an organizational crisis forces members to explicitly examine
> their collective identity.[8]

Identity reformulation is a time-consuming, contentious, and dangerous process,
bringing the daunting prospect of actually destroying the organization in its wake.
Organizations typically avoid addressing their identity drift, therefore, unless a
severe crisis of some sort has left them no other alternative.

Studies of identity formation and change have usually focused on these
dynamics in schools, hospitals, and other nonprofit service organizations.[9] But
denominations and denominational groups are subject to the same dynamics. As
with their schools, hospitals, and social service agencies, the initial identities of
sponsoring religious groups were strongly influenced by their founding relationship
with their institutions. In subsequent decades, religious sponsors, too, were subject
to identity drift, at least partly in response to changes in their own organizational
fields. To understand and recognize this drift, however, it is necessary to examine
how religious institutions had shaped their sponsors' identity in the first place.

The Founding Identity of Virtuoso Groups

Of Catholic Religious Orders

The officially-stated purpose of Catholic religious orders, as in most faith
traditions containing organized virtuoso groups, has always been the spiritual
perfection of the individual virtuoso. Teaching the young, ministering to the poor,
or nursing the sick may have been activities in which some medieval nuns or
mendicant friars engaged, but they were ancillary to the orders' primary purpose.[10]
Only after the late sixteenth century were Catholic religious orders established
primarily to perform some institutionalized service. Catholic theologians such as
Ignatius of Loyola and Vincent de Paul had articulated a "reformed Catholicism
[which] incorporated many of the welfare policies advocated by humanists and
Protestants," and each had begun a hugely successful religious order—the Jesuits
and the Daughters of Charity—specifically to teach, nurse, and care for the poor.
In the following centuries, the service-oriented model developed by Ignatius of
Loyola and Vincent de Paul became the standard one:

Here we see the birth of female lay communities which were transformed into religious communities. In the beginning of the eighteenth century, unmarried peasant women living in the same village formed groups of three or four that would establish a civil contract before a notary. These contracts regulated their communal life, stipulated the goods of each one, the mutual aid for which they were responsible, *and what tied them together: common work, opening a school, a pharmacy, a hospice, or a hospital for the village.*[11]

The new French teaching orders of the seventeenth and eighteenth centuries specifically stated in their constitutions that "the first end and principal aim" of their monasteries was the instruction of young girls. The traditional monastic goal of personal spiritual perfection was de-emphasized.

By the nineteenth century, the vast majority of extant Catholic religious orders of women had been founded to do specific charitable works in the context of formally-organized institutions.[12] Despite this fact, however, official Church doctrine continued to insist that the primary goal of these groups was the spiritual perfection of their members and that the services they offered were secondary. Consequently, both purposes were often listed in the orders' constitutions, and entering cohorts of novices were taught that the two were inseparable: that one furthered one's own spiritual development by diligent service in the order's institutions.

This study's eleven focus groups of older, retired sisters reflected this belief. When asked to describe how they had viewed the purpose of their order when they had first entered it, six groups mentioned the official goal of spiritual perfection. All six, however, linked this goal to the order's service of others:

- I really came just to save my soul, and anybody else I could on the way.
- Isn't it that the primary end of religious life in those days was to save your own soul? That's what all the vow books said (Focus Group 1.6: Active and retired sisters).[13]

- What the constitution used to say. Helping others and taking care of our own souls, or however it said.
- Sanctification, it used to say something about our sanctification in the ministry to others (Focus Group 3.3: Retired sisters).

An additional five focus groups cited the particular institutional services their order had performed, but *without* mentioning the official primary goal of individual spiritual perfection:

- To educate.
- Health care and education.
- Those were the two principal ministries.
- A lot of what we're talking about went on in both of those institutions (Focus Group 1.3: Active sisters).

- To teach or be in a hospital or an orphanage [laughter] Those were the three good—
-Those were the three big ones (Focus Group 3.2: Retired sisters).

In contrast, *no* group cited individual spiritual perfection as their order's primary goal without mentioning some form of service as well.

In the Catholic religious orders, therefore, the performance of particular services in an organized institutional context was viewed by the members as a primary reason for the group's very existence, on at least an equal plane with the traditional purpose of fostering the members' own spiritual virtuosity.[14] The amalgamation of these two theological articulations of Catholic virtuoso spirituality —that one saved one's own soul by the selfless service of others—was written in the formal constitutions of the orders, as well as on the hearts and minds of those who, attracted by this vision, chose to enter them.

Of the Protestant Deaconesses

Protestant deaconess groups had also been founded for charitable service, usually, but not always, in an institutional context. The Kaiserswerth deaconesses were originally established for hospital work, and were imported to other countries for the express purpose of taking charge of Lutheran hospitals there. According to the annual report of the English Wesleyan deaconesses, their order existed "to supply qualified and devoted women-workers to towns, villages, mission circuits, or churches, either in the United Kingdom or abroad."[15] The Methodist Deaconess Society, established in 1895 in Buffalo, New York, defined its purpose as "1.) The collection and training of Christian young women and lone widows to the exercise of Christian benevolence, and 2.) the establishment and support of institutions in which deaconesses may give their services for the welfare of suffering and imperilled humanity."[16] Likewise, the various women's missionary societies in Protestant denominations were established for the express purpose of supporting the schools, hospitals, and orphanages in which the deaconesses and missionaries served.[17]

The original Protestant articulation of denomination-sponsored social services did not, however, include saving one's *own* soul through these works. While Catholic charity in the Middle Ages had focused primarily on increasing the donor's prospects of salvation in the afterlife, the reformers taught that *all* Christians, enlisted and organized by the civil and religious authorities, were to aid the poor, the sick, and the ignorant, so that they might become "active and useful members of the Christian commonwealth."[18] Thus would the entire society, not merely the individual donor, be sanctified.

None of the three focus groups of deaconesses mentioned the idea that they had expected to advance in their own personal spirituality through their service:

(Interviewer: What would you say was the purpose of the deaconesses at the time you became one?)
- Service.
- Commitment.
- And commitment, yeah.
- Long-term commitment.
- Working with people.
- Working out your Christian faith through the profession which you have chosen and doing it under the direction of the Church (Focus Group 4.1:Retired deaconesses).

For the deaconesses even more than for the sisters, therefore, the primary purpose of their office was the performance of service under church auspices.

The Ongoing Formation and Persistence of Internal Identity

Institutional service not only shaped the identity of women's virtuoso groups at their inception. It also permeated the training and work lives of subsequent generations of their members, thus giving them "a similar grounding and focus as they approached their ministerial work."[19] The hospitals, orphanages, and schools were also the sisters' and deaconesses' homes. Their daily interactions while nursing, teaching, or caring for orphans, as well as after the work day was over, thus reinforced their distinct *esprit de corps*, as well as nurturing bonds of friendship:

> [S]isterhood organized the lives and outlooks of individual sisters. Their letters and journals show affection among women whose paths crossed many times. Sisters lived in dormitory-like quarters in their motherhouse or small subcommunities in distant locations. Annual retreats gathering large numbers of sisters at the motherhouse and assignments to new locations allowed sisters to renew acquaintances and share memories. . . . The values and realities of the community created within it an institutional memory that cemented their identity and calling.[20]

In the Protestant missionary training schools, students

> traded accounts of their work in city missions and settlement houses, prayed and worshipped together, and avidly followed the accomplishments of those who had graduated before them, particularly those who had served as foreign missionaries. Through letters and return visits, alumnae became big sisters in an extended school family.[21]

The older sisters and deaconesses in the focus grouups cited numerous incidents in their initial training that had deepened their bonding to each other and to their order:

> - I remember when, well, there were three floors in the dormitory where I lived and you got all kinds of smart answers when you called to one of the floors. And one time I answered, "Seventh heaven, which angel would you like to speak to?" and it was the House Mother. [laughter]
> - That's better; it could have been "Joe's Bar." I did that once. [laughter]
> - It was a matter that we were still human beings, we enjoyed a good joke, we needed to be loved, we needed to be appreciated, and we needed fellowship. I have heard a lot of raving about the wonderful fellowship [we had] (Focus Group 4.1: Retired deaconesses).

> I enjoyed those years [of the novitiate]. As much heartache as we sometimes had to face, we had so much fun. It was a good time. And we got into trouble over silly stuff. . . . You know, like sneaking down to the refectory and getting cartons of milk and bringing them back to the dorm. . . . And it was a wonderful thing. It was innocent. We had a wonderful time (Focus Group 3.10: Active sisters).

> One of the things that sustained us in our five years together in the novitiate—our peer group gave us such support. We cried together, we laughed together. We are still good friends (Focus Group 1.3: Active sisters).

Similar bonding interaction also occurred later on, in the schools and hospitals where the sisters and deaconesses served:

> Friday nights were special when we were young sisters. We would always meet down in the basement and starch the caps [which went under our veils] and guimpes. And it was kind of like letting our hair down. You could make a lot of noise down there (Focus Group 3.2: Retired sisters).

> [While leading the prayers one morning], it was October 6th, the feast of St. Bruno, and I said, "St. Bruno was a monk, and he led his monks through a rocky and mountainous dessert." [laughter] I couldn't stop laughing. All I could see were marshmallows and sticky, uh, fudge and well, everybody laughed. . . . I was afraid I was going to get scolded, but I finally stopped laughing by biting on one of my fingers (Focus Group 3.2: Retired sisters).

> [At our hospital, there were] about fifty sisters there at one time. . . . And we had a big dining room and all the young sisters sat at the lower table and we had more fun. It was a great place. We laughed. It was just a good community place, really (Focus Group 3.3: Retired sisters).

The focus groups remembered this institutionally-fostered togetherness with nostalgia:

> Whenever we had so many sisters involved in schools and hospitals, we had such a group of sisters living together. . . . Like my years at St. Joseph's school, there were twelve of us living together and I just have so many happy memories of that

community aspect that I said to somebody one time, I would just love to be able to go back to that sometime. I mean, there's a lot of the old way that I wouldn't want to go back to, but certainly some of those memories of the sharing and the good times that we had, I would just like to go back to today (Focus Group 3.11: Active sisters).

I go back in my own case to X Convent and X High School. That's where you formed these friendships that were lifetime, because it was a matter of throwing all your energies—and we lived together as well– there was a kind of totality of life that had to do with both the living and the working and then the connections we made with each other (Focus Group 2.6: Active and retired sisters).

Of the 27 focus groups of sisters and deaconesses, 21 mentioned similar experiences which had fostered friendship and a common spirit among them.

Although the women in the missionary societies did not experience the bonding that came from living together, several cited similar experiences occurring during the course of their activities in the society. One African American focus group remembered traveling to their district meetings in a neighboring state:

Our meetings were separate from what our [white] counterparts had. We did not go to their meetings. We had our own meetings, and I can remember going to them in [state]. We went to the college there for our meetings and so forth. That's when we drove up and had our hallelujah good time (Focus Group 5.9: Mission society).

Most (7) of the nine focus groups of the missionary society mentioned the fellowship fostered by their common activities:

The thing that attracted me all through the years was the care and concern of the women in the church and particularly in the [mission society]. They seemed to have an uncanny ability to make you feel wanted and accepted, and I wish that this could be projected and given to the younger women today. I'm not sure how to transfer that (Focus Group 5.1: Mission society).

The closeness fostered by these interactions gave a sense of belonging and support that sustained the members in stressful times. This was mentioned by 28 of the 36 focus groups of sisters, deaconesses, and mission society members:

- The other thing was the tremendous supportive fellowship within the Deaconess community. . . . And when we went through tough times, there was always, because I remember this particular climactic time in my life when things were really, really rough, and the Klan was out there and all that. And I got a call from one of the deaconesses, the head of an institution, saying "I heard about it; I'm there with you." You know, that fellowship, that kind of support.
- And see, I've always been fortunate, when I was at X High School, there were six or seven of us there. At Y School, there were three or four or five, something like that. So I wasn't one that was alone somewhere in a community center (Focus

Group 4.2: Retired deaconesses).

And we were very supportive of each other. I remember for months, I was always going to [leave the convent and] go home. And Sister Catherine, who was a year older than I was, used to take me down to the basement and sit me on the trunk and say, "Now, Ann, you can stay for one more day. Just stay for tomorrow, that's all you have to stay." Well, obviously, 66 years later, I'm still here. But we were very supportive of each other (Focus Group 3.1: Retired sisters).

We've had ups and downs in [the local mission society chapter], but this is a very strong church with a lot of women who are willing to give you the time—We've got older women, middle women, younger women, and everybody's willing to work together and I think that's the strength of who we are. And I think that's why, through a lot of turmoil in our church, this group of women was able to continue (Focus Group 5.6: Mission society).

We knew poverty, first hand. Up in [rural town], for instance, we'd be up at the crack of dawn and make thirteen fires. One in the convent and the rest in the school. But, you know, we use the word hardship, but we had such a good time doing those things (Focus Group 1.1: Retired sisters).

The common service activities which each group's members performed, therefore, strengthened their bonds of friendship and their sense of common purpose. And, in turn, the reinforced friendship and purpose which the sisters, deaconesses, and mission society members received from their institutional service helped to strengthen their commitment to the group.

Recruitment and Internal Identity

Finally, the institutions shaped the sponsors' identities through the way they attracted new recruits. Catholic orders which staffed upscale private academies, for example, tended to attract novices of a higher socio-economic status than those which staffed orphanages. The Kaiserswerth deaconesses began to attract more educated and middle-class women to their ranks once they expanded from hospital work into educational institutions.[22] American Catholic sisters and Protestant deaconesses serving German, Irish, or Slavic immigrants drew entrants from the ethnic group they served. Over time, each group's internal identity took on a particular flavor from the predominant class or ethnic background of the members who had been recruited through its institutions.

In addition to attracting women of a certain class or ethnic group, the sisters' institutional service also affected both the public and private identities of their order by attracting women who expected to perform professional service in an institutional setting, and who preferred this career choice over motherhood or an individual profession:

Well, I think in those days, too, as a young woman, if you weren't married, single, a nurse, um, or a teacher, there was no avenue for a woman. A religious avenue actually was the only way you could be a more professional person. I mean, the things in social work and all these things that exist now, all these, uh, things that work with government and states and counties and all that. I mean religious [sisters] did most of that . . . You know, there were just these few ways . . . It gave you the avenue to be a professional person (Focus Group 1.4: Active sisters).

I've heard a lot of sisters say it. That the reason they came to the Sisters of X was to serve God in a group of people who also wanted to love and serve God. And a lot of sisters have said that, as a person who had a desire yourself for personal holiness, you would reach out to others to help them through the ministries to be good, holy people (Focus Group 1.1: Retired sisters).

The mindsets which these women brought to their orders helped shape and reinforce the group's culture—which, in turn, attracted the next generation of like-minded women.

Both the sisters and the deaconesses tended to see an intimate connection between their work and their religious call:

- It was just part of the life, what you were supposed to do.
- This was, this was exciting.
- That was our apostolate, you know, your teaching was what you were sent out to do, God wanted you to do that (Focus Group 3.4: Retired sisters).

I had a struggle about whether I wanted to go overseas [as a missionary] or stay at home [as a deaconess]. But after I went to seminary, we helped to educate the students . . . I was thrilled and felt that it really was my calling. We made a map of the world and then we would put ribbons on everywhere we had educated or trained one of the students (Focus Group 4.1: Retired deaconesses).

For myself, I've liked every place I've been. There's always been good things about every job. And I've always looked forward to the next thing. And I think I feel the same way with my spiritual life. It has been a growing process, and every place I go there's something there that's new and different and it calls forth, it intensifies my relationship with God, so I just think it's been a good time, since the beginning (Focus Group 2.2: Retired sisters).

Most, in fact, found it difficult to separate one from the other:

- It was all very integrated.
- I didn't make that dichotomy, it was all of a piece.
- Yes.
- Yes (Focus Group 2.6: Active and retired sisters).

In summary, these educational, health care, and social service institutions shaped the internal identity of the orders who sponsored, staffed, and supported them. When asked to articulate what their order's or society's central purpose had been in the past, most members cited the provision of institutionalized service. The distinctive character of each group was shaped by the social class or ethnic group served by the institutions (which were the primary sources of new recruits), and through the *esprit de corps* fostered by the sisters' or deaconesses' early training and subsequent lives together. In turn, these common bonds gave the sisters, the deaconesses, and (to a certain extent, at least) the mission society members the strength to persevere in difficult times, thus further contributing to the survival and growth of their order or society.

Forming the External Identity of the Sponsoring Group

The external identities of the virtuoso religious groups were also shaped by their institutional service, since this service was, one historian notes, "the public face of private philanthropic enterprise."[23] The Catholic sisters' nursing activities during the Civil War, as well as during the recurring cholera, typhus, and diphtheria epidemics which ravaged nineteenth century U.S. cities, were instrumental in dissipating nativist prejudices against them. By 1900, Protestant diatribes against nuns as agents of Rome and slaves of priests had been replaced by almost universal admiration of their devoted service and their business acumen.[24] In nineteenth century England, evangelical suspicion of the "popish" Anglican nuns was greatly lessened by "the heroic self-sacrificial actions of the sisters, whether in cholera epidemics, slum parishes, or in caring for orphans and the elderly poor."

The sisters in the focus groups shared similar stories of how their institutional service had affected the public identity of their order:

> I found it in [city], too, the thanks to all the sisters that have been up there for these one hundred years. That there's such a level of respect and appreciation for the sisters and what the sisters have done and what their presence in [city] has meant over all the years. I chuckle to myself, because we've had some characters around, but, still, there's that respect (Focus Group 1.6: Retired and active sisters).

> - I was up at the city planing commission yesterday . . . and I got up and told them I was a Sister of X. I frequently do that and people do know us.
> - A lot of them from their grade school experiences or their family being taken care of at the hospital.
> - I think there's a trust there (Focus Group 2.3: Present and former leaders).

> I can give you an old, old experience. It used to be when we were in the habit and we were in the center of downtown, you never went up to a store on Main Street without meeting people that you had had as patients. Or people who were familiar with the sisters who were trying to take care of sick people at the hospital. And they would say, "Oh, my mother was at St. Mary's Hospital." That kind of thing

(Focus Group 3.6: Present and former leaders and staff).

During their time of service in hospitals, schools, and orphanages, the religious orders were well known and, for the most part, respected in the larger community.

In contrast, the nineteenth century deaconesses were often much less visible in their hospitals, since these institutions were founded and overseen by male clergy and philanthropists. In many denominations, it was these men, not the deaconesses, who comprised the public face of the institutions. Possibly in consequence, therefore, the external identity of the deaconesses in these denominations was less well defined than that of Catholic sisters.[25]

The lack of a tradition of organized virtuoso service within Protestantism also impacted the image of the deaconesses. As one delegate to the 1888 Methodist General Conference, which first authorized the office of deaconess in the northern church, remarked, "I do not think that there is one man in this conference who really knows what the term 'deaconess' means."[26] The focus groups of deaconesses noticed a similar identificational vagueness today:

I've noticed a big difference between [denominational jurisdictional areas]. I went from [state], were there are deaconesses everywhere . . . and moved to [another state]. When I went in and introduced myself to my minister—he's a wonderful minister—he introduced me as a deacon candidate to the congregation. Because he had no idea what a deaconess was (Focus Group 4.3: Active deaconesses).

To the extent that the sisters and deaconesses were known through service in their institutions, the public, external, identity which they gained in this manner also influenced their *internal* identity. Church leaders and the laity often believed that teaching or nursing by a sister or deaconess was superior in quality to the same activity performed by a hired lay staff member.[27] This public belief could then become an additional part of how the orders' members viewed themselves:

I think there was a certain pride in, if someone did well, some school did well, you sort of, um, well I—there was a reflection from that to yourself, because you belonged to that group that did so well. The hospital did that well, or the sisters that were successful. You thought, "Oh, that's great!" you know (Focus Group 3.4: Retired sisters).

Their institutional service thus profoundly shaped both the public and private identities of the religious groups. Their "success" was judged, both inside and outside the Church, by the success of their institutions.

Forming the Identity of the Larger Denomination

As important as they were in forming the external and internal identities of the orders and mission societies, institutionalized mission services were also key factors in shaping the identity—and sometimes in catalyzing the very existence— of entire denominations. Many congregational-polity denominations had originally adopted a centralized structure at least partly in order to run their institutions more effectively.[28] Often, a denomination's educational institutions were key actors in shaping its distinctive vision and theological stance. According to several historians, the Baptist system of higher education had a foundational impact on Baptist religious identity, synthesizing otherwise disparate trends and beliefs through a common commitment to the mission of education.[29] Among Mennonites, Harold Bender, the dean of the Biblical Seminary at Goshen College and a key educational leader within the denomination, authored a seminal essay on "The Anabaptist Vision" and edited a four-volume *Mennonite Encyclopedia*. Through these activities, he and his fellow academics were a key factor in centering Mennonite identity in Anabaptism rather than in evangelical fundamentalism:

> For Mennonites it ... became a manifesto for a postwar identity. In time "Anabaptist" identity became a Mennonite folk myth. Perhaps its power was that it allowed Mennonites to continue a strong sense of peoplehood and distinctiveness even as many began shedding older boundary-markers such as plain attire.[30]

Similarly, Seventh-day Adventist colleges were instrumental in articulating a distinctive Adventist identity.[31] Valparaiso University and St. Olaf College once performed a similar function for the Lutheran Church Missouri Synod and the Evangelical Lutheran Church of America, respectively.

In addition to providing the theological and organizational underpinnings for a denomination's beginning, educational institutions have also helped develop its public and private identities in a variety of other ways. Many colleges provide ongoing support for their denomination's identity through their research activities. Goshen College's Mennonite Historical Library is an internationally-recognized church resource, and Goshen also sponsors many major church-wide events.[32] Baylor University has established a Baptist Studies program and a Center for Christian Ethics, has co-operated with the Baptist General Conference of Texas to start a Center for Ministry Effectiveness, and has hosted numerous BGCT events, seminars, and workshops on its campus. Notre Dame houses the Cushwa Center for the Study of American Catholicism. The Ohio Wesleyan University's library houses a Methodist history collection, and another Wesleyan college regularly conducts a think tank for denominational leaders. Valparaiso University continues to support centers, institutes, and programs that explore the Lutheran perspective on contemporary issues.[33] Religious colleges have also served as homes for scholarly publications that explore the relationship between denominational thought and societal developments: *Spectrum* (Seventh-day Adventists), *Dialog*

(Mormons), and the *Mennonite Quarterly Review*, for example. Theologians in denominational colleges and universities—especially if a denominational seminary is located there—have helped articulate and spread official religious perspectives to both clergy and laity in the local congregations.[34]

A denomination's connections with its educational, health care and social service organizations have also helped nourish and transmit strong communal bonds, a common world view, and a collective memory across generations. It is difficult, one Australian writer remarked, even to discuss the development of the Catholic Church in that country without also mentioning the Catholic school system there:

> More than any other single factor, the schools are the key to understanding the religious life of Australian Catholics. From the first decade of the twentieth century, the majority of Catholics were products of parish schools. What religion they imbibed there became the standard and foundation of whatever else followed.[35]

In addition to the explicit grounding in denominational culture provided to children by these religious schools, institutional sponsorship afforded other ways of developing a common *esprit de corps* among members. Fund-raising endeavors by mission society chapters in local congregations for "their" hospital in China or school in Appalachia helped reinforce a sense of direct participation in, and loyalty to, both the denomination and its missionary endeavors.[36] Denominational colleges also served as agents of inculturation for Catholic and Seventh-day Adventist students in adapting to the larger society, strengthening their religious affiliation while simultaneously providing a safe environment in which to experiment with new ideas and practices.[37] By offering a religiously safe opportunity for a medical, legal, or business education, denominational universities have kept generations of doctors, lawyers, and businessmen within the church. In turn, the continued presence of these active, educated professionals gradually affected the socio-economic aspects of a denomination's internal identity.

In addition to shaping the *internal* identity of a denomination, its colleges, hospitals, and other institutions have also been a very visible *public* face that focused its organizational identity in the larger society. "Education and the strong support of educational institutions," for example, were considered both by members and by outside observers to be among "the historic and theological hallmarks of . . . Presbyterianism," thus imparting a definite aura of intellectualism to the denomination as a whole.[38] The good will generated in the nineteenth century by the sisters' hospitals augmented the reputation, not only of the sisters, but also of the larger Catholic church.

Conclusion

The schools, hospitals, orphanages, and settlement houses which were operated by church-affiliated groups such as Catholic religious orders, Protestant deaconesses, or Protestant women's missionary societies, have shaped both the public and private identities of these groups—and of their parent denominations—in many key ways. Operation of these institutionalized services was the catalyst for the original establishment of the virtuoso groups and, sometimes, for the formal coalescence of the denomination itself. Training for and working together in these institutions fostered continuing group bonds among the sisters and deaconesses; time spent as a pupil or patient in one of these institutions also fostered denominational loyalty and commitment in succeeding generations of lay congregants. As several researchers in the Church of the Nazarene put it:

> The colleges and universities of the Church of the Nazarene are part of the soul of the Church of the Nazarene. Just as they have been shaped by the denomination they have in turn shaped it. The denomination and its educational institutions are actually unthinkable apart from each other. They have so extensively educated the lay and clergy leadership of the denomination that when one thinks of himself or herself as a Nazarene, he or she usually includes his or her educational experience in the mix.[39]

Finally, the schools, the colleges, and the medical or nursing schools were instrumental in raising the overall educational level both of the orders which staffed them and the denominations which channeled students to them. Over time, this affected both the internal identity/ethos and the external image of the order or society as well as of the larger denomination.

As strong and important as they were, however, these identificational influences were largely taken for granted and unexamined, both by the denominations and by the women themselves, under the pressures of day-to-day problems. "They were," as one focus group member noted, "part of the air we breathed. . . . We did very little to study our own history and tradition. . . . It was presumed. It was the air you breathed" (Sisters' Focus Group 2.6). As a result, the orders and denominations did not anticipate the identity shifts that might occur once their connections to these institutions changed.

In addition to their role in shaping the orders' organizational identities, however, the schools, hospitals, and social service institutions also affected their sponsors in other ways. The following chapters will explore these additional aspects.

Notes

1. See Wittberg (2003) for a review of this literature with regard to Catholic colleges.

2. Overall, in 1900, only 10-15 percent of the faculties at Catholic colleges were lay (Leahy 1991:100). While the deaconesses usually comprised a smaller proportion of the staffs at their hospitals, schools, and social service agencies, their witness and service was nevertheless great.

3. A point made by Contosta (1995:28), Gallin (1999:113), and Gleason (2001:4) for Catholic schools. Beaty (2002:119-120) makes a similar point regarding the staffing of Baptist colleges by ministers and active Baptist lay elites.

4. Contosta (1995:30).

5. Goia and Thomas (1996:372). Italics added.

6. See Albert and Whetten (1985:269), Goia and Thomas (1996:381), and Martin (2002:113), for these definitions. See Albert and Whetten (1985:269) for the effects of the gap between public and private organizational identities.

7. A point made by Albert and Whetten (1985:270-76). In "holographic" organizations, all members simultaneously subscribe to these disparate identities; in "ideographic" organizations, various subgroups among the members may each adhere to a different one. See Albert and Whetten (1985:274-75) also for the references in the rest of this paragraph.

8. Albert and Whetten (1985:277).

9. See, for example, Albert and Whetten (1985), Sloan (1998), Kraatz and Zajac (1996), Feeney (1997), and Young (1998). Only recently has Finke (2004) attempted to analyze *denominations* in these terms.

10. See Wittberg (1994:111, 133-34) for additional documentation for these assertions with regard to medieval orders. Mendicant orders, notes Grell (1997:49), were "primarily geared to saving souls, and only as a consequence of that were they concerned with practical charity." See Grell (1997:48) for the sixteenth century religious orders mentioned in the next sentence.

11. Diebolt (2001:37). Italics added. See also Hickey (1997:142-149) for examples. See Rapley (2001:220) for the aims of the French teaching orders discussed in the following sentence.

12. See Brewer (1987:38), Diner (1983:133-34), Madden (1991:201), Wittberg (1994:86-88), and Hogan (1996:146), and for examples. According to Walsh (2002:18, 21), only 11 percent of the Catholic religious orders in England at the beginning of the twentieth century were not active in teaching, nursing, or social services.

13. The focus group excerpts are identified in the following manner: the first number of the focus group designates the particular order or society from which the focus groups were drawn. The second number designates the specific focus group itself. Thus, Focus Groups 1.1 and 1.2 are two groups drawn from the same religious order; focus groups 1.3, 2.3, and 3.3 are from three different orders. Ellipses (. . .) indicate that words have been omitted (usually for clarity of sense), while long dashes indicate that the speaker herself suddenly changed a topic or trailed off. Initial short dashes indicate a change of speaker. All names of individuals or places are pseudonyms.

14. The same was true for Anglican religious orders: Dunstan notes that "being useful to society" became a deeply-imbedded aspect of their identity (Dunstan 2003:340).

15. Quoted in Golder (1903:199). See Nelson (2001:134, 138) for the Kaiserswerth deaconesses.

16. Quotation from Golder (1903:286). See also Dougherty (1997:5-6) and Tatum

(1960:235).

17. See, for example, Isham (1936:14), Tatum (1960:13, 25), Meeker (1969:2-20), and Higgenbotham (1993:74-75) for documentation of this assertion.

18. Kouri (1997:177).

19. Morey (1995:74).

20. Anderson (2000:67). See also Kauffman (1995:152-3).

21. Brereton (1981:181).

22. See Thompson (1989) for the influence of academies on the social class of sisters, and Prelinger (1986b:224) for the importance of schools for attracting middle-class women to the Kaiserswerth deaconesses.

23. Luddy (2001:15). Dunstan (2003) makes the same observation for the institutions run by Anglican religious orders.

24. Coburn and Smith (1999:193) and Maher (1989:138). Know-Nothing Senator Robert M. T. Hunter, for example, publicly retracted his previous anti-Catholic and anti-convent statements at a meeting in Baltimore in 1855 (see Nelson 2001:41). See Dunstan (2003:339) for the quotation in the next sentence.

25. See Nelson (2001:139) and Golder (1903:289) for the absence of the deaconesses from the public identity of their hospitals. In the Methodist Church, in contrast, the deaconesses who worked in the institutions of the Woman's Home Mission Society were not subordinated to male administrators and were more visible to the larger denomination.

26. Quotation in Golder (1903:321).

27. An assertion documented by O'Donnell (1988:261), Leahy (1991:97), Moylan (1993:79), and Walch (1996:172), and Dougherty (1997:135, 231). See Dunstan (2003:341) for judging the success of religious orders from the success of their institutions.

28. See Harrison (1959:35-48) for an example.

29. See, for example, Leonard (1997:533) and Shurden (1981).

30. Schlabach (2000:23). See also Toews (1996). For the essay itself, see Bender (1944).

31. Vance (1999:70). See Benne (2003:210) for the Lutherans.

32. Albert Meyer, personal communication.

33. See Burtchaell (1998:316) and Stoltzfus (1992:91) for the Wesleyan examples, Beaty (2002:133) for the Baptists, and Benne (2003:211) for the Lutheran organizations. Meyer (forthcoming) describes the think tank role of church colleges in more detail.

34. Sharot (2001:230).

35. Campion (1987:141). See also Cleary (2001:20). See Fulton (1997:117) for a similar point regarding U.S. Catholics.

36. Hill (1985:48).

37. Gleason (1995:91) and Leahy (1997:50) make this point for Catholic institutions; Lawson and Carden (1983) and Vance (1999:70) for Seventh-day Adventists. Benne (2003:207-208) makes a similar point for Lutherans.

38. Meyer (2000:82). See also Maher (1989:147) and Nelson (2001:41).

39. Lambert et al. (2002:149-150).

Chapter 3

Effects on Recruitment

In addition to shaping the identity of the sponsoring denomination or denominational group, religious institutions have also been essential channels of recruitment. A wide range of historical literature documents the ways in which the schools, hospitals, and social agencies catalyzed denominational growth and also attracted new generations of women and men to the ranks of the religious virtuosi themselves.

Recruitment to the Virtuoso Group

To the Catholic Religious Orders and Seminaries

Religious institutions have traditionally been a key channel for membership recruitment to the order which staffed them. As far back as the sixteenth century, the new Catholic religious orders had been attracted to hospital service at least partly because these early institutions also housed foundlings and orphans who could ultimately be recruited to their ranks. Similarly, an important incentive for male and female religious communities to found schools and colleges in the nineteenth century United States was to attract vocations from among their students.[1]

> Establishing a "college" [for young men] commended itself, not only because it filled a genuine social need and thereby gave the [men's] religious community meaningful work to do, but also because it brought in income, *served as a recruiting agency for the order*, and in general constituted a nucleus from which the community could grow.[2]

John Carroll, the first American bishop, stated that his main reason for founding Georgetown College was the recruitment and training of priests for the infant

Catholic Church in the United States.

Recruitment was an especially important consequence of the sisters' service in their residential academies and colleges, where their "particularly intense" and intimate interaction with their students led many young Catholic women, and even some of the Protestants, to join their order.[3] During the first half of the twentieth century, it was not unusual for ten to fifteen percent of each graduating class at Catholic women's colleges to enter the community of sisters who taught there.[4] The sisters teaching in convent schools also organized spiritual clubs, or "sodalities," among the pupils, which "provided another source for the steady stream of aspirants" into English, Irish and American orders.

When the U.S. public school system began to separate high schools from colleges in the late nineteenth century, the Catholic colleges and academies continued to follow the European combined model of a six- or seven-year course of studies. This reluctance was primarily for recruitment reasons:

> The high school years . . . were the most fertile years for cultivating vocations to the religious life as a priest, brother, or . . . sister. With demonstration of this fact always at hand, Catholic college managers were horrified by the thought that the principal source of clerical supply might escape their control.[5]

When it became obvious that their amalgamated curriculum could no longer be sustained, the orders set up separate boys' and girls' high schools so as not to lose contact with youth. The annals of these high schools, as well as those of the parish-based elementary schools, were careful to enumerate each year's vocations to the priesthood or sisterhood from among their alumni.[6] The sisters' colleges and nursing schools were also fertile sources of new entrants to the orders. As late as 1962, a sister wrote in the Rosemont College Journal: "There is a general agreement that an intimate connection exists between the spiritual programs [of our] colleges and high schools and the number of vocations to the priesthood and religious life."[7]

The sisters in the focus groups reflected on the importance of the orders' schools and hospitals for their own recruitment:

> (Interviewer: What first attracted you to enter the Sisters of X?)
> - They taught us.
> - I was in the nursing school.
> - Everybody else was in grade school, high school, college.
> - That was the feeder.
> - Sisters Mary, Ann, and I [points to two other members of the focus group] all went to the same school, where Sister Mary is now the principal (Focus Group 2.6: Active and retired sisters).

> I went to school here, to the academy, and what attracted me was the spirit among the sisters. I used to see them—we had a canteen, and it was open from 3:00 to 3:30, something like that. Then after that, the sisters would go in. You could hear

them in there. They'd have an ice cream cone, they'd be laughing and talking and I thought that would be so wonderful, you know, just that spirit among them. Or sometimes they would be on duty and I'd see two or three of them laughing and talking together and I just thought that was great. So that's really what attracted me, initially (Focus Group 1.6: Active and retired sisters).

In twenty of the 24 sisters' focus groups, the participants listed contact with the sisters working in their schools and hospitals as a primary reason why they themselves had joined the order.

The variety of institutions which the orders operated—nursing schools and orphanages as well as elementary through post-secondary education—exposed them to a wide spectrum of potential recruits. Orders would deliberately seek to open schools in certain areas—upper middle-class neighborhoods of large cities, for example—in order to attract young women from "better" economic backgrounds.[8] The orders also printed pamphlets and books describing their community's history and the type of works they performed. These were made available to students in the schools and parishes where they worked. Young women, by choosing an order specializing in a particular type of work, were able to choose, and be educated for, the profession that best suited their interests and abilities.[9]

At least some of the sisters in the focus groups mentioned that they had chosen the particular order they had entered because it specialized in a certain type of service. A sister in an order with a large number of hospitals remarked:

I wanted to be a nurse. I knew that, if I joined the Notre Dame sisters [who specialized in teaching], I would be stuck [nursing] in their infirmary for the rest of my life (Focus Group 2.4: Retired sisters).

Others valued the opportunity to interact with members in different fields of work, even if they were not personally involved in such works themselves:

I came wanting to teach, but I also knew that the Sisters of X were a community that had health care and education. That was different from [other religious orders in the city, which] were totally health care or totally schools. And that was attractive, not that I ever wanted to be in health care, which I'm in. But there was that breadth— (Focus Group 2.6: Active and retired sisters).

However, the sisters' expectations of entering a particular professional field were not always fulfilled. The speaker in the preceding quotation came intending to teach and ended up in health care. A sister in another order had the opposite experience:

Well, I already knew what sisters do and what the Sisters of X did. We have two hospitals and any number of schools. . . . I remember, though, telling the Mother Superior that I did not want to teach, that I wanted to nurse. . . . Well, the first thing she did was to send me out to a school in [city] (Focus Group 1.6: Active and retired sisters).

The orders' institutions were thus important recruiting factors because they acquainted young women with the sisters who taught them, and because they offered specific professional opportunities at a time when other options were limited for women. But many recruits were not attracted by a specific occupational choice, but simply by the general idea of religious service as a way of doing something significant in one's life:

> - I grew up where there were a lot of sisters, in Lowell, Massachusetts—just tripping over each other, sisters and priests. I thought, "I'd like to go where I'm more needed."
> - Where there's not so many.
> - [Southern state] seemed to be the place.
> - Less than one-half of one percent of the population was Catholic at the time (Focus Group 1.6: Active sisters).

> I entered because I saw this service being given by the Sisters of X to me and to other people, and I thought that was a good thing to do for God in a special way (Focus Group 3.8: Retired sisters).

> I wanted to do something significant with my life and to do good things for other people, and that's what got me here (Focus Group 3.11: Young sisters).

Acquaintance with the nuns in one of their institutions may have been important in channeling a recruit to one order instead of another, but many of the sisters in the focus groups emphasized that a deeper feeling of God's call came first:

> Well, I came to the convent because the Hound of Heaven wouldn't let me alone. I really did not want to be a sister. I was happy doing what I was doing. I don't know what it is, but I think that when God calls you, He must do something special for you (Focus Group 1.1: Retired sisters).

> - I didn't know any nuns. I felt a call and I wanted to save my soul. That was the main part.
> - I think it's a mystery. I think God puts you where he wants you, because I was taught by the Benedictines, I was taught by the Charities, I had never seen a Sister of X . . . and yet I ended up here (Focus Group 1.4: Active sisters).

> [As a child], in my prayer after Holy Communion, I always asked God to let me know what He wanted me to be. And I kept praying that it would fall true. And then when I was in high school, I thought more about it. I didn't have sisters [as teachers when I was growing up]; I went to a public high school. . . . And when I was in teacher training, I kept up my prayer. I felt sure that I wanted to be a sister, but I didn't know what kind (Focus Group 2.4: Retired sisters).

Overall, sisters in nine of the 24 focus groups mentioned being attracted to their order through attending its institutions; seven groups mentioned a generalized desire to do God's work, and six mentioned a felt call to religious life independently of institutional service. In four groups, all three motivations were mentioned.

To Protestant Clergy, Deaconesses, and Mission Societies

Denominational colleges and training schools were also important in recruiting men and women to Protestant virtuoso groups. It was a common observation that a strong correlation also existed between attending a denominational college and the likelihood of becoming a missionary.[10] Special programs existed at these colleges to encourage young women to become deaconesses and missionaries; the Student Volunteer Movement, for example, was the source of more than half of the Protestant missionaries sent overseas from North America.[11] Other institutions besides colleges also served recruitment purposes: the Lutheran deaconesses at Kaiserswerth founded an orphanage "specifically to supply recruits for the deaconessate—genuinely parentless daughters for the surrogate family." The various missionary training schools and hospitals also channeled recruits to the deaconess programs. The Dorcas Institute, which trained German-speaking nurses for Bethesda Hospital in Cincinnati between 1908 and 1931, was one such school. As its administrator, John Albert Diekman, noted, the institute served as the preparatory school for the deaconess mother house, and as the primary source for new German Methodist deaconesses: "Where should the deaconesses come from without the Dorcas Institute? We see little hope for accessions to our ranks for the German deaconesses unless we maintain a school of our own."[12]

Both focus groups of retired deaconesses cited the role of denominational colleges and missionary training programs in attracting them to their order:

I worked at X College, where they trained a lot [of deaconesses]. . . . I began to go to their meetings, and one thing led to another (Focus Group 4.1: Retired Deaconesses).

My particular contact was when I was a sophomore in college, and through my [student mission group]. During that period of time, I felt a calling to what we called in those days "full-time Christian service." And so I transferred to [the missionary training school] as an undergraduate, to get my degree, and of course I met a number of deaconesses there, and even worked with them later on as a [two-year volunteer] (Focus Group 4.2: Retired deaconesses).

Their denomination's two-year volunteer program (here abbreviated 2YR) was a common path directing the deaconesses to lifetime commitment:

- You know, it's interesting: when you're looking around this table, I'm in the [2YR] class of 1957-1959. [Points to participants] 2YR, 2YR, 2YR.

- I believe all of us are.
- I was not.
- Four were. It's interesting to see how many came out of that program.
(Focus Group 4.2:Retired deaconesses).

The women in this volunteer program worked in a variety of the institutions which the deaconesses staffed and the mission societies supported. This experience acquainted them with deaconesses and their works:

- I was a 2YR for two years. I had been a teacher in public school for ten years, and then I went as a 2YR to [place], and it was a home and school for girls.
- I was 2YR. I taught at X school, six year olds.
- When I got interested in 2YR and all, I hoped to go to Y High School and I was thinking of it. My sister Sheila had worked at Z Neighborhood House (Focus Group 4.2: Retired deaconesses).

As with the sisters, it was the opportunity to become more intimately acquainted with older deaconesses in the training schools and as a volunteer with them in the various locations they staffed that attracted young women to become deaconesses themselves:

(Interviewer: What first attracted you to become a deaconess?)
- The deaconesses. That's all I have to say, that's true.
- Well, I became a deaconess, I think, in relationship with Mary Jones and Betty Smith and some persons that I knew as deaconesses (Focus Group 4.1: Retired deaconesses).

While institutions played a key role in attracting new deaconesses, individual chapters of the women's mission societies in local congregations also assumed a special responsibility for recruiting and training young women for full-time church service. They often paid for the schooling—even the medical education—of potential missionaries.[13] Many chapters also contributed information about missions to the Sunday School curricula in a deliberate effort to attract potential missionary recruits.[14]

In addition to the efforts of the local chapters, the national offices of the mission societies also concerned themselves with recruitment to the ranks of deaconesses and missionaries, as an essential part of their overall responsibility for co-ordinating the denominations' efforts in Christian Education:

The way in which it was implemented was through the [mission society] organization at several levels. There were people [in the mission society administration] for whom Missionary Personnel, Missionary Recruitment, was a primary organizational responsibility. There was another category of workers, called "Youth Work," or "Student Work," where you kept track of the kids that were going through college and you tried to funnel them into student organiza-tions on campus, you tried to keep track of them, you tried to offer them vocational opportunities . . . to keep the whole broad vocational opportunities of the Church before them. We had a program—either two or three years, short term programs—which was subsidized to the point that the kids went on stipends for a contracted period, clearly with the intention of giving them the opportunity to express whatever kind of service vocation they thought they were interested in, and to do some good work. And many of them came back to go on for further training and to become missionaries and deaconesses (Individual Interview: Retired deaconess).

In addition to working to increase the number of deaconesses and missionaries, each local chapter of the mission societies also recruited the next generation into its own ranks, for example by sponsoring "Children's Bands" to cultivate enthusiasm for church mission work in the next generation. As participants in one of the mission society focus groups recalled:

- I first got involved when I was a teenager, because, you know [the missionary society], when I was a senior in high school they paid part of my way for a trip to Washington with the [denominational] youth group.
- It seemed like I went with my mother to missionary meetings all the time. We had at that time a Little Lambs for children—I don't know the age limit. I had my membership in that, and then you were promoted to the younger people, maybe to high school, and then, when we had the [denominational] Service Guild for those that were employed, I belonged to that.
- I didn't remember until you said that about going to Washington, DC, but when I was in high school, I went to the school of missions and at that time, where I grew up in [state], you went to a college and spent the week there, and that was sponsored by [the mission society] (Focus Group 5.1: Mission society).

The mission society and deaconess focus groups echoed the sisters in citing the general attraction of doing "God's work" as a primary motivation for joining:

It's a wonderful place to have in your life. The spiritual nourishment and you get a sense of direction. The involvement with the rest of the world; missions are important and the ideas of the Church are important (Focus Group 5.5: Mission society).

And also, the women had been very traditionally mission-minded, and this was something that was very much important in my upbringing, and my history and background was missions and so this was one reason I got involved (Focus Group 5.6: Mission society).

I think it was the sense of a lifetime commitment to mission that drew me. I saw that in the women who were deaconesses stronger than in the women who were not. And I wanted that. I wanted to express that (Focus Group 4.1: Retired deaconesses).

I had been teaching school for ten years. I wanted to work with [the denomination]. I thought, I want to do something with the Church that they need doing. So I looked into it (Focus Group 4.2: Retired deaconesses).

As with the sisters, the deaconesses also articulated their strong sense of being called by God:

> I worked for the church as an employed worker for twenty years. And then I had a religious experience that, for me, said, "Sharon, you must, you know, as a statement, as an affirmation of your calling, of your desire to serve and be identified as a follower of Christ." I needed to do something else and then, of course, knowing deaconesses as I had through the years, for me that said—that's what I must seek (Focus Group 4.2: Retired deaconesses).

All three of the deaconesses' focus groups cited this feeling of call and the general attraction of service. Six of the nine mission society focus groups also stated that they had joined their local congregation's chapter out of a desire to become involved in mission work.

The sisters, deaconesses, and mission society members varied in their prevalence within their respective denominations (the sisters and mission society members were much more numerous than the deaconesses were), and in the different commitment levels expected of them (the sisters and deaconesses were celibate and had traditionally lived communally,[15] while the mission society members married and enjoyed relative financial and personal autonomy). Nevertheless, recruitment to all three groups depended in essential ways on their schools, hospitals, and social agencies. The sisters' and deaconesses' students and co-workers, first of all, came to know and appreciate their lifestyle through interacting with them in their institutions. Since the larger denomination valued the institutional services the sisters and deaconesses provided, denominational officials and laity actively channeled promising recruits to them. Finally, the need to staff or fund their sponsored organizations also spurred the sisters, deaconesses, and mission society members themselves to recruit new members to their own ranks. As chapter 9 will demonstrate, however, once the sisters and deaconesses no longer staffed their traditional organizations, it became harder for the rest of the denomination to figure out exactly what they did, or why their services were important. And promising young lay women were less likely to meet them.

Recruitment to the Denomination

In addition to attracting recruits to the ranks of deaconesses, sisters, or missionaries, denominational institutions also helped attract and retain members within the denomination itself. Orphanages and schools, both Catholic and Protestant, had as their avowed purpose the rescue of vulnerable, parentless children from the twin dangers of irreligion and heresy, and of attaching them to the true faith.[16] At least one historian has noted the impact of the Sunday School Movement in catalyzing the elevenfold growth in the U.S. Presbyterian Church between 1800 and 1837.[17] In any country where the two faiths co-existed, an active competition existed between Catholics and Protestants to draw off converts from each other via their institutions.

The institutions also sparked increased commitment among those who were already church members. The women's missionary societies argued that mobilizing churchwomen to support the home and foreign missions would, by a "reflex influence," invigorate the sponsoring church and the women's own spiritual lives as well.[18] More recently, Mennonite scholars have argued that their denomination's colleges have been indispensable in strengthening and preserving the Mennonite rank and file in their faith. "Nearly 80 percent of the Mennonite young people who come to our colleges stay in Mennonite churches throughout their lives. . . . The figures for 'keeping our own'—or participation in any religious body after graduation—are much lower for Mennonites who go to other colleges."[19] Similarly, various studies of Seventh-day Adventist children attending that denomination's schools have found that between 80 percent and 100 percent of them were ultimately baptized as Adventists.[20] "Participation in a separate educational system is an expected (or at least desired) component of the Adventist experience." By fostering marital endogamy, the schools help keep the next generation in the faith as well.

In addition to attracting and retaining rank and file members, religious institutions also fostered a new leadership cadre for the sponsoring denomination, both on the local and on the wider level.[21] A faculty member at a Presbyterian college "nicely illustrated the historic contribution of [his] college to church leadership by recalling members of his graduating class who went on to such positions as the Dean of Duke Divinity School, the presidencies of two Presbyterian seminaries, and the presidency of Union Theological Seminary in New York."[22] Baylor University's Ministry Guidance Program counsels approximately 1800 students who are interested in pursuing ministry vocations.[23] Lutheran colleges are expected to encourage their students to consider the ordained ministry and to steer them to Lutheran seminaries. Five of the past seven moderators of the Mennonite Church have been faculty members or administrators at Mennonite schools, and the promotional literature of these schools has regularly emphasized their role in training such leaders. The United Methodist Church has traditionally required prospective candidates for the ministry to have at least some explicitly Methodist postsecondary education, either by completing their undergraduate studies at a Methodist college or else by attending a Methodist seminary.

Local and denominational lay leadership was also fostered by the institutions. For example, former missionaries often staffed and directed the mission boards at denominational headquarters, or served in denominational colleges.[24] As late as the 1970s and 1980s, the "overwhelming majority" of the women in denominational leadership in the United Methodist Church had first been active leaders in the United Methodist Women—the modern incarnation of that denomination's home and foreign mission societies. Among both Catholics and Protestants, the graduates of denominational colleges usually returned to active participation in local congregations and church agencies, where their presence "made a tremendous difference in the quality and quantity of church life."[25]

Negative Effects

For the deaconesses and sisters, however, the demands of institutional service might also drive recruits away. This was especially true if the sponsoring group's need to fill particular institutional positions took precedence over a new recruit's desires and aptitudes. The sisters' focus groups were emphatic that such policies resulted in stress:

> - I think some came through OK. I was assigned . . . to teach French. I had had one course of intermediate French in college, and I happened to do well in it; so I learned it real well to teach it. But I think it was a two-edged sword. Some people came through it and grew, said to themselves, "I would never have done this; I love it." But others were—[Respondent's voice trails off]
> - When I first started teaching, I had [to teach] a number of religion courses. . . . I had never been in a Catholic school; I had never had religion [courses]. I was terrified.
> - I would say I was pretty terrified the first year.
> - I cried every Sunday night, my first year of teaching, and Sister Mary and I counted the days to the end of the school year.
> - It was their expectation that you do what you had to do. And you did.
> - But I was not only told to do it, they also told me not to let anybody know that I was scared about doing it or that I needed any help. That was a very—when I look back on it—I had anxiety attacks, and it was awful. From a psychological point of view, when I look back on that, it was not good psychology (Focus Group 2.6: Active and retired sisters).

Another source of stress was being overworked in order to meet institutional staffing needs. This, too, was a frequent complaint:

> I got sent to X Hospital in [city], and was made operating room supervisor, which was a trauma. So for three years, I was at X Hospital and had the operating room with no head nurse when I got up there, and sixty surgeons. But later, I [also] assumed the emergency room and the central supply department. So I had three departments. And that about burned me out (Focus Group 1.5: Active sisters).

In all, 23 of the 27 focus groups of sisters and deaconesses mentioned the negative impact of being sent to an assignment without adequate consultation or preparation. Thirteen of the 24 sisters' focus groups also mentioned the additional stress of overwork.

For this reason, the sisters approved of more recent policies that allowed them a choice in where they worked:

> Because, if you remember when we could choose to do what we wanted to do, practically everyone got out of education? I mean, lots of sisters were in education who hated it. Because they were *put* in education. If you go back and look at all the sisters that were so unhappy, as soon as that chance came they were, you know, they opted to get out pretty fast (Focus Group 3.5: Active Sisters).

And eight of the sisters' focus groups mentioned that these stresses—overwork, or the disappointment and frustration of being assigned to jobs that they had neither the aptitude nor the desire to perform—had driven promising recruits from their order:

> There were 52 of us in the novitiate and some of the people that left, you know, some of them were moved into nurses [who wanted to teach] and some of them were teachers that wanted to be nurses. There were too many nurses, so they took them out and put them into teaching and, I mean, that wasn't where they were coming from. I love teaching, and I love what I'm doing now, totally, absolutely. But, if you were put into a job or a grade that you didn't like—(Focus Group 3.10: Active sisters).

> - I have to say that when I first went out, and talk about not being prepared for things, when I was assigned to teach piano and have the choir and everything else, I mean, it was not exactly all a joyful piece.
> [Several voices] No. No. It was awful.
> - It was absolutely traumatic. . . . Pretty much in my life, [these experiences] turned out to have some positive effects, in terms of challenging me to do things that I might not have chosen to do, or to find out that I could do things that I didn't know [I could do]. But the danger was that they could break you.
> - Exactly.
> - I think it may have broken some of those who left.
> - Sure (Focus Group 2.6: Active and retired sisters).

The daily stresses of common living in the institutions where they worked, while often a source of togetherness and friendship, also took their toll on the sisters' ability to do their jobs well:

> There were about, I think, there were eight sisters . . . and it was a very small convent. You had sheets separating the beds in the room I was in, and then everybody had to walk through our room to get to their room, which was in the back. So you could never plan on going to sleep until you were sure—let's see, there were [counts on fingers] 1, 2, 3, 4, 5—about five or six who slept beyond us (Focus Group 3.4: Retired sisters).

> You know what else was hard was [lesson preparation]. You had to study [together] in one place, especially if you were [an] elementary school [teacher]. And this one would maybe have emphysema or asthma or a bad cold and that one

would be—and of course you had only a half hour, 45 minutes to prepare all the subjects for a class. It was terrible, you could not concentrate. All you could do was put page numbers down and, you know, words, vocabulary. You could not prepare your lessons (Focus Group 3.9: Retired sisters).

Surprisingly, only these two of the 24 sisters' focus groups mentioned these stresses of daily living. Both coupled their comments with the observation that they had had happy times despite the crowded living conditions. Unlike the descriptions of the stresses attendant on overwork and the lack of preparation, none of the sisters cited the stresses of common living as a factor in alienating new young members.

Conclusion

Religious schools, health care institutions, and social service agencies were thus important, not only for shaping the identities of denominations and denominational groups, but also for attracting and retaining—or alienating and repelling—the groups' members. The bonds formed with students and co-workers in these institutions were pivotal in drawing new recruits to the ranks of the sisters and deaconesses. Other recruits who had had no previous experience with the sisters' or deaconesses' institutions were nevertheless attracted to them because of the unique opportunities they offered for church service. At times, however, the stresses of overwork or placement in an unsatisfactory position drove away some of the members. For the larger denomination, the schools, hospitals, and social service agencies helped attract new converts, retain current members, and train both lay and ordained leaders. Both church officials and the heads of the order or society were well aware of the recruitment benefits of these institutions, and worried about the negative impact of losing them.

But their institutional involvement brought about still other effects for the women's virtuoso groups. The following chapter will describe how this involvement influenced the power of the orders and the individual members, both within the larger denomination and in society at large.

Notes

1. See Palmer (1999:98) and Contosta (2002:141) for these assertions.

2. Gleason (1995:83), italics added. See also Contosta (2002:141). See Heft (2003:36) for John Carroll's motivations for founding Georgetown College.

3. Coburn and Smith (1999:167-72).

4. Ebaugh (1993:95-98), Oates (2002:174), and Conway (2002:13) make this observation for the United States. At Chicago's Rosary College, an average of eleven graduates each year entered the Dominican order of sisters who taught there; 13 percent of

the first 23 graduating classes at St. Catharine's College joined the sisters. In nineteenth century English and Welsh convent schools, 20 percent of the students joined the sisterhoods who had taught them (Walsh 2002:126). Rapley (2001:165) makes a similar observation for the French convent schools on the seventeenth and eighteenth centuries. See Walsh (2002:151) for the quotation in the following sentence.

     5. Annarelli (1987:33). See also Brewer (1987:5-6), who makes a similar argument for the sisters' academies.

     6. See, for example, Dudine (1967). The archives of the St. Joseph Sisters in St. Louis contain similar material. See Walsh (2002:7, 139, 151) for recruits from colleges and nursing schools.

     7. Quoted in Contosta (2002:141). See a similar quotation from 1917 in Oates (2002:174-5).

     8. Thompson (1989).

     9. Luddy (2001:13). See also Coburn and Smith (1999:171) and Walsh (2002:151). For orphanages as recruitment sources, see Coburn and Smith (1999:210).

     10. Hill (1985:128) and Field (1974:52) make this point.

     11. According to Friedman (1985:115), the most active educational institutions in the southern states for recruiting and training women missionaries during the late nineteenth century were Richmond Women's College, Judson College, Bessie Tift College, Hollins College, and Greenville College. See Phillips (1974:101) and Tatum (1960:321) for the information about the Student Volunteer Movement. See Prelinger (1986b:220) for the Kaiserswerth deaconesses.

     12. Quoted in Dougherty (1997:128).

     13. Hill (1985:65). See Boyd and Brackenridge (1983:65) for the national offices' efforts.

     14. Isham (1936:33), Brereton and Klein (1979:308), and Boyd and Brackenridge (1983:46). See also Phillips (1974:101) for the role of youth organizations in missionary recruitment.

     15. The "total institution" model (Goffman 1961) of communal life was more applicable to the lifestyle of the sisters than of the deaconesses. And deaconesses were free to leave the deaconessate to marry, if they wished. After the mid-twentieth century, it became possible, in many denominations, for deaconesses to marry and remain deaconesses, an option still not available to Catholic sisters. These changes have moved the deaconess lifestyle away from that of the sisters and closer to that of mission society members.

     16. See, for example, Walsh (2002:32), who documents this purpose for nineteenth century England and Wales.

     17. Miller (1985:151). See also Jones (1999:218) and Dougherty (1997:13) for further documentation of the competition between Christian denominations through their institutions.

     18. Hill (1985:66).

     19. Graber Miller (2000:3-4). A footnote to this article (2000:12) notes that, while 80 percent of those who attend Mennonite colleges remain Mennonites, only 60 percent of those who do not attend college at all remain Mennonite.

     20. These studies are cited in Vance (1999:67). See Vance (1999:667) also, for the quotation in the following sentence, and Vance (1999:132) for the role of schools in encouraging marital endogamy.

     21. Marsden (1994:53), Shepherd and Shepherd (1998:418-420), and Graber Miller (2000:3) give examples of this.

     22. Stoltzfus (1992:61). Between 2/3 and 3/4 of the chief executives of the United

Presbyterian Church in the U.S.A. from 1923 to 1959 had been educated at denominationally-affiliated colleges (Reifsnyder 1992:272).

23. Beaty (2002:133). See Durnbaugh (1997:362) for the information about the Mennnonites later in this paragraph. See Benne (2003:208) for the information about the Lutheran colleges.

24. Field (1974:52). See Campbell (1975:46) for the quotation on the United Methodist Women in the following sentence.

25. Stoltzfus (1992:109). See Davidson et al. (1997:102) for a similar assertion regarding Catholics, Meyer (1974) for Mennonites, and Trotter (1987:136) for Methodists.

Chapter 4

Effects on Power

Every organization exists within an environment composed of other organizations, on whom it depends to provide the raw materials, clients, personnel, and other resources needed for its survival and growth. According to Resource Dependency Theory, organizations and their administrators must maneuver for favorable positions *vis à vis* the other actors in their organizational fields, using their own resources to gain power and influence over the others. The winners in this competition obtain opportunities for "changing, as well as responding to, the environment. Administrators manage their environments as well as their organizations, and the former activity may be as important, or even more important, than the latter."[1] Organizations which lose in these struggles become vulnerable to the whims and desires of outside stakeholders, and forfeit a great part of their control over their own destinies.

Denominational groups such as religious orders or missionary societies are organizations, and therefore subject to this same dialectic of power and dependency. To what extent did their ownership and administration of schools, hospitals, and social service agencies affect the resources and power available to these religious groups and to their individual members?

The Power of Virtuoso Groups

Control of the Institutions

Women's virtuoso groups have varied in the amount of power that they possessed over the various institutions in which they served. In the early eighteenth century, the Daughters of Charity, a French Catholic religious order, staffed and administered over two hundred health care institutions in that country. Although,

89

in theory, they were supposed to defer to the medical staff, in practice these doctors were rarely around. The sisters performed minor surgical procedures, ran the apothecary, and controlled most of the other medical services their hospitals provided. The French Revolution temporarily displaced the sisters from their hospitals, however, and upon their return they had much less power. Nineteenth century French nuns ran only the religious and housekeeping departments of the hospitals in which they served. In contrast, American and Australian nuns in the late nineteenth and early twentieth centuries owned their hospitals outright and held overall authority and responsibility for both policy formation and operating decisions.

> A superior led the community of nuns in a hospital, and she had control over the management and direction of the facility. Her authority was supreme, and little was done without her permission. A number of sisters served as hospital trustees, while others were supervisors of the different floors and departments. They all reported directly to the superior.[2]

Examples of the sisters exercising this power are numerous:

> Sister Lidwina became superior of Holy Cross Hospital in Salt Lake City. As superior, she set admission policies, protected the hospital's assets, and promoted the hospital to the press and public. She controlled equipment purchases, nursing assignments, and filing procedures. . . . Most importantly, she approved all applications for admission to the attending hospital staff and dismissed physicians whose competence she questioned.[3]

> In 1899, Sister Blandina Hooper reviewed the performance of doctors in the light of the number of private patients they were bringing to the hospital. Those doctors who failed to bring in private patients were sacked. Finally, at the end of 1899, Sister Felicita McNulty abolished the medical board and renegotiated all contracts for the year 1900. She brought matters under control through mandated monthly staff meetings, at the first of which she appointed the chairman of the committee (no elections!) to create by-laws, a constitution, and a procedure for the selection of medical appointments. Importantly, she renegotiated the terms under which doctors could charge their private patients, making it more profitable for private medical practice.[4]

As another example, the sister administrator of St. Joseph's Hospital in Paterson, New Jersey, demanded the resignation of the entire hospital staff because they wanted to choose their own chief surgeon. A local newspaper quoted her as stating that the basic question was "shall supervision and control of the medical staff rest with the sister directress, or shall the power to make appointments and fill vacancies be exercised by the physicians serving on staff?"[5] Similar tensions between the sister administrators and the hospital medical staff existed in Australia.

Organizational power was not confined only to the sister who ran the hospital.

The order's presence pervaded all levels of administration and staffing. Sisters "automatically had a position of authority, extending from the superintendent, director of nurses, chief dietician, librarian, and chief X-ray technician, to the head of the surgical and laboratory technicians. At least one or two sisters worked in each hospital department."[6]

Protestant deaconesses did not own their hospitals and were not represented on the boards of directors. Nevertheless, they wielded considerable authority: "the Oberin was to be looked upon as the executive head of the hospital and household. All admissions and discharges of patients, or permits for temporary absence must pass through her hands."[7]

The religious sponsors also possessed differing amounts of power over their schools. For Catholic sisters, educational arrangements varied from country to country: in nineteenth century Ireland, the sisters owned almost all their schools; in France during the same period, the majority of sisters were employed in the public school system.[8] In the United States, sisters staffed both parish grade and high schools—which they did not own—and private academies and colleges, which they did.[9] The priests or bishops who owned the parish school buildings and were financially responsible for their upkeep negotiated with a religious order to provide the instruction. It was often unclear who had the authority to assign a given sister to a school or to move her to a new assignment, and superiors often clashed with the male ecclesiastics over this issue. Moreover, by the early twentieth century, many dioceses had created the position of Superintendent of Schools (almost always filled by a priest), together with a diocesan school board composed entirely of clergy, "to investigate the schools in their districts, examine the teachers, test the pupils, reform the discipline and remit the results" to the bishop.[10] This further limited the autonomy of the sisters teaching in parish schools. Protestant deaconesses also did not own the schools they staffed: these were usually owned by the denomination or, among the Methodists, by the women's missionary societies.

The Catholic religious orders had more control over their own academies and colleges. As late as the mid-twentieth century, the sisters exercised this control in several different ways:

1. The religious order might be the parent corporation that owned the college's property or facilities.
2. The religious order might run the college as one of its activities.
3. The religious order might furnish most of the personnel, administrators, and faculty for the college.
4. The religious superiors might comprise all or most of the board of trustees.
5. The religious superiors might move the order's members to or from college positions without consulting the college's administrators.
6. The religious order and/or its superior might exercise various types of financial controls over the college.
7. The superior of the order might also be the college's president.[11]

Many orders exercised a paternalistic control over the smallest details of their colleges. Few, if any, written guidelines existed concerning which policy decisions were the responsibility of the order and which were the responsibility of the college trustees—a moot point, when the trustees were all members of the order. Major decisions were often made by the superior's fiat.

The social service institutions originally founded by the sisters, deaconesses, and missionary societies were a different story. Both the Protestant and Catholic women had largely lost their control over these institutions by the early twentieth century. Unlike the academies and hospitals, the orphanages and settlement houses could not raise their own revenue in fees for services, and depended instead on charitable donations. And raising money for the "hopeless"—the handicapped, the chronically poor, incurables—was often more difficult than for causes that could show tangible signs of success.[12] After 1900, the women might still own the buildings, but control over the fund-raising had passed either to male ecclesiastical authorities or to the State. Most Catholic dioceses established social service departments run by a priest, and hired lay, credentialed social workers to oversee the sisters' work. Protestant denominations also moved to centralize administration of their social agencies under male control. By the mid-1960s, only the women's mission societies in the Methodist Church retained even partial control over the financing and administration of their social service institutions.

Power in Church and Society

Control over their institutions gave the women's groups a degree of power and influence in the larger society that was unusual for their sex. It also enhanced their power *vis à vis* the larger denomination. As one historian of nineteenth century Catholic religious orders in the United States noted:

> Bishops and priests came to have a healthy respect for the power of sisters, and with good reason. The sisters were important influences in the Catholic commu-nity and ran most of the Church's charitable institutions. In disagreements, the sisters fought for their rights and usually won. Then, too, they could and did vote with their feet, or threatened to, when the occasion warranted it.[13]

The threat to withdraw institutional services was a potent one, since most nineteenth century American dioceses were "desperately short of personnel."[14] A bishop's or priest's career depended, in part at least, on his ability to provide educational, health care, and social services to the Catholics in his diocese or parish, and the sisters were needed to staff these institutions. In the language of resource dependency, the nuns controlled a valued resource which the clergy needed. As a result, pastors rarely expelled sisters for any reason since, as one priest wrote, "it would be impossible to get sisters" to replace them.[15] Furthermore, many superiors would refuse to replace another order in a school until they could find out why the first group had left. The superiors of an order would also refuse a bishop's request to open a girls' high school in an area if they thought it would hurt another community's school. "The Mothers Superior were not about to let the clergy play them off against each other if they could help it."[16] In a similar fashion the early women's mission societies were able to obtain recognition from Presbyterian ministers because the latter realized that these societies would be useful in increasing the membership and the fervor of the local congregation.

By providing these valuable institutional services, the religious orders and women's mission societies could sometimes accumulate surplus funds—another source of power and a rare experience for women. By the early 1900's, the Wisconsin Dominican sisters owned $600,000 worth of real estate in seven states and the District of Columbia. The La Crosse (Wisconsin) Franciscan sisters provided over $76,000 in loans to the bishop and priests for diocesan building projects.[17] Another Franciscan order of sisters in Rochester, Minnesota, provided $40,000 to build the hospital that later became the Mayo Clinic. The sisters' good reputation with the people they served was a powerful resource that could be wielded in fund raising, even in competition with ecclesiastical authorities:

> It was almost like we were in competition with the Bishop of the diocese. Because the people knew what the sisters did in the care of the sick, and the Bishop resided in [another city] . . . The people who gave money gave it to the sisters and the Bishops weren't getting any (Focus Group 2.6: Active and retired sisters).

Nineteenth century Protestant women's missionary societies also gained power within their denominations through the provision of valued resources. By becoming an officer in one of these societies, a woman could control impressive amounts of corporate money at a time when individual women were legally denied control of their personal finances. The women officers served as employers, invested the society's money in stock, and served on the boards of the agencies they owned or sponsored—all occupations normally reserved for men.[18] Through their societies, therefore, the women gained ecclesiastical power by the sheer weight of their numbers or the power of their financial contributions. Even in the early years, before 1892, the first sixteen women's societies had raised $5,940,045. In 1900, the funds raised by the women's missionary societies accounted for between 25 percent and 33 percent of all the money collected for the foreign missions in the various denominations. By 1970, the United Methodist Women alone were raising $30 million per year. The women were well aware of the power implications of the resources they provided to the denomination. As the author of one mission society's handbook noted: "All this represents power! Women power! Money power! The money is and has been raised by women, is managed and appropriated by women, according to policy directives previously determined by women."[19]

By supporting women missionaries, the missionary societies also helped insure that, by 1900, over 60 percent of all missionaries were women.[20] As with the Catholic nuns, therefore, the Protestant women's missionary societies provided key resources of money and personnel which the male denominational officials needed and made numerous attempts to control. In 1876, for example, the (male) Executive Committee of the northern branch of the Methodist Episcopal Church recommended that the Women's Foreign Missionary Society combine its funds with larger church revenues. The women refused to do so: "We regard closer financial union as prejudicial to our interests, in short, such a change would be disastrous."[21]

By the early 1900s, however, many women's missionary societies began to lose this power source, as they were subordinated to male-dominated denominational mission boards.[22] The Presbyterians consolidated all seven of their foreign missionary societies in 1920. The women's groups became auxiliaries of the denomination's Board of Foreign Missions, which made all appropriations and disbursed all funds. Baptist and Congregationalist women were similarly subordinated to male-run boards and lost control over both their funds and mission personnel. Only the women's missionary societies in the various Methodist denominations managed to retain some autonomy and control over the funds their members collected.

> After about the 1960s, Methodism was the only group that really maintained a separate women's organization with the kind of power and authority – the control of our money, the ownership of property—all the rest of the groups got pulled into a coeducational effort of some kind in the denomination. Which really made women's work invisible, if not totally lost (Individual Interview: Retired deaconess).

Even within the Methodist denominations, the women's control was constantly threatened. For example, a 1910 merger in the Southern branch of the Methodist Episcopal Church between the Women's Missionary Council and the larger denominational Board of Mission—without consulting the membership—subjected the women to the male-dominated Board in key decisions. The women were extremely reluctant to accept this re-organization, and acquiesced only because they feared that the alternative would be complete subordination. Throughout the nineteenth and early twentieth century, the relationship of the Methodist women's missionary societies to the larger denomination remained "one of the most delicate and perplexing problems" the women had to face.[23]

Youth work was another source of power, since it supplied future members both to the denomination and to the women's societies. Again, the women's missionary societies had to resist attempts by the larger denomination to remove this responsibility from them and lodge it elsewhere in the central bureaucracy. The leader of one society argued that "if the Society was to be a living organism, continuing, as its intent was, until the last woman and child had heard of the Redeemer, young people and children must be within its ranks."[24]

By 1930, however, the women's jurisdiction over youth work had been removed in many denominations:

> It was difficult for women involved in the changes, which took place so radically

and so suddenly . . . to understand the manner in which such change had occurred. The fact that the General Conference provided for women members on the General Board of Christian Education was small comfort to those who felt their interests in and contributions to the missionary education of young people had been ignored and cut off without warning.[25]

For the Methodist societies, a further change occurred in 1964. The three Methodist churches which united in 1940 had combined their respective Home and Foreign Missionary societies into a national agency (the Women's Division of the Board of Missions) to co-ordinate the activities of the local women's societies and service guilds. In 1964, however, responsibility for missionary projects and programs was removed from the Women's Division to other (male-dominated) parts of the Board of Missions. The women were given a certain number of seats on these other bodies, but they were no longer able to exercise complete control:

> In 1964, when this whole structure that I am describing moved from one part of the Board of Mission to another part. . . . Everything that [the United Methodist Women] had been doing was supposedly continued. But for them, it was at an arm's length. . . . The Women's Division, the entity that had been doing all this management, all this recruiting, all this placement, raising all the money—the administration of all this work and the handling of the personnel, was now off in another department where they were no longer the majority and where you had a lot of persons who didn't really know or understand the women's history—some of whom were hostile to it (Individual Interview: Retired Deaconess).

Although they still owned and operated some three hundred pieces of property in 1960, the women now had only partial control over the money to run them:

> Well, we control some of the finances. . . . The Women's Division has more authority over the expenditures of its money than it had in the past. This is one of the changes that occurred two years ago. See, [between 1964 and 1996], we sent roughly six million dollars from the Women's Division over to the unit that was doing mission in the U.S. and we sent another six million dollars from the Women's Division to the unit that was doing mission outside the U.S. Some of our members were over [on the boards of those units] helping make decisions [concerning the expenditures], but it was not a majority of our members and it was not a majority of that [unit's] committee (Individual Interview: Retired Deaconess).

As an observer at the time noted, women were under-represented in the General Conference, on the Conference Boards, and in the Executive Staff of the United Methodist Church, comprising fewer than a quarter of the positions there.[26]

In addition to the loss of church power for the United Methodist Women, the Methodist deaconesses were also affected by this organizational change:

> The total system of education, recruitment, training, and placement once

supported by the Women's Division was dismantled in the 1964 restructuring. A consensus emerged that the transfer [of responsibility for the deaconess program] contributed to the increasing decline of the national church's understanding and appreciation of deaconesses and home missionaries. The Program Office of Deaconess and Missionary Service functioned on a constantly diminishing budget, salaries of workers remained low; agencies and institutions verged on bankruptcy; male pastors increasingly headed agencies traditionally administered by deaconesses.[27]

A deaconess in one of the focus groups mentioned the loss of power and resources at the local level that resulted from these re-organizations:

It used to be all women on our boards at community centers. When I went to [state] in 1970, men were dominating the board of directors and they loved it. . . But it was the women who had started it, who had funded it, and everything else. But the men suddenly came in when the structure changed to the [denominational board] rather than the women operating these places (Focus Group 4.1:Retired deaconesses).

Or, as one Methodist historian put it:

Credit for the changed status of women [within the denomination] goes to the vision, sense of organization, self-reliance, and religiously-rooted self-respect of the leaders and members of the Women's Foreign Missionary Society. Without the personal initiative and sense of call of these women, there would have been no specific Methodist Protestant missions. Women began and inspired the work; they learned and grew from it too.[28]

The summary pattern across the denominations, therefore, was that, as long as the sisters, deaconesses, and the missionary society leaders had controlled the funding and personnel for their institutions, they were able to exercise a group-based power in the larger denomination. Whenever they lost this control, their power as a denominational group was correspondingly diminished. But, as the following section will show, the need to train and educate their members to serve in these institutions was also a powerful source of *individual* empowerment.

The Power of Individual Members

Running their institutions empowered individual sisters, deaconesses, missionaries, and women's society members, first of all, by providing them with professional occupations unavailable in the larger society. Baptist and Presbyterian women missionary doctors found "that there were more opportunities overseas than on the home front."[29] Catholic religious orders also offered more opportunities for women than were available elsewhere. "Indeed, since their early days in Ireland, sisterhood had been a most successful strategy for women who desired respect, independence, and social mobility without losing their traditional identity and kinship."[30] This assertion has been documented for Catholic religious orders of women in many other European and North American countries during the nineteenth century.[31]

Spurred by institutional needs, the leaders of the orders and societies actively developed their members' administrative skills. As early as the 1870s, the Daughters of Charity were training their members on how to conduct meetings of corporate boards and keep records. Similarly, in the 1880's, the leaders of the Presbyterian women's missionary societies published educational documents to train their members in parliamentary procedures.[32] Religious superiors placed young sisters with older mentors: "The skills of new recruits, once training was completed, were honed by strategic placements. . . . 'Who would be a good person to send on this difficult assignment? Who needed more guidance and would benefit from working with a more experienced individual?'"[33] As a result, nineteenth and early twentieth century sisters, deaconesses, and mission society members showed great executive ability, at a time when this was unusual in women. Some of the sisters:

> established three or four hospitals from nothing. They knew how to raise loans from individuals—many of their mortgages were from 'friends.' They understood the way government worked and what funds were available from the county or state. . . . Basically, they knew how to do business, raise money, and build support, how to deal with the clergy and the medical profession. They did this their entire working lives, without the distraction of family cares, training a new generation of sisters in their wake.[34]

Similarly, the women in the mission societies displayed "extraordinary organizational skills" in building, funding and operating schools, hospitals and social service agencies. "Their new-found ability to run such enterprises was a surprise to [the members] themselves."[35] The public speaking skills which the missionary society women developed also opened the door to their speaking in other church settings. Their increasing participation in these mission societies "influenced the Church to reflect on issues relating to women in a way it had never done before," and to support higher educational opportunities for them. Church leaders such as Josiah Strong affirmed women's authority in social issues as an essential part of the Church's work in building the Kingdom of God. Women, Strong concluded, were "indispensable co-workers with men," performing "authentic and essential forms of Christian ministry."[36]

Initially, the women had so much work to do that there was no time for either professional or spiritual training.[37] After teaching and nursing professionalized in the late nineteenth and early twentieth centuries, however, informal mentoring was no longer enough. Both the nuns and the deaconesses felt pressured to acquire academic credentials in order to validate their professional qualifications:

> For the first generation of deaconesses, a call to vocation sufficed as grounds for

admission to the training schools; for the next generation, religious conviction alone was judged insufficient qualification. Whereas women with little or no formal schooling had been welcomed to the ranks, now a high school diploma was deemed a must.[38]

Both the sisters and the deaconesses, therefore, began to upgrade their "in-house" training schools to full-fledged colleges, in order to insure that all of their members were adequately trained. By mid-century, most of the deaconesses were expected to acquire professional credentials *before* entering the diaconal probationary program.

The Catholic orders, however, found this more difficult. A 1952 survey found three critical obstacles to the sisters' professional education: 1.) the amount of *time* needed to complete these degrees, in the face of pastors' and bishops' increasing demands for more sister-teachers, 2.) the *cost* of higher education, especially since, in about half of the orders, the annual cost of living per capita exceeded the average annual salary of the teaching sisters, and 3.) *lack of understanding* by both the clergy and the orders' own superiors as to why all this education was needed in the first place.[39] Many bishops and priests thought that education for elementary teachers, especially, was a needless extravagance: "Bishop John W. Shanahan of Harrisburg, PA, told the Sisters of Mercy in his diocese that 'the eagerness for higher education would diminish the religious spirit' of their institute, which was supposed to be devoted to the care of the poor."

As a result of these difficulties, most young sisters in the 1930s, 1940s, and 1950s were sent to fill positions in their order's hospitals and schools before completing college. Many finished their degrees on the "Ten Year Plan," studying on weekends and during the summers. The older sisters in the focus groups were able to cite numerous instances when they had been given administrative responsibilities without adequate preparation:

When I became operating room supervisor, I had no preparation. Here I am a brand new graduate—five to six years out of nursing. So here I'm going up hardly remembering what I'd learned and I found myself in this position and it was like I was studying every night. Trying to remember, trying to think of procedures, trying to think of instruments, trying to play a role. It was awful (Focus Group 1.5: Active sisters).

- I was only in [the Sisters of X] nine or ten years, I didn't have a college degree, and I was made principal of two schools. And I went to the Mother and said I had never had a course in administration. "God will help you, and the Holy Spirit. Pray every day."
- I was in the same situation. I did get [an administration degree] after I was in it, but initially you used your common sense and consulted people who had experience and prayed hard (Focus Group 2.2: Retired sisters).

They sent me to take charge of the orphanage and that was social work and I had never had any social work. And I was supposed to be the superior, the child care co-ordinator, the principal of the orphanage (Focus Group 3.9: Retired sisters).

Similar stories were recounted in seventeen of the 24 sisters' focus groups. In most, however, the speakers ended by concluding that they had been successful in their administrative positions. Many even felt that having had "real world" administrative experience prior to beginning formal academic training had been beneficial:

- Well, I would say I was trained on the way. [laughter] I was made a principal and then after a couple of years, I began working on a graduate degree in education administration. I have to tell you, I didn't feel that that was a disadvantage, because I already had hands-on experience and I could more easily apply the pie-in-the-sky kind of things that you're taught. So I sort of enjoyed that I'd had the experience and then got into the training.
(Interviewer: What about the hospital positions?)
- I was well trained in the laboratory and knew that I would probably be in a supervisory position, but I never found it a problem. . . . You learn by experience, that some things are—I think that whether you had been trained in it or not, you would face the same kind of problems that I faced along the way. Sometimes you made mistakes and sometimes you didn't. But I think it went well, and I know that I did a good job (Focus Group 1.6: Active and retired sisters).

- Well, interestingly enough, I'm going to say this and I'm going to say it humbly, I was a very good principal. And it would never have been a job I would have sought, outside the convent. . . . I enjoyed being in the classroom when I was there, but I liked being principal better. But, I went in and I didn't sleep the whole first year I was there. I couldn't stop my mind when I went to bed at night, I reprocessed everything, all day long. But, I turned out to be a very good principal, which I consider to be an act of grace.
- I think we all went through that (Focus Group 1.3: Active sisters).

In 1954, the U.S. women's orders, at the instigation and with the help of the leading Catholic colleges and universities, established the Sister Formation Conference to facilitate the educational preparation of the young nuns.[40] This was an additional way in which the orders' colleges, as a group, helped empower the individual sisters. The SFC collected and disseminated information concerning the best programs of higher education for sisters and opportunities for financial aid, announced workshops, suggested bibliographies for postulants and novices, and commissioned articles on education.[41] Gradually, and with much struggle, the orders managed to retain their young sisters at the motherhouse until they had completed their education or nursing degrees. By the 1960s, "sisters were among the best-educated cohorts of women in the country and highly active in their professions."[42]

The need to staff and administer their colleges lent a further impetus to the orders' educational efforts. In order to fully accredit these institutions, the sisters needed to send some of their members for post-graduate training. This had a profound impact on the orders as a whole, and on the individual sisters as well:

> The significance of the liberal arts college phenomenon for the intellectual life of U.S. women religious can scarcely be exaggerated. It propelled nuns into study for advanced degrees. Dependent to some degree upon individual ability, interest, and postgraduate opportunity, it incorporated them into the intellectual circles of academe.[43]

The orders spent thousands of dollars on advanced education for the sisters slated to teach in their colleges.[44] Superiors applied for scholarships for promising young nuns. "It was a huge investment made on each prospective faculty member."[45] Several authors have argued that the orders would not have considered such an investment without the spur of institutional need.[46]

And neither would the individual members. The sisters responding to one recent study of Catholic colleges stated that they owed their achievements to their superiors, who had seen creativity and potential within them that they themselves had not. They believed that their lives and their ministry would have been diminished without the institutional spur to pursue post-graduate education.[47] The sisters in the focus groups agreed:

> I never knew what a versatile woman I was until I entered the convent. I've taught every grade but the first, even including college. I've worked in the hospital and in many different types of [Sisters of X] institutions: the orphanage, our military school, high school, hospital corporation, and regular parish school. I've had an awful good time doing it (Focus Group 1.1: Retired sisters).

> - I see myself this way: I'm in the [Sisters of X]; I've had the jobs I've had because the [Sisters of X] called me to do them. And I've put myself in a place where I could be called, and that's what I'm saying about the importance of having collective commitments. . . . At least for my life, it worked, to draw me out into doing things I wouldn't have had the nerve to do on my own.
> - Me neither (Focus Group 2.3: Present and former leaders).

In addition to their formal academic training, the sisters also continued their tradition of mentoring each other "on the job," as the older, more experienced sisters shared techniques of teaching and administration with those who had recently completed their studies:

> Well, I was just new out of going to [the diocesan teachers' college], and I just appreciated listening to the other sisters talk. And they were always willing to—they would tell you the stories that happened in their class and it kind of helped me to know how to do things in my class. That was a big help (Focus Group 3.3: Retired sisters).

> I was really blessed because at St. Luke's, we had double grades . . . . Each of us had an experienced teacher, you know, to work with. Like, I worked with Sister Mary. So every Saturday afternoon, we spent time doing lesson plans together.

And she would come in at least once a day to see how I was doing, because we both taught fifth grade (Focus group 3.1: Retired sisters).

Thank God for Sister Jane, because when I got there, she decided that I didn't know anything about the hospital and I should go through every department in the hospital for a week. Which I did. At least it gave me an overview of the hospital—thank God for that, because I didn't know anything. And then one day, they had a Board meeting . . . and they came back and told me I was the new director of nursing services (Sisters' Focus Group 1.5: Active sisters).

There was, I think, a nurturing among us of each other, but also from the [order's] leadership in wanting to encourage the sisters to get the kind of training they needed . . . to move on or move up or become more involved in what they were doing. There was a real personal interest in the sisters (Focus Group 2.5: Active sisters).

Of the 24 sisters' focus groups, 22 mentioned the empowering effects of the education and mentoring they had received, which had prepared them for service in the order's institutions.

Local chapters of the Protestant women's mission societies have also offered opportunities to develop skills in public speaking, fund raising, and organizational management. The Women's Foreign Mission Society was created, not only to liberate women in non-Christian lands, but also "to provide outlets for the energy, ability, and leadership of American women."[48] Histories of the nineteenth century associations document the skills and self-confidence gained by the society members and (especially) by their leaders:

The Church permitted the women's organizations, through which they came to a greater appreciation of their abilities and self-worth. This new confidence and altered self-understanding were essential in encouraging the women to seek greater authority and independence in the denomination.[49]

More recently, a publication of the United Methodist Women noted:

Have you ever considered, for example, the amount of work done and the skill and patience required by a district treasurer of the UMW? She may handle as much as $30,000—$50,000 annually, receiving that money from 75 to 125 different treasurers, in payments that come quarterly and at miscellaneous other times. Or the work of a conference secretary of program resources? She usually has two very strenuous work periods each year when materials are displayed and sold at the annual meeting and the School of Christian Mission.[50]

As with the Catholic sisters, the women in these mission societies actively mentored each other in the needed administrative skills.

I was with the older women, with Mrs. Jones, and I was the youngest thing. But even so, with the generation gap, it was a very, very pleasant experience. And from that experience, I wanted to learn as much as I could about the organization. [emphatically] *And I did.* I became the Vice President of our local group here. I became the Vice President of the district and then I became Vice President of the conference level. And I remember the joy we had the first time we went to the Assembly in [city]. We didn't know what the experience was going to be, but it was a magnificent one with about 10,000 women! (Focus Group 5.9: Mission society).

In recent times, several mission societies have initiated training seminars specifically to prepare women for denominational leadership roles.

In previous decades, therefore, owning, running, and financing their sponsored institutions had provided an avenue to denominational power for both the Catholic and the Protestant women's groups. Loss of control over these institutions, which began as early as the beginning of the last century for many denominational mission societies, had profound and detrimental effects on these groups' ability to influence church decisions. Additionally, the demands of institutional sponsorship had spurred the leaders of the orders and societies actively to seek out and train talented new members in a host of administrative and professional skills, training which the members might not have considered pursuing on their own. In an era when few other opportunities were available to women, their institutions gave Catholic religious orders, Protestant mission societies, and deaconesses a way to develop and exercise their talents—and an arena in which to exert actual power.

This power could be exercised in the larger society as well as in the denomination. The leaders of the nineteenth century women's missionary societies had frequently intervened with the Federal government in issues such as prohibition, the treatment of native Americans, and polygamy in Utah.[51] Their institutional resources and their administrative expertise gave weight to their opinions. To a certain extent, this is still true today among the Catholic religious orders:

- Over the years, we had a sister who served on the city council, was mayor pro tem, our sisters have been on different boards and organizations. We have invited people to meet here: some of our civic groups.
- We've had interaction with the other churches, too.
- [Order's residential home for severely retarded children] has done a lot of outreach. . . Those things are really public institutions. . . . Many of us serve on different civic organizations or are involved in projects and things like that (Focus Group 1.6: Active and retired sisters).

- I know that [the order's institutions] can get funding from the government, because the Sisters of X and [another order] are behind it, and they know it, and that's important.
- And they know that there will be no waste of the people's money (Focus Group 2.1: Active sisters).

- [When I went to the city planning commission] I was speaking to get what I wanted and I said I was a Sister of X, and they listened.

- They all dropped their pencils.
- The Sisters of X are known for getting things going and making them work, institutionally. Years ago, some study identified us as the builders of institutions. In some ways, that's still true (Focus Group 2.3: Present and former leaders).

In like manner, sponsored institutions have also served to increase the larger denomination's societal influence. Institutional networks of educators, social workers, and health care professionals have frequently pressured the National Conferences of Catholic Bishops in the U. S. and Australia to take public positions on various governmental policies which they otherwise might not have taken. By interacting with the presidents of Catholic colleges, the CEO's of Catholic health care systems, and the boards of Catholic social service organizations, bishops have gained the background knowledge and motivation to speak out in the public arena on issues affecting these institutions. The institutions themselves lobby government, both on the state and national level. Catholic Charities USA is by far the largest non-governmental provider of social services in the United States, with an annual budget of $2.5 billion, fourteen agencies, and a paid staff of 47,532. It maintains a permanent lobbying staff in Washington, DC, to influence social legislation.[52]

Power, Class, and Division

The impact of institutions on the power distribution within their sponsoring denominations and denominational groups might not be totally positive, however. Many also were sources of division. As was noted in Chapter 2, all organizations accumulate additional goals and identities over time. These identities may be blended in a "holographic" manner, such that each member of the organization subscribes to the entire amalgam, however inconsistent it may be.[53] Thus, a worker in a denominational institution might think of himself or herself as a *Catholic* doctor/nurse/hospital administrator, a *Mennonite* historian/biologist/college president, or a *Lutheran* social worker. These combined identities often served to retain professionals in the denomination who otherwise might have left.[54] However, an amalgamated religious/professional identity such as these could also cause gradual but fundamental changes in the internal culture and operation of the denomination or sponsoring group, and, indeed, in its founding definition of religious virtuosity:

> The sisters' move into higher education often challenged their convent training and religious ideals. Taught to be humble and self-effacing and to avoid singularity, sisters had to compromise if not reject these values to complete M.A.'s and Ph.D.'s in secular institutions that challenged them to compete, excel, and strive for individual awards and accomplishments.[55]

As a result, the sponsoring group's members may become confused as to how the competing expectations of religion and professionalism are to be applied in their daily lives.[56] "Holographic," or combined, goals may thus become more difficult to sustain over time.

On the other hand, the "ideographic" form of dual identity reflects a situation in which various subgroups in the institution or the sponsoring religious group have come to subscribe to different and incompatible organizational identities. For example, a denomination's representative on its college or hospital board may be committed to advancing the institution's religious identity and insuring that it operates according to denominational principles. But the actual personnel and administrators of the organization may feel a stronger identification with their professional counterparts in secular institutions—if, indeed, they identify with the denomination at all.[57] Or professionally trained sisters might desire to attend a conference with their lay colleagues rather than one of the order's internal meetings. In such cases, the result may be division and conflict within the sponsoring religious group, or between the sponsor and the institution.

Divisions in the Sponsoring Religious Group

Several historians have noted that the need to educate members for professional positions in their schools and hospitals quickly led to a "meritocracy of ability" in U.S. Catholic religious orders which replaced the medieval European distinction between choir (noble) and lay (peasant) members.

> Ironically, just at the time that [the Sisters of St. Joseph] discontinued their classist distinction between choir and lay sisters in 1908, it was necessary for some sisters to be singled out and propelled into positions of academic prominence and achievement if they were to accomplish their goals in women's higher education. Formal education, not socioeconomic level, became a new source of tension within the community. Sisters who earned graduate degrees created a new distinction, and at times it must have been difficult to mesh the religious goals of uniformity and solidarity with the "special status" awarded to college faculty.[58]

By the early twentieth century, the Sisters of Providence required all of their novices to pass an examination before being sent to teach. The grades in these examinations led to a kind of caste system based on literacy, academic preparation, and/or facility for book learning. Instead of the sisters being all more or less at the same level of preparation, the new emphasis on formal education "promoted some subtle divisions in the community, the effects of which were felt for years to come."

In orders which performed several different kinds of work, there might also be divisions between the hospital sisters, the school sisters, and those who served in the orphanages. The latter group usually had the least prestige. One's status within the order might mirror one's position in the order's institutions: principals and hospital administrators had higher status than teachers and nurses. Hospitals were ranked in prestige as well: administering a large, wealthy, urban hospital brought higher status within the order than administering a small, rural one. Teaching in an elementary school had less prestige than teaching in a high school, and both were less prestigious than teaching in the order's college.

> In elementary education there was always the caste system, so I could speak to that from living as a grade school principal in a high school convent. It was definitely the *high school* convent. There was an impression that if you were a nurse or in high school you were—"better," I'll use that term—better than elementary school teachers (Focus Group 3.6: Former leaders and staff).

One focus group noted that, while the sisters teaching in the elementary school had to prepare their lessons for the following day together in a single room, under the watchful eye of the convent superior.

> - The high school teachers were able to study in their rooms. That was hard.
> - Yes
> - That was really, that was painful (Focus Group 3.9: Retired sisters).

A retired hospital sister in another focus group noted that the nursing sisters, too, were given more freedom and autonomy than the elementary school teachers were.

In addition to inequities in freedom and autonomy, factions within the sponsoring religious group might contest over the distribution of resources. Mission societies in the late nineteenth century often argued over the amount of support which could be given to the home versus the foreign missions, and whether the two goals could be combined in one organization.

Divisions in the Larger Denomination

In addition to their possibly divisive effects within the sponsoring group, religious institutions might also serve as sources of division in the larger denomination. Establishing colleges often divided a church into classes—the educated elite vs. the masses. The elite were seen as contemptuous of ordinary believers, which the latter intensely resented:

> "A religion that didn't appeal to any but college graduates," [William Jennings] Bryan huffed, "would be over the head or under the feet of 99 percent of our people. The God I worship is the God of the ignorant as well as the God of the learned man." Both the scientist and the biblical critic were portrayed as holding, in effect, that religious truth belonged to the domain of the highly educated expert.[59]

By retaining a new class of educated members within the denominational ranks, colleges might create economic and political divisions. Wealthy lay professionals —doctors, lawyers and the like—who had been educated in denominational colleges might contest with their poorer and less-educated co-religionists over issues of church governance, and feel that their larger tithes entitled them to a greater voice in denominational decision-making.[60]

In addition to the *intellectual* elitism expressed by a denomination's educated members and the *economic* elitism displayed by its professional members, the virtuosi operating the institutions might also come to be seen as a *spiritual* elite. This might inhibit less spiritually-advanced lay members from becoming active in church works themselves. Several historians have noted, for example, that the initial domination of social services by sisters in Catholic countries had hindered the development of lay women's benevolent societies comparable to those developed by Protestant women, thus forestalling the development of church power by women *not* in religious orders.[61] Finally, while most Catholics and Protestants respected and admired religious sisters, deaconesses, and missionaries, some— especially after the mid-1960s—also resented the implication that these virtuosi were somehow "better" than other church members. This resentment could become an additional source of division.

The women's institutional service sometimes sparked conflict between the members of these societies and the clergy or the male-dominated mission boards. After the absorption of their financial and decision-making powers into the larger denominational structures, the women often found that they had "virtually no input" into how the fruits of their labors would be used. In some local congregations, the minister would even appropriate the women's mission funds for his own local building projects.[62]

In many Catholic parishes, this power struggle was played out between the sisters who ran the school and the pastor of the parish:

> Well, when I was in [city], we taught for nothing. We had to earn our salary. And so we had to make candy and . . . we had paper drives to make the money for our salaries. Cause the pastor said he didn't have any money. . . . So, one year, a principal who was sent there said she wouldn't do this. So she only lasted one year. But the next year the principal was told to ask the pastor for the last year's salary. . . . And she asked him and he said, "You can have it if they earn it." So we had to earn two years' salary in one (Focus Group 3.4: Retired sisters).

> Then the pastor was, uh, you know, one of those "noted" pastors. And he, uh, our superior was an older sister, very calm and cool and collected and just a darling nun. And he took a liking to some of the other sisters, and he did all his business through these other nuns. So the superior never knew what was actually going to happen, she'd find out at the supper table from one of these sisters, what was coming off (Focus Group 3.4: Retired sisters).

Local tensions between ministers and the women's missionary societies were also mentioned in some mission society focus groups:

> We didn't have a minister who was really with it, as far as we were concerned. And that didn't work out well. Now we're on our feet again, because we have a wonderful staff now (Focus Group 5.6: Mission society).

- And there are some ministers who don't like the [name of mission society].
- Right, right.
- About 25 percent of them (Focus Group 5.5: Mission society).

Some of the retired deaconesses recalled similar difficulties:

- Some of us have experienced being conscious of God's presence and direction in ways that the others don't, or that the power structure hasn't, and if my God-consciousness has to be held up to someone else to be approved by comparing it with theirs, then I've failed.
- Yours and mine are both a personal relationship with God. It doesn't matter about anybody else.
- No, but sometimes the powers that be want to crack down and say, "Hey!" (Focus Group 4.2: Retired deaconesses).

In addition to fostering intellectual, economic, and spiritual divisions, denominational organizations might spark other types of conflicts as well. Religious colleges and universities—especially if they harbored a seminary or training school for virtuosi—often incubated theological or liturgical changes which their graduates then attempted to spread to the more conservative mainstream.[63] Sometimes this could be good for the denomination:

The music faculty . . . contributed to church music by active leadership in compiling two major new hymnals produced co-operatively with other Anabaptist-derived groups, and by helping Mennonites make a transition to some use of instruments in worship while, at best, still preserving a strong a cappella tradition.[64]

On the other hand, the students and faculty at denominational colleges were the most exposed to ideas and values from the larger society and they were often in the vanguard of those wishing to liberalize standards of dress, diet, entertainment, or reading matter.[65] As another example, a religious institution or its staff might advocate the extension of church or virtuoso membership to previously excluded population groups. Hill notes that there was initially much opposition within Protestant denominations to the idea of creating the roles of missionary or deaconess for women; similar opposition had occurred in the seventeenth century Europe when Catholic sisters first left their cloisters to teach and nurse.[66] Protestant efforts to educate the poor in eighteenth century England contradicted the prevailing belief that God had created this class to remain poor, dirty and ignorant. American home missionaries to the rural South and Southwest challenged entrenched caste systems of the 1930s, 1940s and 1950s by educating African Americans and Native Americans. Later in the twentieth century, the leadership of the women's missionary societies in many U.S. Protestant denominations were more likely than the average member to favor the admission of women, ethnic minorities, and, sometimes, gays to church positions that had formerly been closed to them. All of these activities led to internal dissension, both within the virtuoso groups and in the larger denomination.

> One thing concerned me personally—last year I was listening to a Christian radio
> station and I heard that [the mission society] was supporting a homosexual group
> in a high school in Salt lake City. And that concerned me a whole lot, because our
> church had been very public about its stand on homosexuality as far as ministry
> goes, and then I heard this on the radio. And I never read anything about it in our
> local [denominational] papers or anything, but I wanted to not be a member any
> more, once I heard that because that's not something that I would support at the
> local level, and then somebody that I send money to is taking a stand on this and
> so I don't know that much about it but that's what I heard come across the radio,
> that the [mission society] had supported this action in this high school. That
> concerned me (Focus Group 5.2: Mission society).

> You know, in the society around us . . . the lottery is OK, and I know that on the
> national level [denomination] is not in favor of gambling, and, uh, so every time
> it comes up for voting there's always a bunch of activity, and it got through this
> time and so many are worried about families and counseling families that have
> trouble, you know, with gambling. And there's the gay/lesbian movement and
> people are worried, well, what is this going to do to the family, or is it going to do
> anything to the family and what are we going to do about that, if we do anything
> about that. And there are so many things like that, and then the abortion issue,
> well, should we, and at the national level it's supposed to be pro-choice, but then,
> also people say, "Well, I really cannot vote for that, so, should I be pro-life?"
> (Focus Group 5.3: Mission society)

Four of the nine mission society focus groups raised such concerns.

Conclusions

The institutions sponsored, staffed, and administered by religious groups have thus
had wide-ranging and profound effects upon the groups themselves. The orders of
sisters, the offices of deaconesses, and the lay women's mission societies often
owed their very existence to these institutions: they had originally been founded
precisely in order to run them. The sisters' and deaconesses' institutional service
continued to shape their group identity throughout subsequent generations of
members—but it also, eventually, caused their identity drift. Institutional service
attracted new recruits—but overwork and lack of preparation sometimes drove
them away. The women who ran the institutions gained power by doing so, both
within the fields of education, health care, and social work, and also *vis à vis* the
larger church and the society—but this power was often contested and sometimes
removed. Young members were pushed to develop skills and talents they had not
known they possessed—sometimes, however, at tremendous personal cost.
Institutions sparked the formation of entire denominations and kept subsequent
generations within the fold—but also fractured denominations and denominational

groups into classes and warring factions.

Given the immense influence of their institutions on the sponsoring groups, therefore, one might predict that the loss or attenuation of their mutual relationship might have equally profound results. Before analyzing these results, however, it is necessary first to outline the way in which the connections between religious sponsors and their institutions were broken.

Notes

1. See Aldrich and Pfeffer (1976:83).
2. Wall (2002:24). See Jones (1999:232), Risse (1999:292), Cleary (2001:46-47), and Wall (2002:26) for the information in the preceding paragraph.
3. Wall (2002:25).
4. Nelson (2001:46).
5. Farren (1996:46). See Cleary (2001:46-47) for Australia.
6. Risse (1999:524).
7. Nelson (2001:139).
8. See Clear (1987:105) for Ireland, and Langlois (1984:383) for France.
9. See, for example, Deacon (1989:389) for staffing figures for Wisconsin Catholic schools in the nineteenth century. Deacon (1989:353) also mentions the authority conflicts described later in this paragraph.
10. Pfau (1934:17).
11. This list is taken from Gallin (1996:18-19).
12. Beaver (1968:29) makes this point for Protestant social and mission works.
13. Ewens (1981:107). See Deacon (1989:350-80) and Thompson (1991:148) for specific examples of this exercise of power.
14. Byrne (1986:259). See also Deacon (1989:140-45), Nolan (1989:88), Thompson (1991:148), and Nelson (2001:107) for the shortage of sisters in nineteenth century Catholicism. See Ewens (1981:107) and O'Brien (1987:346) for examples of sisters withdrawing from a school, or even a diocese, if they were displeased. See also Langlois (1984:415) and Rapley (1990:86) for similar examples in other countries.
15. Deacon (1989:351). See also Wittberg (1994:86-87) for further examples.
16. Deacon (1989:137). See Miller (1985:55) for the Presbyterians.
17. See Deacon (1989:111, 250, 333, 389) for these figures; Farren (1996:74) for the figures on the Mayo Clinic.
18. See Beaver (1968:106), Boyd and Brackenridge (1983:35) and Ginzberg (1990:50-62) for the information in this paragraph.
19. Campbell (1975:88). See also Brereton and Klein (1979:308-9) for examples.
20. Hill (1985:14).
21. Quoted in Isham (1936:32).
22. See Brereton and Klein (1979:312), Keller (1981:255), Noll (1981:223-26), Shadron (1981:262-67), McDowell (1982:126-31), Boyd and Brackenridge (1983:52-57), Hill (1985:49-53), and Higgenbotham (1993:157) for instances of this power struggle in various denominations.
23. See Tatum (1960:30) and Isham (1936:30).
24. Quoted in Isham (1936:33).

25. Tatum (1960:53).

26. Campbell (1975:45-47). This proportion was too small for the women to exercise any meaningful control over the disbursement of the funds they had collected.

27. Dougherty (1997:264).

28. Noll (1981:232).

29. Weber (1986:302) makes this point for Baptist missionary doctors. Boyd and Brackenridge (1983:170) for the Presbyterians. Brereton and Klein (1979:308-309) and Cnaan et al. (1999:196) make the same point.

30. Risse (1999:516). See also Clear (1987:5, 19) and Nolan (1989) for similar assertions regarding Irish sisters.

31. See Langlois (1984:643) for France, Bukowczyk (1988:24) for Poland, Prelinger 1986a:163) for Germany, and Hill (1973:254, 272) for England.

32. See Nelson (2001:52) for the Daughters of Charity; Boyd and Brackenridge (1983:40) for the Presbyterian women's missionary societies. See also Walsh (2002:158).

33. Nelson (2001:54).

34. Nelson (2001:54).

35. Quoted in Boyd and Brackenridge (1983:37). See Boyd and Brackenridge (1983:166, 101) also for the quotation in the following sentence.

36. Wendy Edwards (2003:40-41).

37. Golder (1903:279) makes this point with regard to Methodist deaconesses.

38. Dougherty (1997:xii).

39. Schneider (1986:6-7). See Madden (1991:362) for the quotation in the following sentence.

40. See Beane (1993:4) for the role of the NCEA College and University Department in the beginning of the Sister Formation Movement. For the movement itself, see Beane (1993), Kolmer (1984:23-26), Schneider (1986, 1988), Quinonez and Turner (1992:6-10), Gleason (1995:226-34), and Daigler (2000:129-31).

41. A list of the SFC's publications and other activities can be found in Kolmer (1984:23-26) and Schneider (1986:19-20, 25).

42. Nelson (2001:162).

43. Kennelly (1996:51). See a similar argument for the professionalization of nursing in Nelson (2001:132).

44. In 1911, for example, the Sisters of the Blessed Virgin Mary sent six sisters to the Sisters' College at Catholic University. This cost them $6,000 – the *total* year's earnings of 30 teaching sisters (Gleason 1995:95). By 1919, Sisters' College had taught 1,800 sisters: 214 got their BA degree, 115 got a Master's; and 12 a Ph.D. (Murphy 1988:132).

45. Coburn and Smith (1999:186). See Daigler (2000:75) for examples among the Sisters of Mercy.

46. Kennelly (1996:60) and Daigler (2000:196) make this point.

47. Morey (1995:86, ftn.). Compare Daigler (2000:221).

48. Keller (1981:251). See also Hill (1985:4).

49. McDowell (1982:117).

50. Campbell (1975:75). See also Isham (1936:34), Hill (1985:4), and Ginzberg (1990:38) for specific examples.

51. Boyd and Brackenridge (1983:38). See also Kemeny (2003:226-27).

52. Coleman (2000:1-2) and Coleman (2001). See Cleary (2001:26) for Australia.

53. See Albert and Whetten (1985:270-76) for this terminology.

54. Vance (1999:73) makes this point for the Seventh-day Adventists: 40 percent of Adventist men and 33 percent of Adventist women have earned college degrees. Adventists

are disproportionately represented in professional and skilled occupations.

55. Coburn and Smith (1999:186). See Flanagan (2005:56) for a similar complaint today.

56. See Cnaan et al. (1999:70-86) for a description of the gradual separation between religious and professional views of social workers, for example.

57. Albert and Whetten (1985:271) note this possibility.

58. Coburn and Smith (1999:186-87). See also Kennelly (1996:44). See Madden (1991:72) for the Sisters of Providence.

59. Cherry (1995:173). See Numbers and Larsen (1986:456-7) for educational stratification among Seventh-day Adventists.

60. Lawson and Carden (1983) give examples of this for Seventh-day Adventists.

61. Moloney (2002:41, 47) makes this point.

62. See Boyd and Brackenridge (1983:61, 63-75) for examples of this.

63. Leahy (1997:59) and Chaves (2004:134-39) give examples.

64. Schlabach (2000:24).

65. See Lawson and Carden (1983) and Durnbaugh (1997:359) for examples.

66. Hill (1985:39). See Rapley (1990:6) for seventeenth century French opposition to Catholic sisters leaving their cloisters. See Cnaan et al. (1999:100) and John T. Smith (1998:2) for opposition to educating the poor beyond their station in life. See Van Liere (1991:23) for attempts to challenge racial inequality in the American South. In the past, however, the opposition died down once the groups were actually formed and the value of their works became evident.

PART III

INSTITUTIONAL IDENTITY
AND RELIGIOUS WITHDRAWAL

Chapter 5

The Attenuation of Religious Identity

Any number of organizational studies have noted that, over time, denominational schools, hospitals, and social agencies have increasingly come to resemble their secular counterparts. "It is easy," one author notes, "for the sense of mission and the character of an organization . . . to erode or evolve in inappropriate directions."[1] In the latter decades of the twentieth century, pressing economic constraints, as well as isomorphic pressures from government agencies, professional associations, and clients, have rendered the day-to-day operations of the sisters' and the missionary societies' sponsored organizations less and less religiously distinctive. In addition to these larger environmental changes, the number of sisters and deaconesses working in the organizations has also declined, sometimes quite dramatically.

As a result, some religious groups have relinquished their institutional sponsorship entirely, vesting ownership and control in lay boards or in the denominational hierarchy. Other groups closed their institutions or merged them with other organizations. This section will briefly chronicle the course of organizational withdrawal by Catholic and Protestant religious groups, and the impact which this withdrawal has had on their former schools, hospitals and social service agencies.[2] Subsequent chapters will focus on the basic theme of the book—the reciprocal impact which the withdrawal has had on the sponsoring religious order or denominational group.

Educational Institutions

The Religious Identity of Protestant Colleges and Universities

The withdrawal of Protestant denominations from the active supervision of their colleges has been ably, and often polemically, charted by many historians and theologians.[3] Between 1910 and 1920, the number of formerly Protestant colleges whose catalogs stated a religious identity or purpose decreased by over one-half. The percentage of students or faculty belonging to the sponsoring denominations steadily declined, the proportion of the colleges' budgets that was underwritten by denominational sources fell to a minuscule amount, and even the nominal presence of denominational officials on the colleges' governing boards dwindled to a small and complacent minority.[4] Faculty teaching at denominational colleges also became more secular, withdrawing from religious associations such as the Faculty Christian Fellowship. Specialized trade journals such as *The Christian Scholar* ceased publication.

The literature postulates several environmental sources for these changes. Some were economic: "pervasively sectarian" educational institutions were not eligible for the Carnegie Foundation's matching grants to fund faculty retirement.[5] Other pressures came from professional associations, which "defined academic excellence almost entirely in terms of the intellectual canons of the research university and its discursive, instrumentalist, and quantitative concept of knowledge."[6] The German research university ideal supplanted the classical liberal arts model which had been espoused by nineteenth century denominational colleges. Proponents of the research university model

> were determined to overcome what they took to be the severe limitations of the college system of education. They believed that the colleges founded before the Civil War were controlled by the sectarian outlook of the Protestant denominations, were centered on a curriculum of classical languages irrelevant to life in the modern world, were preoccupied with the training of ministers, and were so superficial in their course offerings that they neglected new fields of knowledge.[7]

As a result, the presidents, boards, and faculties of the denominational colleges —and even the denominations' own education committees—"tended to be increasingly concerned about their colleges' academic excellence (defined in ways acceptable to the nonchurch educational mainstream) and less and less concerned about their colleges' religious identity."[8] Colleges and universities also became increasingly dominated by graduate and professional programs, which made them more likely to experience fragmentation and dilution of their original religious vision.

Other outside stakeholders—employees, clients, licensing agencies, and church-state watchdog groups —pressed the colleges to use secular criteria in their hiring and curricular policies.[9] As with other types of nonprofit organizations, liberal arts colleges thus found themselves "increasingly market driven," viewed more as service providers to demanding customers rather than as educators.[10] Finally, trends toward ecumenism led some denominational colleges to hire administrators and faculty from other faith traditions, despite the worries of critics that the denomination's core traditions were "slipping away from us."[11]

Many denominations lost interest in their colleges, since it had become less and less evident why they should sponsor them at all:

> The United Methodist Church, in a fit of distraction, passed a resolution in the 1968 General Conference that urged their colleges to consider separation from all Church connections, so that they could survive as independent secular institutions. The Supreme Court decision in Roemer v. Maryland (1976) made such panic premature and misplaced, but it reflected the low estate of higher education in the denomination. The Church could not articulate reasons . . . for its historical mission in learning.[12]

At approximately the same time, the General Assembly of the United Presbyterian Church "recommended that all synods and presbyteries relinquish their control over the denomination's colleges. No one, apparently, dissented."

In addition to the denominational colleges and universities, most of which had served only men,[13] various missionary training schools had been established for women. These schools had initially offered courses only in religious doctrine and scripture, but most eventually added professional curricula in health care, education or social work. Still, their primary emphasis was on training for service, not professional development: "No dedicated soul need be left out. Prospective lay workers were more likely to be turned away for lack of religious zeal than for deficient academic preparation."[14] Many were as likely to offer high school courses as college instruction.

As with the denominational colleges, however, the academic pressures of the larger society pushed the women's training schools also to conform more and more to the secular academic model.[15] This proved an expensive undertaking, since expanded libraries, lab equipment, and academically-credentialed teachers now became necessary. For economy and efficiency, therefore, the training schools for each denomination consolidated at a central location and expanded their programs to offer four-year Bachelor's degrees. Eventually, however, even the consolidated schools became unviable as separate institutions, and many were closed or merged with the denominational men's colleges. The Home Mission Society of the Methodist Episcopal Church, for example, consolidated three of its training schools in Kansas City, Missouri, renaming the combined entity National Training School and, later, National College. In 1964, this college was closed and its records and one member of its staff were moved to Scarritt College for Christian Workers, the training school of the former Methodist Episcopal Church, South.[16] Scarritt College continued as a co-educational senior college and graduate school until 1979, when its undergraduate division closed. It then became a graduate school in church music and Christian education before finally closing altogether in 1988.

The Religious Identity of Catholic Colleges and Universities

Catholic colleges, unlike their Protestant counterparts, were rarely sponsored by the Church itself. Instead, most were owned and operated by a particular male or female religious order, whose members, initially at least, comprised some 90 percent of the faculty and administration. As late as 1960, fewer than 10 percent of Catholic colleges had lay trustees—if, indeed, they had separate governing boards at all. Within the colleges' faculty, "clergy and religious held almost all top-level positions . . . outside of business and professional schools."[17]

But the orders' numerical dominance in their faculties could not be sustained. Between 1940 and 1981, the percentage of lay faculty increased from 30 percent to 75 percent at the College of St. Catherine, from 27 percent to 82 percent at Trinity College, from 35 percent to 95 percent at Villanova, and from 52 percent to 91 percent at the University of Santa Clara. Overall, by 1965, the faculties at Catholic men's colleges were 80 percent lay.[18] The religious orders attempted at least to hire *Catholic* lay faculty and administrators, but often Catholics with the necessary educational qualifications either could not be found or were unwilling to work for the lower salaries which were all the colleges could afford to offer.

Several Catholic leaders began to worry that this increasing proportion of lay faculty would lead to the same sort of secularization which Protestant colleges had experienced earlier in the century. "In a 1958 editorial, [the Jesuit magazine] *America* praised efforts to grant more responsibility to lay faculty and administrators in Catholic colleges and universities, but it also warned that 'there is a point beyond which delegation obviously cannot go—when this means loss of basic control.'"[19] An internal Jesuit subcommittee report written in the same year wondered:

> Are we building toward a lay university in which the Society provides the legal ownership, the president, a few top administrators, a few trustees and counsellors, but for the rest and for the most part the administration and the instruction is in the hands of lay men?[20]

Despite these doubts, however, the trend was irreversible. By 1968, the Jesuits comprised only 27.5 percent of the faculties at their colleges and universities. By 1998, this figure had fallen to 4 percent. Only 3 percent of the full-time teaching and research faculty at Notre Dame in the late 1990's were members of the sponsoring Holy Cross order.[21] The same trend applied to administrators. Already in 1981, 25 percent of Catholic colleges had lay presidents; by end of the century, over half of the presidents were lay and several were not even Catholic.[22]

The final and culminating change was the transfer of the colleges from the orders' control. In 1967, the presidents of the top 26 U.S. Catholic universities met at Land O' Lakes, Wisconsin, to formulate a statement on the role of Catholic universities in North America. The resulting "Land O' Lakes Statement" affirmed the universities' institutional autonomy and adherence to academic freedom. In other words, Catholic universities, like their Protestant predecessors, now pledged themselves to conform primarily to accepted, secular academic standards. Increasingly, their emphasis shifted from "the apostolate of *Catholic* higher education" to "the apostolate of *American* higher education."[23]

The Land O' Lakes Statement also recommended that the colleges and universities be incorporated separately from their sponsoring religious orders. The first to do so was St. Louis University, whose president, Robert Henle, SJ, was the statement's author.[24] Between 1967 and 1977, 98 percent of all Catholic colleges and universities followed suit. At the same time, board membership shifted: "By 1977, lay people outnumbered clergy and members of religious orders on the boards of at least 77 Catholic institutions of higher education."[25] Almost 20 percent of the boards were also chaired by lay men. By the late 1990's, the orders were finding it difficult to fill even the statutory minimum of board positions reserved for them. One study predicted that, within ten years, over 25 percent of Catholic colleges would have no members of the founding order at all, either working on campus or serving on the board of directors.[26] Several colleges have already formally discarded their Catholic identity and become private, non-sectarian institutions.[27]

As with the Protestant colleges and universities a generation earlier, these changes were facilitated by external isomorphic pressures. New state and federal policies had been drafted concerning the eligibility of religious schools for government grants. Among these were the Supreme Court's 1966 Horace Mann decision regarding federal funds for higher education, and the formation of New York's Select Committee on Aid to Private Education chaired by McGeorge Bundy of the Ford Foundation. The "Bundy Funds" provided $800 per student to non-sectarian colleges.[28] Several authors have noted that, in the 1970's, 21 percent of Catholic colleges dropped the use of the word "Catholic" from their legal documents and their publications in order to qualify for state or federal funds.[29]

Such "secularization" of religious institutions, however, is not merely a passive response to outside isomorphic processes. As recent scholars have noted,[30] it is also a conflictual process championed by interested inside actors. Many of the faculty and staff at Catholic colleges—both religious order members and lay—agitated vigorously for these changes. Many had earned their graduate degrees from secular universities and had absorbed the expectations of academic freedom and professionalism current at these institutions. They questioned whether a religious presence was appropriate if Catholic colleges and universities wanted to join the mainstream of American higher education, and they faulted the Catholic colleges for adhering to a backward and inferior standard. Journet Kahn of the University of Notre Dame, speaking at the American Catholic Philosophical Association in 1957, complained that Catholic universities were still operating under the assumption that the primary goal of higher education was the development of religious piety.[31] Previous generations, of course, had never questioned this assumption.

Faculty unrest erupted at several campuses over these issues.[32] Some of the lay faculty attacked the competence of the religious order faculty and administrators. Institutions were urged to abandon their "Catholic ghetto" mentalities and embrace accepted secular standards of professional organizations and associations. The religious habit and the Roman collar were seen by religious order faculty as divisive and as obstacles to true fellowship with their lay colleagues.

Even those administrators who were members of the sponsoring religious orders pressed for their independence. As Father Hesburgh put it: "I knew that, if I were going to see Notre Dame grow into a first-rate Catholic university, I could no longer have to get permission from [the order's superior] every time I needed a new lawn mower."[33] The complexity of higher education administration was beyond the expertise of most religious superiors, who were less and less able to provide effective oversight of the order's members who ran their colleges. By 1970, for example, the presidents of the Jesuit colleges and universities managed to escape from the oversight of the Jesuit Educational Association (which had been composed of the order's provincial superiors), and formed the Association of Jesuit Colleges and Universities (which was composed of the presidents themselves).[34]

The rest of the members and, at times, even the leadership of the orders were unprepared for these changes. Often, the members had not even been informed ahead of time. Numerous studies describe the sisters' sadness, even years later, over the "loss" of their colleges.[35] This sadness was also reflected in the focus group interviews. Two of the religious orders in the focus groups had closed their colleges; one had done so quite abruptly. In this latter order, four of the six focus groups spontaneously mentioned the pain that this closure had caused:

> - The only thing I think of is the pain that's involved every time we've closed a sponsored ministry. [Several speakers: Yes. Yes.] It's been a death and dying. And it's been real, a real hurt, a hard hurt, as well as the loss of a place to minister and the loss of effect on people in the area.
> - Especially when you are close to it. Every day you hear it.
> - That's been a real strain. I think it's helped us grow, but it's been very painful because to close the college, to close the school, to close this, that, and to sell this and to get rid of that. So that's been painful (Focus Group 1.4: Active sisters).

> - I think a very traumatic event for us was the closing of our college. Not that everybody worked in the college, but it was a traumatic experience.
> - It was an abrupt thing in a sense. We knew we were struggling, the college—but at the same time, it was something that happened overnight. So it was such a shock to everybody (Focus Group 1.5: Active sisters).

The third order's college was still operating, but it was separately incorporated, and neither the President nor most of the faculty belonged to the order:

> It's a great loss, I think. You have a sense of mourning, you know, in a way. And especially at the college, you know. As a student, having all those marvelous sisters teach us [speaker names several sisters who had taught her at the order's

college]—you know, just one great teacher after another. And you really felt that it was a Sister of X college that you were going to. But I don't think that's the case at all any more. And, and I think it's still sponsored by the Sisters of X, and you do have some good Sisters of X over there teaching—very dedicated Sisters of X teaching there. . . But, you know, you couldn't call it a Sister of X institution (Focus Group 3.4: Retired sisters).

Some of the orders' superiors had believed—naively, Daigler says—that the changes would not affect the fundamental religious identity of their colleges.[36] Others, such as the international leader of the Jesuit order, were not so sanguine. Pedro Arrupe wanted to know how a university could claim a Jesuit identity if the head of the Jesuits had no control over it.[37] And, as early as 1974, the Vatican authorities had begun to express concern that the universities' property was being transferred to lay boards without first securing the permission required by Canon Law. By the 1980's, Rome also fretted that the universities were losing their essentially Catholic character. This concern culminated in the 1990 publication of *Ex Corde Ecclesiae*, Pope John Paul II's apostolic constitution on Catholic universities, which attempted to secure the Catholicity of higher education by subjecting their theology faculties, at least, to episcopal oversight. Since 1990, the bulk of the literature has focused on how and whether, after the past forty years, the universities can retain and foster their Catholic identity.[38] This mirrors a similar literature on ways to increase the religious identity of Protestant colleges.[39] But the impact of the changes on the religious sponsors, now more and more removed from their colleges and universities, has rarely been considered.

The Religious Identity of Grade and High Schools

While most Protestant denominations and denominational groups did not sponsor many elementary and secondary schools, Catholics did. In addition to the private secondary academies owned by the orders themselves, most Catholic parishes in the early twentieth century owned and operated a grade school for the children of parishioners, and most dioceses owned and operated at least one high school. The number of students educated in these schools increased quite rapidly after 1950. In 1949, two million children attended Catholic elementary and secondary schools; ten years later, the total was 4.2 million and climbing. In 1965, the high point, 12 percent of all U.S. students were being educated in Catholic schools.[40] Despite a massive building program and a steady supply of recruits to religious orders during the 1950s, the Church could neither build nor staff schools quickly enough to meet the demand. As one author notes, "It was a crisis of success."[41]

Since the orders could not supply a sufficient number of sisters and brothers to teach the burgeoning numbers of children, pastors were forced to hire at least some lay teachers, despite their increased cost relative to the sisters' stipend and a persisting prejudice against them. Surveys from the 1940's found that lay teachers in Catholic elementary and secondary schools were treated "kindly but not professionally."[42] They were usually young, less likely to possess degrees, received lower pay and fewer benefits than their public school counterparts, and were not involved in shaping school policy. Administrators openly admitted that they intended to replace their lay teachers with sisters or brothers as soon as any became available. Over a decade later, little had changed. "The percentage of lay teachers is as heavy as we ever care to have it," wrote one priest school superintendent in 1960. "In most cases, the best lay teachers do not approach the average Religious in performance. Consequently, we feel strongly that the more lay teachers we have, the less effective will be our schools."[43] But the trend was irreversible: in 1946, 7.4 percent of the teachers in the Catholic elementary and secondary schools were lay; in 1950, 9.8 percent; and in 1958, 23.8 percent. By 1965, there were 80,463 lay teachers in Catholic schools, approximately 40 percent of the total.[44]

The second half of the 1960's saw a pronounced decline in the number of children attending Catholic elementary and secondary schools. In 1965, Catholic schools had educated 4.5 million students (47 percent of the total number of school-aged Catholics in the United States), but by 1968, that number had fallen to 3.9 million. The decline bottomed out in the 1970's, but numbers did not rebound. Throughout the 1980's, only about two million students attended Catholic schools each year.[45]

There were several possible reasons for this decline. The post-war Baby Boom had peaked, and subsequent age cohorts of children were much smaller. Costs rose as the number of religious order teachers in the schools declined. By 1993-1994, sisters, priests, and brothers made up only 12 percent of the faculty in Catholic elementary schools, and 15 percent in high schools. The parishes were often unwilling to subsidize the higher salaries of the lay teachers: in 1969, 63 percent of elementary school bills had been paid by the local parish, as compared to 49 percent in 1980 and 33 percent in 1993.[46] The difference had to be made up by increased tuition, and the more the tuition rose, the fewer students attended. Far-flung suburban parishes often did not have schools; inner-city parishes often had no Catholic children nearby. In addition to these factors, moreover, some vocal critics expressed their doubts about the usefulness and desirability of a separate religious school system. The most famous spokesperson for this viewpoint was Mary Perkins Ryan, whose 1964 book, *Are Parochial Schools the Answer?*, argued that, by sinking so many resources into its elementary and secondary schools, the Church was neglecting adult education and preventing the development of the more mature faith called for by the Second Vatican Council.[47] Other critics charged that, since over 50 percent of Catholic children were attending public schools, the "excessive" focus on the parochial school system was shortchanging the religious education of the majority of the Church's children.

Most of the sisters in the focus groups had lived through these changes. Several commented on the impact which the withdrawal of the sisters had had on the parish schools, both economically and psychologically:

- Well, as far as our elementary schools, I see them being moved on by our lay teachers and lay principals. My school board, now, is in shock because it's finally dawned on them that they probably are not going to get a sister to be principal [when I leave]. We've been talking about that possibility for years and now all of a sudden we're all having a novena said that we will get a [sister] principal. But I think the schools will survive with lay people—the value is there; they see the value, it will continue.

- That's what's happened already in some places, and someone has stepped up to that position.

- Lots of new Catholic schools [are being built], four or five, and only one of them has a sister (Focus Group 2.6: Active and retired sisters).

When the sisters left, we had been in [city] over 100 years. We actually owned the school; it was a Sisters of X school, and after so many years, we turned it over to the parish but we continued on living there and teaching in it. So, three years ago when we left the school—we had a marvelous woman that we chose as principal and she's doing a wonderful job. So when the sisters left, there was like a death. The school is doing beautifully; I'm so pleased with that principal, but to this day the teachers will stop me, the same ones who have been there for years, and say, "We miss the presence of the sisters" (Focus Group 1.3: Active sisters).

As in the case of the colleges, some of the sisters in the focus groups believed that the religious character of their elementary and high schools would not diminish, even though the sisters had left:

For me, it's exciting. It's a very positive step. Though we may look at it as a diminishment of numbers of religious, to see that so many lay people can embrace the Sister of X charism and be excited about it and carry it in their lives [is exciting] (Focus Group 2.1: Active sisters).

Others were more doubtful:

I feel that in the parochial schools, that [spirit] is lost, or has been lost to a great extent, because, for one thing, with the lay teachers far outnumbering what sisters are there, I don't think it's the same at all (Focus Group 2.4: Retired sisters).

By the mid-1990's, the enrollment crisis in Catholic schools was over, and many were even posting a slight increase. Some 2.5 million children attended in 1995, a number which has remained relatively constant ever since.[48] More and more critics, however, were beginning to point out that, despite the admirable job the schools were doing in academics, they seemed to be failing their role of religious education. Liberals and conservatives alike bemoaned the "religious illiteracy" of a generation of students—both their ignorance of basic Catholic doctrine and their unfamiliarity with the papal and episcopal teachings on social justice and peace.[49] And, as with the Catholic colleges, the primary purpose of Catholic grade and high schools was gradually shifting from the religious development of the students to providing high quality academic education.[50]

The question of what it actually means to be a Catholic school has become a more pressing one, both with regard to the content of the subjects taught and the religious affiliation of the faculty who teach them. Can a school be Catholic if the bulk of its finances no longer come from the local parish? If many of its teaching staff are non-Catholic lay persons? If its social studies, English, math, and science courses are taught from the same text books and with the same teaching methods as in the public schools? If religion classes are relegated to forty-five minutes a day? Exactly what makes a school Catholic, anyway? Today, fewer and fewer of the teachers at these schools are Catholic, despite the reservations, and sometimes the active intervention, of supervising bishops and pastors.[51]

While most Protestant denominations owned or operated very few elementary or secondary schools in the United States, some of the home missionary societies did sponsor a few in underserved areas.[52] Many of these were originally administered by deaconesses or home missionaries, although these women never comprised a majority of the staff as the sisters had. In the 1960s, these schools, too, were closed as public schools became available:

> And then, for some reason, they began closing all the schools that had been under the [denomination's women's organization]. Now, sometimes they had their reasons, like out in [school], they were going to close that and the girls themselves fought, Dr. Brown fought, they all fought to keep it, and the girls said, "They'll probably close this and change it into a place for drug addicts and we'll all be back [as inmates] in a couple of years." And that's what they did with it. And now it's gone (Focus Group 4.2: Retired deaconesses).

Few mainline denominations operate primary or secondary schools today.[53]

Conclusions

As an overall pattern, therefore, there were two ways in which the grade schools, high schools, and colleges that were once owned and operated by religious groups have been "lost" to them. Some were closed. Others continued, but with their religious character greatly attenuated. As one critic recently lamented when observing the small Lutheran college of his own student days:

> There was no articulated center that sharply delineated the mission of the college. The theological acuity to do that was simply absent, or was felt not to be needed. Lutheran theology and ethics were not taught. Lutheran history was nowhere to be found. The Lutheran idea of calling was not explicitly taught . . . There was no concerted effort to interrelate the Christian vision with other fields of learning.[54]

Another critic, the president of the General Conference of the Seventh-day Adventists, called on his denomination's colleges to halt their pernicious slide down the slippery slope of secularization, stating, "More Adventist schools, universities, and seminaries are established. These go to the world for accreditation and tend to become secularized."[55] In ringing tones, the president urged his listeners to resist the pressures of contemporary culture:

> Brothers and sisters, this must never happen to [Seventh-day Adventists]! This will not happen to the Seventh-day Adventist Church! It is not just another church—it is God's church!

As established Catholic and Protestant schools moved toward the secular end of the continuum, more religiously-focused colleges, academies and grade schools—Ave Maria College and Law School, Christendom College, Steubenville University, and Spiritus Sanctus Academy for Catholics; Liberty and Bob Jones Universities and a plethora of congregational academies for evangelical Protestants —have arisen to serve the market niche which the former institutions have abandoned.[56]

Health Care

The Religious Identity of Hospitals

Prior to 1900, hospitals were primarily charitable shelters, with their religious purposes clearly evident. After the development of modern medicine, however, they rapidly developed into institutions organized on scientific and business principles. Scientific and business foci predominated in the state and for-profit institutions, but even America's many voluntary hospitals became "economic hybrids, proclaiming a charitable mission while operating like a business."[57] Once dependent on gifts and donations, the hospitals developed into market institutions delivering services to those who could pay for them. "The old rhetoric of paternalism was superseded by the new vocabulary of scientific management and efficiency."[58]

This new method of operation contrasted sharply with how the Catholic religious orders had been accustomed to operate their hospitals. In the mid-nineteenth century, the four sisters at St. Elizabeth Hospital in Appleton, Wisconsin, had

> managed the garden, the cow, the laundry and the cooking, as well as the care of the sick and collecting tours to raise money. . . . Hospital work meant providing a room, clean linens, and nutritious meals. Sisters grew the food, harvested it, preserved and/or prepared it. They sewed linens for beds and [washed them] weekly.[59]

Fifty years later, the sisters' hospitals were still run informally, in much the same way as their colleges were operated:

> As was the norm for Catholic hospitals, the Sisters of St. Mary conducted their hospital business as an in-house affair, and the sisters were signatories of their original articles on incorporation. The sisters comprised the total membership of their hospital boards, and the role of medicine was that of a welcome visitor.[60]

As one historian put it, "the inherently sacred character of caring for the sick and dying . . . had been incarnated in Catholic benevolence . . . with its personalist mission in a homelike setting."[61] It was precisely this informal, spiritually-focused vision of health care that the newer scientific mode of medical practice threatened to replace.

The dialectic between the spiritual and the scientific aspects of medicine continued in both Catholic and Protestant hospitals throughout the first decades of the twentieth century. Many Protestant denominations had originally begun medical work as an adjunct to their evangelization efforts: it was the missionaries' practice of Western medicine that attracted converts to Christianity. By the early 1900s, however, many critics considered medicine too demanding a profession to be interrupted by evangelization. A group of Northern Baptist businessmen responded to these critics by forming a commission composed of representatives from seven Protestant denominations, with a mandate to study the foreign missions. With money supplied by Baptist John D. Rockefeller Jr., the commission investigated missionary organizations in China, Burma, India, and Japan during the 1930's, and eventually published *Rethinking Missions: A Laymen's Inquiry after 100 Years*. This study urged the practice of medicine on more professional lines to free doctors and nurses from the pressure to evangelize.[62]

Catholic hospitals, too, increasingly wrestled with the tension between their spiritual and their scientific goals. This especially affected the sisters who ran them:

> Catholic sisters did not reject modern medicine. They spent hundreds of thousands of dollars to buy new equipment and renovate their buildings and bring their institutions into line with scientific standards. Furthermore, from the beginning of their involvement with hospitals, they deferred to physicians on medical matters. Complications arose, however, if doctors emphasized only medical and scientific function and dismissed the sisters' religious ideals.[63]

To deal with these issues, the Catholic Hospital Association was established in 1915, expressing its concern, on the one hand, that "existing Catholic hospitals were not keeping pace with the rapid advances in medical science and technology required to maintain their accreditation and provide adequate services," while at the same time worrying about the danger "that recent advances in medicine threatened to separate caregivers from their patients."[64] It was not until after World War I, and urged on by the CHA, that more professional standards of administration, patient records, and medical staff qualifications became the usual practice in

Catholic hospitals. This transformation profoundly changed the ways in which the sisters who worked in the hospitals understood their call to care for the sick with the compassion of Christ.

As medical advances made it increasingly likely that a hospital stay would actually cure a patient, more and more sufferers sought admittance to an institution that had once been the repository of the dying poor. Patient loads swelled beyond the ability of the sisters and the deaconesses to tend by themselves. Hospitals were forced to hire more lay nurses, and to hire them based on their educational credentials and technical expertise rather than on their willingness to follow the hospital's religious philosophy.[65] The nuns first began to employ lay nurses on an extensive basis in the 1920s; by the late 1940's, the number of secular nurses in Catholic hospitals was greater than the number of sister-nurses. Hospitals which depended on the labor of deaconesses fared even worse. In the early twentieth century, American deaconesses had "overwhelmingly abandoned nursing." As early as 1924, only 124 of the 810 active Lutheran deaconesses in the United States served in hospitals, in contrast to the situation in Germany, where all deaconesses were nurses.[66]

> The question of Lutheran identity for hospitals . . . became a critical one in the twentieth century. With the decline of the diaconate, rising costs for health care, and in many cases tenuous relationships to the churches . . . the validity as well as the viability of church-owned hospitals became more uncertain.[67]

A similar debate existed in many other denominations, both in the United States and in Europe.

The beginnings of government aid, with the inauguration of the Hill-Burton grants in the 1950's, led to the further expansion of the hospitals and the hiring of even more lay personnel.[68] Catholic hospitals hired their first lay department administrators in the late 1940's, and also formed personnel departments to codify labor policies. As the ratio of sisters to lay staff declined, the orders had to re-examine their most basic assumptions about the spiritual value of nursing as a religious calling suitable for virtuosi: "were the sisters primarily labor or management? And, if the latter, how did their management functions relate to their traditional ministry of providing personal and spiritual care to the sick and dying?"[69]

At approximately the same time, the rise of third-party payers such as Blue Cross necessitated the adoption of more detailed accounting procedures. In its 1953 annual convention, the CHA

> addressed issues surrounding the rapid transformation of Catholic hospitals into businesses. Sound financial procedures were still lacking. Since these institutions now became increasingly involved with federal agencies and third party insurers, their success depended on adequate budgetary planning and the employment of uniform accounting principles.[70]

Throughout the 1950s and 1960s, these isomorphizing government, economic, and professional pressures caused Catholic hospitals to become more and more like their secular counterparts, a process that foreshadowed the secularization of Catholic higher education a decade later.[71]

As with the colleges and universities, the hospitals also became separated from their founding order or denomination. Following the recommendations of the Catholic Hospital Association, the position of hospital administrator was separated from that of the sister-superior of the local convent. Government and insurance payments, as well as separately-organized fundraising campaigns, also made the hospitals increasingly independent of the religious order for financial support.[72]

The hospitals' top administration became increasingly lay. In 1965, only 3 percent of the top positions in Catholic hospitals had been filled by lay administrators; five years later, 23 percent were. In 1985, some 70 percent of Catholic hospital CEOs were not members of the order that had founded the hospital, and, by the late 1990's, over 90 percent of the CEOs and board members of Catholic hospitals were lay.[73] Mergers, too, led to a re-configuration of the hospitals' identity: from Franciscan, Dominican, or Alexian to generic Catholic.[74]

As had been the case with their schools, some of the sisters optimistically believed that the religious spirit of their hospitals could survive, and even flourish, after its transfer to lay administration. As one sister in a focus group put it:

> Our change at X Hospital with the lay CEO certainly went very sweet. When it first happened, they called the lay CEO "Brother Thomas," but I don't think there was much fear in [city] from the different people that I have spoken to, it wasn't "Oh, what's going to happen to the place?" now that we had a lay CEO. I didn't hear a lot of fear (Focus Group 2.1: Active sisters).

Or, a little later, in the same group:

> It goes back to the baptism call of all people. We have recognized the role of collaborating and ministering with our lay counterparts in a much more positive way than we ever saw it before. And, for me, that's exciting. It's a very positive step (Focus Group 2.1: Active sisters).

Other sisters, however, believed that the decline in the number of sisters had changed the character of their order's hospitals—and *not* for the better:

> It seems to me we're constantly struggling now, against culture, against the mores of the world and in health care, to maintain our humanity and mercy and compassion in the face of economic constraints. That is really very difficult. It's like knowing always what the ideal is, but you have the reality to work with, and how do you do it? It's very difficult to keep feeling positive about it when it seems the whole world is fighting against what we stand for (Focus Group 2.1: Active sisters).

I live right across the street from the hospital and I go over there for meals once in a while and the people miss the sisters.
(Interviewer: What about the sisters do they say they miss?)
Oh, [they say that] the sisters did a much better job of running the hospital than the lay people do. They gave us much more credit of knowing the right things to do and how to do it. . . . They miss the family feeling that we had. The sisters did give that feeling of being family and of course now they don't care who they hurt and if this job has to go, this job has to go. They don't care whose job it is or anything, and it used to be that we really—it was hard. I left X Hospital probably about three years after I should have because I did not like the way it was going either. The nurses didn't care. All they cared about was getting a salary. They didn't care about the care of the patient. . . . Someone asked me about that. They said, "How can you continue to stay here when it's like it is?" And I said, "Well, because I know that I have a department that cares and the patients know that we care and I'm not going to leave; they're going to have to fire me." And that's what happened. They fired me. No, they didn't—they just got rid of my department. Our department was one of the first departments to go (Focus Group 3.10: Active sisters).

This speaker may be overemphasizing the difference between the sisters' and the lay nurses' motivation, however. One historian contends that the sister-nurses had been paid full salaries and fringe benefits since at least the mid-twentieth century, and often "projected an image of employment rather than calling."[75]

In 1965, Catholic orders operated 950 hospitals in the United States, containing 156,000 beds and serving 16 million patients per year.[76] The orders also operated 376 facilities for the care of the aged. From this high point, the number of Catholic hospitals began a steady decline, "with nearly 200 abandoned by their congregations in the 1980s because of decreasing numbers of sisters available to manage them." The most publicized of these was the sale of the Jesuits' St. Louis University Hospital to Tenet Healthcare Corporation in 1997. In 2002, there were 625 Catholic hospitals, approximately 10 percent of all the hospitals in the United States.[77] The number of Protestant hospitals, too, declined, as separate facilities were closed or merged. A search of the 2004 American Hospital Directory found 72 hospitals with "Baptist" in their names, 41 with "Methodist," and 19 with "Lutheran."

Some of this decline, of course, was due to the consolidation of individual hospitals into larger systems. In 1979, for example, there were 29 health care systems sponsored by Catholic religious orders. This increased to 54 in 1985 and to 60 in 1988.[78] Since then, the total number of systems has stayed constant (there were 61 in 2002), but they have continued to consolidate with the remaining single hospitals and with each other into ever-larger entities. The 1995 formation of Catholic Health Initiatives, for example, combined the Sister of Charity Health Care Systems, Catholic Health of Omaha, and Franciscan Health Systems of Aston, Pennsylvania, into one entity with a combined annual revenue of $4 billion. Of the twenty Catholic mega-systems, the largest in 2003 was Ascension Health System, which had $6.5 billion in 2001 revenues.[79]

On the one hand, this amalgamation is a survival necessity, reducing administrative overhead and consolidating purchasing and contracting power:

> If you had a hospital here and there was a network-based hospital over there—even though yours is bigger, the network [hospital] can connect up with one over here and one or two over here and the county will say, "I don't want to negotiate with all these little tiny groups. I'd rather go with this one, even though the hospital's older. I'll hook up with them because then I'll only have to negotiate with one person." So that's the advantage that Columbia has. [Interviewer: So what should religious orders do?] What we need to do is hook up together. . . If we hook up a whole slew of hospitals, then you can come in and negotiate for all the institutions in that area with one voice (Individual Sister Interview: Former health care system CEO).

A second reason is to insure the formal authority of the sponsoring religious group over the hospital, at a time when there are not enough qualified group members to fill positions at the local administrative or board levels: "integration into a system can ensure that a sponsored institution will carry on its mission even if the religious community or diocese which founded the institution is no longer able to act as sponsor" of each separate hospital.[80]

On the other hand, however, amalgamation into systems may further dilute the institutions' distinctiveness and the sisters' presence in them:

> Our health care system is unusually high in the number [of sisters]. We have fifteen, plus two or three more in long term care. [Interviewer: Are any of the hospital CEOs sisters?] No. We just lost our last sister CEO (Individual Sister Interview: Health care system CEO).

In addition, several studies have found that hospitals structured into systems tend to become more similar to each other, and to develop corporate-type boards with primarily businesslike orientations.[81] Even the pastoral care staffs have professionalized, with the result that hospitals are often unable and unwilling to limit these positions to the members of the sponsoring order or denomination.[82]

Organizational field pressures have also encouraged the convergence of the hospitals' practices with those of their secular counterparts. As numerous authors have noted, the initiation of the prospective payment system for Medicare reimbursement has led to greater uniformity and common institutional practices among all types of hospitals—religious hospitals included.[83] Medicare regulations have also required hospitals to limit their services to sicker patients, and have subjected them to additional government regulations, more paperwork, and non-sectarian standards for admission and treatment. With mandated shorter stays, it may seem less necessary for a hospital to continue a mission that addresses the spiritual needs of patients.[84] The religious hospitals' day-to-day operations have thus become more similar to those of secular non-profit and for-profit hospitals.

Adventist hospitals today serve meat to patients, perform operations and open the accounting office on Saturday, and do abortions. A *Wall Street Journal* report on Baptist Hospital in Nashville notes that it has severed its connection to the Tennessee Baptist Convention, and that it has agreed to build and operate a $15 million, 18-acre office and training field complex and rent it to the city's professional football team: "Nonprofit hospitals, once bastions of care for the poor and strictly bound by their tax-free designation, are increasingly turning to money-making ventures."[85]

As a result of such isomorphic pressures, it has become less and less evident to the staff, the patients, and the denominational sponsors what religious identity, if any, remains to these hospitals.[86] Sister Mary Roch Rocklage, the chair of both the secular American Hospital Association Board and the Governing Board of her own order's Mercy Health System, recently noted that

> When we [Catholic institutions] took on the mind set of corporate America, we began to talk that way, we looked that way, we acted that way, and we alienated our own selves and our employees. We were acting like "We are market-driven," versus "We are in that market but it doesn't apply to us."[87]

Or, as a Seventh-day Adventist critic pointed out, building such institutions, however necessary for evangelizing progress, has also vitiated the denomination's explicit *raison d'etre*:

> For a movement which still formally commits itself to the imminent end of things ... extensive this-worldly involvement, particularly in institutions and activities which are directed to the preservation and improvement of mortal existence, would seem to pose something of a paradox.[88]

Working in such large organizations, therefore, or serving on their increasingly business-oriented boards, is often alienating to the members of the sponsoring religious group.[89] There is an intense ambivalence among the religious orders about their continued sponsorship of these hospital systems—especially as external events remove them further and further from the sisters' control. One writer compared the orders' institutional ties to the central figure in the movie "What's Eating Gilbert Grape,"

> an exceedingly obese mother of four, [who] says to her son in a moment of reconciliation, "I never wanted to be like this." She had eaten her way to virtual immobility. . . . Do we women religious, as this twentieth century of ours draws to a close, gaze at our corporate body and say to ourselves, "We never wanted to be like this"?[90]

Or, as one interviewee stated:

> I'm sure our hospitals are eventually going to do something, but I don't know

what. . . . And it's getting so big—[Interviewer: What do people think about that—that it's getting so big?] I, I'd like to see us get out of it. [Interviewer: For any reason?] I think it's such big business. We have maybe one sister, a board president only. Maybe two sisters in a hospital. I don't see how we can say it's *our* hospital (Individual Sister Interview: Retired hospital administrator).

Several focus groups agreed:

I was in [city] a few years back. They had, I think, about 600 or 800 beds at X hospital in [city], and I was there one day and someone came in and said, "How many sisters do you have here?" We said six sisters—now you know, six sisters with an 800-bed hospital, it's difficult for them to get around. And right away, he said, "You people don't own that hospital," he said, "with only six sisters there (Focus group 2.1: Active sisters).

I was in [city] and I think we were the first [hospital] to have an administrator that was not a sister. And nobody ever told you that, that, you know, all of a sudden you had that feeling that it was not your hospital any more. Like, I had a key to any door that I wanted to get into, and I would not have used it once we had an administrator that wasn't a sister. It was a, it was just a feeling you had that it was not yours any more (Focus Group 3.3: Retired sisters).

Of the 24 sisters' focus groups, eight expressed some doubt that the religious element could be sustained in their hospitals.

The Religious Identity of Nursing

In the late nineteenth century, nursing was considered a holy calling, partly because of the example of the nursing sisters and partly because Florence Nightingale had deliberately modeled her reform of nursing on the example of the Catholic nuns and the deaconesses at Kaiserswerth. Ideally, it was thought that the nurses in religious hospitals should all be Catholic sisters or Protestant deaconesses. Many of the sisters and deaconesses agreed, and doubted that hired lay nurses could possibly have sufficient religious motivation for the work:

Sister Ludgera stated vehemently that the community should not employ secular nurses whose service was, in her view, inferior to that given by the sisters. Sister Berenice felt that secular nurses might not have had the same religious motivation, but, she believed, it was possible to instill these values through the sisters' training.[91]

In their nursing schools, therefore, the sisters trained both their own novices and their lay students in an atmosphere that strongly resembled that of a monastic house. The training schools for deaconess nurses also attempted to maintain a pervasively religious focus: only women whose motive for nurse training came from a vocational call were accepted.[92]

As the twentieth century progressed, however, nursing became increasingly professionalized. More and more women applied to the training schools, but fewer and fewer saw nursing as a religious vocation. This change bothered both Catholics and Protestants. The executive director of the Catholic Hospital Association, Father John Flanagan, "observed that selfless hospital service—identified with a religious vocation—was being portrayed as being at odds with the new professionalism in medicine and nursing, in fact, as 'something demeaning.'"[93] Deaconesses, too, increasingly expressed concern about the neglect of spiritual training in nursing programs. "The sacrificial element of the nursing vocation, so much a part of the deaconess nurse's identity, struggled to survive in the for-profit world of the medical marketplace."

By the 1960's, the number of live-in schools of nursing began to decline, to be replaced by academic programs at local colleges and universities.[94] This resulted in a further distancing of nursing from its religious roots:

> The status of Catholic training programs for nurses [was] threatened by the new emphasis on university education. . . . While everyone agreed that the old-fashioned nurse had almost disappeared, expectation for personal service and the highest standards of medical and nursing care remained. But how, in the face of continuing shortages of nursing personnel in hospitals, could a more old-fashioned attitude be returned to nursing? Unfortunately, the American hospital environment was rapidly changing. The hospital was no longer part of a monastery, but reflected the cultural and social practices of society.[95]

Another difficulty arises from the ethical dilemmas that frequently accompany modern nursing. Some of these dilemmas spring from the day-to-day operations of a system that is forced to cut costs and staffing.[96] Other issues involve specific denominational proscriptions. Catholic hospitals, for example, are not supposed to be performing abortions, in vitro fertilizations, or even tubal ligations, but many have devised creative ways of circumventing this:

> [Interviewer: What happens if a Catholic hospital merges with a nonreligious nonprofit hospital?] One thing they can do is have a separate piece of property, not owned by this joint network, and they can do these surgeries [abortions and tubal ligations] over there. And it has its own name and is run by a separate foundation. Now, for emergencies, you have a hallway here in case somebody has to go over [to the hospital] (Individual Sister Interview: Former health care system CEO).

To some in the new systems, these tactics may raise ethical issues: "How close can you get to something you regard as wrong before the wrong is your wrong too?"[97]

> The key issue is material co-operation. It gets to the point where you have, uh, questions like, "I'm a nurse. I work part-time here and I work part-time over

there. The only thing I do over there is I set up the equipment." Now, have I
really participated in that because my job is setting up the equipment? (Individual
Sister Interview: Former health care system CEO).

Most denominations have not done sufficient theological reflection on these
problems of institutional ethics. As one Mennonite scholar put it:

> We have considered personal ethics, congregational ethics, and witness to
> government and other secular structures. But, although institutions are central to
> our Church's life, careful thought about how our faith bears on the workings of
> our church-related institutions seems scarcely to have begun.[98]

Those denominations which *have* attempted to address these issues, however, often
find their efforts to "rein in" questionable practices stymied by the economic,
governmental, or professional constraints on hospital practice.[99]

Conclusions

As has been the case with the religious colleges and universities, a plethora of
studies, articles, and books have recently appeared, all questioning whether and to
what extent hospitals can be expected to retain their religious identity.[100] The
prospect is not a positive one. One author outlined no fewer than eight factors that
he considered "profound threats" to religious-based health care, beginning with
"managed care" and "health care as a business," and ending with "mergermania"
and "the obsolescence of the hospital." Denominational officials have fretted about
the issue as well.[101] If religious health care institutions do not remain connected to
their former denominational sponsors, however, the denominations will lose a
powerful resource which has given them a voice in national health care policy in
the past. One study of Catholic bishops in the Netherlands, for example, notes their
powerlessness to prevent that country's liberalization of abortion and euthanasia
laws.[102]

The Religious Identity of Social Service Institutions

Prior to about 1880, the goal of Protestant social service activities was an
essentially post-millennial one: to hasten the promised Second Coming of Christ by
preparing a people fit for Him—sober, diligent, thrifty, and Protestant. The social
services rendered by Catholic sisters endeavored to counteract Protestant
blandishments, and to relieve the stark poverty of Catholic immigrant women and
children. The activities of both were small-scale, personalized, and run by women
—the sisters, deaconesses, and Protestant "friendly visitors"—none of whom either
had, or needed, extensive formal training.

By the late nineteenth century, this began to change. "Starting with the organization of the Associated Charities in 1879, Protestant agencies adopted the goals of system and rationality that the national charity organization movement had touted."[103]

> Of particular concern to the training schools, the informality associated with early city mission and settlement work began to yield to the professionalism of social work. Experience and dedication were not longer valued as highly as the proper credentials.[104]

By 1932, the Rockefeller Commission's *Rethinking Missions* study criticized the professional quality of the social services rendered by Protestant home and foreign missionaries. "It drew a picture of most missionaries as well-intentioned but second-rate professionals, who were beaten down by the bureaucratic demands of denominational missionary boards, who were burdened by the requirement to deliver converts as well as social services, and who were badly trained in the helping professions."[105] The report also questioned attempts to evangelize non-Protestants. In the U.S., Protestant efforts to use social work to convert poor Catholic immigrants also came to be seen as counterproductive.

For greater efficiency, the various denominational agencies in each city were united and placed under lay trustees, usually male. Social work became a female semiprofession, subordinate to the professional leadership of lay males, and was removed from church jurisdiction.[106] "Protestants . . . increasingly viewed the relief of the poor as a state obligation in justice, and, while they continued to support them generously, their denominational charitable agencies gradually became independent of church control."[107] The role of congregations and denominations in social service agencies became less evident. By 1955, a study by the National Council of Churches of Christ revealed that many social service agencies had secularized.[108] As with the schools and hospitals, the secularization process was accelerated by government funding. By the early 1960's, a survey of 407 denominational agencies in twenty states found that 70 percent were involved in some form of government contracting.[109]

Jurisdiction over Catholic social services was also consolidated, although the actual running of many institutions remained in the hands of the sisters. Between 1910 and 1921, most major U.S. dioceses opened Catholic Charities Bureaus. Fund raising was centralized under these bureaus, and credentialed lay social workers were hired to oversee the sisters' institutions. Also in 1910, the National Conference of Catholic Charities was organized. Both the national-level and the diocesan organizations were run by priest directors. Religious orders of women were not even allowed to belong until 1920, when a separate section was created for them.[110] This centralized oversight not only reduced the sisters' control of their social service institutions, but also drove a wedge between them and the laity, who were suspicious that all of this professionalization would erode the religious character of the social services. The credentialed social workers required salaries, and were thus more expensive than the nuns. This increased overhead and resulted in a smaller proportion of the donations actually going to the poor whom the sisters' institutions were supposed to serve.

Tensions arose between the sisters and the social workers. By the twentieth century, the small, informal arrangements by which the nuns had cared for orphans in earlier days had now grown into huge congregate institutions housing hundreds of children cared for by too-few religious staff.[111] In city after city, survey teams of social workers faulted the sisters's institutions for poorly kept records, problems with cleanliness and hygiene, and inferior educational and recreational facilities. A 1920's study of more than eighty Catholic orphanages recommended that the religious sister-superior of the orphanage "insure that the religious and lay members of the staff were well-trained and not overburdened. . . . The superior should have a college education and professional social work training; each member of the staff should have a good general knowledge of child welfare work."[112] Such professionalization was difficult to achieve, however. The sisters felt that the social workers did not appreciate the constraints under which they operated and looked down on their efforts to improve.

As late as the 1940s, sisters who worked in orphanages were the least trained of all sisters, and still put in excessively long hours. One sister recalled a typical day with the teen-aged girls she cared for in a California orphanage during that time:

Well, I probably lived in those days with at least twelve other sisters. And I remember, we got up at 4:00 AM in those days. We prayed in common, we had Mass and spiritual reading—all before I got the kids up for school. They all went to different schools, so I had to get them up and out. And then it would be kind of peaceful for a couple of hours. And then in the afternoon, we [the sisters] would have prayers together and then the kids would come home and we'd be with them until—well, I'd take time out—we sisters had recreation in common. I would come over to recreation and I would think, "Well, these kids are old enough to take care of themselves for an hour." But I'd worry about it, wondering if they were OK. And then I'd go back, and I slept in the dorm with the kids. And if they were out on a date on weekends, I waited up for them, because I wanted to be sure they got in. And I still got up at 4:00 the next day. [Interviewer: While the kids were in school, were you with the other sisters then?] Part of the time. I was in my own department, cleaning, doing the kids' sweaters, which I wouldn't trust them to wash, ironing [laughs] all the little things that needed to be done (Individual Sister Interview: Retired social services worker).

Tensions between the spiritual and professional aspects of social service also existed in the Protestant institutions. As Oscie Sanders, the president of the Deaconess and Home Missionary Conference in 1925, noted: "I am afraid we are losing sight of our real purpose—the bringing of Jesus into the lives of the people with whom we work. I am afraid that clubs and classes, the keeping of records and running of the institutions are taking the place of soul winning. I am afraid that the workers and the secretaries do not understand each other."[113]

By the early twentieth century for the Protestants, and the mid-twentieth century for the Catholics, the same attenuation of religious focus that was affecting the schools and hospitals had also begun to catch up with the social service institutions. And the same environmental pressures could be listed as causes. Agencies were restructured as public benefit non-profits rather than religious ones in order both to be eligible for government aid and to reduce the liability of the diocese or sponsoring group. By the late 1990's, about two-thirds of the budget of Catholic Charities came from government, not church, sources. Most of the staff (between 40 percent and 80 percent, depending on the local agency) were not Catholic; nor were 70 percent of Catholic Charities' clientele.[114] Lay staffs became more professionally credentialed, in part to meet government regulations, which also mandated that religious agencies could not discriminate on the basis of their religion when hiring them.

Government funding had a wide range of other impacts. The need to be certified as a mental health clinic in order to receive government and insurance funds favored large agencies or coalitions of agencies. Clinic status required social service agencies to use standard medical classification systems and to adjust their practices in conformity with medical diagnostic procedures and treatment approaches. This resulted in the medicalization of social work along the lines of a psychiatric, not a religious, model.[115] State and municipal governments also preferred to contract through one umbrella organization for social services; this forced various denominational agencies to organize into coalitions. One denominational organization (such as Catholic Charities or Lutheran Social Services) might serve as the main contracting agency and farm out pieces of the contract to agencies in other denominations, or even to secular non-profits.[116] All this increased isomorphic pressures and eroded denominational distinctiveness among the agencies.[117]

Still another impact of government legislation occurred during the Johnson administration's War on Poverty. The 1964 Economic Opportunity Act mandated that the poor receiving the agencies' services be afforded "maximum feasible participation" in determining how the agencies would operate. War on Poverty programs "initially ignored professionals, indeed were generally hostile to them, under the theory that the poor would develop 'indigenous leadership' and would be the experts in determining what they needed."[118] Church social service programs often responded to this new ideal by shifting service delivery locations away from the church buildings they had previously occupied, in order to be closer to those they served. This further distanced the program from its religious supervisor, geographically as well as psychologically.[119]

The push for local direction especially impacted the deaconesses, who in 1965 still ran many denominational social service agencies. National denominational boards adopted new policies affecting the staffing and administration of these institutions:

> Minorities struggling for equality wanted explanations as to why "white persons" were directors of institutions serving people of color. Personnel issues underwent microscopic scrutiny. Trying to rectify the "shortage" of minority women in the deaconess relationship, the Church failed to be "sensitive to and concerned for its workers of long standing." In the months prior to the 1970 Convocations . . . "white persons" (deaconesses and home missionaries) had lost their jobs as directors of community centers and other agencies, as agencies became locally incorporated and sought indigenous leadership.[120]

Several of the deaconesses in the focus groups and individual interviews cited this policy as a key change in the religious character of the agencies in which they had served:

> The point at which the social changes in this country caught us was the whole notion of indigenous neighborhood leadership. Because, with almost no exception, the deaconesses and missionary corps were white. And almost all of, particularly, the community centers, were in racial/ethnic neighborhoods . . . In the 1960's, remember, that's when the War on Poverty came along and you were building community leadership, indigenous leadership. So the community centers suddenly wanted neighborhood folks to run the center. . . . The white, trained, professional deaconesses were suddenly *persona non grata* . . . . Some of them could find work in the Church in various places, but many of them just went out into secular social work positions or other kinds of things. Not that that was *bad* —but it meant that the kind of corps of workers available to the Church to meet new kinds of crises, new kinds of ministries, were simply not there any longer (Individual Interview: Retired deaconess).

> - Mrs. Jones was working at the national level and she pushed through a reorganization for all the community centers so that, instead of just having [denomination members] on the Board, they had one-third [denomination members] and one-third the neighborhood you were serving and one-third the larger community. So we followed that, let me tell you we did. And we had our first Black director, Black president of the Board, in one of the agencies about ten years ago, and you know, that was a neighborhood person who was president of the Board, which was a very different situation. So that, it wasn't a comparable situation where it was just the [denomination members] talking to themselves.
> - You stopped doing *for* people and began doing *with* people.
> - And training leadership.
> - That was a big thing. To enable people to do for themselves (Focus Group 4.2: Retired deaconesses).

A similar administrative transfer happened in the overseas mission institutions.

As with the hospitals, the bureaucratization and professionalization of denominational social services eroded their religious distinctiveness. Government funding has shifted from grants and contracts to vouchers and other forms of assistance that require non-profits to compete with each other—and with an increasing number of for-profit agencies—for "customers."[121] Greater pressures for accountability—the "effectiveness challenge"—require social service providers to prove they are having an effect. All of this leads to the adoption of an "enterprise culture" by social service agencies, one which emphasizes "identifying a 'market niche,' formulating 'business plans,' and generally incorporating the language and the style of business management into the operation of their agencies."[122] Recent studies have found that church-sponsored social programs do not show significant differences from secular ones, despite their claims to be more "holistic" in service delivery. Nor do they appear to have higher rates of success in meeting the needs of their clients.[123]

In addition to the effects of government regulations, professional standards have also become more avowedly secular:

> The larger ideals of social justice and public welfare will become subordinate in the new social work to ideals that have to do with the effective delivery of specific services in an accountable way: more evaluative research, more budgetary accountability, more specialization, and less ideology.[124]

Or, as another critic put it, a "tacit separation" has developed that has forced religion to the margins of professional social work, and precluded any attempts to acknowledge religion as "a legitimate partner in the quest to improve the life conditions of those in need."[125] As a result, denominational-affiliated social services, while continuing to give lip service to religious ideals, have "rather uncritically" adopted a business model of organizational management.

This loss of distinctiveness leads staff to wonder why the agencies should exist as *religious* agencies at all. In a 1974 poll of Minnesota Catholic and Lutheran social service directors, nearly 75 percent of those responding could not identify any values distinguishing religious from secular social agencies. The religious sponsors, too, questioned whether

> diocesan charitable bureaus, in their eagerness to qualify for designated government funds, were providing social services more congenial to civic and political agendas than to the benevolent preferences of Church members. . . . Charity directors pointedly asked the National Conference of Catholic Charities . . . "How do you Christianize your services when your funding source (particularly the government) is constantly trying to secularize your institutions?"[126]

Conclusions

In a recent article for an edited volume on Church organizations, Thomas Jeavons listed seven basic characteristics to examine in evaluation an organization's "religiousness:"

> First, how religious is the organization's *self identity*? Second, how religious are

its *participants*? Third, how religious are its *material resources* and their sources? Fourth, how religious are its *goals, products, or services*? Fifth, how religious are its *decision-making processes*? Sixth, how religious is its definition and distribution of *power*? Seventh, how religious are the other organizations or *organizational fields* with which it interacts?[127]

The present chapter has briefly outlined how church-sponsored educational, health care, and social service institutions have drifted in identity, participation, and resources from their original ranking on Jeavons' characteristics. With this drift have come increased demands on the (now usually lay) administrators of these institutions, who must balance the "religious distinctiveness" imperative with the "survival imperative."[128] As one critic noted:

> Because of mission vagueness, the actual goals pursued by a nonprofit may reflect managerial preferences, and, through a managerial sorting process, those preferences can be expected to reflect the (revenue and other) constraints faced by prospective managers.[129]

Government regulations, professional standards, and economic constraints have forced the hiring, the day-to-day operating procedures, and the clientele of religious institutions increasingly to resemble those of their public and for-profit counterparts. Their funding increasingly comes, not from their religious sponsor, but from government monies and fees for their services. Alliances and networking arrangements between geographically proximate hospitals, colleges, and social agencies have further eroded the distinctiveness that had once set these organizations apart.

Jeavons' fifth, sixth, and seventh dimensions remain to be addressed. To what extent do the denominational sponsors still remain as active and powerful participants within the institution's relevant organizational field at all? Chapter 6 will describe some of the ways in which both parties attempted to modify, and yet retain, their connections with each other.

Notes

1. Jeavons (1994:124). This is similar to the trend in non-profits in general: see O'Neill (1989), Weisbrod (1998a:298), and Salamon (2003). Albert and Whetten (1985:278) note this for denominational colleges. See also Hollingsworth and Hollingsworth (1986), O'Neill (1989), Ruggie (1992), and Fennell and Alexander (1993) for hospitals, and Oates (1995), Cnaan et al. (1999), Coleman (2000), Chaves (2004) and Salamon (2003) for Social Service agencies.

2. For more detailed analyses, see Hughes and Adrian (1997), Marsden (1994), Burtchaell (1998), Johnson (1992) and Sloan (1994) for educational institutions; Kauffman (1995) and Starr (1982) for health care, and Oates (1995) and Cnaan et al. (1999) for social services.

3. See, for example, Cunniggim (1994), Marsden (1994, 1997), Sloan (1994), Reuben (1996), Cherry (1995), Burtchaell (1998), Hughes (1999), and Schmidt (2003). Sloan (1994:20) supplies the figures in the next sentence.

4. Burtchaell (1998) documents this process for colleges in several denominations. Smith (2003:77-78) notes that, between 1860 and 1930, the percentage of clergy on the boards of trustees of private colleges and universities in the United States dropped from approximately 40 percent to less then 10 percent. Sloan (2002:21) documents the secularization of faculty involvement mentioned in the following sentence.

5. Monsma (1996:35-40), Burtchaell (1998:144), and Smith (2003:75-76) cite this cause.

6. Sloan (1994:204). See also Hellwig (2002:105), Keim (2002:274), and Garroutte (2003).

7. Cherry (1995:32).

8. Sloan (1994:205). See also Carpenter (2002:201) for the secularizing impact of graduate and professional programs.

9. Monsma (1996:98-102) describes some of these pressures.

10. Lambert et al. (2002:156) make this point with regard to higher education. See Salamon (2003:63-64) for a similar observation about non-profits in general.

11. A comment of Paul Williams, a Lutheran pastor and a member of Capital University's (Columbus, OH) board of trustees when, in 1999, this Missouri Synod university hired a Catholic president (Schmidt 2003:199). Similarly, Meyer (forthcoming, p.93) quotes one faculty member who stated in 1997: "I'm the only Presbyterian in our Presbyterian college's religion faculty of twelve. I can't think of anyone in the middle-age group at out college that is behind our institutional mission. I'm not sure we can go back. . . . Unless an institution has an adequate body of faculty members who in some way affirm and live out the mission, it might as well close its doors. It will not be meaningfully church-related for long. Faculty hiring is *the* crucial area."

12. Cuninggim (1994:12). See also Harris (1974:16), who makes the same point. See Longfield and Marsden (1992:119) for the information on the United Presbyterian Church in the next sentence. In 1993, the PCUSA dissolved its Commission on Higher Education, which had been responsible for maintaining the relationship with its colleges and universities. Also in 1993, the Evangelical Lutheran Church in America also entertained a proposal to stop financial support of its colleges. Although the proposal was rejected, the fact that it was even put on the agenda, and by a high denominational official, was significant (Meyer forthcoming:51).

13. The Methodist colleges were an exception to this: several hundred of the 1,200 schools they originally established were exclusively for women. Today, four of the 87 colleges and universities that are still officially Methodist are women's colleges (Burtchaell 1998:260-262).

14. Brereton (1981:181).

15. Brereton (1981) outlines some of these pressures.

16. Scarritt College began as Scarritt Bible and Training School of the Woman's Missionary Society of the Methodist Episcopal Church South. It moved to Nashville, Tennessee, in 1922, and eventually became a co-educational senior college and graduate school (Barbara Campbell, private communication).

17. See Leahy (1991:100, 104) for the information in this paragraph.

18. See Leahy (1991:102) and Gallin (2000:121) for these figures. The sisters' colleges, being smaller and less well-funded, continued to be staffed largely by nuns until well into the 1960's—only 31 percent of their faculties were lay in 1965 (Gallin 2001:3).

19. Quoted in Leahy (1991:100).

20. Quoted in Fitzgerald (1984:162).

21. See Burtchaell (1998:582) for the Jesuits; Gleason (2001:12) for Notre Dame.

22. Hellwig (2002:109). Of the 222 Catholic institutions of higher education in the United States in 2002, 116 had lay presidents and 106 had presidents who were priests or members of religious orders (Holtschneider and Morey 2003). This is in spite of the colleges' tendency to hire presidents from the sponsoring religious order whenever a candidate who was even remotely qualified was available (Holtschneider and Morey 2003:7-8).

23. Daigler (2000:98). See also Tripole (2000:457).

24. Gallin (1996) describes this transfer process for seven Catholic colleges. See Morey (1995:130-131) for the figures in the next sentence.

25. Leahy (1991:106).

26. Holtschneider and Morey (2000b:6), who also supply the information in the previous sentence.

27. These include Medaille College, Villa Julie College, Daemen College, Nazareth College, Marymount Manhattan College, and Marist College.

28. Gallin (1996:23, 102-31) and Daigler (2000:132-36, 197) list these events as precipitating secularization. Rebore (2003:66) lists a countervailing set of Supreme Court decisions that permitted the channeling of Federal funds to religious colleges, but notes that the fear of a possible court-ordered cutoff of the funds was nevertheless "particularly divisive" (Rebore 2003:67). See Monsma (1996:80-98) for a more thorough discussion of the types of government funds available to private colleges and universities, and the changing policies regarding the colleges' eligibility for and use of these funds. Harris (1974:17) notes that the remaining Protestant colleges also felt the secularizing pressure of government policies in the 1960s and 1970s.

29. See Monsma (1996:159) and Gallin (1996:102-31).

30. See, for example, Smith's (2003) edited volume.

31. Gallin (2000:7).

32. See Gallin (1996:27-36; 1999:114) for a case study of conflicts at the College of New Rochelle in New York and La Salle College in Philadelphia. See Gleason (1995:309-12) for similar case studies of St. John's University in New York, and of the University of Dayton. As recently as 1996, Notre Dame experienced a similar faculty uprising when the religious order president of the university appointed a member of his order to the faculty over department objections that proper academic procedures had not been followed (Schaeffer 1997a).

33. Quoted in Gallin (1996:1).

34. The politics behind this is described in Gleason (1993:8) and Fitzgerald (1984:111-118). See also Contosta (1995:164) and Leahy (1991:107).

35. See, for example, Gallin (1996:9, 24).

36. Daigler (2000:132-36).

37. Gallin (1996:50-55), Burtchaell (1998:594) and Fitzgerald (1984:205) discuss Arrupe's reservations. See O'Brien (1994:60) for the Vatican attempts to forestall the secularization of the colleges alluded to in the remainder of the paragraph.

38. See, for example, Shea and Van Slyke (1999), Gallin (1996, 1999, 2000), Gleason (1993, 1995, 1997, 2001), Langan (1993), O'Keefe (1997), O'Brien (1994), and Tripole (2000).

39. See, for example, Benne (2003:208) on the dilution of Lutheran identity in that denomination's colleges. See also Hughes and Adrian (1997), Marsden (1994), Burtchaell

(1998), Johnson (1992) and Sloan (1994). Meyer (forthcoming) notes that avowedly Christian colleges which retain and celebrate their religious identity have grown at twice the rate as institutions whose religious affiliation is more nominal.

40. See Walch (1996:170) and Bryk et al. (1993) for the statistics in the preceding sentence.

41. Walch (1996:170).

42. O'Donnell (1988:256).

43. Quoted in Walch (1996:172).

44. See O'Donnell (1988:264) for the 1946, 1950, and 1958 figures; and the 1966 *Official Catholic Directory* for the 1965 figures. According to the 2005 *Official Catholic Directory*, in 2004 there were 170,000 lay teachers in Catholic grade and high schools, as compared to 10,000 priests, brothers, and nuns. Today, in other words, lay teachers comprise over 95 percent of the teachers in Catholic schools.

45. See Walch (1996:178, 180, 231) for these figures.

46. See Harris (1996:21, 66, 76, 125) for these figures.

47. Ryan (1964).

48. Walch (1996:231). The 2004 enrollment was 2,484,252 (Cieslak 2005:176).

49. See, for example, Deedy (1984) and Scheiber (1984).

50. Michael Cieslak (2005:176) reports a 1996 survey conducted by the National Center for Education Statistics which found that fewer than half of the Catholic high school principals surveyed listed religious development of the students as their school's primary mission.

51. See Sengers (2003) for failed episcopal attempts to prevent non-Catholics from teaching in Catholic schools in the Netherlands.

52. They also, of course, operated hundreds of elementary, secondary, and post-secondary schools in Asia, Africa, and Latin America.

53. An exception is the Seventh-day Adventists, who have always operated an extensive parochial school system. Recently, numerous private religious schools have recently been established by individual evangelical and fundamentalist congregations, primarily to serve the children of the sponsoring congregation's members or of like-minded middle-class parents.

54. Benne (2003:208).

55. This and the following quotation are cited in Vance (1999:91).

56. See Finke and Stark (2001) for the theory behind this process.

57. Risse (1999:471).

58. Starr (1982:161).

59. Moylan (1993:40-41).

60. Nelson (2001:132).

61. Kauffman (1995:190).

62. Weber (1986:305). See also Hill (1985:130).

63. Wall (2002:33).

64. Risse (1999:522-23). See Kauffman (1995:190) and Nelson (2001:132) for the CHA's role in urging professional standards.

65. Risse (1999:542). Catholic hospitals had had a few lay nurses as early as the 1880s, but the overwhelming majority of nurses in the nineteenth century Catholic hospitals were the sisters themselves. See Moylan (1993:79) for the increase in lay nurses in Catholic hosptals in the 1940s.

66. See Nelson (2001:208, ftn.129) for these figures and Nelson (2001:150) for the quotation in the preceding sentence.

67. Lindberg (1986:195-96). See Sengers (2003:536) for the secularization of medicine in Dutch hospitals in the late twentieth century. See also Kauffman (1995) and Starr (1982).

68. See Conroy (1989:152) and Moylan (1993:126), who describe the impact of government aid.

69. Conroy (1989:153).

70. Risse (1999:523).

71. O'Neill (1989:68) notes that the degree to which doctors control the delivery of care is more important than the official legal ownership of hospitals in affecting their identity and day-to-day operations. This has led to standardization across the nonprofit–for profit spectrum as well as between religious and secular hospitals.

72. See Moylan (1993:124,132). Salamon (2003:54) charts the rising percentage of hospital revenue coming from governmental sources.

73. Anthony (1997:58). See Moylan (1993:178) and Kelly (1989:177) for the figures in the preceding sentence. The lay board members were still predominantly Catholic, however: 82 percent in 1991 (Abzug and Galaskiewicz 2001:61-64).

74. Ledoux (2002:185). On page 186, Ledoux also mentions the impact of lay administrators on a hospital's identity.

75. Risse (1999:541).

76. See O'Connell (1986:136) and Nelson (2001:6) for these figures. See Risse (1999:544) for the figures on the declining number of Catholic hospitals in the next sentence.

77. Jones (2003:3) provides these figures. Catholics also sponsored 1,796 continuing care ministries—hospices, home health care, nursing facilities, etc. (Jones 2003:3). See Schaeffer (1997b) for the controversy around the sale of St. Louis University Hospital.

78. Moylan (1993:178). Tuckman (1998:42) lists multiple-partner hospital mergers through 1996.

79. Jones (2003:3). The National Catholic News Service listed 583 Catholic hospitals—which probably reflects inconsistencies in counting branches, mergers, and clinics. Similar consolidation and co-operation has occurred in other countries as well. See Amos et al. (1993:69) for information on Catholic Hospital co-operation in England, Ireland, and Canada. See Jones (1995) for Catholic Health Initiatives.

80. Amos et al.(1993:62).

81. See, for example, Fennell and Alexander (1993:93), Clarke and Estes (1992:961), O'Neill (1989:69), Marmor et al. (1987:222, 229, 234) and Kramer (1987:241).

82. See Sengers (2003:536) for an example of this in the Netherlands during the 1980's, despite the objections of the Catholic bishops, who wanted chaplaincy positions limited to Catholic clergy.

83. See Ruggie (1992:935), Fennell and Alexander (1993:103), and Risse (1999:542).

84. Cleary (2001:96) makes this point.

85. See Langley (1997) for this quotation. See Numbers and Larson (1988) for Adventist hospitals. See also Hollingsworth and Hollingsworth (1986).

86. Salamon (2003:76) notes that this risk to identity is especially strong in health care, more so than other religious-sponsored educational and social service non-profits.

87. Quoted in Jones (2003:3-4). James (1998:281) and Salamon (2003:62-64) discuss the adoption of an "enterprise culture" by non-profits, including outcomes measurement, marketing, and hiring managers with a more for-profit outlook.

88. Quoted in Vance (1999:69-70).

89. According to one critic: "Many institutions today have become complex

organizations, characterized by government regulations, intricate financing, and multiple interlocking corporations. Particularly in the realm of health care, freestanding institutions have been linked to health systems, with numerous layers of management and governance. An individual sister ministering within such a system may wonder what influence, if any, she has on the overall direction or quality of the ministry. The bureaucratization of ministry contributes to a feeling of alienation in individuals who derive satisfaction in ministering from the feeling of being effective—'making a difference'—in the organization" (Gottemoeller 1991:565-66).

90. Knittel (1995:501).

91. Moylan (1993:79).

92. See Dougherty (1997:54) for the deaconess nurses' training; Risse (1999:519) and Kauffman (1995:158) for the Catholic sister-nurses' training.

93. Quoted in Risse (1999: 540). See Dougherty (1997:206) for the quotation in the following sentence.

94. See Risse (1999:538) and Chambliss (1996:72) for a discussion of this development.

95. Risse (1999:522-23).

96. See Chambliss (1996:91-110).

97. Jones (1995:14).

98. Koontz (1997:422).

99. See, for example, Sengers' (2003:536-37) account of the losing struggle by Dutch bishops to control Catholic hospitals in that country and to prevent their becoming involved in abortion and euthanasia.

100. Among these, for Catholic hospitals, see Hehir (1995), McCormick (1998), and Arbuckle (1996). See McCormick (1998) for the quotation in the following sentence.

101. See, for U.S. Catholics, Bernardin (1995). See Sengers (2003) for Dutch Catholics. See Gallagher (1996) for a summary of the U.S. Catholic bishops' statements on health care.

102. Sengers (2003:536-37).

103. Anderson (2000:74). See Cnaan et al. (1999) for a description of the secularization of social work from its Protestant roots.

104. Brereton (1981:193).

105. Cherry (1995:74-75). See Schwartz (2000:81, 84) for Protestant use of social work to convert Catholics.

106. Anderson (2000:64, 75). See also Rosner (1998:311).

107. Oates (1999:6). Reinhold Niebuhr noted that the division of social work from religion is a "Protestant way of doing business" which values lay activity and leadership in the social world and confines clerical leadership to church settings (Cnaan et al. 1999:63).

108. Cayton and Nishi (1955). See Garland (1992, 1994) and Ellor, Netting, and Thibault (1999).

109. Coughlin (1965).

110. Brown and McKeown (1997:54-63). See Oates (1995:90) and Moloney (2002:49) for the information in the following sentences.

111. In 1929, the sisters cared for 54,350 children in 350 orphanages (Brown and McKeown 1997:108). See Brown and McKeown (1997: 98-101) for the information on social workers faulting the sisters' institutions.

112. Quoted in Brown and McKeown (1997:108). See Brown and McKeown (1997:103) for the sisters' reaction.

113. Quoted in Dougherty (1997:176). See also McDowell (1982:25) for similar

reservations among Southern Methodist churchwomen.

114. Coleman (2000:4-5). See also O'Neill (1989:127).

115. See Smith and Lipsky (1998:471) and Popple and Reid (1999:17).

116. Or, in reverse, as Salamon (2003:22) notes, for-profit agencies may obtain the funds and contract out to non-profits. Even the work of charitable fund-raising itself may be done by for-profit fundraising firms.

117. See Coleman (2000:5) and Cnaan et al. (1999:70-86).

118. Popple and Reid (1999:17).

119. See, for example, The CYCLE Program of Chicago's LaSalle Street Church: "Although the move made CYCLE more a part of the community it serves, it further distanced CYCLE from LaSalle; and while this has been an incredibly successful program, the growth of CYCLE and its relocation have meant that the material contribution of LaSalle members to CYCLE has become, in proportional terms, negligible." (Price 2000:68)

120. Dougherty (1997:250).

121. Salamon (2003:18) makes this point.

122. Salamon (2003:24, 62).

123. See Chaves (2004:67) and Popple and Reid (1999:11). This has obvious implications for the new federal "Faith-Based Initiative."

124. Popple and Reid (1999:24).

125. Cnaan et al.(1999:48). See Eby (1997:396) for the quote in the next sentence. Cleary (2001:198) makes a similar point.

126. Oates (1995:171). See also Oates (1995:171-72) for the figures in the preceding sentences.

127. Jeavons (1998:81). See also Bielefeld, Littlepage and Thelin (2002) for another classification attempt to rank the degree of religious affiliation in social service agencies: "Does the provider: provide funds or support to any religious organizations; have an affiliation with any religious organizations or faith traditions; desire, request, or require that staff and volunteers share the same religious belief or faith; include religion or faith as part of any services provided; make organizational decisions guided by prayer or religious texts, documents, or periodicals; and use religious or faith criteria to assign staff to positions?"

128. The terms are Salamon's (2003:76).

129. Weisbrod (1998a:298).

Chapter 6

Sponsors and Institutions: Changing Relationships

As religious schools, hospitals, and social agencies grew in size and complexity, as their day-to-day practices shifted to match those of their competitors, and as the forces of economic competition, government regulations, labor market constraints, and professional credentialism exercised greater and greater influence on their organizational cultures, the longstanding relationships between these institutions and their sponsors also shifted. But, in spite of the importance of each side in establishing the very identity of the other,[1] there has been great resistance to examining this changed relationship in any detail.

In part, this may be due to the current lack of clarity about the exact role of a religious sponsor in the sponsored institution, a lack which is simultaneously deplored and obfuscated. As early as the mid-1960's, no fewer than three separate surveys of Catholic college presidents in the United States found the ambiguous role of the associated religious order to be one of the most pressing problems they faced, second only to financial concerns.[2] A 1985 survey of 22 Catholic health care system CEOs surfaced a strong desire for "a more effective and clearer working relationship with the sponsoring congregation." And this ambiguity, if anything, has worsened in recent decades: a 1998 survey of the presidents of all Catholic colleges and universities in the United States found that 98 percent of them reported organizational stresses because the reduced presence of the college's religious sponsor had not been adequately addressed, and a recent article on Catholic hospitals lists the transition from religious order sponsorship to lay trusteeship as one of the two major elements of these hospitals' mission that they have not fully resolved.[3] Similarly ambiguous relationships have been noted by scholars studying Baptist, Methodist, Lutheran, Presbyterian, Wesleyan, Calvinist, and Mennonite colleges.[4]

Changed Institutional Identities

The Definitional Role of Religious—or of Non-Religious—Staff

It is vital, therefore, to examine the ways in which the institutions' increasingly prevalent adoption of secular models has affected their relationship with their religious sponsors. The first and most important question which must be answered is whether the organizations have been able to preserve any distinctive religious identity at all.[5] One Mennonite author noted that there are several different ways in which a "church-related organization" might be considered "related" to a denomination or denominational group. Churches need to ask whether the relationship was expressed:

- by an ideology that defines the organization's activities as "God's work"
- by official accountability, charter, or by-laws
- by demonstrating religious values in organizational activities
- by receiving Church funds, or
- by restricting leadership positions to Church members.[6]

But, as the previous chapters have shown, the religious ideology that sacralized education and health care institutions as "God's work" has been greatly attenuated, church funds no longer provide a noticeable portion of their operating expenses, and few if any members of the sponsoring church group possess the expertise needed to oversee the increasingly complex and professionalized activities of their staffs.[7] And, because it is difficult to measure amorphous qualities such as "mission" and "values," church-sponsored organizations are vulnerable to the displacement of their original religious goals by secular ones.[8]

Until recently, the religious identity of Church-sponsored organizations was unquestioned and unexamined. The active, daily presence of the sisters or deaconesses, and the active financial and administrative involvement of the mission societies, have certified the religious character of their institutions. According to one study of Catholic colleges:

> One of our consistent findings was the important role that vowed religious play in inspiring positive attitudes toward the institution's Catholic identity. The example set by those faculty members who are vowed religious apparently permeates the entire faculty and sets the tone for connecting with the school's mission. Unfortunately, in this age of declining religious vocations, many religious orders are experiencing difficulty maintaining a significant presence among college and university faculties.[9]

Or, as a Protestant critic put it: "The determining factor in the nature and effectiveness of a Christian university is the faith and commitment of the teacher."[10]

Particularistic hiring and recruitment practices once ensured that the majority of the staff and administrators of an institution would be members of the sponsoring group or of its parent denomination, as would a disproportionate number of the students, patients, or clients which the organization served. Often, applicants were asked to affirm publicly their adherence to denominational creeds before they could be hired.[11] Therefore, it was not necessary for denominational officials, the sponsoring religious group, or the institution itself to spend time outlining exactly what it meant to be a Baptist university, a Catholic hospital, or a Methodist community center. The domination of staffing and administration by the religious sponsor and its parent denomination ensured the organization's religious status. A 1996 study of church-related colleges and universities reported that most denominations have not had strong agencies or offices charged with asking long-term questions about their involvement in higher education.[12] Typically, the denomination's chief executive, who served only a short term, was expected to perform this role. The denominational leaders tended to focus on temporally-limited, and largely academic, goals for the schools, and not on the overall role which the denomination's theology might play in setting and achieving these goals.

But when the sisters or deaconesses no longer worked in denominational institutions, when the bulk of their funds came from government sources or fees for services, when the majority of both the staff and those they served were not members of the founding denomination, then the religious identity of the institution was in jeopardy. As one critic put it, "if an organization cannot insist its staff members be in agreement with its religious beliefs, but must hire persons of other religious traditions and nonbelievers, that organization effectively ceases to exist as a religious organization."[13] On the other hand, as this same critic also noted, without a persuasively-articulated rationale for *including* a religious component in their services—which most denominations had never developed—it became harder and harder for organizations to justify the preferential hiring of religious staff:

> If a religious nonprofit agency or institution is performing certain secular functions that are clearly and cleanly separable from its religious functions, what rationale does it have to defend its practice of hiring only fellow religious believers to perform those supposedly secular functions? Or on what basis can one justify introducing any religious values or practices at all into purely secular programs or activities? If a certain program or activity of a religious nonprofit is purely secular in nature, there is no rationale left to defend insisting on a fellow believer running it.[14]

Or, as a recent study of the Jesuits put it:

> In balance with the talent and determination that qualified lay people bring to the academic job market and marketplace of ideas, priestly ordination has lost much of its rationale as a prerequisite for ministry. Professional credentials have in many cases surpassed apostolic zeal as the criteria for hiring and promotion.[15]

Only about one-fourth of denominational colleges and universities currently give preference in their hiring to faculty who agree with the college's religious orientation.[16] None of the Catholic child service agencies, and only 13 percent of mainline Protestant agencies, give preference in hiring staff to applicants who agree with the agency's religious orientation.[17] Similarly, few if any mainline Protestant or Catholic institutions restrict their services to students, clients, or patients of the same denomination.[18]

The question of retaining a "critical mass" of staff or clients from the founding denomination in a religious institution raises additional difficulties. Such standards are hard to enforce: "[W]hat constitutes a critical mass? Is it 75 percent? 50 percent? One-third? Our calculations set it at just over 50 percent. But what is a professed Catholic? Does a divorced Catholic qualify? Do we monitor weekend Mass attendance?" Should the faculty from the sponsoring denomination, order, or mission society be concentrated in a few key areas (e.g., Departments of Humanities, Religion, or Philosophy in a college), or spread throughout the institution? How essential is it for a college's engineering faculty to be Baptist or Catholic? For a hospital's janitorial or radiology staff?[20]

As the religious diversity of staff and clients increases, the pressure to de-emphasize an institution's religious identity also increases:

> To what extent could students and employees be required to understand, encourage, or support Catholic values? And to what extent were "Mercy values," "Franciscan values," or "Benedictine values" of importance to the members of any college community?[21]

The internal organizational culture often becomes, not simply ignorant of, or indifferent to, the religious dimension of the institution, but actively *hostile* toward it. In recent surveys, for example, college and university presidents have reported that their faculties frequently oppose all attempts to reinvigorate the school's religious character.[22] Or, as a perceptive outside observer put it:

> You know better than I the extent to which the disciplines, not the particular schools, define what is to be considered excellence, organize the subcategories of fields, and control the real loyalties, aspirations, and career paths of faculty. It is not only the problem of the job candidate in economics who is deterred by her discipline from developing a subspecialty in economics and theology, or even cultivating an interest in interdisciplinary conversation of that sort. *It is also the problem of the economics department members who feel that their own reputations vis à vis their discipline's standards (and therefore their marketability) might be tainted by actively recruiting someone with a theological interest.*[23]

This is in stark contrast to the view expressed by one sister, herself a teacher of physics at her order's college, that no field of study is profane "for those who know how to see."[24]

The leaching of religious content has affected even college departments of

Bible Studies (in Protestant colleges) and Sacred Theology (in Catholic colleges). Once, these disciplines not only held preeminent place among the subjects the students were expected to study, they also were considered essential tools in converting students to the faith and/or retaining them once converted.[25] Increasingly, however, both fields have been transformed into academic disciplines, objects of study approximately equivalent to history or philosophy, with no essential link to the personal faith or religious practice of either the teachers or the students.[26] A graphic example is this contrast between course descriptions in catalogs of the same Catholic university, from the mid-1950s and mid-1970s respectively:

> **603, 604: The Dogmas of the Existence and Nature of God, the Blessed Trinity, and Creation**. A study of the apologetic evidence for supernatural faith, the Triune God, creation. An appraisal of modern theories of evolution in light of Papal Encyclicals and Catholic teachings (1955).

> **467: Readings: Poetry and Theology of Earth**. Readings and discussion will focus on various ways the earth has been envisioned by twentieth century American poets (e.g. Frost, Roethke, Wilbur) and theologians. Special attention will be directed to the ecological crisis and the Christian doctrine of creation (1976).[27]

Thus marginalized or simply discarded, the theological foundations of denominational colleges lost all or most of their influence.

In the face of competing pressures from Church, government, and professional stakeholders, therefore, many institutions have responded by "decoupling" their religious identity from their everyday practices.[28] This gives the institutions' administrators the flexibility they need in order to maneuver in sometimes conflicting organizational fields:

> Rather than having one clear measure upon which all organizational activities are justified, the ambiguity of mission, and the multiplicity of constituents, may offer administrators several interpretive options. The organization may be presented differently to various constituencies, with different aspects of its mission and accomplishments highlighted.[29]

Thus, in order to attract the credentialed, high caliber staff and administrators demanded by secular professional standards, a hospital, university, or social agency might downplay its religious identity—while simultaneously *emphasizing* that identity to alumni, foundations, or denominational supervisors. One study found that the heads of some Catholic religious orders have expressed concerns that the presidents and administrators of their colleges were "soft-pedaling" the Catholic identity of these institutions.[30] Another study found that the medical faculty and the faculty of religion in a Seventh-day Adventist medical school were promoting at least two different models of medicine in their teaching, thus segregating the

Christian aspect from the secular medical one. If such decoupling is recognized, however, it may alienate the religious sponsor. In addition, such tactics may render the external religious identity of many organizations vague or non-existent in the eyes of the other actors in its organizational field—and in the eyes of its own employees and clients as well.

The sum total of these internal and external pressures push religious institutions inexorably away from their former denominational connections. As one critic noted:

> Whether the institutions are Lutheran, Catholic, Jewish, Mormon, evangelical, fundamentalist, Adventist, Reformed, Baptist, or of any other faith, commitments to preserve religion must be structural, systemic, and courageous. . . . Institutional leaders who will not make the unfashionable commitment to prejudice hiring in favor of religiously committed faculty, who will not provide the buckets of money required for bringing the competence in religion of at least some of the faculty up to their competence in the disciplines, who treat tenure decisions in exactly the same way as they are treated at the nation's pace-setting secular institutions, must be resigned to witnessing their institutions lose a distinctive religious character.[31]

Needless to say, institutional leaders willing and able to do this are rare.

Defining "Mission"

Buffeted by these pressures, an organization's external and internal religious identity may be further attenuated by the difficulty of explicitly articulating exactly what it is.[32] One recent study found that 41 percent of the presidents of Catholic colleges who were members of religious orders, and 26 percent of the lay presidents, found terms such as "Catholic Identity," or "Catholic Intellectual Tradition" to be vague and impossible to define effectively. At a 1999 conference on Jesuit higher education in the United States, "the participants never came to a consensus on what being Catholic or Jesuit means, or how Jesuit or Catholic values, whatever they might be, can be preserved. A reviewer of the published proceedings called them 'fascinating and indispensable' reading, yet admitted that he could not conclude from them what Jesuit education stood for."[33]

Hospital leaders are similarly uncertain. As one interviewee for the present study put it:

> I see a decline of a [specific religious order] mission and the rise of a "Catholic" mission. The days of a specific Mercy or Charity or Franciscan mission are over. [Interviewer: What does it mean to have a Catholic mission?] To follow the example of Christ and how he related to people. [Interviewer: How is that different from other Christians?] Well, there are certain directives, prohibiting abortion and sterilization, that we follow. Also, uh, I guess I never thought what it was. I do believe in Jesus' gift to have various perspectives—a blend of

Catholic theology and others. Hmmm. Maybe it's not so different from Christian. (Individual Sister Interview: Former hospital system CEO).

While the professional qualifications necessary for a hospital administrator, a counselor in a social agency, or an assistant professor of economics are specifically listed whenever religious institutions publish job openings, the institutions are rarely able to state even minimum standards of theological literacy, or of doctrinal and religio-historical awareness, which the candidates should possess.[34] Often, they do not even attempt to do so.[35] A study of lay administrators in Catholic hospitals noted that:

> These findings raise questions about exactly what types of background and attitudes make the best preparation for board governance, and about whether CEOs/presidents and [religious sponsors] differ on this subject. For example, in terms of background and skills, have business, financial, and marketing skills taken precedence over skills in theological reflection and ethical decision-making? Are lay board members expected to learn about or be versed in theology and/or the delivery of health care services as much as sisters are expected to be able to read financial statements?[36]

As one interviewee admitted, while financial accountability is well-delineated—"If you're making 4 percent operating margin, we can call you to accountability on that"— evaluating the pastoral/spiritual aspects of hospital care or college teaching is far more difficult.[37]

The difficulty of articulating and measuring a religious mission makes it difficult to screen prospective hires. Although recent authors[38] advocate intensive interviewing techniques as a way of "hiring for mission," the present study's interviewees noted that this was harder than it sounded:

> The key is finding the right CEO. And I'm telling you that if you find the right CEO, I've seen some CEO's that would put many of us—I mean, we would be awed at the things that they commit themselves to. But we don't always know what it is we're looking for. [What do you look for in a CEO?] We worked with a firm and we came up with competencies. The CHA [Catholic Hospital Association] has this competency study. We adapted it and we looked for people who had the values we wanted, that had the ability to take risks, that knew something about managed care, could handle this piece of it, had all the values. And we put them through a three-hour interview, testing compatibility, and we found that some people who we thought had talked nice weren't who we wanted. . . . Most people don't go through all that; they just go through resumes and check credentials (Individual Sister Interview: Former hospital system CEO).[39]

Even less often have religious mission criteria been used in *subsequent* personnel evaluations: one author notes that, while some universities have begun to review the performance of administrators and staff on these dimensions, "it is not common to hear about 'firing' for mission."[40]

[Interviewer: If you end up with a CEO that is all business and not pastoral, what happens to the religious identity of the hospital?] It depends on how much—or what we call accountability. You see, I don't think we do a good job of calling to accountability. We really haven't. I'm talking about Catholics in general. There's a reluctance to do that in church ministry (Individual Sister Interview: Former hospital system CEO).

The difficulty of articulating a clear religious identity has thus prevented changing the institutions' staff or clientele to conform with it.

Religious Marginalization and Decoupling

If hiring and promotion criteria are affected by the attenuation of an organization's religious identity, so also are its day-to-day operations. While church sponsors tend to believe that religious values should "quite often and quite appropriately interfere with rational planning and with decision-making" in the institutions, this interference is resisted and ultimately marginalized by managers and CEOs, who have adopted the mainstream professional or business culture.[41] This marginalization of the formerly dominant religious culture, and of those who carry it, may be intensely resented by the religious sponsor:

The assumption is that the only people with sufficient expertise to be on hospital boards are wealthy *men*. But this is based on the incorrect assumption that the purpose of a board is primarily *fund raising*. This may be true for colleges—our college's board meets four times a year and does fund raising. But hospital boards meet *monthly* and still can't keep up with the issues. Still, we put lots of businessmen with financial expertise on boards. They leave the "mission" to the sisters and make all the *real* decisions. Sisters have tremendous expertise in public policy or ethics or communications, but it's ignored and *not* used. When an issue arises, the guys solve it by themselves, using *their* perspectives only (Individual Sister Interview: Former hospital board member).[42]

One Australian study found that the "religious" aspects of human service organizations are seen as the "soft" part of administration, and that "what really matters is the 'hard' stuff of financing the organization and, in particular, competing for funds.[43]

Many institutions have adopted "Mission Statements" as a way to retain the influence of their religious identities in their daily operations.[44] However, as one Mennonite critic notes, while a good mission statement can help an organization focus on its original *raison d'etre*, "by their very nature, organizations seek self-perpetuation and consequently tend to misuse mission statements. The statements often become slogans to garner support, both financial and moral, [from the denomination] and to show that an organization's particular ministry is more important than other ministries."[45] While top administrators may give lip service to the mission statement's effectiveness, middle level managers and the rank and file employees may not agree:

> [Interviewer: How can you make the mission and core values more than just superficial?] At the risk of sounding arrogant, study [our health care system]. We have a straightforward set of core values and mission statements which we have everyone memorize like a mantra. Then we have them take every activity and observe it and make reference to these core values. After six years of this, our values are *yeast*, not icing (Individual Sister Interview: Health care system CEO).

> The Executive Council [of the religious order] gives us these "challenges" each year. For the past two years, we've been unable to figure out what they meant. Both times, I had to call someone on the council and ask them. This [current] one is just as bad. How do I write a response to this challenge? It's stupid! So we're having the annual meeting of our board of directors on how our board participates in this challenge. . . . What does all this mean to a bunch of lay people on a board? These are high-powered people – to think they're even going to be interested in these challenges is to miss the point (Individual Sister Interview: Middle management employee in a social service agency).

It is easy for the sister-administrator quoted above to say "All that is needed is to articulate a mission that is fluid enough that an institution can do what is needed." It is harder to specify to the staff what this means, or to catalyze their full commitment to it. As one teaching physician in a Seventh-day Adventist medical school commented, "I don't remember every detail, but I think most of the mission statements (as this one is, I presume) are very broad and general. You know, it's noble goals and so on."[46] The newly-hired lay administrators may be similarly vague. The board chairman of the largest Catholic health care system in the United States recently bemoaned the "mission illiteracy" of lay administrators, who "have lived most of our lives in the world of secular businesses [and] are comfortable talking about financial and operational performance. . . . But ask us to assess the mission effectiveness of our ministries or the quality of our spiritual care— arguably the distinguishing characteristics of these Catholic institutions—and many of us become tongue-tied."[47]

Many hospitals and colleges have established special "Mission Effectiveness Offices," often at the vice-presidential level, in order to oversee the organization's adherence to its mission. Recent researchers, however, have expressed strong doubts—shared by individuals within the organizations themselves—about the power of such offices to carry out their mandate: "even in colleges that maintain Vice Presidential rank for the Mission Effectiveness officer, there is no guarantee that the position will enjoy institutional prominence."[48] The creation of a Mission Effectiveness Office also allows other administrators or board members to compartmentalize, and therefore ignore, its concerns: as one lay board member for a Catholic college put it, "When it comes to this 'mission business,' I let the good sisters take care of that."[49]

"Out of sight" in a Mission Effectiveness Office "can put mission out of mind."[50] Attempts by denominational officials to increase the salience of the religious mission often have little effect: one survey of thirteen Catholic college presidents noted that none mentioned the recommendations of the papal letter on higher education when asked to list their organizational priorities. A similar study of the CEOs of Catholic hospitals found that they were more likely to list "Improving and Maintaining Hospital Profitability" as one of their highest priorities, while the leaders of the sponsoring religious orders were more likely to emphasize quality of patient care and care of indigent patients.

Religious Controls in Organizational Governance

In the face of all of these pressures to marginalize their religious role, there are several ways in which denominational sponsors attempt to retain some amount of control over their institutions. One is by providing financial subsidies, which gives the sponsor a voice in how these organizations are run. The Wesleyan Church provided $500,000 to $600,000 per year to one of its colleges in the early 1990s. One study found that 91 percent of the Catholic colleges and universities associated with Catholic religious orders reported receiving regular funds from these orders. In addition, many sisters still contribute their services to their schools and hospitals, either *gratis* or at a greatly reduced rate.[51] But the Wesleyan Church's $500,000 was only 3 percent of its college's $14.5 million annual budget, and the donated labor and money of Catholic religious orders is a much smaller—and declining— percentage of their institutions' total funding stream today than it was in the past.[52] This has led to discrepancies between how much influence the religious sponsors think their financial contributions *should* entitle them to exercise over the colleges, and how much influence the college administrators are actually willing to grant them. "Colleges believe that [religious orders] want greater and greater influence and attention while giving smaller and smaller gifts." Meanwhile, the heads of the orders "believe that the colleges do not appreciate the gifts they make, or treat them as well as they treat other donors."[53]

Among Catholics, especially, but also among some Protestant denominations, the sponsor may attempt to exercise control through a mandated presence on the boards of directors. Initially, all board members had to belong to the founding denomination or religious order.[54] Some denominations, such as the Southern Baptists, retain this arrangement in their colleges to the present day. Baylor University's charter stipulates that:

- All Baylor regents must be Baptist.
- The Baptist General Convention of Texas will directly elect 25 percent of the regents.
- Baylor will continue to operate within Christian-oriented aims and ideals of

Baptists, including those of the *Baptist Faith and Message*, adopted in 1963.

In addition, the President of Baylor suggested that:

– the President of Baylor always be Baptist.
– most of the senior leadership of the university be Baptist.
– at least 50 percent of the faculty be Baptist.
– every member of the Religion Department be Baptist.[55]

At Nazarene colleges, most of the faculty are of that denomination, having received their own degrees in Nazarene schools.

Sometimes, religious sponsors retain a specific proportion (usually one-fourth or one-third) of a unitary board. In other cases—including half of the Catholic colleges and all of the Mennonite colleges—there is a "dual" or "two-tier" board system, whereby an upper body composed entirely of representatives of the sponsoring group exercises control over a limited number of key ("reserved") decisions, and a lay board composed of credentialed professionals and influential community actors controls the rest.[56] A certain amount of tension exists over how many reserved powers the religious sponsors should retain: the religious sponsors tend to want more and the lay boards less.[57] Furthermore, "distinctions between reserved powers for Church purposes and reserved powers built into a health care system operation for economic and business reasons are often not articulated or understood. The corporate model with reserved powers may not have a chance to work well; it may frustrate the religious leadership and the laity involved. What appears in the neat corporate documents and organization charts may not reflect reality."[58] In other denominational organizations, religiously-connected members have been replaced by persons chosen primarily because of their money, connections, or professional expertise.

As their influence declines, the sponsoring group's members become "audiences" or "small stakeholders in a large corporation," which operates essentially without their input.[59] Members of the sponsoring group may hesitate to accept a board position, assuming that it takes more knowledge and expertise than they possess:

We recycle the sisters—so at Hospital X we say, "Why, they have so much experience and blah, blah," and so nobody ever says, "Let's bring [other sisters] from other cities for another perspective." Instead, they say, "[The current board members] have such *great* expertise, and nobody else could do this." (Individual Sister Interview: Former hospital board member).

Other groups may shift from an active "sponsor" to a more passive "donor" role— and a comparatively small donor at that.[60]

An additional issue is how much authority *any* board can have over a large institution. In one study, "we could count on one hand the number of times hospital governing boards played a key leadership role in initiating strategic change." This same study predicted that, "increasingly, individual hospital boards will become advisory rather than policymaking in nature."[61] One critic expresses the similar doubts with regard to whether the boards of church-related colleges will be able to safeguard the religious mission of these institutions.

The combination of recycling board members from the religious sponsor and ghettoizing them in "Mission Effectiveness" positions, as well as the increasingly advisory role of the board as a whole, could lead to an oligarchy of control dominated by the CEO or president:

> We have recycled [sisters] over and over, and they are so overwhelmed by rapid and complex changes that they leave it all to the CEO. If the CEO believes in the board's and the order's mission, that's fine, but if not, the board and the order are left in the dust (Individual Sister Interview: Former hospital board member).

It does not appear likely, therefore, that the increased reliance on board membership as a way of maintaining the religious identity of a denominational sponsor's institutions will be sufficient. The original influence of the religious sponsor, once provided by large numbers of members permeating all aspects of the institution's functioning, has given way to formalized board controls. One pair of critics call this "ministry one step removed," in which "the power of lived witness is being supplanted by contractual commitment."[62] The religious sponsor has

> final authority over some specifically defined issues, but little overall influence. . . . All of these governance structures depend on the involvement of at least some members [of the sponsoring group] in the life of the college. Should the [religious sponsor] disappear altogether, or no longer be able to provide effective staffing for designated positions, these solutions will cease to be workable."[63]

Meanwhile, the overall mindset of the board members shifts to the welfare of the institution rather than to its original religious goals.[64] This is often true even of the board members from the sponsoring order or denomination.

The Changing "Sponsorship" Role

When, then, can a hospital, college, or social agency accurately be called a religious organization? In the absence of a dominant religious presence (or, often, of any religious presence at all) in its staff or administration, with religious financial contributions diminished in proportion to other revenues, and with religious actors marginalized on trustee boards or in mission effectiveness offices, some Catholic religious orders have devised formal "sponsorship" relations with their institutions. The term, however, is vague, having "no official status in either civil or canon law."[65] One 1994 study of eight colleges and their associated religious orders found that "The presidents and congregation heads all admitted that the term sponsorship had become almost meaningless for them. They could not agree on a definition of sponsorship, nor describe a single model that had broad use across campuses. They found little in the literature that brought any real clarity to the term, and believed, as a result, that the term sponsorship had outlived its usefulness."[66] One sister interviewed for this study commented that her order had discussed the concept for 25 years and still was unable to define it.

In some settings, "sponsorship" simply refers to the mandated presence of the religious sponsor on the board of trustees which has already been discussed in this chapter. As was noted above, researchers doubt whether such a minority of denominational board members can significantly influence a board, or whether the entire board can influence the day-to-day operations of the institution. Nevertheless, the presence of religious sponsor board members "legitimates" the continuing religious character of the institutions, both to the sponsor and to the wider community.[67]

Still another interpretation of sponsorship implies that the religious order or denomination retains the power of officially certifying an institution to carry the title "Catholic," or "Baptist," or "Franciscan" in its name. Under the 1983 revision of Roman Catholic Canon Law, the diocesan bishop is empowered to decide which of the increasingly secularized social service agencies, hospitals, or educational institutions under their jurisdiction may continue to call themselves Catholic. But most of these institutions were civilly incorporated prior to 1983 with the term "Catholic" as part of their names, and the bishops now have little power to challenge this.[68] Similarly, many Catholic colleges (29 percent according to one study) are subject to a form of accreditation by the sponsoring order in order to be able to use a term such as "Franciscan," "Jesuit," or "Mercy" in their titles. The order is empowered to assess periodically the college's faithfulness to the terms of whatever agreements have been made to preserve the sponsor's mission and identity. "Rarely, however, does the agreement indicate how often the assessment will take place, who conducts it, or whether there is an appeal if a negative judgment is rendered."[69] Critics also note that, while such sponsorship arrangements may impose specific obligations on the college or hospital, they rarely outline the responsibilities of the sponsoring religious order. For example:

> 1.) The buildings of many colleges must revert to the religious order if the college dissolves. The reverse is rarely true.
> 2.) By-laws frequently list ways for the religious order to influence college policy. The reverse is never true.
> 3.) The religious order is often given a voice in the selection of the college's leadership, but the college is *never* given input in the selection of the order's leadership.[70]

One critic makes a similar point for Mennonite schools and colleges.[71]

And the danger of this ambiguity for the institutions is real. It is becoming more and more difficult for the Catholic religious orders even to fill the minimum number of places reserved for them on the boards of trustees of their institutions. Some orders, financially strapped due to the need to provide for aging members, must sell their properties—which may also house the order's college. The limited number of members available for election to leadership of the religious order means that "it might become difficult in the future to find people . . . who understand the implications of [institutional] governance, have a solid understanding of higher education, and are willing to commit themselves to the endeavor."[72] Observers on both sides worry that religious board members might experience loyalties divided between the needs of the college and those of the order. For Protestant colleges, denominational mergers may abruptly change the established model under which the two sides have defined their relationship.[73] As fewer denominational members attend these colleges, they may be less interested in retaining any relationship with them at all.[74]

Conclusion

Overall, the relationship between religious sponsors and their institutions is in a state of change and flux. Yet the reluctance, on both sides, to address this issue means that needed changes are seldom planned ahead of time, and are often triggered by some sort of crisis. For Catholic colleges, the crisis is usually the inability to find a new President from among the members of the sponsoring order when the former sister-president retires.[75] While most Catholic colleges and universities report that, within ten years, no one from the sponsoring order will be serving on campus in any capacity or seated on the board of trustees, over half (59 percent) have no plan for what to do when this happens.[76]

To the extent that the religious identity of institutions remains undefined and dependent on the memory of a few senior staff members, this identity is vulnerable. And this is increasingly the case:

> If it were not for Susan, I am not sure that today there would be a College of St. Mary affiliated with the Sisters of Mercy. Perhaps that statement sounds overly dramatic. It is not intended to be. For a brief period, Sister Susan was the only Sister of Mercy on the faculty of the College of St. Mary. Often, she was called upon to speak to the role of the Sisters of Mercy at the college. . . . Susan kept the fires burning.[77]

More than formalized "sponsorship" arrangements, presence on boards of directors, or generalized mission statements, the religious identity of institutions requires a common culture, one which a majority of the administration, staff, and clientele of the institution believe in and can articulate.[78] Increasingly, there are too few denominational members present in most institutions for this to happen:

> The strategy of basing culture on the memory of a few, in our opinion, is a poor formula for keeping organizational culture vibrant and alive. A generation hence,

the sisters and those who knew them will be gone, and the culture then will be based upon secondhand and thirdhand stories. Memory itself cannot sustain a culture.[79]

However, not only do denominational institutions depend on a critical mass of administrators, staff, and clients in order to retain their religious identity, the sponsoring denomination, religious order, or mission society may depend on a "critical mass" of its members being actively involved in these institutions in order to retain their original identity. As one historian recently put it, the disconnection from their sponsored institutions is a "stunning change" that begs for further exploration.[80] What have been the effects on the sponsors? The next section will explore this question.

Notes

1. Zech (1999:14), Cleary (2001:143), and Hellwig (2002:108), among others, note that the presence of religious orders had been essential for the maintenance and health of Catholic institutions. See Beaty (2002:133), Lambert et al. (2002:144-49), and Stoltzfus (1992:91) for the influence of various Protestant denominations on their colleges—and of the colleges on the denominations. See Wittberg (2003) for a discussion of the reciprocal influence of Catholic religious orders and their colleges.

2. These surveys are reported in Gallin (1996:1,17; 2000:43). See Sanders (1988:25) for the 1985 survey cited in the following sentence.

3. See Holtschneider and Morey (2000b:6) for the colleges; Jones (2003:3) for the hospitals. Cleary (2001:176-77) reports similar confusion regarding the sponsorship of Australian Catholic schools and hospitals.

4. See Beaty (2002) for the Baptist colleges, Schwehn (2002) for Lutheran colleges, Stoltzfus (1992) for Presbyterian and Wesleyan colleges, Carpenter (2002) for Calvinist colleges, Harris (1974) for Methodist colleges, and Meyer (2000, forthcoming) and Sawatsky (1997a, 1997b) for Mennonite colleges.

5. O'Connell (2002:69) makes this point.

6. See Bontrager (1997:331). Noll (2002:89) contends that colleges and universities that wish to maintain or restore their religious identity must hire only faculty who are well-socialized into the sponsoring religious denomination's ethos and immediately dismiss any faculty who question this ethos, raise as much of their operating funds as possible from church and private sources, and aggressively advertise the religious identity of the institution to parents and students. He also notes that this is usually extremely difficult or impossible to do.

7. Cuninggim (1978:17) lists nine alleged marks of church relatedness in higher education: Church ownership, historical ties, board membership, required courses and/or chapel service, creedal conformity, percentage of top faculty and administrators belonging to the denomination, financial support, and student behavior rules. He then proceeds to show that each of these is honored more in the breach than in actuality. Harris (1974) adds sponsorship of campus ministries and donating scholarships.

8. Eby (1997:401). See also Weisbrod (1998a:298).

9. Zech (1999:14). Holtschneider and Morey (2000b:3) quote a 1969 statement of the

Jesuits at the College of the Holy Cross to make a similar point:

> The Jesuit Community of Holy Cross College is the agency by which the Society of Jesus makes the College of Holy Cross a Jesuit enterprise. It represents a commitment of the Society of Jesus's major resource—capable, professional manpower—concentrated into the service of the College of Holy Cross in such positions and with such quality and energy of professional effort that the College will be recognizable in the character of its operation rather than in accidental characteristics of organization. The purpose is to influence a college which will be an outstanding witness to the commitment of the Church to the pursuit and dissemination of truth in all areas of human activity.

Cleary (2001:143) makes a similar point regarding Australian health care and social service institutions.

10. Fisher (1989:119). See also Parker (n.d.:2).

11. Longfield and Marsden (1992:108). See also Gleason (1995:320).

12. Meyer (2000:92, ftn. 5). A similar conclusion had been reached thirty years earlier by the Danforth Commission Report (Pattillo and Mackenzie 1966:276-77).

13. Monsma (1996:149).

14. Monsma (1996:152-53).

15. McDonough and Bianchi (2002:233). See Shea (1999:210) for a description of the push for professionalization in Jesuit colleges.

16. Monsma (1996:74). The figures are actually more stark when they are broken down: only 8 percent of Catholic colleges and 11 percent of Mainline Protestant colleges restrict their hiring to persons of the same religious affiliation; 67 percent of Conservative Protestant colleges do so. While 26 percent of Catholic colleges and 13 percent of Mainline Protestant colleges give some preference to co-religionists, 40 percent of Conservative Protestant colleges do. Consequently, the percentage of co-religionists on college faculties has steadily fallen: from 64 percent to 56 percent at Notre Dame between 1990 and 2000 (Meyer 2000:92, ftn. 6). And the trend is continuing: Meyer notes that only 45 percent of Notre Dame's new hires are Catholic.

17. See Monsma (1996:75) and Hill (1985:125). According to Monsma (1996:75), 45 percent of Conservative Protestant agencies and 43 percent of Jewish agencies give preference to co-religionists in hiring staff.

18. Monsma (1996:74-75, 123). Again, 34 percent of Conservative Protestant universities give preference to Conservative Protestant students, and 36 percent of Jewish child service agencies give preference to Jewish clients.

19. Zech (1999:15).

20. Geiger (2003a:209) also makes this point.

21. Daigler (2000:179). See also Gallin (1996:9) and Gleason (1995:93).

22. See Zech (1999), Meyer (2000:92, ftn. 6), Geiger (2003a:207), and Holtschneider and Morey (2003:12-13) for examples. See also Gleason (1995:93) and Gallin (2000:86).

23. Steinfels (1997:202). Emphasis added. This was noted as far back as 1974, when Monsignor John Murphy, the new executive director of NCEA's College and University Department, commented, "Unfortunately there is considerable evidence that Catholic colleges and universities have many academically credentialed persons on their faculties who are ignorant of, indifferent to, and, yes, even hostile toward the Catholic dimension of these institutions." (Quoted in Gallin, 2000:86) See also Wittberg (2003:274) and Holtschneider and Morey (2003:12-13). Stark and Finke (2000:14-15) note that faculties in the liberal arts and social sciences tend to be the least religious.

24. Duffy (2004:196).

25. Longfield and Marsden (1992:105).

26. See Cherry (1995:89), Gleason (1997:87), Marsden (1997:22), and Carey (1999:66). Ironically, this trend has actually been accelerated in Catholic colleges and universities by the 1990 papal document *Ex Corde Ecclesiae*, which requires faculty in the *Theology* departments of Catholic colleges and universities to receive a "mandatum" from the local bishop certifying their orthodoxy, while faculty in *Religious Studies* departments do not have to do this.

27. Quoted in Schubert (1990: 52, 107).

28. Monsma (1996:116) See Scott (2003:214-215) for a discussion of decoupling in organizations. See Salamon (2003:76) for the pressure on CEOs to do this.

29. Williams (1998:211). See also Weisbrod (1998a:298). Dobbelaere (1982) describes a similar practice for hospitals and welfare agencies in Belgium.

30. Morey (1995:191). See Ramirez and Brock (1996:28) for the Seventh-day Adventist study cited in the following sentence.

31. Noll (2002:90).

32. A point made by Gallin (2000:182) for Catholic colleges, Sawatsky (1997b:192) for Mennonite colleges, and Carpenter (2002:199-200) for Calvinist and evangelical colleges. Mudd (2005:14) makes a similar point regarding Catholic hospitals.

33. Tripole (2004:11). See Holtschneider and Morey (2000a:34-37) for the study cited in the preceding sentence.

34. Eby (1997: 405-6) makes this point in general; Holtschneider and Morey (2003:2-3, 9-11) make it for colleges, and Amos et al. (1993:74-75) for hospitals.

35. One study (Dwyer and Zech 1998) found that fewer than one-third of Catholic colleges and universities indicated in their employment advertising that prospective faculty were expected to support a distinctive institutional mission.

36. Sanders (1988:28).

37. Individual Sister Interview: former hospital system CEO. Daigler (2000:199) makes this same point for Catholic colleges.

38. For example, Rebore (2003:68).

39. An Australian study of Catholic health care CEOs found the same wariness of hiring interviewees who "know how to mouth the right words" (Cleary 2001:198).

40. Grant (2003:62). Coleman (2000:6-10) makes the same point for religious social service agencies.

41. Eby (1997:401).

42. Morey (1995:220) reports a similar objection with regard to colleges. One congregational head stated: "Many board members are men, and business men at that. They think in terms of home and values as one compartment and work and real life and business as another compartment. The nuns are in charge of making sure the values are OK and they are in charge of the money." Another congregation head stated, "The trustees are untutored about the legacy. They understand us as good nuns to be patted on the back. Much of it is partiarchal and patronizing in terms of internal awareness or conviction." (Morey, 1995:220).

43. Cleary (2001:61).

44. Sample mission statements include the following:
"The mission of Baylor University is to educate men and women for worldwide leadership and service by integrating academic excellence and Christian commitment."
"St. Olaf College provides an education committed to the liberal arts, rooted in the Christian Gospel, . . . [and] offers a distinctive environment that integrates teaching, scholarship, creative activity and opportunities for encounter with the Christian Gospel and God's call to faith. . . [combining] academic excellence and theological literacy" (quoted in O'Connell 2002:70).

45. Bontrager (1997:333).
46. Quoted in Ramirez and Brock (1996:23).
47. Mudd (2005:16).
48. Holtschneider and Morey (2000b:8-9) See also (2000a:20).
49. Quoted in Daigler (2000:180). See also Holtschneider and Morey (2000b:8-9).
50. Amos et al. (1993:64). See Daigler (2000:206) and Sanders (1988:18) for the studies of college presidents and hospital CEOs cited in the remainder of this paragraph. Mudd (2005:17) lists similar concerns.
51. Holtschneider and Morey (2000b:10-11). See Stoltzfus (1992:95) for the Wesleyan Church. Another connection is through the donation or use of property: 19 percent of Catholic colleges in one study reported that the religious sponsor owned the land; 16 percent shared buildings with the founding religious order; 20 percent shared utility costs (Holtschneider and Morey 2000a:24).
52. See Stoltzfus (1992:95) for the Wesleyans; Holtschneider and Morey (2000b:11) for the Catholic sisters.
53. Holtschneider and Morey (2000b:4-5). See also Morey (1995:3) and Neal (1984:30).
54. Longfield and Marsden (1992:112) note this for Presbyterian colleges prior to the 1950s; Contosta (1995:28-31) and Leahy (1991:95) note this for Catholic colleges.
55. Beaty (2002:124-5). Similar provisions hold for other Southern Baptist colleges and universities (Beaty 2002:129). See Lambert et al. (2002:143-144) for the Nazarene schools.
56. Holtschneider and Morey (2000b:15-16), and Geiger (2003b) describe this system for Catholic colleges; Stoltzfus (1992:118-120) for Mennonite colleges. Amos et al. (1993:37) describe a similar system for Catholic hospitals. Unlike their colleges, Catholic hospitals are separately incorporated and neither the sisters nor the lay board own their assets.
57. Holtschneider and Morey (2000b:18, 20) and Daigler (2000:199). See also Amos et al. (1993:72), and Cleary (2001:190) for a similar problem on hospital and social service agency boards, respectively.
58. Amos et al (1993:72). See also Eby (1997:403).
59. Hill (1985:167-169).
60. Morey (1995:232) makes this point for Catholic colleges; Hill (1985:159) for Protestant women's mission societies; and Coleman (2000:8) for Catholic social welfare agencies.
61. Shortell et al. (1990:279). See Meyer (2000:86) for the criticism in the following sentence.
62. Holtschneider and Morey (2000b:6).
63. Holtschneider and Morey (2000a:22).
64. Meyer (forthcoming:chapter 21) makes this point.
65. Holtschneider and Morey (2000a:5).
66. Morey (1996:5). Cleary (2001:176-77) found a similar confusion in Australian Catholic education, health care, and social service institutions.
67. Abzug and Galasciewcz (2001:53).
68. Coleman (2000:7).
69. Holtschneider and Morey (2000a:20).
70. Compiled from Holtschneider and Morey (2000b:11-12) and Morey (1996:27, 29).
71. Keim (2002:277). Similarly, Meyer (forthcoming: chapter 20) lists seven specific expectations which church-related colleges typically covenant to meet ("Identify itself as

related to X denomination," "Be regionally accredited," "Consider denominational members in faculty, staff, administration, and student recruitment," "Include the study of religion in the required curriculum," "Seek to provide an atmosphere conducive to religious life and growth," "Provide intellectual resources for the denomination," and "Participate in the denomination's association of colleges and universities"). But the responsibilities of the sponsoring denomination toward its colleges are much shorter and less specific:

1. Communicate to church governing bodies, congregations, and members that the college is X Church related,
2. Work to recruit students for the college,
3. Encourage financial support for the college through congregational offerings and publicizing college capital campaigns and deferred giving plans.

72. Morey (1995:215). See also Holtschneider and Morey (2000b:16) and (Morey 1995:31).

73. Keim (2002:277) makes this point for the Mennonite colleges sponsored by the two largest Mennonite denominations in North America. Each denomination has established and maintains its own colleges, but the models used have been different. A recent denominational merger has resulted in an alteration of the older models.

74. Schwehn (2002:215) makes this point for Lutheran colleges, Stoltzfus (1992:63-64) for Presbyterian colleges.

75. Morey (1995:132). See Holtschneider and Morey (2000a:25).

76. Holtschneider and Morey (2000a:27-30).

77. Quoted in Daigler (2000:199).

78. Holtschneider and Morey (2000b:18).

79. Holtschneider and Morey (2000b:16). Holtschneider and Morey also note that "perhaps the most disturbing finding of this study is the degree to which both colleges and [religious orders] are changing their governance structures in order to solve a much larger problem. The loss of Catholic and congregational culture will not be stemmed by adding an additional tier to the governance structure; assigning additional reserve powers to the congregations; creating sponsorship agreements; or creating offices and officers of mission identity in the congregations" (Holtschneider and Morey 2000a:36).

80. Coburn (2004:25).

PART IV

IMPACTS ON SPONSORS

Organizations not only influence the other institutional actors in their environment, but are also shaped by these other organizations. This is as true for religious organizations as for secular ones. Denominational schools, hospitals, and social service agencies, therefore, were once profoundly affected by the religious orders or mission societies which had founded and/or staffed them, while the orders or societies, in turn, were affected by their relationships to these institutions. Chapters 1 through 4 of this book have outlined both aspects of this mutual influence for the period preceding 1960, while chapters 5 and 6 have chronicled one side of the relationship for the post-1960 period—how loosened ties to the religious sponsor impacted the institutions. The remainder of the book will be devoted to exploring the least-studied aspect: the ways in which their weakened or severed institutional ties have shaped the religious orders and mission societies. Chapters 7 and 8 will explore how the loss of their institutions has affected the religious groups' internal and external identity; Chapter 9 will describe how their primary focal activities have also changed. Chapter 10 will chart the impact on the professional development of individual group members, while Chapter 11 will outline the losses of power experienced by members, their leaders, and the order or society as a whole. Finally, chapter 12 will offer a preliminary analysis of the larger ideological and theological implications of these changes for the individual members, the religious groups, and the entire denomination of which they are a part.

Chapter 7

Impacts on Identity I:
Purpose and Goal

As the previous two chapters have demonstrated, large scale political, economic, and other environmental pressures over the past fifty years have combined to leach much of the "religious" aspect from church-sponsored institutions. As a result, critics argue, the identity of many of these institutions has fundamentally changed. Such identity shifts may, indeed, have been a survival necessity. Nevertheless, this isomorphism among formerly religious schools, hospitals, and social service agencies raises the question of whether they will be able to retain any sort of enduring or distinctive religious identity:

> What does "enduring" mean when changing environments demand that even not-for-profit institutions behave strategically, thus encouraging the malleability of identity and image? What does "distinctive" mean when institutional processes emphasize mimetic behavior as a path to achieving a desired identity and image?[1]

The identities of religious institutions shift, grow, and decay as the reference organizations in their organizational fields change, and as their former religious sponsors become less salient components of these fields.[2] The result has been a diminishment of the organizations' former religious distinctiveness.

At the same time as the missionary societies and the orders of deaconesses or Catholic sisters became a less salient part of their organizations' environments, the organizations became a less salient part of the societies' or orders' own environments. As a result, the orders and societies may become less able to retain an organizationally-based identity and purpose that is enduring and distinctive in its turn.

Loss of Organizational Purpose

Most of the offices of deaconesses and orders of Catholic sisters, as well as all of the mission societies, had originally been established precisely to support or operate the institutions they have now largely lost. The loss of this common focus had profound consequences for their identity as a group of religious virtuosi:

> If what makes me a religious is that I am one of a group of people who perform such and such a ministry, and if nowadays other people who are not in vowed life, who are not celibate, and who are not living in community are doing the same ministry that I am doing, then what makes me a religious?[3]

Or, as one respondent in a recent study of the Jesuits put it, "If the schools and other operations launched by the Society can do well enough on their own, what's left for Jesuits to do?" A member of another religious order wondered whether the institutional ministry his order had performed had been merely "an add-on to religious life," or whether it had been inextricably bound to the very *raison d'etre* of his order's existence.[4] If the latter, what was left when the institutional ministry was gone?

For the most part, Catholic religious orders and Protestant deaconesses have had difficulty finding new roles for themselves within the larger denomination. One study of Catholic sisters noted:

> As religious orders moved away from their mission to teach, heal and offer social services in parochial institutions, they were unable to identify a new niche for themselves in either Church or society. Given the diversity of occupations among members today, it is virtually impossible for religious orders to construct their mission and environmental niche in terms of specific works. Instead, many orders are struggling to redefine their purpose in more abstract ideological terms such as "the witnessing of Christian values," "standing with the poor of society," and "dedication to furthering the mission of Jesus in the world." But these redefinitions of purpose are more difficult to define in terms of their necessity to society.[5]

As observer of Methodist Deaconesses made a similar comment:

> As the Church re-evaluated traditional understandings regarding ordained and non-ordained ministries, the deaconess found herself in a sort of no-man's-land. "Set apart" by the Church as an office did she qualify as a lay worker? . . . Responses to the questionnaire showed that, while deaconesses believed that their office possessed a distinctive quality or character, they found it difficult to pin down. . . . Could not this same thing be said about any full-time lay career worker serving the Church?[6]

Ebaugh calls this condition "organizational anomie"—the sisters in the

Catholic religious order she studied were unable to agree on any but the most general aims as a rationale for their existence.[7] Other studies have found similar confusion among individual sisters and deaconesses: as early as 1968, a study of one order showed that "sisters, both young and old, had little sense of the significance of religious life or the purpose of the congregation in the larger social context."[8] In a more recent national study of the members of male and female Catholic religious orders, 33 percent of the respondents expressed a lack of clarity about their role in the larger church.

Goal Restatement I:
Still Serving Others—Outside the Institutions

The participants in every focus group were asked what they believed to be the current goal, purpose, or *raison d'etre* of the order or mission society to which they belonged. Responses to this question are given in Table 7.1. Despite the anomie described by the outside observers quoted above, the most common response of the sisters, deaconesses, and mission society members was that their groups existed to serve others:

> To relieve misery, to address its causes, but also, in the name of God somehow. Not only in religious motivation, but a whole context that speaks of the care of God for the world and we're sort of the workers in that vineyard (Focus Group 2.6: Active and retired sisters).

> – To feed the hungry, to clothe the naked, to visit the prisons, and so on and so on.
> – Exactly (Focus Group 4.2: Retired deaconesses).

> – I would say it's service, service-oriented.
> – I would have to say, service, social and spiritual (Focus Group 5.3: Mission society).

A large percentage of the sisters' and deaconesses' focus groups also cited a second purpose: to bring the presence of Christ or God to the world, whether through their prayers, their works of service, or the witness of their lives.

> I feel very deeply, it's part of what I said before, but [the order is] a sign of God's compassion and loving care towards His people and His unconditional love. And that through me, through us, God is there for people (Focus Group 1.6: Active and retired sisters).

> This may sound a little bit pious, but I really think as [an order] and as individuals we are called to bring and be the mercy and love of Jesus Christ to those with whom we minister and for whom we minister (Focus Group 2.1: Active sisters).

Table 7.1. Basic Goals of the Order or Society. (N=36)

Goal	percent	N
Service	69	(25)
Bringing the Presence of Christ/God to Others*	50%	(18)
Reference to Official Goal Statement	47%	(17)
Act Together/Support Each Other	42%	(15)
Facilitate the Spiritual Growth of the Members	28%	(10)
Help the Church	28%	(10)
Work for Systemic Change	22%	(8)
Don't know/Activities Too Diverse To Say	19%	(7)
This Diversity Is Good/Helps Us Respond to Needs	17%	(6)

* This category includes bringing the presence of Christ or God through prayer (19 percent of the focus groups mentioned this), through works of service (33 percent), through the witness of one's life (36 percent). Several focus groups mentioned more than one of these ways.

– My relationship with God is my relationship with God, but my relationship with God is, I hope, such that it will make that relationship appealing to other people.
– Uh huh. Your witness (Focus Group 4.2: Retired deaconesses).

None of the mission society focus groups listed this purpose. However inchoate, there seemed to be a feeling among the deaconesses and sisters that their membership in a Church-sponsored order or office gave a special spiritual character to their work.

Other commonly-expressed goals, cited by the mission society focus groups as well as by the sisters and deaconesses, were acting together or supporting each other (42 percent of the focus groups mentioned this), facilitating the spiritual development of their own members (28 percent), and helping the larger Church (28 percent).

– You feel you are a small part of something big.
– That's right.

– and that we are all for the same thing and together, we can do something together (Focus Group 4.1: Retired deaconesses).

We don't need to be a collection of *individuals* doing works that serve the poor, the sick and the ignorant. We need to be—we need for the "us" in it, the collective in it, to in some way shape that service (Focus Group 2.3: Present and former leaders).

That's why I think organizations like this one are so important, because they help you keep your life in balance and to keep your priorities of what's important. Serve God, give back to God first, and then your family and everything else will slowly start to fall back into place (Focus Group 5.6: Mission society).

I think our personal relationship with Christ is the thing that is so important, and if our life will nurture that relationship, then that is what I'm here for (Focus Group 3.8: Retired sisters).

You're called into a relationship with whatever your career is. A church can use you with whatever your career is (Focus Group 4.3:Active deaconesses).

Another common response—occurring in seventeen (47 percent) of the focus groups —was to quote or cite the congregation's official mission statement. One of the sisters' focus groups even dispatched a member to retrieve a framed copy from the wall outside the meeting room and read it aloud. In one focus group of the Protestant women's mission society, the framed statement was on the wall inside the meeting room; the group turned toward it and read it together.

Some groups noted, however, that their members served in such a wide variety of ministries that it was difficult to give a single goal or purpose:

– See, like usually you had the schools and hospitals, everybody was interested in that. It was an altogether different way of living, you know?
– Right.
– Now it's so. . .
– It's hard to say what would be the basic goal (Focus Group 3.4:Retired sisters).

Many worried that this vagueness might be detrimental:

I think if we were asked—everyone has their own niche now and if somebody said, "Now the Sisters of X are going to be da-da-da," how many are going to give up what they're doing to be part of the da-da-da? You know. And is that right or wrong? Wise or unwise? (Focus Group 2.2: Retired sisters)

– I think that's a part of it, that people are so scattered in their issues.
– What I've liked most is the diversity [of membership]. The challenge in that is meeting all the needs of such a diverse group (Focus Group 5.3: Mission society).

Other groups, however, celebrated their diversity and strongly resisted any attempts to articulate a single, specific group goal:

> - Well, I think [the goal] is to go wherever we're needed. . . . Before, we were just education, hospital, pretty much. But now, I, I'm sure there's hardly anything that we're not in.
> - That we're not doing.
> - And we've been encouraged by the community to do this. I guess over the years, we've learned that a sister does better, is healthier, when she's doing a ministry that she wants to do. I mean, a lot of sisters who were put in education hated it and got out as soon as they could (Focus Group 3.5: Active sisters).

> I'd say [that our goal is] to do what we were instituted to do from the very beginning. To respond to needs in this world. And I think that's why our ministries are so diverse, because there are so many needs (Focus Group 2.1: Active sisters).

> In our [local chapter of the mission society], the unique part is that we have a diverse group of women. We've got older women, middle-aged, women, younger women, and everybody's willing to work together, and I think that's the strength of who we are (Focus Group 5.5: Mission society).

Linking their own group's identity to sponsorship of specific organizations was almost completely absent in the responses, cited by only one focus group (a mission society). Two other focus groups mentioned general types of activities (elementary education, a Christmas bazaar), but cited no specific organizational focus for them. This was in strong contrast to how the oldest focus group members had responded when asked what the *original* purpose of their order or society had been (See above, p.61-62).

Some interesting differences emerged in the purposes cited. None of the mission society focus groups mentioned witnessing to the presence of God, and none of the deaconess focus groups quoted an official written goal, cited spiritual growth, or fretted about the diversity of their ministries. Several purposes were unique: only the sisters' focus groups mentioned continuing the work of their orders' founders, bringing about systemic change, or empowering the laity to take their places, while only the mission societies mentioned socializing/making friends.

It is significant that there was only limited agreement—even within focus groups of the same religious order or mission society—on what the group's goals were. This was especially true for the mission society focus groups. While it may not be valid to make sweeping generalizations from a small and non-representative sample, the African-American mission society focus groups were more likely to cite the traditional goal of "helping support the missions" than the white groups were.

There may also be inherent contradictions in some of the more commonly cited goals. While eighteen (75 percent) of the sisters' focus groups mentioned witnessing to the presence of God/Christ as a primary purpose of their order,

Table 7.2. Basic Goals by Group Type. (N=36)

Goal	Sisters Focus Groups (N=24)	Deaconesses Focus Groups (N=3)	Mission Society Focus Groups (N=9)
Service	75% (18)	100% (3)	33% (3)
Being the Presence of Christ/God	71% (17)	33% (1)	0
Reference to Official Goal Statement	50% (12)	0	56% (5)
Act Together/ Support Each Other	50% (12)	33% (1)	22% (2)
Facilitate Members' Spiritual Growth	33% (8)		22% (2)
Help the Church	29% (7)	66% (2)	11% (1)
Don't Know/ Too Diverse To Say	25% (6)	0	11% (1)
Continue Founder's Work	54% (13)	0	0
Societal Change	33% (8)	0	0
Empower Laity	21% (5)	0	0
Support Missions	0	0	56% (5)
Socializing	0	0	56% (5)

fourteen (58 percent) also noted that losing their institutional presence had rendered them less visible to give *any* witness at all:[9]

> Can there be a Sister of X presence in the next several, maybe another decade, when there have not been X-sponsored ministries? I know we could do it individually: wherever one [sister] is, that's where [the spirit of the Sisters of X] is. But, still it does not have the same effect that a *group* of people doing

something would have (Focus Group 1.2: Present and former leaders).

> We have lost an identity, because there aren't any sisters working full-time in visible positions at [the order's hospital] (Focus Group 3.6: Former leaders and staff).[10]

Similarly, although two of the three focus groups of deaconesses cited "helping the Church" as a key goal of their office, one of these same two groups (plus the third group) also fretted about the lack of understanding among church authorities of what a deaconess was.

> There aren't any other deaconesses in my [district] either. And when I try to explore my relationship with [the denomination], once the deaconess relationship ended at the [mission society national office], they went into this limbo. And they're still trying to get out of it (Focus Group 4.3:Active deaconesses).

> [The denomination's reorganization] kind of weakened the whole understanding of the deaconess order. People were confused and concerned about that (Focus Group 4.1: Retired deaconesses).

Finally, the sisters' focus groups were more likely to cite "serving the poor" or "working for systemic changes that would alleviate poverty" as goals than they were to cite "serving the Church." This raises the issue of the continuing identity of the sisters' orders *vis à vis* the larger denomination, which, in prior days, had been largely mediated through their institutional service. The lack of an institutional base

> cuts [Catholic orders] off from their own history as well as from the patriarchal history of the Church it seeks to critique. This understanding turns its back on the colleges, universities, schools, hospitals, and other institutions that were the life blood of many congregations, a great source of their own pride, and vehicles for many of their most important works.[11]

As one researcher noted, there may be less of a constituency within Catholicism to support religious orders which are focused primarily on societal change and helping the non-Catholic poor than had formerly existed for the sisters when they were teaching and nursing Catholics who needed their services.[12]

Some critics have fretted that the sisters themselves may have become estranged from the church to which they nominally belong:

> How can we care so passionately about Roman Catholic identity in our institutional ministries and sometimes seem so cavalier about it in our congregational identity? Do we suffer from a kind of ecclesial schizophrenia? Is it more important that our ministries assert and affirm a relationship with the Catholic Church than that our Institute [of the Sisters of Mercy] assert and affirm it?[13]

In a manner similar to the way in which their schools, hospitals, and social service agencies have become increasingly distanced from a church identity, the religious orders and deaconesses, too, may have loosened their ties to the larger denomination.

Goal Restatement II: Personal and Spiritual Growth

Some critics have charged that, with the loss of their institutions, religious sponsors have refocused their identity and purpose to emphasize facilitating and supporting their members' own personal and spiritual growth while they labor in a variety of church and secular occupations.[14] One pair of authors have dubbed this "the individual and therapeutic community":

> On the one hand, in the wake of the disorientation following Vatican II, the Society of Jesus has undergone what anthropologists call a revitalization movement. The interior life of the Jesuits has been made over. . . . The contemplative side of Jesuit life appears to have been turned around. The record on the activist side, especially as it concerns the corporate thrust of the order, is less impressive.[15]

"An individualistic style of thought," Moran contends, "pervades almost the entire terrain of religious life."[16] In this, the orders are imitating a pattern critics have noted throughout American society:

> Observers who believed that Americans were focusing too much attention on the self argued that therapy, Alcoholics Anonymous, and popular psychology fundamentally contradicted a deepening understanding of spirituality. Some worried that people who were interested in self-expression were not interested enough in social problems or were too individualistic to be guided by the counsel of religious communities. . . The call to quit focusing on one's inner self is thus linked to the hope that Americans will get involved in politics, in volunteering, or in working for social justice.[17]

These criticisms, however, were *not* supported by the focus group interviews. Fewer than half as many of the focus groups mentioned spiritual or personal growth as a goal or purpose of the Catholic religious orders of the mission society, as compared to the number citing service (the sisters' focus groups) or helping the missions (the mission society's focus groups). The deaconesses did not mention spiritual growth as a group goal at all. The sisters might also argue that, traditionally, the primary purpose of their orders has *always* been the spiritual advancement of its members and that, if anything, the fact that only 33 percent of their focus groups now cite this purpose is a great decline from the percentage which would have mentioned it in the past.

> That's what [my novice director] told me. She said, it is first your relationship with God, developing and growing in your relationship with God, and then your ministry comes second, and then your life in community comes third. And that's been my—I think that I still hold to that (Focus Group 3.9:Retired sisters).

The sisters and deaconesses also emphasized that the spiritual support they received through their membership in their orders was essential in enabling them to perform their works of active service:

> I don't know of any more humbling, and at the same time, empowering statement to make than to sit in a meeting where you go around and introduce yourselves and, you know, to say "I'm a deaconess of the [denomination]." And I, that just gets you through a lot of tough spots, to know you are a part of this power-ful—not powerful in the worldly sense, you know—[trails off] (Focus Group 4.1: Retired deaconesses).

> Then you realized that God was calling you to this, and you're going to get through it, and that He's going to support you. . . because the work is all-consuming, you know—teaching or whatever else you do. I think it was the spirit of [the order] involved, too, that was the strength and powerful energy that I felt through all the years of the work (Focus Group 2.2: Retired sisters).

> Those are things you can't do by yourself. The Lord just lets you do that (Focus Group 1.1: Retired sisters).

> I think I pray more now, real prayer, because some of the [shut-ins that I visit], I walk down the hall and I say, "Dear God, give me the strength to come back just one more time (Focus Group 3.12: Active sisters).

External Identities

The schools, hospitals, and social service agencies not only had helped to define the purpose of the order or mission society to its own members, they were also a key component in the image which outsiders in the denomination and in the larger society had of these groups. Institutional ministries gave visibility to the otherwise hidden lives of the nuns.[18] They defined a place for the deaconesses and mission societies in Protestant denominations otherwise suspicious of organized women's groups.

The sisters in many of the focus groups frequently commented on the loss of their public identity:

> I think numbers make a difference. So that, as there are fewer sisters who are really active in that institution, I do think that the sense of the sisters' presence does decline, even though there are efforts made to promote who the Sisters of X are. For example, at X Medical Center, a lot of work has been done since I was

there to even put concrete symbols around that would remind one of the Sisters of X. Still, I think that the decline in the numbers of Sisters of X means that, on a day-to-day basis, many people will not have a contact with a Sister of X. They might come through the doors and read, "The Sisters of X Welcome You," and that's all the exposure they'll have to the Sisters of X all day. I think that the way we see ourselves and the way we see our identity . . . is very different from the other people who work and minister in these institutions (Focus Group 2.5: Active sisters).

We've lost our identity . . . I've had priests say, "That's really a great loss to the community. That's why you're not attracting people, because they don't know who you are. They appreciate what you're doing, but there's no way for them to know"—Oh! In fact, my own brother. One of my brothers has a granddaughter and he made the statement, "You know, poor Elizabeth, she's going to Catholic school but she doesn't know who sisters are" (Focus Group 3.7: Active sisters).

In several focus groups, however, the sisters engaged in a spirited debate over whether their order had lost its identity or not, and, if it had, whether this was a good or a bad thing:

[Interviewer: What about the order's public image? Is that any different?]
- Oh yes. Very different. I think we have a better image today, really, because we're more involved with the public.
- We're much more visible.
- Before, we were kind of like the little ladies in black on this hill—
- For those who knew we were here.
- And unless you came to school here, the civic community had very little interaction with us (Focus Group 1.6: Mixed active and retired sisters).

I think when we were [assigned to a ministry] and there were large groups of us together working in the ministry, it was seen as a Sister of X ministry and probably not so much emphasis on the individual. I think in our present reality, it's—especially when we're working with lay people, it's broadened our sense of self-empowerment and our ability to collaborate with others. But I also think it's broadened our perspective on what we're about in the ministry of the Church and not just the ministry of the Sisters of X (Focus Group 3.6: Former leaders and staff).

In the absence of an institutional base, the responsibility for the order's identity now rests on the individual sister or deaconess. When asked how their orders had changed, nine of the 24 sisters' focus groups mentioned having an increased personal responsibility for keeping their order's image before the public. It was unclear, however, how effective this would be:

The Sisters of X have had to fight so hard just to prove their existence, in a sense. I loved what I was doing, and I felt proud to be a Sister of X, but it was getting harder and harder when fewer and fewer of us were there [in the order's hospital]

(Focus Group 2.1: Active sisters).

And now, I find that what I'm doing, I have to work harder and maybe more consciously at identifying so that who I am as a Sister of X and how does what I'm doing right now fit in with that. Because, for the most part, I'm working in a place where there aren't any other Sisters of X at all (Focus Group 3.11: Young sisters).

After some of the Catholic religious orders had sold their hospitals or colleges, they placed the proceeds of the sale in a foundation to support new works. This was seen as a new way to maintain the public identity of the order *vis à vis* the larger society:

I think that one of the things that has helped us to continue a different presence is the foundation we set up after the sale of our health care facilities. Because we have limited it to the geographic areas which were the primary service areas for the health care facilities we formerly had. And I think that, in that particular tool, we have been able to carry on the spirit of the Sisters of X, and I think that we have become known somewhat in that circle (Focus Group 1.2, Present and former leaders).

That's a whole identity of our community that's lost, our identity with all those institutions. . . . So we are freer in a sense, aren't we? And we do have the Sisters of X Foundation that we are doing wonderful things with in [state]. So that's a good side to it (Focus Group 3.4: Retired sisters).

Others, however, objected that their foundation's funds and collaboration efforts were not as effective as the institutions had been in preserving the order's external identity:

I think we're talking about a different kind of [identity]. . . . The Foundation is serving a huge need and a great ministry, but I think we are looking for something more similar to when you really became very closely involved with people. Like [our former presence] at the college, that's the sort of thing we were talking about (Focus Group 1.2: Present and former leaders).

An identity tied to a foundation presence might even be negative:

-- You have fund raising for all these ministries when you've got a foundation that could help support this and a lot of people are angry about that. A lot of people do not understand it, and that is a question that comes forward, "Why should I fund you when you've got a foundation?"
-- They will tell you, "I will give my money to an organization that does not have the financial support that you do from the Sisters of X Foundation. So many people who have donated to [the order's residential facility for severely handicapped children] for years are no longer supporting them, and this year alone, we have to raise over a million dollars. It's going to be cutting it close

(Focus Group 1.5: Active sisters).

Recruitment

The internal and external identity of the sisters, deaconesses, and mission society members also has implications for their success in recruiting new members. To begin with, groups that are unclear about their own purpose or goals often resist inviting others to join them. A few (2) of the sisters' and deaconesses' focus groups specifically expressed their reluctance to invite new members:

> [Interviewer: If someone were thinking of entering the Sisters of X and they asked you why they should do so, what would you say?]
> - I'd hesitate.
> - I would think it very difficult (Focus Group 3.9: Retired sisters).

> [Interviewer: If someone were thinking of becoming a deaconess and they asked you why they should do so, what would you say?]
> - I don't want to answer that.
> - I don't either.
> -We've really had so much upheaval. I just don't know really where we are (Focus Group 4.2: Retired deaconesses).

In addition to the difficulty that a lack of *internal* identity poses for motivating the order or society to recruit new members, the *external* identity of the order or mission society—its image in the larger denomination—also has implications for recruitment.[19] All three deaconess focus groups mentioned that the larger denomination did not really understand what a deaconess was, or, worse, did not even know that such an office existed:

> I was told that the deaconesses were dead, but that I could become a diaconal minister. [general laughter] So I started the diaconal minister track, but never fit in, so I asked again and they said, "No, the deaconesses are gone" (Focus Group 4.3: Active deaconesses).

Six of the nine mission society focus groups mentioned a similar lack of understanding:

> I think that we are very rigid about not opening up information channels to the young people. There are so many young people who have no concept of what the [mission society] stands for and what work they do, and I think we need to educate them in order for them to want to come in with us (Focus Group 5.6: Mission society)

> - We have a fall speaker to get people in, and the reason we do that is so people realize that the [mission society] does more than the image of what a mission

society is.

[Interviewer: What is that image?]

- The image seems to be that they're older ladies who sit around and do church things. Whatever that means. And most of the time, people don't have any idea what that "church thing" means (Focus Group 5.5: Mission society).

Two of the sisters' focus groups noted that, without their identification with distinct institutions, outsiders had difficulty distinguishing between the different orders:

[Interviewer: Do you find among the staff or the kids that they know or can tell the difference between the Sisters of X and the Sisters of Y?]

- I don't think the children would know it necessarily. The parents might (Focus Group 2.5: Active sisters).

I don't think that Sister of X sponsorship is going to be [in our hospital] once we continue to be out of the picture. It will be Catholic, and I hope it will still have the same good reputation. I do hope they miss the Sisters of X. I think that personality, which each [order] brings, I think that is what will not be present in the Catholic ministries of the future. I think it will be more generic, if you will (Focus Group 2.6: Active and retired sisters).

In seven other focus groups of sisters and some of the individual interviews, respondents noted that it was becoming different for outsiders to see anything distinctive about being a sister at all.

[Interviewer: How is being a sister-teacher different from being a lay teacher?] I don't think there is any difference today. And the children, they don't seem to distinguish between the two (Individual Interview: Retired high school principal).

Denominational Identity

In addition to the impact of institutional loss on the religious sponsor's identity, the identity of the larger denomination may also be affected. Without concrete institutions to represent and define a denomination to outsiders, it may be hard to describe exactly what distinguishes one denomination from another. Formerly distinctive doctrines may become eclipsed in favor of assumptions drawn from the larger religious scene: one Mennonite official worried that, in the absence of a strong influence by his denomination's colleges on many local congregations, a number of pastors and church leaders have borrowed expectations from evangelical churches (e.g. Biblical inerrancy) that are foreign to the Mennonite tradition. Some critics have questioned whether, in the absence of church-sponsored institutions, the evangelical movement can maintain a stable, long-term tradition:

The evangelical resurgence of the past half-century has unintentionally chipped away at the power and influence of the institutional church. . . . The result is that fewer evangelicals than a generation ago stand in a religious tradition that can provide ballast and long-term orientation. . . . Devaluing the church enfeebles Christians in two respects: it cuts us off from the past, and it relieves us of accountability. . . . Evangelicals have difficulty seeing themselves as responsible and accountable to the church. . . . The very structures of evangelical life are attuned to the intense individualism of American culture.[20]

Similarly, recent research has shown that young Catholics are more likely to be active and orthodox believers if they have attended Catholic high schools and colleges.[21]

In the absence of an institutional presence in education, health care, or social service, therefore, denominations may increasingly become viewed as privatized, spiritual "self-help" groups, whose teachings individual seekers can mix and match at will. Chapter 12 will explore this possibility and its implications in greater detail.

Conclusions

Overall, the public identity and purpose of the sisters, deaconesses, and mission society members, both within the denomination and in the larger community, appears to have become more ambiguous after the loss of their institutional ministries. The schools, hospitals, and social service agencies which these groups had once financed, staffed, and administered had made a profound impact on how the sisters, deaconesses, and mission societies were viewed, not only by their own members, by also by the denomination and the larger society. The imposing silhouettes of their buildings against a city's skyline, the services they provided to generations of pupils and patients, the pervasive presence of cohorts of identically-dressed teachers or nurses laboring inside—all served as symbols of the group's and the larger denomination's identity. Today, this iconic presence is attenuated or gone. While the focus groups continued to cite service of others as the purpose of their order or society, this service was less likely to be expressed through the specific church-run organizations of old. As a result, the focus groups were less able to define a common purpose for their order/society, either in the denomination or in the larger civic community.

In addition to their iconic or symbolic function, however, the institutions shaped the common identity of the sisters, deaconesses, and mission societies in another way. Working together in such organizations helped develop an *esprit de corps*, the common culture which was an essential part of who these women were. The next chapter will examine this second contribution in further detail.

Notes

1. Goia and Thomas (1996:371). See also Tuckman (1998).

2. Bartel (2001:379) and Goia and Thomas (1996:395) make this point.

3. Himes (2000:16). See also Moran (2004). See McDonough and Bianchi (2002:186) for the quotation in the following sentence.

4. O'Malley (1997:14).

5. Ebaugh (1993:41).

6. Dougherty (1997:243-244).

7. Ebaugh (1993:87).

8. Moylan (1993:174-5). See also Dougherty (1997:230-231) for similar problems among Methodist deaconesses. See Nygren and Ukeritis (1993:190) for the study cited in the next sentence.

9. This is not the same answer as line 7 of Table 7.2 (although it sometimes occurred in the same focus groups). The latter response listed in the table referred to the inability of the respondent to enunciate a specific goal for the order or society; the former answer refers to the perceived ability of the order to provide a visible witness to that goal.

10. It should be noted that, in 2 focus groups of sisters (both drawn from the same order), participants felt that their order had become *more* visible after losing its former institutions. This was a minority opinion, however, and partly due to the new institutions the order had recently begun:

> I think what happened on our campus, too, was we closed our college and we made our buildings available to a lot of different services, and we changed a lot of attitudes, at least in a better understanding of who the sisters are and what their mission is. Because of all the different things that are on this campus, it was very obvious that we were concerned about children, children on the street, runaway teenagers. [Residential facility for handicapped children] was always a part of this, but the foundation also, the ministries that our foundation is funding now, the people that are part of these ministries, which are so diverse (Sisters' Focus Group 1.5).

11. Morey (1995:99).

12. Ebaugh (1993:41).

13. Gottemoeller (1995:35).

14. See Moran (2004:307), who makes this charge for Catholics, and Wuthnow (1994; 1998:150), who makes the same observation about church groups in general.

15. McDonough and Bianchi (2002:187).

16. Moran (2004:309-310).

17. Wuthnow (1998: 150-151). See also Putnam (2000:149-152), who makes a similar point.

18. Soher (2003:5).

19. A point made by other observers: see Brinkman (2005).

20. Hatch and Hamilton (1992:29).

21. Davidson et al. (1997:102). This does not seem true of attending Catholic grade schools, however (O'Connor, Hoge and Alexander 2003).

Chapter 8

Impacts on Identity II:
Common Life and Culture

In addition to their role as iconic representations of their sponsoring order or society—both to the members themselves and to the surrounding community—schools, hospitals, and social service agencies also provided locales in which "communities of memory" could develop. Through their common experiences of working together, and—for the sisters and deaconesses—of living together "above the store," members grew connected to each other as they shared the mutual histories and practices that defined "who we are" and "how we do things here." The sisters, deaconesses, and mission society members thus constructed "a tradition and a past that [were] continually retold to members through ritual and story but also through interdependent sharing and decision making."[1] Communities of memory must remain living and vital if a group's bonds are to continue healthy and strong. But what happens when the settings and activities that once fed these communities of memory are no longer available?

Identity and Mutual Support

On a sheer physical level, the Catholic religious orders' withdrawal from their schools and hospitals has meant that opportunities for more than two or three sisters to live and work together in the same setting are now rare to non-existent. Active deaconesses are even more widely scattered. Some orders may still possess a few large buildings where ten or more persons may live under one roof.[2] However, their inhabitants often work at varying and disparate occupations during the day and may rarely see each other:

> Since Jesuits have come to do so many different things, since their work has become more specialized, and since so many Jesuits have settled into retirement, virtually no large communities built around an encompassing corporate

mission—secondary education, for example— remain.[3]

Many sisters were evicted—sometimes abruptly—either from parish convents which were slated by the pastor for another use, or from expansion-minded hospitals desiring the space the nuns had once occupied. Few alternative living situations in the mainstream housing market were able to accommodate five or ten adults on such short notice,[4] and the sisters often found themselves with only one- or two-bedroom apartments to choose from. This limits the size of communal living groups that are possible, such that, today, 69 percent of sisters live alone or in groups of two.[5] In addition, these settings also provide "no room for guests, potential new members, or even one's own community members. There is no room for a common prayer space, and no room to welcome groups of guests."[6] This is in spite of the fact that, in one recent survey, a plurality of sisters (45 percent) preferred living in a group of between four and seven persons.[7]

Five of the sisters' focus groups noted that living in smaller groups, with persons working in widely-varied ministries, often hindered their communal bonding:

> In my house, and I'm afraid there are a few others that have the same thing, we have three individuals living in the same house. We all do different work. I'm doing some tutoring, and one is working in the hospital in pastoral care, and the other one is the president of our foundation, and we say our [morning prayers] together in the morning, we might have one meal together—ordinarily we don't—and after supper one goes to her room with her media center and the other one goes to her room with her books. They've both been talking all day and want silence, so I ramble around the house and do lots of different things. . . . But the thing is, there is—in my house, we are three individuals living different lives (Focus Group 1.1: Retired sisters).

All three of the deaconesses' focus groups agreed:

> – This is one of, to me, one of the radical things that changed. People talk about a fellowship, and we had a fellowship through this organization. But you don't become a deaconess now because of the fellowship, because that same fellowship just isn't there.
> – That's right (Focus Group 4.2: Retired deaconesses).

> I have a difference in terms related to the training, I think. Deaconesses, so many of the deaconesses, they all went to school together and lived in community, they worked in the community centers. . . . And now I went to school here, but I didn't go to school with anybody else that was becoming a deaconess (Focus Group 4.3: Active deaconesses).

On the other hand, sisters in at least one of the focus groups claimed that their more recent experience of living in ministerially heterogeneous communities was preferable to living and working together in the same place:

Well, one thing [that has changed] is the living situation, certainly. When you were on a particular mission with a particular group, all of which were pretty much doing the same thing, it's limiting, in some ways, at least of what you share. And so you each slept and talked that particular ministry. And I know I found it so much more enriching when the house was full of [sisters doing] a variety of ministries that we could share and support each other, and it was a whole different atmosphere, then, of community living—I do think that it was enriching to us personally to be surrounded by people in various ministries. If you didn't do it, at least you understood it and supported it and were broader because of it (Focus Group 3.6: Former leaders and staff).

Communal identity was once simply assumed, an integral part of working and living with the same individuals day-in and day-out. As the preceding quote shows, this may not always have been an unalloyed good. Still, the sisters and deaconesses generally felt that their common ministries had fostered a valuable common bond that was more difficult to achieve today:

And so, that's a difference in terms of the deaconesses that are my peers, we didn't train together, we've never lived together, and thus we've had to build relationships in a different way, in terms of trying to stay connected and to become a community. . . . It's frustrating at times; you've got to make that effort to keep up with people (Focus Group 4.3: Active deaconesses).

Thirteen of the sisters' focus groups and one of the deaconesses' focus groups mentioned that each individual sister or deaconess now bears a greater personal responsibility for keeping up her connection to the larger order.

Often, however, these efforts to remain connected may appear to infringe on one's work obligations. Ten of the sisters' and deaconesses' focus groups noted that their work activities had had a negative impact on their ability to connect with the other members of their orders:

I live by myself now, but previously when I lived with another sister . . . I found it extremely difficult to, as far as the living of religious life, to be home at X time and to be there for supper and to have the energy to try to communicate and be present. I love what I'm doing, but I'm very tired when it's over. Each day, I can hardly make it to the parking lot (Focus Group 2.6: Active and retired sisters).

I have to admit that, at times, I do find my ministry something of a distraction to my vocation, in that being in youth ministry and working the hours that I work, doing the kinds of work that I do, it's really busy, it's very active when you're dealing with teenagers, and it's very much evenings and weekends, which is also very much community time. And there are times when I feel like I'm pulled in two or three different directions at once, and I go, "When is a good time for community prayer, where is the time for personal prayer?" You get home at 10:30 or 11:00 at night and how do you balance all of that? How do you make it work? (Focus Group 3.11: Young sisters).

For those whose job also requires them to live singly or at some distance from their order, staying connected may be even more difficult. As a result, the sisters' and deaconesses' actual, day-to-day relationships may be primarily with people who are not members of their order.[8]

> For me, living in [state] now, it's different. Always before, I was living in [another] jurisdiction, where there were always deaconesses around, and I'm the only one in [state] and so it's a little bit more isolated. I've got to be more conscious of the email and the letters and reading the stuff that comes from the deaconess program office and all. And this is more important now than it was six years ago (Focus Group 4.3: Active deaconesses).

Such geographical difficulties were mentioned by two of the three groups of deaconesses, but by only one group of sisters. Another sisters' group countered that geography was not determinative: members could "distance" themselves even when they lived in the same area.

Communal Support Systems

When asked how life in their order had changed after the ties to their institutions had been severed, a loss of mutual support was one of the sisters' and deaconesses' most common responses, mentioned by 79 percent of the sisters' focus groups and by two of the three deaconesses' groups:

> - I don't feel the mutual support we once felt in our ministry. You know, in community, we all knew what everyone was doing, and we're not always that aware of what other sisters are doing now.
> - That's what I miss, being able to share with the sisters the little things that happen through the day, and the hardships and disappointments and little things that I don't seem to be able to share with my lay counterparts (Focus Group 1.3: Active sisters).

In addition to a lack of mutual support, participants in all three of the deaconesses' focus groups, and in twenty of the 24 sisters' focus groups, also mentioned a loss of group cohesion:

> I would disagree a little bit with the idea that we know sisters better today. It may be my fault, but I don't know as many sisters today as I did in the years when we were more formalized, because we had to return to the headquarters [every summer] and we got to know almost everybody in the community. And today, you know, I'd say three-fourths of them I can't put a name on. Does anybody else have that problem? (Focus Group 2.4: Retired sisters).

Table 8.1. How Community Life Has Changed (N=36)

Change Mentioned	Sisters Focus Groups (N=24)	Deaconesses Focus Groups (N=3)	Mission Society Focus Groups (N=9)
We have more responsibility now:			
for group identity	45.8% (11)	0	0
for professional growth	62.5% (15)	100% (3)	0
for our connection to the group	54.2% (13)	33% (1)	0
We have more group cohesion	25% (6)	33% (1)	0
We have less group cohesion	83.3% (20)	100% (3)	0
There is still much group support	62.5% (15)	33% (1)	0
There is less group support	79.2% (19)	66% (2)	22.2% (2)
There are fewer memories	29.2% (7)	66% (2)	11.1% (1)
We have more individual freedom:			
which is good	83.3% (20)	33% (1)	0
which is bad	20.8% (5)	0	0
More consultative leadership	41.7% (10)	0	22.2% (2)
Less dedication to a place or ministry	25% (6)	0	55.6% (5)

I think there's a real effect, though, on the newer members. . . . I go back in my own case to the convent of X High School. That's where you formed these friendships that were lifetime, because it was a matter of throwing all of your energies—and we lived together as well—there was a kind of totality of life that had to do with both the living and the working, and the connections we made with each other. So, the newer members are looking for what is the heart of Sister of X life, and . . . they don't see everybody working in Sister of X institutions, and they don't have the sort of formation in that that we did. So I think it's causing us to ask some real questions about how to incorporate the newer members and how they might have those relationships that we got just because we worked so hard together (Focus Group 2.6: Mixed active and retired sisters).

The opinion that there was *more* cohesion after losing ties with their institutional ministries was much less frequently expressed, occurring in only seven of the 27 sisters' and deaconesses' focus groups.[9]

Common Memories

Their experiences of living and working together also built up a reservoir of common memories in the older sisters and deaconesses. Several focus groups of retired sisters and deaconesses regretted that the younger members would not have a similar store of common memories:

- The other thing, too, was that so many of us went through [deaconess training college] for our training. And that was a bonding kind of a thing, that training. [Interviewer: How are things different now? I don't suppose the current deaconesses go through that.]
- They don't. They can get their training wherever. You know, and commissioned wherever.
- I don't think they are ever going to have that bond (Focus Group 4.2: Retired deaconesses).

One thing, the young sisters don't have the experiences that we had by living together, you know. And we have stories that we tell and all of this. And I keep thinking that they won't have any of these stories to tell (Focus Group 3.4: Retired sisters).

The younger members, too, have expressed a felt lack of the bonding caused by common service in one of the order's institutions.[10]

As a result of this attenuation of the orders' common life and culture, many young people today are less willing to join them.[11] Ten of the 24 sisters' focus groups mentioned that their lack of common life was deterring potential members:

- The literature today is telling us what people want, what Generation X wants are three things, essentially: community, structure, and prayer. And—

- We can offer all three.
- They're not looking for ministry. They say, "We can do ministry without being in [a religious order]." And it's true, people do marvelous ministry without being in [a religious order] (Focus Group 1.2, Present and former leaders).

For new people coming into the community, the attraction is not [the works the order sponsors], because they don't see the works as much any more, so I think the attraction for the new people coming into the community is to live a religious life. That life of prayer, of being at a comfort level with other people who are willing to share their spiritual journey with you (Focus Group 2.5, Active sisters).

The interesting aspect that came up this year with us is Mary Smith. She liked the Sisters of X immensely and was very interested in [our foundress] and so forth. But what she told us was that she found herself drawn to community and prayer. And her observation was that the Sisters of X, she felt, put ministry first. She felt that . . . prayer and community . . . are secondary to the ministry. And one of the things about community which you really can't argue with, is that she felt she really wanted to live in community with a group of people. And yet, as she looked around [city], just at how many [Sisters of X] were living alone or in twos . . . So she felt that was a difficulty and she ended up deciding [to enter] a monastery (Focus Group 3.5: Active sisters).

Yet, without their institutions, the orders may be hard-pressed to provide the communal experiences they perceive new recruits to be searching for.

Increasingly, the sisters, deaconesses, and mission society members must experience their feelings of common bondedness, not through common work in or for a sponsored institution, but as a deliberately created and separate activity.[12] Not all of the sisters were enthusiastic about the effort required to do this:

- We had a discussion at [the order's governing assembly] this summer about the newer members wanting [to live in] an intentional community, and they want it to be intergenerational, and I'm scared to death that they would ask me [to be a part of it]. . . . But I'm full of conflict about that. I want them to have what they need—
- and want
- and want, and especially what they need, but I don't know how much sacrifice I'm willing to make to cause that intergenerational part to happen. I could go over there occasionally, but I don't know that I could live in it (Focus Group 2.3: Present and former leaders).

And, as the remainder of this chapter will show, members working outside their order's institutions may be less free to take time off to organize and participate in community-building activities.

Since the mission society's members had never been expected to live communally, their perceptions differed from those of the sisters and deaconesses. Still, the focus group participants valued the increased sense of unity and mutual support that came from working together on a common project:

- We have older workers who have been [in the local mission society chapter] for twenty years. It's a great fellowship for all ages.
- There's some women that I never see at the church, because, you know, we have so many services and all that. But you go to the rummage sale, you see them all (Focus Group 5.4: Mission society).
- There's something about having [a fundraising event] and all the working together in the church. I mean, people that don't even want to do it and end up doing it, they'll have a smile on their face. But basically it's a good feeling and you need those activities to keep people working together.
- Don't you get to know at least three new people?
- Oh yes! Sure you do!
- Absolutely! (Focus Group 5.2: Mission society).

Often, what was valued in the mission society's service projects was precisely the camaraderie that such joint efforts supplied.

We've also become good enough friends that we socialize, we had cooking class outside the church a few weeks ago, and so it's kinda become a social group too, with the focus still on volunteerism within the church (Focus Group 5.4: Mission society).

As with the sisters and deaconesses, however, the mission societies now had to focus specifically on creating the common bondedness that before had been a natural by-product of their service activities. Six of the nine mission society focus groups mentioned at least some purely socializing activities when asked to describe their local chapter's activities:

- I don't know if [that chapter is concentrating on] service now. When I was there it was not a service [chapter] It was for the mothers and maybe they would do [one mission-related activity] but it was not—if you didn't want to be into it, that was fine.
- It was not anything but social. Keeping mothers sane (Focus Group 5.3: Mission society).

I would have to say that probably most of the chapters are in existence for personal relationships. I mean, they're—it's not like we're not doing productive things, but the reason the women are involved is because they have a personal group of people to get together with and like those five, six, or seven women (Focus Group 5.5: Mission society).

Instead of the camaraderie arising from common participation in mission-supporting activities, therefore, mission society members created activities focused solely on intra-group support:

The most important position in [respondent's former mission society chapter] was "care and concern." They kept track of everybody that's in the hospital and made reports, sent out cards, and that kind of thing, and kept everybody, you know, in touch with each other (Focus Group 5.4: Mission society).

This concentration on camaraderie and mutual support, while attractive, can also have a down side. It may cause the local chapters to appear—and, in fact, actually to be—exclusive. One of the focus groups was composed of women who had deliberately chosen *not* to join the mission society chapter in their local congregation, but had decided to establish a spiritual book discussion club instead. Without the spur of common activities, the group was less willing to accept new members into what had become a closed circle of friends:

- I would be uncomfortable, though, to bring somebody that didn't know anybody else in the group.
- I would bring someone who is a good friend, but I would not bring a casual acquaintance.
- It would have to be someone that I knew very well (Focus Group 5.7: Book discussion club).

In addition, some of the mission society chapters had also become set in their ways, which was also a deterrent to new members. One member of the book club had not felt welcome to join the mission society chapter in her church:

I would definitely be interested in joining the [mission society] if there was a group that met at a good time and was interested in doing something. But there doesn't seem to be—plus, they don't seem to want anybody new. [general laughter] I mean, I know a lot of women in the [mission society] and they're very nice women, but they don't—I don't know anybody that's been invited. A lot of these local groups have been together as a cohesive group for many years (Focus Group 5.7: Book discussion club).

Four of the nine mission society focus groups and one of the sisters' focus groups mentioned this tendency to become an exclusive clique:

Some of the older women have held offices for so long that it's sort of like a rotation. They are not really letting any new people in. OK, they say they *want* new people, but—[others nod] (Focus Group 5.8: Mission society).

I think, in smaller churches, . . . they might have a [mission society chapter] which is run by the ladies that have been running it for the last thirty years, and after a while, you kind of lose interest in—not that you don't respect what they're doing and everything, but you kind of have to—[trails off] (Focus Group 5.4: Mission society).

Working in or for the institutions, therefore, may have been a spur to more inclusive membership, while cohesion based on conscious personal contacts may more easily become exclusive of potential new recruits.

Commitment to the Group's Needs

If members of a religious order or mission society no longer feel the sense of mutual support and cohesion that the active involvement in their own institutions had once engendered, will they, in the long run, be able to maintain their commitment to these groups? Recent studies of other organizations have found that "members may recalibrate the strength of their organizational identification when work contexts and comparison groups change."[13] As their order's or society's ties to its former schools, hospitals, and social service agencies loosened, other loyalties and obligations began to compete for members' time and attention.

For the Catholic religious orders, one source of competition has stemmed from the increasing "parochialization" of their members' activities. Instead of working in their own schools or hospitals, Catholic sisters increasingly serve in diocesan offices, or else in local parishes as pastors,[14] directors of religious education, pastoral associates, and the like: "The increasingly widespread insertion of religious into diocesan and parochial positions, *to the point where such commitments take precedence over involvements in the lives of their [orders]*, is a growing phenomenon."[15] When all sisters had worked in their own schools and hospitals, weekends or some other agreed-upon time might be deliberately left open for the orders' own assemblies. Weekends are, however, precisely the time when parish work is most demanding. It has become more and more difficult to find meeting times which can accommodate an ever-wider set of ministerial obligations.

The active members of both the Catholic religious orders and the office of deaconess have also begun to feel competing loyalties to other poles: their families, their co-workers, their clienteles. Since the late 1950s, deaconesses in some denominations have been permitted to marry and yet remain deaconesses. The one focus group of active deaconesses, therefore, noted the pull of family ties:

> It's hard, though, particularly if you're married. I had a very difficult time meeting my educational needs in order to become a deaconess. The only thing that was offered to me was to travel to a seminary and go for two weeks of intensive study and leave my husband and three children (Focus Group 4.3: Active deaconesses).

Similarly, the mission society focus groups unanimously agreed that one reason for the lessened participation of younger women was the competing demands of work and family.

Professional ties have also competed for the sisters' and deaconesses' loyalty. Even the few nuns and religious priests or brothers who still occupied positions in their orders' colleges or hospitals often felt stronger ties to the professional guild in which they had been trained than they did to their own orders. Where colleges or hospitals once were "ministerial subcultures" within the larger culture of the orders that had staffed them, such institutions now foster competing professional subcultures and loyalties *outside* of the order.[16] One study of Holy Cross College found that the older faculty—both the lay professors and the Jesuits—"were dedicated teachers and passionately loyal to Holy Cross." The younger faculty, including the younger Jesuit faculty, "were loyal to their professional field first of all" and sometimes chose professional obligations over commitment to their order.[17]

In addition to the professional staff, the Catholic religious order administrators of these institutions also underwent a similar shift of loyalty:

> In 1960, [Jesuit college administrators] were men who were usually but not invariably credentialed as academics. Their task was to govern the local Jesuit community, preside over the college or university for a short span of years, answer for their performance to their religious superior and then move on to another assignment. By the end of the decade, the presidents were specifically trained as academics.[18]

These men now rose to administration through academic, not religious order, career tracks; they were hired for indefinite appointments and, when they moved, they took up other positions in higher education. They were free from responsibility for, and to, the local Jesuit house, and were primarily accountable to lay boards. "The new presidents are more professional than their predecessors. They tend to form closer bonds with fellow educators than with fellow religious, with alumni than with students, with donors than with scholars."[19] Such men had "informal immunity" from being assigned by their superiors to other positions, and their independent power bases thus limited the demands which their order could make on them.[20] At least one national study found that this situation has made it difficult for the supervisors of religious orders to exercise the amount of leadership over their members that they had enjoyed in the past, and, as a result, few now even try to do so.[21]

Three of the sisters' focus groups were composed of present or former leaders within their orders. These women were keenly aware of their reduced power over the rest of the membership, and of the difficulties this engendered:

> Well, I could say right off the bat, I think we moved from a very autocratic kind of leadership, wouldn't you say, to a more participative kind of leadership. I mean, that's the only way you can do it—they'd kill you otherwise. [general laughter] I mean, definitely (Focus Group 1.2: Present and former leaders).

> - I think, as I reflect on leadership in the past and leadership now, regardless of who's in it, I think leadership has to be much more accountable to the community than they did in the past. [Before], everybody didn't feel like they had to know everything, and now we all feel like we want to know what's going on and participate in decision-making.
> - We struggle to find how to have that happen, most of the time (Focus Group 2.3: Present and former leaders).[22]

In contrast, the rank and file, by and large, celebrated the change:

> - I'd like to say this one thing, too, about the changes that we've experienced. And this, to me, has been a positive one, that we have collaboration in our jobs, that we have discussion and it's open. I think we're treated in a more adult fashion than we used to be, which I appreciated. We have dialog and our needs are respected and our weaknesses are respected and our strengths are respected and I find that a very positive change and one that I appreciate.
> - I would ditto the same thing. It's very comfortable to be told what to do and when to do it. It's much more challenging this way (Focus Group 1.5: Active sisters).

This delegation of authority and responsibility to individual members, however, has made it extremely difficult for the orders' leadership to do any long-term strategic planning. They cannot be assured that any of the members will be willing actually to serve in the order's institutions, since they can no longer be required to do so. In the words of an older Jesuit:

> The provincial could no longer effectively assign ministers if they were no longer acceptable to the ministries they were assigned to. With that came gradually an unforeseen diminution in the corporate identity of the society. The irony was that this was happening at the same time . . . when we began to engage in planning programs and we adopted the Arthur D. Little model, which was a highly rational model based upon management by objectives . . . [yet] the power of anyone in the congregation to manage this was being diminished by the structural changes we were experiencing.[23]

The leaders' focus groups made similar comments:

> And the hardest thing about leadership, to me, was to try to make a difference, to do some leading while presiding over all this chaos. [General laughter, comments of "Yeah"] . . . I do have a vivid recollection of the fact that when I was the [leader of the order], I endeavored to have conversations about whether we just individually choose our ministries or if there's some element of taking the community's viewpoint into consideration. Maybe I had the kind of shock you [points to another sister] had, you know—you almost dare not raise the question (Focus Group 2.3: Present and former leaders).

In one mission society focus group containing several former district officers, the participants also worried about the society's ability to elicit long-term commitments from its members:

> In the traveling I've been able to do [as district officer] and so forth, it's a world-wide trend. It isn't limited to just one area, and the reason the women give is . . . they have too many other things to do and all they want is short-term kind of activities. They don't want something like [the mission society's traditionally-sponsored drug treatment facility], that you've got to do for the long term.

[Interviewer: what would a short term activity be?]
Doing something right now, and you're done with it, you don't have to worry about it the rest of the year, OK? And I think that's why we're giving up a lot of our property and a lot of the homes and things that we have been taking care of all these years, is because that's long term (Focus Group 5.9: Mission society).

Therefore, however helpful sponsored institutions may have been for fostering communal bonding in the past, the sisters, deaconesses, and mission society members are no longer able to use them for this purpose. This does not seem likely to change in the future, as isomorphic pressures prevent a return to the institution's communal role.

Organizational Pride

Another way schools, hospitals, and social service agencies once united the members of the orders or mission societies was through their vicarious identification with the accomplishments of these institutions. The extent to which members derive a sense of "collective self-esteem" from the successes of the organization to which they belong is, however, a dynamic process which fluctuates as their contact with other reference groups increases or decreases. Eventually, contacts with other actors in the organizational field may shift one's identification and pride away from whether the sponsored institutions do well or not.[24]

Some of the sisters in the focus groups still felt a strong identification with the schools and hospitals where their order had once served:

I think it is really part of my own understanding of myself, that even when I was not serving in a Sister of X institution, I always took pride in the institutions that existed, whether they were in [city] or around the nation. There is a way in which I identify when I see a Sister of X hospital, a Sister of X school, a Sister of X college: "That—that's me, too!" It's not just about what *I'm* doing (Focus Group 2.1: Active sisters).

But this is less and less often the case:

- You know, I couldn't tell you what goes on at the [order's] college, hardly, if I read their paper. There's this sense of pride, you know. It did something for the individual, too, you know. That's, that's what I see is missing.
- Something intangible, it's hard to describe, that's gone.
- Yeah, there's a spirit that you had then that's not in existence now.
- Yeah (Focus Group 3.4: Retired sisters).

Some of the mission society members, too, felt less identification with the success of institutions in which they had once been highly involved, and were therefore less willing to support them:

> I think there is probably a lack of knowledge and a lack of education in each one
> of our [local mission society chapters] to keep us informed of what's going on at
> the state level. You know, we just focus on the local and [if] we have a meeting
> when the officers report on their district meetings or whatever, it's usually not
> well-attended and not well listened to. I mean, it seems like a drone, "We did this
> and we did that." From my point of view, it's not interesting (Focus Group 5.2:
> Mission society).

> We have a financing system in our whole church where each congregation is
> supposed to pay a particular amount into the operation of the general church.
> And, uh, we've had things over the past 25 years where, if you don't like what the
> church is doing, you withhold your money. Um, technically, that's illegal and it
> has some ramifications, but, you know, that's what happens, and we don't have
> a way of punishing, really. So that unrest is there, along with, I think, the whole
> feeling in the country today—get away with Big Government, get away with Big
> Brother, get away with whoever is looking over your shoulder. But I still think
> there are things for centralized structures and denominations as a whole to do that
> individuals and congregations cannot and will not (Individual Interview: Retired
> deaconess).

In his recent book, *Bowling Alone*, Robert Putnam notes that American society
as a whole is losing its traditions of communal bonding and voluntary group
activity. As a result, he argues, our daily lives are less connected to each other, with
detrimental results to our safety, health, and happiness.[25] The focus group responses
appear to indicate that religious orders and societies, too, may be feeling a similar
decline in "community," as a direct result of their decreased opportunities to
support and serve in their former institutions.

Conclusions

In addition to their iconic/symbolic value, therefore, the various institutions once
run and supported by the sisters, deaconesses, and mission society members had
also served as places where they could develop a distinct *esprit de corps*, fostered
and sustained by their common activities, common memories, and feelings of
mutual cohesion and support. Members felt a vicarious pride in and identification
with the growth and success of these institutions. Loyalty to the institution was, in
a real sense, also loyalty to the sponsoring order or society. As ties to these
institutions weakened, fewer opportunities were available for community-building
interaction. Competing professional and local loyalties began to drain time and
energy which had once been focused on the order or society. Members were no
longer as likely to feel a thrill of proprietary pride when speaking of the successes
of "our" clinic, college, or hospital. Loss of these institutions thus had a pro-

foundly weakening effect on the sponsoring group's identity, which was only partially offset by the development of new roles and activities in other arenas.

The loss of their institutions had other impacts as well, however. Chapter 9 will explore how changing the focus and setting of the sisters', deaconesses', and mission society members' activities had unexpected ramifications for their *performance* in these activities.

Notes

1. Wedam (2000a:232). See also Coleman (1987:208, 213) and Wedam (2000b:110).

2. This is truer of the male orders, which had been more likely to own their schools, than it is of the women's orders.

3. McDonough and Bianchi (2002:172).

4. Many cities also have zoning regulations which prohibit more than two unrelated adults from residing in the same house.

5. Gottemoeller (2005:273).

6. Bertrand (1998:10). See also Schneiders (2001:237).

7. Reported in Gottemoeller (2005:273). In addition to the 45 percent who preferred to live in a group of 4 to 7 sisters, 11 percent preferred to live alone; 14 percent preferred to live with one other sister, 12 percent in a group of 3, and 18 percent in groups larger than 7.

8. Schneiders (2001:27) makes this point.

9. The opinion that the amount of mutual *support* had increased was more common— occurring in 16 of the 27 focus groups. Still, this was fewer than the number of focus groups (23) claiming less support.

10. In a publication aimed especially at young women in Catholic religious orders, one writer noted that "sharing both life and ministry . . . has been a great way for me to get to know the sisters and to better understand the mission of the congregation" (Soher 2003:5).

11. Bertrand (1998) notes the importance of common life and prayer in attracting young recruits to Catholic religious orders; West (1991:6) notes the importance of "fellowship: in attracting young recruits to the United Methodist Women."

12. Matthes (2003:7) makes this point.

13. Bartel (2001:379).

14. A role not restricted to ordained males—see Wallace (1992).

15. Gottemoeller (1997:127-8). Italics added.

16. Morey (1995:7).

17. O'Brien (1994:125). See Daigler (2000:183) for a similar observation on the Sisters of Mercy and their colleges. See also McDonough and Bianchi (2002:167), Morey (1995:2,7) and Gallin (2000:125).

18. Burtchaell (1998:484).

19. Burtchaell (1998:709).

20. Burtchaell (1998:583-4). See also Ebaugh (1993:108-109) for a similar assertion about sisters in professional roles.

21. Nygren and Ukeritis (1993:39-59).

22. One former leader, however, felt that this was a definite improvement: "I think the pressures of leadership have changed. . . I remember my first day on the governing board,

we're sitting here approving these physicians in [our hospital in a city on the other side of the country] and I'm thinking, "How do I know these physicians are really qualified? I'm taking someone else's word and why are doing this in [the order's headquarters city]? So I think as the responsibilities shifted, the nature of the pressures changed also. I saw these as primarily administrative responsibilities, and I think they detracted a bit from the exercise of leadership because we were so bogged down in management, and therefore the creative aspect of leadership and the engagement of the members was very limited. I see that very different in today's reality" (Sisters' Focus Group 3.6: Former Leaders and Staff).

23. Quoted in McDonough and Bianchi (2002:246).

24. See, for example, Bartel (2001:384).

25. Putnam (2000).

Chapter 9

Impact on Activities:
The Shift from Institutional Service

Chapter 6 has already documented the pronounced decline, both in the total number of sisters and deaconesses serving in religious institutions, and in the percentage of the institutions' staff and administers which these devoted women comprised. Additionally, however, the percentage of the active membership within the orders who are still serving in such institutions, as compared to those serving elsewhere, has also declined. One 1991 nationwide survey of Catholic male and female religious orders found that one of the strongest trends in the sisters' service was a shift "*from* works owned or sponsored by the institute *to* unsponsored works, while another [was] *from* institutionally based services *to* non-institutionally based services and *from* church-related services *to* non-church related services."[1]

Even in the fields of education, health care, and social work, the majority of currently active sisters and deaconesses no longer serve in their own traditional institutions—or, in some cases, in religious institutions at all. Of all the Sisters of Mercy involved in higher education, for example, only 54 percent were still serving in that order's own colleges by 1990.[2] As early as the 1940s, fewer than two-thirds of all deaconesses and home missionaries were serving the Methodist Church. By the 1970s, local and regional activities such as sponsoring retreats, enrichment workshops, and training experiences for the members of the women's missionary societies were tending to overshadow the traditional goals of learning about and raising funds for global ministries.

The members of the focus groups reflected, to some extent, this pattern of shifting away from institutional service. Of the 107 sisters in the focus groups who were still active, about half (52) worked either full- or part-time in the schools, hospitals, and social agencies traditionally staffed or sponsored by their orders. An additional 27 sisters worked in other Catholic settings not sponsored by their order, usually in local parishes. Five sisters were employed in secular organizations.[3] In the focus group of active deaconesses, participants were distributed evenly between work in traditional denominationally-based positions, local congregation work, and work in settings outside of the denomination.

Chapter 6 has documented the impact which the sisters' and deaconesses' reduced religious presence has had on their institutions. The primary focus of this book, however, is the reciprocal effect on the orders and mission societies themselves. How has their employment in new, non-institutionally-based, occupations affected the sisters, deaconesses, and mission society members?

Reduced Commitment to Institutional Maintenance

The participants in the sisters' focus groups unanimously agreed that they used to feel a sense of ownership regarding the schools and hospitals in which they served, whether or not these institutions had legally belonged to them:

> - The institution we have been speaking of, and that the two of us continue to minister in, was not officially a Sister of X-sponsored institution until two years ago. [Before that], we actually administered it for the Archdiocese. But it *felt like* [an X institution].
> - Yes
> - Yes, it did (Focus Group 2.1: Active sisters).

> - I think we felt we owned it. Yeah, we always said "our schools," you know, because they were staffed completely by sisters; you didn't even have lay teachers in the first nine or ten years I was out. And so you thought of it as, as yours. The question of whether we "owned" it or not—I don't think it ever even arose. It was simply our mission.
> - We didn't really mind whether we owned it or not.
> - No, no (Focus Group 3.1: Retired sisters).

Similar sentiments were expressed in ten of the 24 focus groups of Catholic sisters.

The schools and hospitals were, in a sense, "family businesses," in which everyone was expected to pitch in with whatever needed doing:

> We worked together, we did things together, and we never really measured—and I find, today, that's something that I see missing in people coming along. It wasn't a measurement, but, you know, if Sister Mary said to me, "I need help with this," and if I was free, that would not be a problem and we all kind of pitched in. I remember, up in the kitchen, we kind of, like, all helped each other. People didn't walk off and leave each other (Focus Group 1.3: Active sisters).

> When we first started out, everybody was kind of gung-ho because we were all living together, and when you started school at the beginning of the year, you knew you had that whole force with you. . . . You just knew that all the bulletin boards needed to be put up, everything had to be cleaned, and you don't have that

today. It's a different feeling when you're going about your business, when you're dealing with a lay faculty because of their own contributions or limitations. You kinda just—It was a game when you first started out (Focus Group 2.6: Active and retired sisters).

I think that's the way it was in the beginning, that was one of the strong points, was the teamwork in our institutions. You know, we were the ones that did everything. And so, we worked together and, and it was really great to see what we were able to do together. Whether teaching or orphanage or whatever. I think that was one of the good things in the early days (Focus Group 3.2: Retired sisters).

In contrast, the present bureaucratization of their institutions has rendered them much less attractive to the sisters and deaconesses. As several thoughtful observers in both denominational and academic settings have noted, the bureaucratization of church institutions usually has the effect of increasing the distance between one's faith and one's work: organizational administrators must make morally ambiguous decisions which may have bad, or at least unforeseen, effects; the amount of time and effort which must be spent on "money-grubbing" is seen as illegitimate; and workers begin to feel that they are merely cogs in a large structure over which they have little control.[4] A sister who administered a large Catholic hospital admitted to the *Wall Street Journal* that "one-half of my brain is what's the right thing to do; one-half is a clinking cash register."[5] This distancing between religious calling and the bureaucratic demands of one's profession is not confined to religious orders in North America: one Argentinian Jesuit, speaking at an international conference on Catholic religious orders in Rome, listed the "dulling" of the sense of vocation by professionalism, efficiency, and productivity as a key way in which modern culture has impacted religious life.[6]

Working in such large and impersonal settings can be profoundly alienating, especially if, as Weisbrod notes, new administrators are hired whose primary backgrounds have been in the private business sector.[7] Participants in several focus groups mentioned feeling this alienation:

[Interviewer] You seem to be indicating that it was different to teach in a denomination-sponsored—
- Very different. Very different.
[Interviewer] In what way?
- Uh, you don't have the support, you don't have the security, you don't have the connection with the other workers. Well, when I left X Hospital, which was a [denomination]-related agency, I needed to stay in [state] to take care of my dad. So I took a job with a state agency school for retarded people and my supervisor kept telling me, over and over and over again, "You've got to learn a new chain of command." A new chain of command. [Distastefully] And it *was* a new chain of command. [Several others nod.] (Focus Group 4.2: Retired deaconesses).

- I think one of the frustrations I have in the hospital is that, as we move more and

more away from the sisters' ownership of it, it's becoming more and more a job. Where our whole system was always a ministry. And so, it's becoming more and more a business, and I've heard that about all health care.
- I would agree with your frustration about the hospital. I see our schools becoming big business, too. . . . And it pains me when I see all that went on, all the sweat, blood, and tears that we put into the schools and how much we loved them, and we started Catholic education in [state], our community did, and then to see it turn into this. One of our sisters, who was the [diocesan] superintendent of education, with one secretary, covered the entire diocese and visited every school at least twice a year. We now have three superintendents who seldom visit the schools, if ever, and don't know what's going on—don't even know the people working there. It pains me very much to see how our schools have gone in the direction they have gone (Focus Group 1.3: Active sisters).

The bureaucratization of non-profit institutions may also lead, at times, to daily compromises that workers, clients, and funders consider unsavory, morally ambiguous, or in conflict with the organization's basic mission.[8] Such compromises can affect the support which the religious sponsors are willing to provide.

This new institutional wariness was reflected in the focus group interviews. Several sisters expressed the fear that their orders could no longer exercise sufficient control over their institutions to prevent them from engaging in activities that were contrary to their religious mission:

I know that all life is compromise, but you now you just, when you're in the middle of it, and I'm in senior management, and I'm at the board discussions and the budget discussions—you realize that those are things over which you have very little control. The question is, do you chuck that and say, "OK, let's try to get into a situation where we can really have control"—and the truth is that we won't ever be there—or do you use where you are to be a platform to serve, even though it's not a perfect situation? (Focus Group 2.6: Active and retired sisters).

This feeling that the institutions were slipping from the sisters' ability to control, or even influence, has been a pervasive theme in other studies as well:

– We at X College . . . no longer have much impact on students, because of our diminished presence in classrooms and administration. Most students graduate without seeing any Sisters of Mercy in action, and without any knowledge of the history of the community at X College.
– Older [lay] faculty share our values, but the newer ones don't even have much (if any) contact with us.
– It is increasingly difficult to influence our sponsored ministries since our [order's] numbers in key positions are diminishing.[9]

As a retired board member of her order's hospital's noted in one of the preliminary interviews:

Now this would be my problem if I were in administration [of the religious order] these days: how much do you turn over to other people and how much do you know what's going on? [Interviewer: Is that a problem that they have to deal with a lot?] I think it is. Personally, that was a reason why I wanted to get off the boards. My last evaluation for the administrator whose board I was on at the time—he was a great man, his evaluations were great, but he was so *involved* with everything outside the hospital, like, oh, commissions, merging for this, clinics for that, and taking on another hospital here. And that's what your top administrators *have* to do these days. Collaborate with everybody and everything you can, but I—and my evaluation wasn't just for him, it was a trend I saw with our religious community and not just us, but any Catholic hospital—we turned over so much responsibility and things to people that we can't be hands-on. They do have great people under them. And they have to let the people perform. But I said about this particular one: he, like all of them, was building a real empire for himself. And I said, "You don't want a person like that unless they *are* good. And they're going to go out and do all these things. But at the same time, when he gets a better job offer, he could leave *tomorrow* and leave every responsibility off to the sisters." And I just think that it's an awful lot of responsibility to take on, when you're not sure you know what's going on in it (Individual Sister Interview: Former hospital CEO and board president).

Thirteen of the 24 sisters' focus groups and two of the three deaconesses' focus groups expressed similar concerns about their reduced ability to control their institutions' drift toward bureaucratization and secularization:

Most people in most institutions no longer feel loyalty to the institution because they don't feel the institution can be loyal to them. It's beyond many institutions, where they are governed by finances and the government and so I find that among most of my lay colleagues, I don't find the kind of loyalty you found in the past to an institution. . . . It's become—I mean, America has become more and more individualistic and it's more and more "I have to look out for myself," and it's very hard when you're the only [sister] in the group and you feel responsible for the morale and the attitudes and trying to bring a positive atmosphere. . . That's gone beyond even the institution's control. You're governed by all kinds of surveyors and insurance companies (Focus group 2.1: Active sisters).

There is a growing distaste in the orders and mission societies for service in these increasingly bureaucratized institutions. This is reflected in a theology that increasingly devalues such institutionalized activities in favor of "hands-on," personalized service. As one Mennonite theologian expressed it, "to institutionalize certain tasks of the body of Christ is to distort, or at least reshape, our understanding of that body."[10] One recent, and widely read, Catholic theologian claimed that:

After the [Vatican] Council, many religious congregations experienced a strong desire to divest themselves of institutional holdings, especially large schools, hospitals, agencies and even mother houses or other centers of government. The motive was primarily to jettison some of the "baggage" they felt impeded them from discerning and responding to new needs. Vested interests buttressed by historical attachments and the non-negotiable commitments of their financial resources and personnel had made them maintainers and mangers rather than risk-taking missionaries. *While some of the divestment may have been too hasty and perhaps ill-planned, the basic instinct was . . . very sound.*[11]

Members of Catholic religious orders in both North America and Europe, therefore, began to devalue institutional service in favor of more personally-fulfilling, individualized service to the poor. As one Irish author noted:

> The closure of their institutions by religious [orders] was also the product of new social attitudes. Corporate achievement was no longer the most significant goal. The first half of the twentieth century had been a time for organizations and uniforms and being part of a team. . . . Joining a group and wearing a uniform were encouraged. . . . In contrast, the post-1945 era would turn its back on such identities and encourage individualism, personal achievement, and fulfillment.[12]

Many saw their institutions as stultifying and hierarchical remnants of a past which they would be better off without. Several of the sisters in this study agreed:

> I'm sure our hospitals are going to do something, but I don't know what. You know, it's something different every day. And it's getting so big . . .[Interviewer: what do people think about that?] I, I'd like to see us get out of it. [Interviewer: For any reason?] I think it's such a big business. We have maybe one sister, a board president only. Maybe two sisters in a hospital. I don't see how we can say it is *our* hospital (Individual Sister Interview: Former hospital administrator).

Local chapters of Protestant mission societies, too, are now less enthusiastic about underwriting institutional maintenance in preference to direct, local aid.

Participants in some of the focus groups regretted this prevailing impulse to discard institutions:

> I understand the purpose of the schools had gone, but now, same with the children's homes, they were closing those, and now social services is begging for them to have some homes for the children, you know (Focus Group 4.1: Retired deaconesses).

> - The [mission society] used to own buildings where they would house poor people who were unable to take care of themselves.
> - Yes.
> - But now [mission society] is getting rid of all their property.
> [Interviewer: Do you think that's a good thing or a bad thing?]
> - I think it's bad.
> [Interviewer: Why?]
> - Who's going to take them over?
> - Are they selling them?
> - That's one of the things that they are saying. That they aren't gong to own

property any more. If you remember, the most giving and mission-minded people in the [denomination] were the women, from the very beginning. If the women were not there doing the mission, I'm not sure the men would have thought about some of the things that were being done. The women kept before them the things concerning women and children. That was our emphasis. . . . That's the concern I have, is that the things that we had been doing we are going to lose (Focus Group 5.9: Missionary society).

Increasingly, however, many of the focus group members expressed the feeling that individualized service outside of a religious institution was just as sacred a calling as working in a denominational organization—if not more so:

- The fact that my bread wasn't paid for by money that came from 475 Riverside Drive didn't mean to me that I wasn't in the place that God wanted me to be in.
- That's true.
- Yes. (Focus Group 4.2: Retired deaconesses).

A good part of our struggle as Sisters of X has been to stay with the situation that has become so complicated in health care. I say that as an outsider to health care. But then there is a place where you have to wonder, should we shake the dust from our heels? Especially as we grow older and have less energy for bullshit. So these are just things that go through my mind (Focus Group 2.1: Active sisters).

Whether or not the sisters and deaconesses in the focus groups celebrated or bemoaned the fact, however, the overall trend has been that fewer and fewer of them are able—or willing—to find employment in the schools, hospitals, and social service agencies where their predecessors had once labored almost exclusively.

Parochialization

Where, then, do the sisters, deaconesses, and mission society members focus their efforts? Many who still wish to minister in a church setting often find themselves doing so in local parishes. For Catholic men's orders, this "drift of manpower out of their schools and colleges and into pastoral ministries" has made their members' lives more like those of diocesan priests.[13] Catholic sisters, too, have found a larger percentage of their membership serving in parishes as directors of religious education, pastoral associates, or even as "pastors" in the absence of a priest. Within the focus groups, almost as many of the non-retired sisters served in parishes (22 in 10 different focus groups) as worked in the orders' schools (23 sisters in 10 groups). Only eight sisters still taught or filled support positions in Catholic grade schools; another four were principals there.

Another tendency has been to concentrate on *spiritual* services, often distanced from any institutional setting:

Table 9.1. Employment of Active Sisters and Deaconesses

	# Sisters	# Deaconesses
Elementary Education (Catholic schools)		
Teaching	2	
Administration	4	
Support Staff*	6	
Elementary Education (public schools)		
Support Staff*	1	
Elementary Education (private schools)		
Teaching	1	
Secondary Education (Catholic schools)		
Teaching	5	
Administration	2	
Support Staff*	4	
Other Education (not in schools)		2
College Education (non-sponsored)		
Support Staff*	1	
Faculty	1	
Health Care		
Nursing		
in sponsored hospital	0	
in outlying sponsored clinic	2	
Administration		
in sponsored hospital	7	
in another hospital	1	
Chaplaincy/Mission Effectiveness		6
Other health care**		
in sponsored institution	9	1
in other institution	2	
Parish Work	22	2

Continued on next page

Table 9.1—Continued

	# Sisters	# Deaconesses
Social Service		
in sponsored institution	4	1
in another institution	1	1
Church administrative position		
(diocesan or other admin)	2	
Full-time leadership of the religious order	4	
Part-time leadership of the religious order	4	
Internal service position		
within the religious order***	13	
Private practice, free-lancing, student	3	

* Includes librarian, guidance counselor, office staff, alumni relations.
** Includes music therapy, physical therapy, social work in hospitals
*** Includes archivist, receptionist, office work, other staff

> Spiritual direction is replete with Godtalk. "It's easier being in pastoral or social work to see ministry and priesthood and the Society as integrated into everything I do," a 56-year-old associate pastor says. . . . In contrast to all this hands-on pastoral work, the figure of the pastor-in-the-classroom as a model of Jesuit pedagogy and scholarly achievement, has not quite passed from the scene. But it has seen better days.[14]

For example, eight sisters in the focus groups worked in health care administration, but an almost equal number were in hospital chaplaincy or pastoral care positions. Only two were engaged in actual nursing, and both of these were in an outlying clinic.

The deaconesses in the focus groups had had a different experience. Until the middle 1960s, they had worked in the schools, clinics, and community centers sponsored by the missionary societies of their denomination. A denominational re-organization and a change in its institutional policies abruptly deprived most of them of these positions:

> - I'll never forget when the change came. [In the past], when we were trying to

recruit deaconesses, we could say, "You're offered a job, you'll always have a job, you'll have a pension." and so forth. And then all of a sudden you could not assure them a job, you could not assure them a pension.
- That's right.
- Nothing (Focus Group 4.1: Retired deaconesses).

Two of the active deaconesses in the focus groups worked in local congregations of their denomination, another worked in the denomination's retirement home for deaconesses, and one in a denomination-sponsored social work agency. The rest worked in social work or educational programs that were run either by other denominations or by state agencies.

Tensions often exist between the sisters or deaconesses and the church—both in the larger denomination and also in the local congregations which they have to face on a day-to-day basis:

My second frustration is I also work with the parish staff and I think that working collaboratively is a big frustration for me. You try to help people who want to love the Church as much as you do, but on the other hand, you're not the one that makes the total decision. I don't have the power that the parish staff, certain people, do. So that's frustrating (Focus Group 2.5: Active sisters).

- I think sometimes for me the frustration comes between dealing with the pastoral needs of the teens I work with and dealing within the legal structures of the Church, and sometimes the two are just diametrically opposed. The tension can be really healthy, but it can also sometimes be frustrating.
- I think I'd like to ditto the restrictions. . . . I'm not saying I want to be ordained, but for me it's frustrating that we haven't changed with the changing times to minister to these people (Focus Group 3.11: Young sisters).

Six of the active sisters' and deaconesses' focus groups, when asked to cite what was frustrating about their current work, mentioned such conflicts.

This tension has led to questions, in some focus groups, about whether denominational officials even cared about the continued existence of the sisters and deaconesses:

- I wonder if they [the young deaconesses] feel that the church is supporting them. How much they feel the support of the church or what it is that does hold them together, the young people just being commissioned.
- There was really a great deal of concern, I feel, on the part of the deaconesses about what is happening. And when we would ask the question again and again, and I was on a national committee at that time, "Does the Church really want us?" And we couldn't get an answer. Quadrennium after quadrennium, and there was just no answer. (Focus Group 4.1: Retired deaconesses).

The other thing I would like to see, I would like to see a relationship within the conference. There's been no acknowledgment of my commissioning other than a letter from the bishop. . . . And every time I'd go to the Annual Conference, there was no room for me, no registration material for me, nothing. I asked my church pastor if there was anything I could do for the church and he said no (Focus Group 4.3: Active deaconesses).

Dealing with the denominational bureaucracy is also frustrating:

I applied to the [denominational central headquarters] and wanted to teach English as a second language in the X Program in China. And I called [headquarters] to get an application, [pauses] and I called [headquarters again] to get an application, and [pauses meaningfully, others laugh] and so I finally got this application, and when I got it, it was in January of 1990 and I had like, I think, like 24 hours to fill it out because it was due. And it was, you remember, a nine- or ten-page application, and I think I stayed up all night trying to do the best answer I could and I turned it in and I waited and I didn't hear anything and so I called them in February and they were like, still processing. And I called them in March, and they were like, "Oh, we processed your application and you have an interview as a [U.S. missionary] today." And I thought I applied for ESL internationally. But they said, "Oh, those slots are filled." And so I went, when it came time for this interview. In May, I called again to get information and it came to me at my address, but it had another woman's name on it [laughter] (Focus Group 4.3: Active deaconesses).

A basic dichotomy thus exists in both cases: on the one hand, a larger percentage of active sisters are working directly in parish-based ministry, but they are experiencing more frustration with the official Church as a result. Deaconesses express a desire to work more closely with their local and regional denomination, but are put off by cumbersome bureaucracy and a lack of support from church officials. In each case, the resulting tension may further distance these women from their denomination at a time when few institutional ties remain to draw them together.

The mission societies experienced another type of parochialization. Frequently, the moneys raised by local chapters were used, not by the missions or social services they had traditionally supported, but by the local congregation. Five of the nine mission society focus groups mentioned this diversion of funds:

- At one time, our [local chapter] had enough that we bought parlor furniture.
- But that isn't supposed to be done.
- And we furnished the kitchen, too. We supplied a lot in the kitchen (Focus Group 5.1: Mission society).

[Interviewer: So you've raised money for the capital campaign fund?]
- Oh, yes.
- That's over and above the regular budget.
- Not only do [our local chapters] give a lot to charity, but they have helped to put bricks and mortar into this building and—
- there's been a few years in the past that the church would not have made the apportionate payments without [our mission society chapter's] giving them the

money. (Focus Group 5.3: Mission society).

- Our budget is just around $30,000. . . . Some of that goes to our district pledges, and then a lot goes out to the community. And a lot goes toward missions within this particular church. For example, we might support preschool choir robes or educational materials or world mission work for a group that goes on mission trips.
- What did we give away last year—$19,000 or $20,000?
- My gosh, I think our budget was around $25,000, and in addition to that, we raised $80,000 for the new [church] building (Focus Group 5.4: Mission society).

Note that this is against the mission society's official policy, as one focus group, which contained a district official, pointed out:

- Now, Judy, is it a rule that we are not to take any money, like the money we made on the cookie walk, we are not to take that money and do anything for the [local] church with it?
- That's right.
- That's right. Every dollar—The only time you can do that is if you do it not as [the mission society].
- Right. Once it goes into the books of the [mission society], it has to be used by the guidelines of giving, and I'm not sure what percentage. It used to be 60 percent went for missions, and that meant you sent it to [the mission society headquarters], 25 percent stays within your local community for missions, and 15 percent is what you use for programming and membership development (Focus Group 5.6: Mission society).

While all nine of the mission society focus groups did engage in the organization's traditional activities of supporting home and foreign missions, over half also assisted local, interdenominational, or even secular services (e.g., a battered women's shelter, the Interfaith Hospitality Network, Habitat for Humanity, etc.), and a third also engaged in service activities for their fellow congregants.

Job Security

As religious institutions adopted more mainstream hiring practices, the members of the sponsoring group had to compete with lay professionals for institutional positions which once had been reserved exclusively for them. In Protestant women's mission societies during the early twentieth century, the rise of a "Science of Mission" led to replacement of the mission societies' volunteer members by professional social workers, newsletter editors, etc., even if these new professionals had had no previous missionary experience.[15] Catholic institutions were slower to shift preference from religious to professional qualifications. Prior to the 1970s, if the members of the sponsoring religious order had prepared themselves to fill a staff or administrative position, they could reasonably expect to be hired for it. In fact, as was noted in Chapter 4, the sisters in the focus groups were sometimes *less* qualified for the positions they filled than a lay professional would have been, but they were hired anyway.

Today, this is no longer the case. The current hiring process at the Catholic as well as the Protestant institutions favors the most professionally credentialed applicant, irrespective of religious affiliation.[16] As a result, and sometimes with no advance warning, many sisters now find themselves without a job. "In some cases, this resulted from sudden congregational losses of institutional ministries, which left religious 'jobless.'. . . In other cases, [the sisters] finished education undertaken to prepare them for positions in their order's institutions and saw these institutions disappear or be turned over to others just as they were ready to assume responsibility for them."[17]

Protestant deaconesses had similar experiences. In one denomination, academically-qualified deaconesses were even deliberately *excluded* from service in their denomination's institutions:

> Trends in missionary personnel disfavored deaconesses. By 1978, new, "fresh" personnel programs grew because they carried "no historical baggage" and smacked of "relevance.". . . The President of the southeastern Jurisdiction reported to the National Committee her concern that some deaconesses and home missionaries were "being told to find their own jobs." To ask deaconesses and home missionaries "to go find their own jobs" betrayed their covenant with the church.[18]

In the new administrative structure, no office was specifically charged with the issue of what to do with personnel displaced by the new policy. The plight of the deaconesses thus got little attention.[19]

In several focus groups, participants noted that this loss of job security had been upsetting:

> - A person who becomes a deaconess now, sometimes they go out and get their own job.
> - That's right.
> - They have no support of the local church. They might be working in a factory—
> - That's right.
> - and have no support of the local church, or the local [women's missionary society] or anything. And that's so different from what we knew.
> - Yeah, because we really knew we were set. We were supported and had a job (Focus Group 4.1: Retired deaconesses).

> When it came time to, to make their own decisions and hunt jobs and all that, it was traumatic. . . . It was terribly hard for some sisters. You lost that support, you know, that you'd always, you'd lived with so many years (Focus Group 3.2: Retired sisters).

In thirteen focus groups, several sisters and deaconesses also noted that they were now unable to find work in their former institutions, even as volunteers, because of the extensive bureaucratic procedures required:

> Because the laity is so educated these days, we have—sisters don't have any more jobs. Like in the parish, it's hard to get a job in the parish. . . . You can't look to the school, because you're out of the schools, and you can't look to the church community because they've already got the jobs filled with lay people. (Focus Group 1.4: Active sisters).

> - But the difficulty now is that you can't always do those kinds of things unless you have all these credits after your name, you know. I think that's a big thing that has changed. It's that kind of a spirit of, "Well, I can do that, so let me do it," you know. But they *can't* always let you do it because there is some kind of report that has to have something on it.
> - That's even true at [order's infirmary/retirement facility for its own sisters] for pastoral care, I'm sure.
> - I'll bet.
> - Sisters have been willing to visit the sick and pray with them. But as far as doing the charting, they've got to be chaplains; they've got to be trained. And so, that's been a changeover in attitude and adjustment for people. And of course Pastoral Care would like, as an organization, they want to be taken seriously as health care people and that makes sense, so it does require education (Focus Group 3.5: Active sisters).

Others in the sisters' focus groups mentioned additional complications. For example, in these new, more bureaucratized ministries, even those that had traditionally been theirs, they could now actually be fired:

> I still feel ownership of X High School [order's school, where respondent currently teaches], but I'm not exactly sure that we own X High School any more. So I might really be working for someone else now. It's like being on a little bit different limb, because I keep thinking, if I go too far out on the limb, I could, somebody could fire me. I mean, that's a possibility. I'm not terribly worried about that, but it's an interesting thought that has, um, that's just there, now (Focus Group 3.5: Active sisters).

> I said, if they want to get rid of me, they're going to have to fire me, because as long as the patient knows there's someone who cares, I'm going to be here. No matter what happens. And that's what happened. They fired me. No, they just got rid of my department. Our department was one of the first departments to go. (Focus Group 3.10: Active sisters).

This led to worries of unemployment and age discrimination—a new feeling for the sisters—and to the fear of being "trapped" in their current occupation:

> - But there's a fear there, too, like after it's closed, your job is gone. And there's

a feeling that you'll never, that you won't be able to find one, or what kind of job. Will they take me now?—especially if you're getting old.
- In your 50s or even your late 40s (Focus Group 1.4: Active sisters).

This is a question that gets right at where I have spent a lot of thought and have had a lot of concern over the past number of years, because it goes back to something [another focus group participant] said about not moving now. Particularly as one gets older and has more experience than previously, you're less hireable because you're too experienced, too educated, and too old for all the positions. . . . It makes finding a position very difficult if you want to change (Focus Group 2.5: Active sisters).

When I went on sabbatical, I never realized how difficult it would be at the end of the sabbatical time to begin another ministry. Up to that point, people were asking you to come [and work for them], and there was a sense that I was one with this ministry and that I would always have a position in our community. And then you take a sabbatical and you realize that things have changed so much outside that you're not sure you did the right thing. Even though the sabbatical year was the most wonderful year, you're not sure it was the right thing because what is there after it? And so, like those people who have been in the same ministry for 25 years—I know I'm not a 25-year person, but there's a fear inside of me now to let go of the ministry that I'm in because I don't know what's next (Focus Group 2.1: Active sisters).

There was a certain amount of nostalgia for their vanished security, and a worry about the implications of the new, competitive system:

- All these years we had somebody tell us where to go and what to do when we got there, there was somebody in charge to guide us through and tell us what we're going to do. And we felt safe and secure with this. And now we have to go out and ask for a job and apply for a job like anybody else.
- We didn't get fired. [laughter] (Focus Group 1.6: Active and retired sisters).

In all, eleven of the 24 sisters' focus groups and two of the three deaconesses' focus groups mentioned issues of job security. None of the mission society focus groups mentioned this; it has been several generations since the agencies they supported financially had also depended on their volunteer labor for staffing and administration, and none of them expected to be given such positions.

New Members and Institutional Service

As Chapters 3 and 7 have already described, the sisters' and deaconesses' institutions had once been an important channel drawing new recruits to the order. The high schools, colleges, and hospital nursing schools offered an opportunity for the young women studying there to get to know the sisters and deaconesses on a closer and more personal basis, and to become sufficiently familiar with their lifestyle to be attracted to it. Even for those not personally acquainted with sisters or deaconesses, the visible presence of their schools and hospitals was an iconic symbol of the purpose and identity of their order.

In contrast, sisters and deaconesses in several focus groups mentioned that, without this visible presence in their schools and hospitals, it was now harder for potential recruits to learn about them:

> So we don't have a real presence in that hospital. So that's different. I guess I would have to say that the lack of sisters, the lack of presence, you know, groups—that others can see us and say, "See how they love one another. See how they live together." That was what influenced most of us, I think. Most of us came from our college. We saw the sisters, we saw how they lived (Focus Group 1.1: Retired sisters).

Without the visible evidence of working in a specific institution, it was also hard for potential recruits to see what was different about the life of a sister or deaconess, when compared to that of any religious lay person. Many new recruits were already employed in professional service occupations, and they were well aware that providing a ministerial service no longer distinguishes sisters from laity. More and more, therefore, recruits to Catholic religious orders—even to the active, "apostolic"orders—list *spiritual* rather than *service* reasons for joining:

> [Recent entrants] express their purpose not so much in terms of service but in terms of community; that is, they seek to fulfill personal needs of belonging to a meaningful group that shares similar values, especially those of Christian living. Unlike the outward focus of earlier eras, today's recruits seem more focused upon personal spiritual development.[20]

To the extent that the new entrants are interested in service works at all, they do not want to work in the order's institutions, much less administer them. One national study found that, whereas 38 percent of the oldest cohort of Catholic sisters, brothers, and religious order priests had advanced degrees in education, only 15 percent of the youngest cohort did.[21] A similar study of Catholic health care, done in the mid-1980's, found that the "general picture was one of continuing decreases in the numbers of congregation personnel available for/interested in the health care ministry." Of the 51 sisters training for health care positions who were interviewed for this study, only twelve were training for top management posts and eight for other management positions. In comparison, 25 were training for direct service, usually in pastoral care.

The sisters in the present study agreed:

> Because of the big business aspect that's gotten into hospitals in the last few years, the young sisters, at least in [our order], who would be capable to go into these kinds of roles, that does not turn them on. And so, they are getting their

masters in whatever—they might get an MBA or they might get a nurse clini-
cian's masters—but they want to go out and go into the clinics, where they have
more contact (Individual Sister Interview: Former social service administrator,
present member of her order's council).

This sentiment was echoed in the focus groups:

[Interviewer: Are there any people coming up that are interested in becoming a
CEO of one of your institutions?]
- No. Not among the people we have.
- No.
- And a lot of them are [entering the order] because they want to do individual,
hands-on work. They want to get out of the corporate world (Focus Group 2.3:
Present and former leaders).

Given the lack of preferential hiring for sisters and deaconesses, even those
entrants who want to work in an institutional setting may be constrained to accept
positions in organizations not affiliated with their order or denomination. Some of
the sisters in the focus groups argued that they could still witness to the identity and
goals of their order while working as individuals in non-Church settings. However,
several admitted that they deliberately *concealed* their affiliation with the order, at
least initially:

Now, I'm in the public school system and I went in under "Miss Smith" and I did
that—they didn't ask me to—but I did that because I just wanted to be treated as
this individual person. Also, I wasn't sure how public school parents, as it were,
or teachers, the staff, personnel, administration would accept that title, and so
then, when I went in, I went in as "Miss Smith," but I just felt so accepted for me,
not for being a Sister of X and so on (Focus Group 3.7: Active sisters).

When I'm out in the field working with clients, and especially when we're
working with persons living with AIDS, I never go into the home identifying
myself as a sister. And I found I needed to do that because many individuals who
are living with AIDS are homosexual and they know what the stance of the
Church is and right away they tend, you know, there's that feeling that they're not
going to be accepted. "You're coming to care for me only because you have to"
(Focus Group 3.11: Young sisters).

In a few instances, respondents mentioned that identification with their order
was detrimental to effective ministry *even in its own sponsored institutions*:

It was very hard to minister when I first went into a Sister of X-sponsored
organization to do pastoral ministry . . . it was the first time I ever did anything
for our [order] and I was flabbergasted—And nobody would talk to me, nobody
would share anything with me. It was very hard for me to do a lot of the pastoral
ministry with the staff because I was "one of *them*," they didn't know if they
could trust me. I don't know where it came from, and it still exists (Focus Group

3.11: Young sisters).

The impact of job diversification on the sisters' and deaconesses' ability to recruit new members is, therefore, mixed. On the one hand, they have lost the visibility they formerly had. And individually-based occupations are not an adequate substitute: the sisters and deaconesses working in them are often indistinguishable from the rest of the staff. On the other hand, at least some sisters claimed that continuing to work in their traditional institutions was no solution either. Their numbers have become so few that their distinctive presence has been diluted. And, since isomorphic pressures have forced administrators of religious schools and hospitals to make often unpopular decisions, the few sisters who continue to work there often bear the brunt of staff or client dissatisfaction with policies they had no hand in shaping. The youngest sisters were, therefore, much less likely to value serving in these institutions and preferred to work elsewhere.

Strategic Planning

As a result of the gradual attenuation of the institutions' religious identity and the marginalization of their mission concerns, as well as of the increasing alienation of younger members from institutional service, there is often a profound disjuncture between the needs of institutional sponsorship and the willingness and/or ability of the sponsoring group to meet them. This makes it hard to plan for the group's future. Large-scale structural trends—professional specialization, increased market competition in both education and health care, and the erosion of institutional control by the order—have resulted in "the sense that ministry is what goes on locally and rather haphazardly in the midst of larger, barely comprehensible forces."[22] In this fragmented institutional environment, there is little opportunity, or incentive, for co-ordination and planning by leadership:

> Perhaps most noticeable is the absence of a vision and a comprehensive plan for the education of young members. Individual choice and personal option, rather than a structured plan, seem to guide most decisions about ongoing education, and these choices are usually not tied to a clearly articulated mission. Consequently, ministerial focus with deliberate and specified goals is lacking.[23]

As one administrator of her order's college put it:

> We will have only 22 sisters [in our order] under 65 by 2010, and I guarantee you that none are interested in corporate ministry. In hindsight, when we all began to get enamored of social justice and individual ministries in the 60s and 70s, we took our [novices] and made sure they had experiences in the central city, etc. But no one invited them to go into an institution and shadow an administrator or someone working there. Now there seems to be no interest, and, for most, no background that would be viable without years of education, for most of our

ministries within the corporate context.[24]

The staffing needs of the orders' traditional institutions—or of the larger denomination—are now rarely considered in Catholic orders, either in the training of new members or in the employment of already-educated members. One study found that survey respondents, when asked to rank 30 priorities to consider when choosing a ministry, gave *least* importance to "Maintaining sponsored institutions" and "The priorities of the diocese or archdiocese." The study's authors noted that this represented "a dramatic shift from the early days in the United States when congregations came to this country to meet the particular needs of the diocese and to do that ministry quite visibly in the name of their particular congregation."[25]

These trends show no sign of changing. When asked their future work plans, the sisters' focus groups contained six mentions of interest in serving in their orders' own institutions:

> If I reach the point where I am either told or realize that I am not effective in the classroom any more, then if there is a position that I can serve in the school, I would like to stay. If not, I would like to go to the Mother House and serve out there. Whatever, wherever they want me to work (Focus Group 3.5: Active sisters).

In contrast, there were over twice as many (16) mentions of interest in serving elsewhere:

> Part of my dream has been to have this big van that will have a counselor, nurse practitioner, chaplain, a clinic, like a holistic van. Take it up through the hollers in the mountains (Focus Group 1.4: Active sisters).

> I'm not planning on a change in ministry any time soon, but as I look to the future I expect [I will do] some pastoral ministry but not as focused on young people as I age and the need to work with adults becomes much more of a piece of me. But I'm not sure it's even going to be in a church setting (Focus Group 3.11: Young sisters).

> [Interviewer: What are your plans for after you leave office?] Well, one has always been to go down to Mexico and work in one of our missions. Another would really just be to get involved in some direct project with the poor. [Interviewer: You wouldn't go back to your order's hospital?] No, I don't see that, unless it was some kind of program attached to it. . . . If I did any direct kind of health care, you know—I still have my nursing license—it would be more like home health care (Individual Sister Interview: Former emergency room supervisor and present member of her order's council).

> I'd prefer direct service as opposed to administration. I think I've administered all my life and maybe it's time for somebody else to come in and do those kinds of jobs (Individual Sister Interview: Former social services administrator, present

member of her order's council).

Conclusions

The reduced involvement of the sisters, deaconesses, and mission society members with their traditional institutions has gone hand-in-hand with a reduced interest in such activities. It is difficult to say which came first:

> I'm wondering, if we look at our statistics—there aren't as many people in Sister of X-sponsored institutions: what does that really mean? Is it because of the things that we were just saying, that the hands of the institutions in many cases are tied, in terms of a person securing a position there? Or is it because they really don't believe in that? Because the majority of our sisters are not serving in [our] institutions, but, *would* they [if they could]? (Focus Group 2.1: Active sisters).

Whether due to unwillingness or inability, however, the result is the same: the movement of the sisters and deaconesses out of these institutions and the failure of ministering there to appeal to the orders' new recruits, in comparison to the attractiveness either of personal, individualized service or of more spiritually-focused, monastic groups.[26]

The substitution of individualized service and spiritual development for institutional commitments implies profound shifts in identity, recruitment, future financial stability, and a host of other issues for the orders, which many respondents cannot even begin to address:

> There isn't enough energy to face these questions . . . I think what hasn't happened and what I would like to see happen is that the Sisters of X haven't had a good discussion about what our mission is in health care. Any discussions we *have* had have tended to be on what to do with our institutions. . . . It's too hard to start something [new] and it's too esoteric, so I don't think we will get a discussion about the future of health care. Instead, there will be continued angst about what to do with institutions—which will be in the hands of a few people to decide, but which will be part of the [order's] corporate anger toward its inevitable decline (Individual Sister Interview: Former board member of her order's hospital system).

Or, as the leader of one community poignantly stated in her focus group:

> It was a lot more fun to open things, in my opinion, more exciting. . . . You pull back, you sell, you pull back, and this person leaves, and I'm leaving—And I do think we need to regroup at some point and find a way to—It is a question that we need to face head-on and then really search for something that the sisters can get excited about and be a part of, and be out there again (Focus Group 1.2: Present and former leaders).

The anomie discussed in Chapter 7 thus hinders the orders' ability to elicit sufficient enthusiasm from their members either to maintain existing organizational commitments or to enter into new ones. In a self-reinforcing feedback loop, lack of organizational involvement generates the very anti-institutional mindset that inhibits further involvement.

Notes

1. Cited in Morey (1995:89). See also Waring (1985) for a similar finding.
2. Daigler (2000:49). One 1985 study of Catholic sisters' colleges in the U.S. found that 1360 sisters had served in these institutions in 1973-74, but that, ten years later, only 991 did so. By 1990, the study projected a further reduction—to 843 (Waring 1985, quoted in Gallin 2000:216). See Dougherty (1997:223) and Campbell (1975:102-111) for the information on the Methodist deaconesses and mission societies.
3. The remainder worked in support services at the orders' mother houses (13 individuals), or held leadership roles in the orders (8 individuals). One was a full-time student. See Table 9.1.
4. Wolfteich (2002:94-98). Harris (1998:193) makes a similar observation that the attraction of welfare projects is opportunity they provide volunteers for self-development and autonomous decision-making. But if outside pressures force these to become more bureaucratic, "the commitment and enthusiasm of the volunteers may melt away. Even though such sponsorship reflects project success and offers the possibility of expansion with less responsibility, it may also take from volunteers what they most value; the ability to control the project and run it according to their own preferences." See also Young (1998:197).
5. Langley (1997).
6. Juan Libanio, SJ, quoted in Flanagan (2005:56).
7. Weisbrod (1998b:57). See also James (1998:287), who makes the same point.
8. Young (1998:197).
9. Quoted in Daigler (2000:183-184).
10. Bontrager (1997:333).
11. Schneiders (2001:270-271). Italics added. See also Moylan (1993:175), Sanders (1988:24), and MacDonald (2000:14).
12. Dunstan (2003:346-6). See also Moran (2004) and Schuth (1996:17) for a similar observation about American Catholic orders.
13. McDonough (1992:10). Non-ordained religious brothers, who had rarely served in parishes, were completely marginalized by this shift (Sammon 2001:218). See Wallace (1992) for Catholic sisters serving as pastors of parishes.
14. McDonough and Bianchi (2002:198-9).
15. Hill (1985:92).
16. See Morey (1995:227-228), Daigler (2000:199), Gleason (2001:15), and McDonough and Bianchi (2002:233), for examples to support this statement.
17. Schneiders (2001:236).
18. Dougherty (1997:164-165).
19. Barbara Campbell, personal communication.
20. Ebaugh (1993:101).

21. Nygren and Ukeritis (1993:116) for this study. See Sanders (1988:5,22) for the study of Catholic Health Care.

22. McDonough and Bianchi (2002:195).

23. Schuth (1996:17).

24. Personal communication 1999.

25. Morey (1995:88) describes this study in greater detail.

26. According to Nygren and Ukeritis (1993:114), contemplative, cloistered religious orders are gaining new members at a proportional rate that is over twice as high as that of the active orders which are still involved in institutional ministries.

Chapter 10

Impacts on Personal
and Professional Development

When the orders and the mission societies were first founded in the nineteenth century, their members had believed that they were embarking on a holy endeavor whose success would bring about the Kingdom of God, as well as their own progress in virtue. For the early nuns, deaconesses, and missionaries, therefore, their teaching, nursing, and social work had been a *calling*, not merely a job or profession. Religious dedication took precedence over mere technical proficiency in these tasks. As an early study of sisters, written in the 1940s, put it:

> To the Sister, her religious life itself is her "profession," the term actually used to denote her separation from the secular world. The end of her whole life towards which she constantly tends, is her religious perfection. Teaching fits into that pattern only inasmuch as it can, by its faithful and conscientious discharge, glorify God and sanctify her soul.[1]

Similarly, the earliest Protestant missionaries and deaconesses also ascribed to an ideology of self-immolation in the service of the unevangelized poor. In such an ideology, developing one's own intellect and talents might be de-emphasized, or even viewed as spiritually dangerous. Critics felt that it fostered unseemly pride and self-will, thus diminishing the humility and obedience idealized as virtues for religious women.[2]

By the beginning of the twentieth century, however, this attitude had changed among the Protestant missionaries and deaconesses:

> Through a process of professionalization in missionary training that parallels the introduction of business methods into mission administration, this melodramatic ideal yielded to a view of missionary service as a career option akin to teaching, nursing, or social work. . . . Women who made mission work a career in the new era of modern missions placed greater reliance on their professional competence

225

and less on the prayers of laywomen than had their predecessors.[3]

Somewhat later in the century, Catholic religious orders also were encouraged by Pope Pius XII himself to give their sisters professional training equal to or better than that of their secular counterparts. In his 1952 address to the International Congress of Major Superiors, the Pope urged:

> In the training of your sisters for the tasks that await them, be broadminded and liberal and admit of no stinginess. Whether it be for teaching, the care of the sick, the study of art, or anything else, the sister should be able to say to herself, "My superior is giving me a training that will put me on an equality with my secular colleagues." Give them also the opportunity and the means to keep their professional knowledge up-to-date. This is important for your sisters' peace and for their work.[4]

As a result of this emphasis on professional education, the sisters and deaconesses became some of the most educated women of their time. By the 1960s, all deaconesses were professionally credentialed—mostly with degrees in social work. The sisters were more likely to have trained via their order's apprentice system; still, however, 35.4 percent possessed Bachelor's, 21 percent Master's, and 1.7 percent Doctoral degrees in 1965. By 1982, almost all sisters had their undergraduate degrees, and 43 percent had Master's degrees as well.[5] The percentage of sisters with at least a Master's degree rose further—to 80 percent—by 1990. As the institutions run by Catholic religious orders began to value the pedigree of an applicant's professional credentials as the primary criterion for hiring and promotion, however, fewer of the sisters earning these degrees received them from a Catholic university.[6]

Hidden in these figures were several other worrisome trends. Neal noted that, while there was "a noticeable increase . . . in the number seeking the professional credential, the Master's degree," there was only a slight rise "in those gaining the independent scholar degree, the doctorate."[7] For the most part, the sisters and deaconesses had gotten their advanced degrees, not out of a theology that valued learning for its own sake, but because this knowledge was needed for staffing a school or hospital. The needs of the orders' institutions, therefore, had been the primary spur to their members' educational advancement, and once the orders' ties to these institutions loosened, there was little incentive to spend time and money on advanced degrees.[8] Among Catholic orders which still possessed colleges in the 1980s, 64 percent had at least one member who had earned her Ph.D. during that decade. Among orders without colleges, however, only 36 percent had a member who had attained this educational level.[9] Even among the orders with colleges to staff, the number of sisters earning advanced degrees declined. In the Sisters of Mercy, for example, 93 women were pursuing doctoral degrees in 1962, as compared to 34 in 1996.[10]

At the same time, those sisters and deaconesses who *did* have the same credentials as the lay professionals with whom they worked began to expect commensurate salaries and benefits. The deaconesses experienced this shift in the 1930s and 1940s:

> Seeing the church's employment policy as a possible cause for so many women workers leaving its service, Deaconess Barnwell told the gathering: "It is not selfishness or lack of spirit, or sacrifice, but common sense, that makes young people ask, 'What of the future?' They have a right to demand fair employment practices on the part of the church just as the church has a right to demand higher standards of its workers."[11]

Catholic sisters began to receive comparable salaries and benefits with their lay counterparts somewhat later: in the 1950s for hospital sisters and the 1980s and 1990s for most elementary and secondary school teachers.

The present chapter will consider the effects of institutional loss on the personal and professional development of the sisters and deaconesses and, to a lesser extent, on the mission society members. On the one hand, without the "spur" of institutional staffing needs and with no coherent theology that valued intellectual development for its own sake, the orders' members might be less likely to seek advanced education at all. On the other hand, the sisters and deaconesses who *did* gain professional and doctoral degrees might be more likely to identify with their secular colleagues and less likely to identify with the other members of their orders. This may have been especially likely as they began to fill positions outside of their order's traditional institutions.

Declining Intellectual Focus

Although their colleges had been a driving force behind the orders' efforts to send at least some of their sisters to study for advanced degrees during the early and mid-twentieth century, the push for higher education was still suspected of having negative side effects. Even as the orders responded to Pius XII's challenge in the 1950s, there had remained the lingering belief among many sisters, priests, and bishops that "too much study rendered a nun's virtue suspicious."[12] Among older members, there was often resentment of the "elitism" of those with doctorates, and anger at the cost of their prolonged education—which was borne by the rest of the sisters.

This tendency to discount the spiritual value of intellectual pursuits actually increased in the 1960s and 1970s, after the Second Vatican Council. The Superior General of the Jesuits, for example, announced his intention to convince some of the brighter young men in his order that direct ministry to the deprived was a more appropriate ministry than scholarship and teaching. Increasingly, younger Jesuits engaged in an active campaign to replace their order's intellectual apostolate with social programs.[13] As the women's religious orders began to espouse similar ideas, intellectual pursuits came to have a negative connotation among many sisters, who saw them as elitist and outdated symbols of religious life.

Loosening the orders' ties to their colleges and universities, therefore, only exacerbated a trend that was already underway. As one study in the mid-1990s noted:

> The seeking of advanced degrees, once a driving force in congregational renewal, became unpopular. It is not surprising, therefore, that only 4 percent of the women religious respondents to the National Survey of the *Religious Life Futures Study* have doctoral degrees.[14]

The same study noted that the former caste system, whereby sisters with the highest education had been given more prestige, had now almost completely reversed. Instead of feeling inferior to the sisters still teaching in or administering their order's colleges, the sisters working in the new, direct-service ministries thought of themselves as more powerful, more up-to-date, and more respected in their order, even though they often had less formal education.

In many Catholic orders today, therefore, while there may be a value placed on practical, professional education to fit onself for a particular ministry or service, there is less value placed on learning for its own sake. As one Jesuit critic noted:

> There is a serious problem with what I would call a few anti-intellectuals [among the Jesuits]. . . . To become a serious, contributing scholar in American academic intellectual life, that has to be a lifetime's work. And the Jesuits' lifetime work is peace, justice, and the transformation of society. Some of them make it through to an academic orientation in their lives; most of them simply don't have the desire for it. They have other, competing desires. . . . Here among the faculty at the university, Jesuits who become serious scholars are relatively few. Most of them are not interested in scholarship. They're very good teachers, they care deeply about the institution, and they work hard for the institution. . . . but the life of scholarship is not there.[15]

Another Jesuit claimed that, as a result:

> American Jesuits at present do not have anything like a coherent operative philosophy or rationale for the intellectual life or for our insistence on a well-trained ministry in all our apostolates. . . . I do not find that anything now compels widespread consent among Jesuits to our historic and present commitment to the intellectual life and a learned ministry.[16]

Similarly, a Benedictine college president criticized her order's move away from higher education: "This view that 'I will serve dinners to the poor' is partly a repudiation of the intellectual life."[17]

Like the Catholic sisters, the deaconesses had established their institutions of higher education primarily for training those in church-related vocations. The primary curricula at the various nineteenth century training schools for deaconesses and missionaries included bible study, nursing, early childhood education, and social work.[18] Even when some of these schools became accredited as three- or four-year, post-secondary institutions, their leaders continued to resist the temptation to make them into just another liberal arts college. After the training schools were closed, subsequent candidates were expected to earn their professional certification prior to joining the program, and their formal deaconess training was confined to somewhat haphazard courses in church history and doctrine. The younger deaconesses noted that even this minimal academic training in religion and spirituality might be set aside if the needs of the ministry required it:

> When I came through, you were supposed to have, I guess you had to have a masters degree in the area in which you were going to work, and a commitment to your faith, or something similar to that. But they didn't have any actual required courses and I'd gone to a [denominational] college, so I'd only had one class of philosophy and one class of Old Testament and nothing more. And then we were supposed to go to deaconess orientation after the commissioning, [but] we were trying to start a program in the summer in [state], so we wrote and said, "Is it OK if I miss orientation in order to start this?" and they said, "Pick whichever one you want." So I never went to deaconess orientation or anything (Focus Group 4.3: Active deaconesses).

Among the sisters as well, new entrants today are expected to be already professionally trained in a career. What training they receive as part of their initial formation period tends to focus primarily on theology, ecclesiology, and spirituality, and *not* on intellectual or professional development:

> Formation today is described as a "busy" process that does not attend to or encourage integration of the intellectual life with communal life and ministry; therefore, the attitudes of the young toward the life of learning are becoming more negative. They often see intellectual activity as elitist and not in harmony with concern for the poor.[19]

Some observers have worried that the young recruits will not value what their training does not emphasize.[20] One study of Catholic religious orders found that the percentage of the membership valuing advanced education decreased with age: while, in general, 59 percent of the sisters surveyed believed that it was important for their order's future that some members have Ph.Ds, only 46 percent of the youngest members agreed.[21]

When the focus groups were asked about how their order or society had changed and what the participants now found fulfilling about their membership in it, ten groups mentioned opportunities for spiritual or personal growth as compared to three groups (one group of sisters and two of the mission society) that mentioned the opportunity to learn new things. The opportunity to develop and use their talents was, however, a frequently-named source of *job* satisfaction among the active sisters and deaconesses:

> [In my former job], I was bored, it was terrible. But anyway, I kind of found [the order's residential home for severely handicapped children]. I found it, or they found me, I'm not sure how it all came to be, but that has been the total opposite. I've been allowed to do different things, to experiment, to try my wings at different aspects—some things I did well in, some things I totally blew, but at least I was allowed to try and to have different experiences. And that's been the difference for me (Focus Group 1.5: Active sisters).

> Also, the whole multi-media, how that enters in, like students will email me that they can't come to class—Putting web pages together. We're into Web CT, which is course tools where we can—like, I just last week figured out how to put quizzes online for them to take. And so it's like in a sense, so many different things, in a sense it's so much harder because there's so much to learn. . . . It's just like it's much busier than I expected, but rewarding because, as you said, I'm learning (Focus Group 3.10: Active sisters).

The sisters, deaconesses, and mission society members in the focus groups, therefore, did not necessarily disparage intellectual achievement. The active anti-intellectualism noted by some critics did not seem to be present. Still, knowledge seemed to be valued more for its practical utility than as a good in itself. Only six individual sisters or deaconesses, in all of the twelve non-retired focus groups, were still involved in post-secondary academic settings—and only one of these, a sister who had founded and was running a theological institute, mentioned having an ongoing commitment to the intellectual life. Most appeared to see their education as a means to an end rather than an end in itself.

On a more subtle level, it may also be noteworthy that the purely academic degrees received by members of Catholic religious orders now tend to be in theology and religious studies, rather than in English, chemistry, or mathematics.[22] This may contribute to the increasing compartmentalization of religion from secular disciplines. At the very least, there will be few in the religious orders able to follow Teilhard de Chardin, Joseph Fichter, Edith Stein, or Gerard Manley Hopkins in integrating religion with the physical and social sciences, philosophy, or literature.[23]

Mentoring For Leadership

In an earlier era, being a sister, a deaconess, or a member of a mission society provided the women with opportunities and training for leadership roles, both in the sponsored institutions and in the group or denomination itself. A sister profiled in one study noted that her own history illustrates the importance of mentoring to leadership:

Everything in my life that expanded my world, learning, and made me go beyond myself was initiated from outside myself because someone said, "You will do this." or "We want you to do this." Left to my own devices, I probably would not have thought of those things. They would not have been within my categories.[24]

Twenty-seven of the 36 focus groups also mentioned similar mentoring for leadership:

My husband and I were in youth work at our former church, and worked with them and had a good rapport with them. One of the ladies was on the Executive Board, and she put my name up to be the secretary of youth for the [city] district (Focus Group 5.1: Missionary society).

I started as a teacher at [school] in [city] and went home for vacation and came back to be congratulated because I was the superintendent, to my surprise (Focus Group 4.2: Retired deaconesses).

I was assigned as a principal at the age of 28. Two years later, I started studying administration. So I probably could have taught the classes I took (Focus Group 2.5: Active sisters).

While a few had had formal education for their leadership roles, most were—at least initially—mentored informally into them:

I had to [get my degree in administration] in order to become a member of the American College of Hospital Administrators, which it was called at that time. It took four years to do that, and then Sister Mary and I got our membership at the same time, because she was assisting me and then she went away to school to get her masters in administration and took my place (Focus Group 2.6: Active and retired sisters).

I was a district officer when I was 18. I've learned a lot and the older women helped me. But I was almost overwhelmed because there was so much and I was so young. Then later on, when we [respondent's pastor husband and herself] came back from seminary, I did two or three different offices (Focus Group 5.5: Mission society).

In contrast, twelve of the focus groups noted that such mentoring opportunities were rare today, both for administrative positions in their sponsored institutions and for leadership within the order/society itself. For the current leaders of the religious orders, this deficiency resulted, in part, from the lack of opportunities to know the members in their newly-dispersed living situations:

- I think, too, that in the past, the way the [orders] were, we called forth people more than we do today. . . . But, I'm not so sure that we do that any more—that we help people think about what they could do and encourage them to do it. To take other kinds of steps.

- I wonder, today, we don't view people . . . as we did before, because we lived closer and we could see the giftedness of them and some of that is fading out. . . . I wonder when people come after me how much I really know of their ability. What hasn't been tapped? Helping to tap that (Focus Group 2.3: Present and former leaders).

One of the things we were talking about the other day is the fact that we really no longer have schools which were a training ground, you know, for principals who began to learn how to lead, or hospitals where you had people in administrative positions, or the college. We don't have any of those places any more, so I don't know where people will learn some of the skills of leadership, and where the community will have the opportunity to observe those sisters in leadership, too. I think that's going to have an impact on us. We haven't felt it just yet, but we will (Focus Group 1.2: Present and former leaders).

Or, as one young sister put it, "There's no way in the order to show what you can do, other than scut work like organizing the transportation for a community gathering."[25]

In addition, the lack of the institutional work settings has limited the informal mentoring opportunities that used to be available there:

When I started as assistant dean of students at [the order's] college, I got the support and mentoring—not so much in the counseling that I was doing, but in the professionalism and the ethics and, you know, those kinds of things that you learn at an institution. And I miss, somehow, the fact that I'm not getting to mentor somebody else that's coming along now (Focus Group 3.7: Active sisters).

I think, for my generation, one of the things we have—I was really close to my grandmother, and she was active [in the mission society], and so that's what attracted me. But just the multiple generations, the care and support and hearing what it was like, I don't have another way of getting. And I think other people of my age are missing that, if you are just with other moms of little kids, you miss getting that (Focus Group 5.1: Mission society).

In the absence of these opportunities for informal mentoring, few formal training procedures have been established by the sisters or deaconesses to take their place:

[Interviewer: Is there a mentoring program for leadership or administration for any of these institutions?]
There's a mentoring process that is instituted as far as the folks that are interested in being part of board representation for the various institutions. But, not, I wouldn't say, as part of our formation as Sisters of X.
- No.
- No (Focus Group 3.11: Young sisters).

Instead of either formal or informal mentoring programs to train new recruits for institutional leadership, the orders now rely on the private discernment and preferences of each individual sister or deaconess:

> Everybody has an opportunity to look at themselves and their gifts and find out what is the desire of their heart for ministry. And our leadership is very willing to be dialogical about that. And that is such a beauty. . . . Look at the richness of each of these sisters. Everybody is pretty happy about what they're doing right now, and there's a fulfillment (Focus Group 1.5: Active sisters).

> I think we've gained a great deal of a more individual responsibility, which I think puts that much more of a burden on our own reflection and our own decisions. You used to be able to just go wherever you were told to go . . . but now, I think there's a great deal more responsibility on us, at least I feel that. If I decided to make a change at one time or another, it's always a lot of soul searching and a lot of really examining my motives and examining my gifts and my weaknesses and trying to see is this really [what I am called to do] (Focus Group 3.12: Active sisters).

As was noted in the previous chapter, however, there is a lack of input from the orders' leadership in this private discernment process. This makes it difficult, if not impossible, for the order to assure its institutions of the continued availability of sister administrators, even if these organizations would still prefer to hire a sister in top management.[26] Some of the orders' leaders regretted the diminished opportunities for actively placing sisters in their institutions, but seemed unable to articulate a way of changing this situation:

> I think that it's kind of related to your other question about mentoring and so on. I think that for the community and its members to have responsibility for institutions such as we have in our history and in our present, and the expectation that "We're going to raise up leaders," "We're going to see to it that people get prepared to run them"—there was a richness to that. We had some ambition as a community that maybe we don't have any more, or we don't have to the same extent. Just because every other hospital has a male CEO doesn't mean *we* have to have one (Sisters' Focus Group 2.3: Present and former leaders).

In addition to lack of mentoring opportunities, there has also been absence of a theology or spirituality that values administration. This sometimes makes sisters reluctant to apply for these positions:

> - There may be a cultural issue at work. I think that there are some inhibitions to wanting a top job. You know, it's sort of like it doesn't go with being holy [laughter]
> - I never thought of that.
> - And maybe I'm wrong.
> - No, I think you're right, because how many of us have applied for the things we got? That's the point I'm trying to make.
> - Yes.

- Today, you have to apply, you have to say, "I think I'll do this," and go after it. But we didn't have to do that [in earlier days]. The superior sent us (Focus Group 2.3: Present and former leaders).

One Australian author has noted the absence of specifically religious training programs for health care or social service administration in that country.[27]

Thus, as the present administrators of the sisters' institutions age and retire, there is no one "in the pipeline" within the order to take their place:

[Interviewer: You have a lot of Sisters of X at [the order's home for profoundly retarded children]
We do, but Sister Ann's 82, and Sister Jane is going to be 70 pretty soon. I mean, she's got a few more years, five years maybe, and she'll be 70. I'm not too far away [from 70] myself, you know, and I look behind me and there's nobody coming up who wants to take responsibility for these kinds of institutions any more (Focus Group 3.10: Active sisters).

With no visible successor in the wings, some sisters felt constrained to remain in their current positions, even if it was no longer professionally or spiritually fulfilling for them to do so:

- I think, "I've been here 29 years, and should I stay or should I not stay?" And that goes every year. "Am I doing a good job or not, am I fulfilled?" . . . I have chosen to stay where I am because I don't really feel like, at my age, to start a new place or start a new thing. And I also feel very fulfilled there, and—
– Can I ask you a question, because you're in a situation in a school that we've had since it started. It used to have a lot of Sisters of X there, and now there's just you and one other sister, and you've been there for 29 years, Mary's been there 30, just the two of you.
- For just the two of us, we've been there probably about 10 years, just the two of us together.
- But I think, I want to ask—in that discernment you say you have to think about, how much does the fact that, if you leave, Mary would go, too, and that's the end of the Sisters of X [in that school]. Does that enter into your decision?
- Oh, it enters into our decision all the time (Focus Group 2.5: Active sisters).

Loss or consolidation of institutions also reduces the variety of job opportunities available to the sisters if they *do* decide to leave:

It's the case where one hospital owns practically the whole medical environment of [city] and all the towns around it, even into [neighboring state]. So, consequently, if you quit, where are you going to go to work? You don't have an opening. There are two hospitals that are run like that and one is as bad as the other (Focus Group 1.1: Retired sisters).

The other thing that changed for me was, at least in [city], I used to kind of travel every seven years or so from [the order's] east side [high school] to [the order's] west side [high school], to east side, to west side. And now I'm on the west side [and the east side high school was consolidated with another high school]. I don't know at what point I came to the realization that, really, if I want to teach—and I do—uh, this is really it, now. Um, and I like [the high school where the respondent currently teaches] but I'm really aware of, like, if I wanted to continue what I'm doing, which I do, this is probably it, you know (Focus Group 3.5: Active sisters).

As a result, some see a stagnation developing which stifles rather than fosters the development of new skills for leadership.

In addition to reduced opportunities for leadership in professional positions within the order's institutions, there are also implications for the leadership of the religious order itself. Once the sisters have earned their credentials and actually obtained their positions through a competitive hiring process, they are often reluctant to leave these jobs in order to serve in the leadership of the order.[28] Ten groups of the active sisters were asked whether they would consider such a leadership role in the future: in four groups, at least some of the respondents were open to such a possibility but, in nine groups, many respondents were reluctant to accept such a role. Of the latter, some respondents cited age as their reason for refusing (7 groups), or felt that they did not possess the requisite skills (7 groups). In eight of the nine groups, however, respondents cited job-related constraints that hampered their ability to give time to leadership in their order:

I wouldn't want to do it full time and give up my ministry (Focus Group 1.4: Active sisters).

Well, people who were young enough to do it, know that once their term or terms are over, they're going to have a very difficult time finding a job because they'll be at that age when people aren't hired (Focus Group 2.1: Active sisters).

Once you leave a ministry, today, it's pretty much like you've left it for good. You're not likely to be able to go back into it, and that's different from the past. And the other question is, if you are, for example, the Sister of X presence in an institution that we value, is it more important for you to maintain that, or to put your name in for election? And those are pretty serious discussions (Focus Group 2.5: Active sisters).

A few worried that the leadership pool of prospective candidates for leadership within the order was shrinking:

What we're hearing around the room right now is a concern. . . . Our community needs to look at that because, in the last election, there were three positions and only three candidates (Focus Group 2.5: Active sisters).

The Catholic sisters thus face reduced opportunities for leadership develop-ment. The mission society members, in contrast, face increased opportunities, of a certain kind, at least. A denominational reorganization in the mid-1960s had removed much of the society's administrative responsibility for its educational, health care, and social service institutions. This resulted in a shift in focus, as the society's leadership began to place less emphasis on its mission organizations—which it no longer completely controlled—and more on what had formerly been ancillary activities. According to a former leader in the society:

> There were two areas [of the mission society's activities] which had also been there through all these years, which I have not yet mentioned—one was the whole area of social action. We had been very, very active in that. But it was—I use the word "secondary," and I don't like that word but I can't think of another one to use. . . . And then [the second area was] the organizational maintenance, the preparation and interpreting of materials, the going to meetings, the training of leaders, the program materials—that was an important function, but it existed to make the other happen. Well, with all the administration of the mission projects gone, social action and organizational development became the two new really big pieces (Individual Interview: Retired deaconess and former mission society officer).

This shift of focus is evident in a book about one denominational mission society written in the mid-1970s.[29] In contrast to earlier works written about the same society,[30] there were few, if any, mentions of the specific organizations sponsored by the group, or of those who headed these institutions—primarily because they had been shifted to denominational control and were no longer under the society's jurisdiction. Most of the text's pages were devoted to describing how the society as an organization operated and how its money was raised and distributed. The women who were profiled in the book's pages were selected because of their leadership roles within the mission society itself; any leadership roles they may also have occupied in the institutions formerly sponsored by the society were rarely mentioned.

Still, there was some evidence in the focus group interviews that not all of the rank and file were interested in filling a more active leadership role in the denomination, or in the mission society itself.

> - Susan and I attended several times, district functions, and it was very discouraging.
> - And you have to get in your car and maybe drive to [distant town] or somewhere.
> - But that wouldn't even have been it. It's just that when you go to a meeting, just like anything else, and you're taking your time and your effort, you want to come home with something that you can share with your local [chapter] or with your church.
> - Often you come back with nothing.
> - Nothing. Even negatives.
> - When you go to a district meeting, then we sat and listened and if I remember, at one of them, the president came here and listened to this meeting and the vice

president was there and my opinion as we were driving home was, "Well, wasn't that special." [laughter] So we just kept doing what we'd been doing. I didn't find the meeting very interesting at all. . . . It just seemed not relevant to the cares of the church (Focus Group 5.5: Mission society).

Professional Identification

Most of the members of religious orders not only have earned their professional certification from secular institutions, but also, in increasing numbers, are employed at institutions which are not owned by their order. Some observers have worried that careers in non-religious settings have eclipsed the sisters' commitment to the orders in which they still formally hold membership:

> The lack of opportunities to deepen meaning and a sense of belonging can result in sisters immersing themselves in life-giving experiences that are completely outside the context of congregational life. This can eventually lead to becoming marginal within one's own congregation. In my conversations with younger women religious, I have seen this marginalization make it hard to sustain one's call to religious life.[31]

At least one study has found that many sisters have drawn "lines in the sand," whereby they were committed to retaining membership in their order only so long as it did not interfere with their careers.

This finding of marginalization and disinterest in their order's concerns can also diminish the loyalty which members may feel to its institutions, even as they continue to serve in them. Those who wish to continue working in religious settings may engage in parish or denominational work.[32] For these, their identity as a sister or deaconess may be primarily an instrumental one; it gives them extra credibility for the church career which is their first commitment.

While no active sister or deaconess in the focus groups expressed this feeling of detachment, they were aware of its dangers. A few noted that they had specifically turned down career positions—often high-ranking and prestigious ones —precisely in order *not* to become marginalized within their order or society:

> - When I left [the order's hospital], to go to [an administrative position at another order's hospital in another state], I was down there for seven years and it was a positive experience, but that's where I experienced somewhat of a crisis being 600 miles away from the Sisters of X. . . . I could see that, over a long period of time, those bonds could get looser and, in fact, we did have a sister in our community who did stay away for so long that she just—[respondent trails off] And I would think of her a lot and think about how I care more about being a Sister of X than being a CEO. So eventually, when it was right, I came back to this area because I really needed to be among the Sisters of X.
> - What's interesting is, I've had, some people have contacted me about job

opportunities and things, but the ones that have been geographically far away, I can't even think about them. And so, what I've learned is that . . . I'm not inclined to relocate, like, to Notre Dame, for example, where there are no Sisters of X nearby. And so I suspect that I'm going to have to be much more cautious in what I decide to do and what I don't decide to do because I know those are important things for me (Focus Group 2.5: Active sisters).

Many cited similar instances where other sisters had drifted away from close contact with the order:

- With many of us working in jobs alone, . . . you can become very isolated . . . and you can lose consciousness of really knowing one another or having that unified connection. And that's a type of community. You have to rethink individually, more individually now, and make the choices to be part of community, or you can sit out there for the rest of your life and not have that. And it's a real struggle. I know I've done it for a while in places.
- Been isolated?
- Been isolated. It was almost survival. And when you're working alone in jobs and without support of others, it's not always that easy. You're making choices, you're making new friends, you're making all sorts of new assumptions, and you're swinging it alone (Focus Group 2.3: Present and former leaders).

Conclusion

A subtle but important effect of the loss of institutions on the sisters, deaconesses, and mission society members has been a redirection of the amount of encouragement or aid which these women receive for their personal and professional development. On the one hand, the sisters receive less mentoring for leadership roles, either in their own order or in their institutions. Even orders which affirm the value of their institutions take few practical steps to put this affirmation into practice:

I think you'll agree with me that it would be hard to say what difference that statement [of institutional affirmation] has made! We have no programs of recruitment, mentoring, exchange, or promotion of sisters in ministry; no programs of leadership development or succession; no programs of mission assessment or enhancement.[33]

In contrast, the mission society members now receive *more* mentoring, but for leadership within the denomination, not within the institutions. The following chapter will explore whether this mentoring focus has actually increased the women's power and leadership within the denomination or not.

In addition to lack of mentoring, there is often a pervasive dissociation among the sisters and deaconesses between their formal professional training and their spiritual training, with the former left almost solely to each individual's discretion and preference. In the absence of a coherent theology validating the spiritual worth of either administrative or intellectual pursuits, fewer members are eager to engage in such activity, especially when compared to hands-on service. This has produced, at times, an anti-intellectualism or anti-managerialism that further marginalizes the minority of members who are still committed to developing academic expertise or managerial skills. These women, therefore, often identify more and more with their professional colleagues, and less and less with the other members of their order.

A reduced emphasis on personal and professional development might also impact the members' and the orders' power, both within the parent denomination and in the larger society. It is to this topic that we now turn.

Notes

1. S. Bertrande Meyers, quoted in Morey (1995:73). See Dougherty (1997:206) for a similar ideology among Protestant missionaries and deaconesses.

2. For example, one nineteenth century bishop told the Sisters of Mercy in his diocese that "the eagerness for higher education would diminish the religious spirit" of their sisters, who should be devoting their time to the care of the poor. This incident is recounted in Madden (1991:362). See Oates (1994:97; 2002:179) for similar incidents.

3. Hill (1985:123-4).

4. Quoted in Ewens (1989a:172).

5. Neal (1984:32). See Schuth (1996:14) for the 1990 figures.

6. McDonough and Bianchi (2002:233). According to Cooke and Chinery (1995:33-35) 77 percent of the Ph.Ds earned by sisters in 1951-61 came from Catholic universities. This fell to 30 percent in 1971-1990.

7. Neal (1984:32).

8. Vance (1999:73, ftn.24) notes that institutional investment has had a similar effect on entire denominations. As a result of Seventh-day Adventist emphasis on higher education and on staffing its own schools and hospitals, Adventists are disproportionately represented in professional and skilled occupations. Forty percent of Adventist men and 33 percent of Adventist women have at least a college degree. Black and Hispanic Adventist men are even more likely than White Adventists to graduate from college. It is doubtful if this would be the case without the spur provided by the Adventist institutions.

9. Schuth (1996:18). Schuth also notes (1996:18) that, if an order had a college, 72 percent of the members said that it was important for the congregation's future that some members have Ph.Ds. If the order did *not* have a college, only 38 percent said it was important.

10. Daigler (2000:179-80).

11. Dougherty (1997:223).

12. Kennelly (1996:62). See Schuth (1996:12) the sisters' resentment of the elitism of those with Ph.D. degrees.

13. This is documented in Fitzgerald (1984:192), Burtchaell (1998:583), and Shea (1999:216-217). See Puzon (1996b:3) for the sisters' view of this.

14. Morey (1995:90).

15. Quoted in McDonough and Bianchi (2002:228). See also Burtchaell (1998:582) for similar attitudes.

16. Coleman (1990:11-12).

17. Quoted in Morey (1995:225).

18. Dougherty (1997:94-96). See Dougherty (1997:150) for the following sentence.

19. Schuth (1996:22).

20. This is not a new worry. Those in charge of the education of young sisters in the 1950s also fretted that their charges found study less appealing than active service.

21. Schuth (1996:14, 16). Schuth also found that, in their answers to an open-ended question about "the two most important factors affecting your intellectual growth," 19 percent said that it was their own curiosity and desire for self-improvement that had motivated them, while 18 percent cited the availability of educational resources provided by the order and only 12.5 percent mentioned the active tradition of the order and its encouragement of learning (Schuth 1996:15-16).

22. Cooke and Chinery (1996:40) note that the percentage of earned doctorates in theology and related disciplines is approaching 15 percent, while the percentage of earned doctorates in science and math fell from 24 percent in the 1930s to 6 percent in the 1980s, and to 0 in the 1990s. See Daigler (2000:79) for a description of this trend among the Sisters of Mercy.

23. Haughey (1999).

24. Quoted in Morey (1995:226).

25. From a personal telephone conversation with the author. This sister was a graduate student in sociology who ultimately earned her Ph.D.

26. Ebaugh (1993:109) makes this point.

27. See Cleary (2001:209).

28. Nygren and Ukeritis (1993:179) note a similar lack of interest in leadership positions within the orders they studied.

29. Campbell (1975).

30. For example Isham (1936), Tatum (1960), or Meeker (1969), where the majority of the chapters describe one institution after another.

31. Matthes (2003:7). See also Schneiders (2001:380), who makes the same point. See Ebaugh (1993:108) for the study cited in the next sentence.

32. Gallin (2000:125). Harris (1998:178) notes similar difficulties with volunteer workers in Protestant churches. Ebaugh's interviewees (1993:108) made the observation reported in the following sentence.

33. Gottemoeller (1995:35). See also Schuth (1996:17), who makes a similar point.

Chapter 11

Power

What impact did institutional loss have on the power of the orders and mission societies—and of the individual women who belonged to them? In general, members of subordinated groups have used two tactics, which we might label "Integration" and "Group Hegemony," to obtain and hold power in the larger society. Integration tactics involve attempting to obtain equal hiring and promotion opportunities for group members within the so-called "primary labor market" of an area or an organization.[1] Group Hegemony tactics, on the other hand, refer to attempts by members of a subordinate group to create separate organizational fields of action, free from the "glass ceilings" that limit their careers in mainstream organizations. Several wide-ranging bodies of literature address the relative effectiveness of each of these tactics.[2]

Within the study of women's power in religious denominations, most researchers have studied the "integration" tactics whereby women attempt to enter the primary labor market within their denominations through access to the ordained ministry. Formal acceptance of women's ordination has occurred at various times during the last two centuries, depending on the particular denomination involved. In some denominations, notably Roman Catholicism, it has not happened yet. Consequently, researchers have been able to compare the formal integration of women into the ranks of the ordained across denominations with widely varying lengths of experience with the policy. The symbolic impact of an ordained woman celebrating the central rituals of the faith does have tremendous importance for a denomination. Recent studies have noted that, in denominations where only men can give sermons, counsel congregants, or preside at liturgy, they will employ language, symbols, and metaphors which resonate more strongly with their male congregants than with their female ones.[3] On the other hand, numerous researchers have found that, even in denominations with strong and long-established official support for ordaining women, the glass ceiling persists.[4]

Other researchers—primarily, but not exclusively, historians—have investigated women's "group hegemony" tactics in religious denominations: separate women-founded and women-run activities which provide alternate sources of church power and influence.[5] There are several levels on which gender hegemony can operate. One is the local congregational level, where all-female Bible study groups or mission society chapters may provide networking opportunities, leadership experience, and control over valuable financial resources that women can parcel out to the local church or the larger denomination as they see fit. As one study of a pair of fundamentalist Christian congregations put it:

> Female newcomers to Bay Chapel or Mount Olive rapidly discover that, for them, the congregation as a whole is not the sole provider of religious goods. Alongside the male-dominated symbolic world of overall congregational life exists a parallel symbolic world administered totally by women. The plethora of women's ministry programs simultaneously establishes and nurtures female enclaves, separate sociocultural networks of women.[6]

These networks, Brasher felt, provide the women with a "valuable source of religious alterity and institutional power."

At the denominational level, group hegemony studies could list the religious orders and mission societies established and run by a denomination's women. These associations rapidly became essential to the mission of the larger denomination, which gave the women power. "Because of the power of the purse and of their personal presence, [mission society] women gained rights of representation on various Church boards."[7] One historian notes that Roman Catholic sisters "were among the most liberated women in nineteenth-century America. They were self-supporting, owned property, were well educated, held administrative positions, lived in a community of women, and were free from the dominance of husbands and the responsibility of motherhood. Often they were envied by their Protestant sisters for their independence and hailed by businessmen for their acumen."[8]

Finally, of course, women might break away to form a separate religion or sect, free from male influence altogether. Several historians have noted the tendency of new sectarian or cultic groups, which often gave women more authority than established religions, to attract a disproportionately female following.[9] Today, too, studies of Wicca and other new religious movements have noted their attractiveness to women.[10]

At the first and second of these three levels, the ability to run or finance the schools, hospitals, and other institutions needed by the larger denomination has thus been a powerful resource possessed by sisters and mission society members. What, therefore, might be the effects on these women of the loss or attenuation of their links to these institutions? Are integration tactics such as possessing access to ordination sufficient as an alternative source of power and influence for the women in a denomination, once their separately-controlled institutions are gone?

Power Within the Order or Society

The first impact of institutional loss has been on the power which the order's or society's leaders were once able to exercise over the rest of its membership. Since, in the past, their institutions had continuously needed to be staffed and administered, the leaders of religious orders necessarily retained the power to allocate their members to these tasks. Organizational need thus took precedence over an individual member's personal preferences. All of the retired sisters and deaconesses in the focus groups had experienced simply being sent, without consultation, to serve in a particular institution.

> When I was a student at the X College for Christian Workers in [city], that was the rule. You make an application to be a deaconess or a missionary and you go where the Board sends you. Now, at that point, none of us felt that that was an injustice. We went where the Board sent us. We wanted to serve and we accepted that without fighting (Focus Group 4.2: Retired deaconesses).

> - We had to wait until after breakfast on August 15.
> - You'd see the Mother Superior get up from the head table, and you'd know she was going to post [the assignments for the coming year]. And you were probably serving breakfast and couldn't leave, and you were dying—
> - Our names were on the board and you'd hear somebody scream—[laughter]
> - And that's another thing, you know. You had to leave your trunk packed when you left [the school where you had previously been stationed] for the summer, because you might not go back to that convent again.
> - Every June, you packed as though you were leaving, because you never knew (Focus Group 1.3: Retired sisters).

As these two quotations show, the sisters and deaconesses once accepted the authority of their leaders as part of their religious calling. Among the Catholic sisters, the prevailing ideology was that superiors were given a special "grace of office" that enabled them to make wise decisions.[11]

In the three focus groups of Catholic sisters who either had been or were currently serving in leadership positions in their orders, there was unanimous agreement that such power no longer existed:

> It used to be that the leadership could assign sisters to the schools. . . . There's been a real shift in what is considered to be the sisters' purview of authority; we can't assign them, number one, because the person has to fulfill the job qualifications. But it used to be you didn't have to fulfill any job qualifications. If the superior thought you belonged in a job, you saw your name on a sign on August 15 and you went. That was our [vow of] obedience. So that has changed tremendously (Focus Group 1.2: Present and former leaders).

While the leaders, for the most part, approved of this change, some also voiced the worry that the pendulum had swung too far toward individualism:

I think one of the pros of the evolution of the style of leadership is that the sisters feel ownership of the decisions that are made, for the most part. One of the cons, in my mind – take for example, uh, ministry decisions. Placement of sisters. It's no longer the same as it used to be, and nobody wants to go back to that. There is a concern, perhaps, that the leadership is the last to know about what is happening. The tendency is not to know how to call this person [to a particular job or position], or, when you do call this person, she will say, "Well, my spiritual advisor says," or "My therapist says," and then, you know, what happens to the call in this? What's the involvement of leadership in that call—is it only to confirm [what the individual sister has already decided], or do we lose the sense of inviting the calling forth of the gifts of the sisters by carrying it to the extreme? (Focus Group 1.2: Present and former leaders).

The leaders had liked being able to wield their order's power to effect positive changes. When asked to name particular sources of job satisfaction, all three focus groups of sisters who were the present and former leaders of their orders mentioned the ability to shepherd particular projects to completion, whether inside or outside of the order:

One of the things I enjoy doing is making it possible for other people to do the things that they can do. Making decisions so that they can fulfill their ministries and their lives in the community. That's probably the most fulfilling thing. And then I—when a really good idea comes forth, and you see that idea coming to shape, and eventually come to fulfillment. That excites me (Focus Group 1.2: Present and former leaders).

One of the things that I think has been really fun about [being in a leadership office] is the choices you can make. We have cultivated some new ministries, we have, in recent years, had a little more money to be able to make available. You get to make some choices about that. That's the fun part (Focus Group 2.3: Present and former leaders).

In our Ministry Foundation, we have so many opportunities to learn what people are creating and initiating because of the grant application process, so just working with them . . . and right now conducting training workshops for grantees and applicants. . . . Probably the most rewarding experiences are the site visits: I've had the opportunity to visit Sister Mary's project in [city], and to see the commitment of those people and their willingness to do so much themselves just to change the circumstances of their lives has been very rewarding. Just being responsible for the allocation of resources that are so significant is overwhelming sometimes, and you pray that the decisions you are making, along with the board, really are fulfilling our mission and that we are creating new ways of serving, with and for people (Focus Group 3.6: Former leaders and staff).

Rank and file sisters in other focus groups expressed similar sentiments about leadership opportunities in their work.

The leaders' focus groups admired the strong superiors of the past as women who had gotten things done, while they themselves often felt limited in their ability to exercise similar leadership. Their decisions were "circumscribed by trying to anticipate the consequences of the action on the various segments of the order," in order not to alienate an increasingly individualistic membership.[12]

[When I got to be president of the National Federation of several Sister of X orders], I had a very strong council who expected me to do nothing without it being decided by the group. And there were some rather tricky things to do in that period. Where Rome moved in from the outside and only wanted to deal with me—so that, you know, I can tell that story as the kind of story that pertains to me personally, but I think that it does address a general movement that maybe we're all going through: This leveling out of the leadership roles and yet wanting to be led (Focus Group 2.3: Present and former leaders).

The relative powerlessness of the orders' leaders within the order was often evident to the rest of the members. As a result, some of the younger sisters expressed a reluctance to move into such limited, frustrating, and ultimately powerless positions:

- Well, it seems like we keep going in the same direction, which is why I wouldn't take [a leadership position]. Instead of going in new directions.
- It's hard to turn those thing around. I thought by being a [local] leader in our [area] too, we do things, we're trying to do things with a new direction but it's hard to know how to do things, it's just really hard to do (Focus Group 3.7: Active sisters).

Administration was seen by some sisters as further removed from hands-on ministry, and therefore less desirable:

With leadership today, I don't think they are right here with us, like they used to be, because they go to so many [Federation] things, so that's one reason I don't think I would do well in leadership because I don't enjoy flying and I would miss a lot of the meetings [which leadership has to attend] (Focus Group 1.4: Active sisters).

This unwillingness further exacerbates the leadership shortage noted in chapter 10.

Power Within the Workplace

As chapter 4 has noted, the sisters, deaconesses, and mission society members had once possessed real power within their own institutions, at a time when few other sources of power were available to women. An interesting comparison might be made with the still-active sisters' and deaconesses' present jobs—to see whether these positions offer similar opportunities for developing the women's talents and leadership abilities or for exercising power. The twelve focus groups of currently-active sisters and deaconesses were asked to list what they found to be most fulfilling about their present work. The most common responses to this question—cited by over three-fourths of the groups—were meeting important needs, being a spiritual presence, and serving people. In contrast, most of the "power-related" sources of satisfaction—opportunities to learn new things, to use one's talents, or to bring about change—were cited by fewer groups:

Nevertheless, in half of the active focus groups, at least some members felt fulfilled by having the power to catalyze institutional change:

> Actually, there are a lot of challenges in health care today, but I think it's really exciting to be able to know that you are doing a good job, or your staff is really doing a good job, that whole quality issue—and that it's different from other facilities that, you know, say they provide the same care. And the whole mission piece is, you know, making that come alive in a way that both patients, families and the staff know what that means. (Focus Group 2.3: Present and former leaders).

Four of the individual sisters (in three different focus groups) who cited facilitating institutional change as a source of satisfaction were working in their order's own institutions; three were working either for another order's institutions or for the local diocese.

To the focus group participants who valued the power to make a difference in their organizations, losing this power was especially galling. This frustration was voiced by sisters in nine of the twelve active sisters' and deaconesses' focus groups:

> I've been in my job such a short time that I probably don't have as much perspective, but what I find challenging is, having had the opportunity in the past to be able to set direction and to have more control over operations, [now] I don't have any control and so I am more a cog in a very large organization, and I see lots of opportunities for improvement and I don't have an opportunity to have much impact on that. So I have to constrain my desires (Focus Group 2.5: Active sisters).

The sisters' and deaconesses' lack of institutional power was exacerbated by a growing gender disparity in the lay leadership that had been hired to take their places: whereas the sisters' and deaconesses' tenure in administrative positions had meant that their institutions were run by women, they were now, for the most part, administered by men.[13] Respondents in several focus groups expressed a concern about the erosion of women's power in the institutions they had formerly controlled:

> - One of the things that I find frustrating is what I see as a kind of irony between a value that we espouse and a reality in our institutions, and it has to do with the

Table 11.1. What Do You Find Fulfilling About Your Present Work?
(Asked of 12 Active Groups)

	%	(N)
Meeting an important need	83%	(10)
Being a spiritual/emotional presence to those served	83%	(10)
Being present in the local area	75%	(9)
Serving people	75%	(9)
Bringing about change		
in the institutions	50%	(6)
in society	67%	(8)
Ability to facilitate the accomplishment of projects	58%	(7)
Personal fulfillment		
learning new things	42%	(5)
using my gifts and talents	58%	(7)

role of women. I think lots of us consider ourselves somewhat feminist, but, as our positions have been filled by people who are not members of our [order], in 90 percent of the cases they're filled by males. Now I just think that that says something. . . . I feel that there's an irony that somehow we really stand for women moving forward in ministry, in the Church, in influence, but it's males, for the most part, who are governing our health care institutions.
- This is sort of related to what everybody [else] is saying here, but in [comparing] the situation where I am, being formerly sponsored by the Sisters of X, where all the staff was sisters and all the administrators were sisters, to the present situation. You have a male principal and assistant principal, and the head of all the departments, except one, are men and the majority of the faculty are men. When you were talking about the little bit of control that you have, well, you can divide that a little bit further if you lose the sponsorship role (Focus Group 2.6: Active and retired sisters).

The operation became local. The emphasis was on putting the boards in the hands of the local organizations, and not managed or influenced greatly by the national [mission society] leadership (Focus Group 4.1: Retired deaconesses).

And one community center director said, "What do we owe the [mission society] or the [denomination]? They fund only 3 percent of our budget (Focus Group 4.2: Retired deaconesses).

Since the general culture of the religious sponsors has devalued authoritative styles of leadership, some of the sponsoring groups' leaders, while nominally the supervisors of the male lay administrators in their institutions, may be reluctant even to exercise their remaining authority for fear of being labeled "authoritarian."[14]

In other cases, the women's institutions were merged with other, male-run, denominational entities. The power in these new, merged entities was *not* seen as equally shared. In one instance, the sisters' college had merged with a nearby Jesuit university:

I worked at Y University for twelve years [after the merger], and for me it became more and more difficult, because there were fewer and fewer sisters who felt welcome there. Jesuits are just overpowering, besides being chauvinistic. . . . And so, the Sisters of X have had to fight so hard just to prove their existence in a sense. I loved what I was doing, and I felt very proud to be a Sister of X, but it was getting harder and harder, when fewer and fewer of us were there (Focus Group 2.1: Active sisters).

The merger of the separate women's mission societies with denominational mission boards also diluted the women's power, since their representation on the merged boards was always less than a majority, and the women were never chosen for top positions.[15] This further reduced their ability to influence the institutions they had formerly controlled.

Power Within the Denomination

In the past, the women's power within their respective denominations was largely exercised through "gender hegemony" tactics—they controlled the institutions and resources needed by the larger denomination. As this control lessened, women have increasingly sought power through "Integration" tactics—filling primary labor market positions in local congregations and in regional judicatories. Protestant women entered ordained ministry; Catholic sisters, while officially barred from ordination, nevertheless served as pastoral associates, directors of religious education, and even as pastors of parishes lacking an ordained priest.[16]

Have these new "Integration" paths to power within the ecclesiastical mainstream been as effective as the separate, "Gender Hegemonic" paths were in the past? In the opinion of many focus group participants, they were not. When the sisters and deaconesses in the twelve active focus groups were asked what they found frustrating about their current jobs, many complained about a loss of power, not only in their institutions, but also in the local churches and in the larger denomination:

> I share the frustration of the male-oriented Church at this point, and I have difficulties with the [priests] who are very pre-Vatican II in their thinking. You are trying so hard to move your parishioners into the post-Vatican II Church, and you have people who are almost fighting you. I work with a deacon who is extremely pre-Vatican II and doesn't want to do anything except be seen in the limelight of the celebration, so it can be very frustrating. (Focus Group 1.3: Active sisters).

> We used to have, you know, our own board of missions. And then it became [one part of the denomination's] board of global ministries [which was divided into] the Women's Division, the National Division, and the World Division. And the women who had been administering their projects, raising the money, recruiting the staff—I mean, doing the whole thing—had to turn it over (Focus Group 4.2: Retired deaconesses).

It is true that at least some participants in ten of the 27 focus groups of active and retired sisters and deaconesses also mentioned having had positive relationships with the ordained clergy with whom they had served. In all of these cases, however, these were *personal* relationships: i.e., they depended on the idiosyncratic characteristics of the individuals involved:

> Thank God for my pastor who allows me to do everything and doesn't stand over my shoulder looking at what I'm doing. That's been a real blessing to have someone who gives you credit and lets you do what you want and stands beside you. So, I've found the job very interesting and exciting. (Focus Group 1.3: Active sisters).

In contrast, seventeen focus groups mentioned *negative* relationships with the ordained clergy, and, for twelve of the seventeen, the difficulties were seen as systemic:

> To me, there's not always clarity about what a deaconess is. It's squishy, and I look at it from a legality point, in terms of what the [denomination's official rules] say. What we are and what the Bishop does and what we have the right to do and it makes me furious and there's a part of me that asks, when do we suffer in silence and when do we—in the face of whoever we need to be in the face of—read them [the rule book] and say, "This is what the [rules] say." (Focus Group 4.3: Active deaconesses).

> Everything is given to [the seminarians] free, no obligation to repay, or anything. Which cultivates the attitude that they're not very service-oriented at all, nor are they learning any kind of stewardship. (Focus Group 1.3: Active sisters).

The sisters who had once held administrative positions in their own institutions found it especially difficult to work in parish-level positions where they were legally barred from the full pastorate:

> After being in a leadership position, being at a hospital, I think I have developed some skills, organizational skills, administrative skills. And when you want to transfer these into a parish ministry, you meet with a great deal of opposition. "We tried that; it won't work." Stuff like that. Or to try to initiate things when you're working in a situation where the pastor is ill or doesn't see the need, that was hard for me (Focus Group 3.6: Former leaders and staff).

On the other hand, several of the deaconesses' focus groups noted that ordination was *not* a more effective path to denominational power. The glass ceiling was still very much in evidence:

> Well, I'm very grateful I was not called to ordination because, when I look at what some of my friends are going through who were women who were called to ordination, they are having one heck of a time. The "good old boys' club," they refer to it as [laughter] (Focus Group 4.3: Active deaconesses).

As table 11.2 shows, loss of power and influence was not the most frequently-cited source of frustration in the focus groups. Nevertheless, restrictive church rules and difficulties with the clergy were mentioned almost half of the time, even though no question had specifically asked about this.

Table 11.2. What Do You Find Frustrating About Your Present Work?
(Asked of 12 Active Groups)

	%	(N)
Difficulties with the population served	67%	(8)
Lack of time	58%	(7)
Restrictive Church Rules; Difficulties with Clergy	42%	(5)
Lack of funds	42%	(5)
Excessive paperwork	42%	(5)

The focus group interviews, therefore, indicate that integration of the women into the larger denomination's primary labor market, in contrast to their hegemony within a separate set of institutions, may not have increased their ecclesiastical power. Numerous studies of denominations that ordain women have found that women seminary graduates receive less-desirable first positions, and that the gap between male and female ministers only widens in subsequent years.[17] Within denominational bureaucracies, integration of women may not ensure equality either. For one thing, the sheer number of administrative and professional layers in denominational bureaucracies has increased, diluting the women's voice.[18] Immediately after one denomination's attempt at integration, the participation of women on its newly-merged conference boards and agencies was less than 25 percent, and only 13 percent of the lay delegates to its General Conference were women.

Viewing the aftermath of the switch from Group Hegemony to Integration, therefore, one early author concluded that:

> 10. The present structures of society, especially ecclesiastical structures, are male-oriented. It is not easy for women to participate.
> 12. Where organized women's groups have been removed from a visible policy-making and power-sharing role (in other denominations) the following things tend to occur:
>   a.) male chauvinism increases
>   b.) the status of women declines
>   c.) The image of the *laos* is distorted.
> 13. For the sake of the whole, as well as for ourselves, the denomination needs to maintain an organized women's group which exercises real power. Otherwise, women will have to reorganize later, under more difficult circumstances.[19]

As their ties to their former institutions diminish, that portion of church women's power that was tied to these institutions also decreases. It is interesting that one recent article on how to foster the religious identity of Catholic health care institutions nowhere mentions a role for Catholic religious orders.[20] The formerly powerful role of these women in the Church, a key result of their presence in their institutions, is now so attenuated that it can be passed over without comment.

Power in the Larger Society

Finally, the women's loss of their own institutions has meant the loss of a certain kind of power in the society at large. One recent author noted that the Catholic health care ministry is the largest not-for-profit health care system in the U.S., as Catholic Charities is the largest social service agency and Catholic schools the largest private educational system. "Size never proved anything, but there is something to presence. If one seeks to influence, shape, direct, heal, elevate, and enrich a complex industrial democracy, *it cannot be done simply by the integrity of individual witness. It is done by institutions.*"[21] A sister in one of the preliminary interviews echoed this observation:

> One of the things that would be lost [if our order gave up its institutions] would be the power institutions have. There's just something about an institution that can give a punch that maybe an individual cannot. Maybe it's the advocacy role of the institutions; it's got the power to reach powerful people more so than an individual might have (Individual Sister Interview: Former elementary school principal and present member of her order's governing council).

Sisters in one of the leaders' focus groups agreed:

> - If you don't have corporate works, I think it's harder to exert power in any particular situation.
> - I think there's a tremendous gap in the visibility, the influence, the ability to attract others—
> - The ability to bring about systemic change without the stable institutions we can bounce off of (Focus Group 2.3: Present and former leaders).

Many of the mission societies had always used their organizational power to influence social policy, beginning with the Temperance Movement of the late nineteenth century.[22] The Woman's Division of the Methodist Church, for example, had a third department in addition to ones for Home and Foreign Missions: the Department of Christian Social Relations and Local Church Activities. Through this department, Methodist women advocated for numerous social causes throughout the 1940s and 1950s: the repeal of the Chinese Exclusion Act, the extension of Social Security to domestic and farm workers, and the enactment of anti-lynching legislation.[23] The department also conducted national seminars on a variety of issues, including the rights of women within the denomination itself. Prior to the loss of their institutional ties, however, these activities were seen as secondary to fund-raising for mission work. This balance has now reversed:

> When we lost that major focus on institutional ministries, [when] we lost our management and control of institutional ministries, we didn't lose our statement of purpose, our working around ministries with women, children, and youth. We simply, I think, expanded our understanding beyond—way beyond—institutional ministries. We took on other things in other countries and we took on things here. . . . We got into the J.P. Stevens boycott or the Nestle boycott, or we did some things with political skills workshops, teaching women how to do things in a political setting (Individual Interview: Retired deaconess).

> One of the things that I like to focus on is the fact that I think the [Mission Society] is on top of things. For instance, there's a campaign that's coming out again about the ecological aspect of what's going on . . . no use of Styrofoam, no use of plastics any more. All these kind of things they keep before the women so

that we can have a world to live in in the 2000's, you know, and we're not self-destructing. And that's what I like also about the Church, about our organization. They keep these issues before the ladies and so that they can buy into it . . . that the person at the local level can buy into this rather than everybody at the top making decisions (Focus Group 5.9: Mission society).

But many of the members resist or ignore such activity. One of the mission society focus groups contained a regional official, who took advantage of her chance to offer the other participants information on the society's social action programs:

- Are any of you interested in social action? Have you gotten involved in the men and women's Division of Social Action? I can provide [information on] that.
- No.
- Yes, I'd probably be interested to see. You know, when I joined the church, I was interested in what the denomination's doctrines are and things like that.
- What are you talking about?
- Mount Olive Pickles. They're trying to get them to negotiate with unions and pay their wages to the guy that picks the pickles, the cucumbers, and they're refusing to negotiate.
[Interviewer: Are there any of the local chapters that you're involved with that are doing anything on these kinds of issues either internationally or locally? You know, like protesting unfair labor practices?]
- Outside of the [general office] I don't think it's happening (Focus Group 5.2: Mission society).

In several cases, the local members held opinions and values on a social issue that conflicted with the activist stance of the leadership. Dissent on external issues surfaced in six of the nine mission society focus group interviews:

On the national level, [the denominational policy] is supposed to be pro-choice, but then, also, people say, "Well, I really cannot vote for that, so, should I be pro-life?" Well, the Church isn't going to tell you, but there are many who are backing that. So I think that's part of it, people are so scattered with their issues. (Focus Group 5.3: Mission society).

We're trying to get the younger people interested in us and more up-to-date, you know, 2000 and all this. It's a new generation, I guess. Also, we are doing more social things rather than mission things.
[Interviewer: What kinds of social things?]
We're doing things like, we're getting into—almost meddling in other folks' business as far as moral things are concerned. Mission to me is different than social issues (Focus Group 5.9: Mission society).

But it's just—I want to know that what I believe the [denomination] is locally, is what the [denomination] is districtwide, statewide, and nationally. I want to know that what I'm saying I'm a part of and what I believe in is the same and so it concerns me that a national group may be saying "We're supporting this" when a local group isn't aware of it (Focus Group 5.2: Mission society).

Such alienation also began to be reflected in the official publications of the mission societies, many of which had been reconfigured to reflect the new social emphases. In *response*, the magazine of the United Methodist Women,[24] for example, allusions to conflicts and disagreements over the organization's direction began to appear in editorials almost as soon as the first issue appeared; by 1974, four of the ten issues contained such references. Some of the letters to the editor were even more blunt:

I wish to express my disapproval of the article "Tell It Like It Is" in your first issue of *response*. I do not believe an article like this can enrich lives or help us as we serve the United Methodist Church. . . . It can only breed larger problems and is a definite aid to Communism. [The author] did an excellent job of condemning his country and his elders (*response,* April 1969).

Being of conservative mind, but not a radical, I read [article] with interest. . . . It strikes me that the author, and your magazine in reprinting the article, exhibit a strong bias against conservative or right wing in favor of the liberal or left-wing (*response*, May 1969).

It seems to me that your new magazine is too one-sided. It puts too much emphasis on the social needs of poor people and people with social problems, but says very little about their spiritual needs (*response*, June-July 1969).

I only today picked up *response* to look at the stories published therein in May, 1973. As I read, . . . I was appalled and disillusioned. . . . First, let me say, if you are a "Women's Liberator"—that's your business; but must you bombard us, the readers, with your propaganda? (*response* October, 1973).

One writer claimed that readership in her state of Wisconsin had dropped 24 percent due to objections to the magazine's new focus (October 1969).

Other letter writers, however, took issue with the critics of the magazine's stance:

I feel urged to answer those who write to you complaining about response, asking that it be geared as it was ten years ago. Really, how could it be helpful for this day if it did not challenge us to ACTION? Spiritual material, more Bible, is fine, but if it makes us feel smug and satisfied, then we are not alive, growing Christians (*response*, March 1971).

I am always disturbed when Christian (?) Women get so violently angry at such articles as "The Time of Lettuce." My personal feeling is that our church leaders and writers are often today's prophets, and I hate to think that we who are supposedly enlightened don't heed any better than the people in Bible times. (*response*, May 1973).

I would like to take exception to the writers who objected to some of the prayers from other faiths in the photo story "People at Prayer." We cannot present a true ecumenical face to the world if we are to include only those whose prayers come within our understanding and approval (*response*, May 1973).

In spite of these controversies, the tenor of the magazine did not change. By the 1990s, it showed an actual *increase* in articles devoted to potentially controversial external issues: the death penalty, welfare reform, health care funding, and the like. At the same time, however, the denomination's divided voice vitiates the power the members can mobilize in the larger society to address these issues.

Conclusion

Loss of their institutions has thus seriously lessened the ability of women to wield "group hegemonic" power within their denominations or in the larger society. In many denominations, this power has not been replaced by integration of the women into formerly male-dominated roles in the larger church. And, without their institutions, the ability of the women to influence local and national government policies must now depend solely on whether the order or society can continue mobilizing its members to speak with a united voice. In many cases this, too, is increasingly difficult to do. Even internal power—the authority of the leadership over the members—has been reduced.

But do these changes—loss of identity, loss of intellectual focus, loss of power—actually matter, outside of the women's groups themselves? Should the rest of the members of the denomination, or of the larger society, care whether these groups change, stagnate, or go extinct? It is to this question that we now turn.

Notes

1. See Doeringer and Piore (1971), Piore (1972) and Salaman (1981:109-110) for an explication of Dual Labor Market Theory.

2. First of all, one could cite the studies of ethnic hegemony in the economic structures of American cities (e.g., Light 1972; Kim 1981; Light and Bonacich 1988; Waldinger et al. 1990; Jiobu 1989). According to this literature, immigrant ethnic groups which managed to win control over all aspects of a particular economic niche—Koreans and small grocery stores in Manhattan, Chinese and stationery shops, or Japanese and specialized farming—are able to use this dominance to secure employment for co-ethnics, to buffer themselves and their community against the vicissitudes of the larger economy, and ultimately to force the "center" actors of society—city governments, labor unions, chambers of commerce—to take them seriously. In contrast, ethnic groups which fail to develop their own separate economic base, but press instead for integration into the societal center, often encounter "glass ceilings" that inhibit their rise to power and influence.

A second body of literature has focused on the rise of women entrepreneurs—primarily in response to the continuing "glass ceiling" in mainstream American corporations (Powell 1999; Smith 2000; Carr 2000). While the majority of this literature simply describes the characteristics of the individual women who choose to found their own companies, a limited number of studies indicate that women achieve greater power and independence by entrepreneurship than by working in male-dominated corporations. See Moore (1999:382-383) for a good summary of these studies.

3. Brasher (1998:66-67). See also Chaves (1997:14-37).

4. See Carroll et al. (1983), Lehman (1985, 1993); Clark and Anderson (1990), Schmidt (1996), Chang (1997), Charlton (1997), Chaves and Cavendish (1997), Nesbitt (1997a, 1997b), Zikmund, Lummis, and Chang (1998), McDuff and Mueller (1999).

5. See Isham (1936), Tatum (1960), Meeker (1969), Ewens (1981), Keller (1981), McDowell (1982), Boyd and Brackenridge (1983), Oates (1985), Prelinger (1986a; 1986b), Deacon(1989), Ginzberg (1990), Higgenbotham (1993), Bartholomeusz (1994), McNamara (1996), Brasher (1998), Daigler (2000), Wall (2002)

6. Brasher (1998:13). See Brasher (1998:20) for the quotation in the following sentence. See also Higgenbotham (1993) and Griffith (1997).

7. Lehman (1993:14).

8. Kenneally (1990:43).

9. See, for example, Hill (1973:214-217), McNamara (1996:420-423), and Ranft, (1998:63-64).

10. See, for example, Berger (1999:37-40) for Wicca, and Palmer (2000) for new religious movements.

11. Ebaugh (1993:62).

12. Ebaugh (1993:109). Cleary (2001:216) further speculates that the larger culture devalues firm authoritarian leadership styles in non-profits, in favor of more collaborative leadership. This may further prevent the sisters from exercising their authority.

13. According to Holtschneider and Morey (2000b:6), orders of men choose male presidents to head their colleges 89 percent of the time, while congregations of women choose male presidents 52 percent of the time (See also Daigler 2000:181). Sanders (1988:13) makes a similar observation for hospitals.

14. Cleary (2001:216) makes this point.

15. Hill (1985:167-90) and Campbell (1975:18) make this point.

16. See Wallace (1992). Women held nearly half of all administrative and professional positions in U.S. Catholic dioceses in 2003, according to a report released by the U.S. Bishops' Committee on Women in Society and in the Church [*America* 2004, volume 191:(1):6].

17. See Chang (1997), Royle (1982), Lehman (1985), Nason-Clark (1987). See also O'Neill (1989:41).

18. Harder (1997:380-81) notes that the number of paid administrative personnel of the General Conference Mennonite Church headquarters mushroomed from only one in 1946 to 31 by 1963, and has continued to increase since that time. See Campbell (1975:45) for the figures in the following sentence.

19. Campbell (1975:50-51). This author noted that the statement quoted above was "part of a longer statement made to a general church committee that was looking at total reorganization of the Church and suggesting that the Woman's Missionary Society might be eliminated, merged with the lay men's group, or greatly diminished in its policy-making body. This was a defense for our continued existence" (Campbell, private communication).

20. Hehir (1995).

21. Hehir (1995:2). Emphasis added.

22. See Edwards and Gifford (2003).

23. Stevens (1978:33). See Stevens (1978:41) for information on the department's seminars.

24. *Response* succeeded the society's previous publication, *The Methodist Woman*, which was itself a successor to a series of denominational publications stretching back to 1869.

Chapter 12

The Transformation of Religious Virtuosity

For the past two hundred years and more, Catholic sisters, Protestant deaconesses, and the women in denominational mission societies exemplified a novel, service-oriented version of religious virtuosity. Perhaps uniquely in the panoply of faith traditions across the centuries, this "inner-worldly" virtuoso spirituality had also become inextricably tied to institutional service. After the original, spiritual meanings attached to teaching, nursing, and social work had diminished, these institutions became the essential remaining link between engaging in these now-secular occupations—which any professional lay woman or man could do—and the women's religious virtuosity. It was not because the sisters and deaconesses taught, nursed, or engaged in social service that they were seen as religious virtuosi; it was because they did so together in specific denominational institutions—institutions that, in turn, derived their religious identity from the women's presence. It was not the fact that mission society women collected and disbursed charitable funds at home or abroad that was their most salient characteristic; it was that they did their fund-raising together as an organization, and that the causes they supported were embodied in institutions that their societies officially sponsored or owned. It was through their schools, hospitals, and social service agencies that the deaconesses, sisters, and mission society members responded to their religious call; each institution was, as one sister put it, "a living example of our mission and vision statements. It is the place where we put our words into actions, our lives on the line."[1] The institutions were an essential and unquestioned component of the *virtuoso* identity of the sisters, deaconesses, and mission society members, just as the women's sponsorship was an essential and unquestioned component of the institutions' religious identity.

259

Ideological Weaknesses and Unanswered Questions

When the relationship between a denominational sponsor and its institutions is so completely taken for granted, however, the task of explicitly articulating this relationship—especially as it changes over time—is often neglected. Several scholars have noted this neglect in traditionally Protestant and Catholic institutions of higher education.[2] Similar neglect may have occurred, however, within the sponsoring groups themselves. As a young sister in one of the focus groups commented:

> I think our involvement, our corporate involvement in institutions bodily, just business-wise, has changed dramatically, and I think it's also changed the flavor and the shape of our [order].
> [Interviewer: In what ways?]
> In some very obvious ways. In my own immediate experience, I'm not part of a household of 17 or 20 or 100 people. I've lived in a smaller group setting. . . . So I bring a very different experience of community, and in some respects a very different experience of ministry than other folks in the Sisters of X who are twenty years older than I am (Focus Group 3.11: Young sisters).

Later, another member of the same focus group noted:

> The question that you raised of who I am as a Sister of X, given that we don't have all of these institutions, what does it mean, is it a life-giving question? Because it gets to the heart of who we are as [an order]. What is our charism, what is our call, what is our mission? We can't take for granted what our call, or our mission, is. I certainly don't as a newer member, take that for granted. It's changing too quickly. It looks different even in the short time I've been in the Sisters of X. And so the questions that have been raised here are significant, hard questions that are important to us (Focus Group 3.11: Young sisters).

By and large, however, the Catholic orders, the Protestant deaconesses, and the mission society members have had only limited success in grappling with these questions. There are several reasons for this.

The first difficulty is the current lack of a compelling theology which is supportive of religious institutions and, consequently, of a virtuoso spirituality based on institutional service. The nineteenth century post-millennial theology that had once celebrated Christian institutions as essential building blocks for the coming reign of God—and the workers and administrators in these institutions as true religious virtuosi engaged in endeavors of cosmic significance—is no longer persuasive. In fact, a key component of late twentieth and early twenty-first century Western society is a profound distrust of *all* types of institutions: governmental, business, educational, and religious.[3] Large, complex organizations—even large, complex, religious organizations—are now seen as spiritual negatives, decoupling and sequestering the deepest existential and ethical questions of life from their daily operations.[4] Most of the focus groups expressed opinions that resonated with the words of a leading Mennonite educator: "Do Anabaptists have a theology of institutions?"[5] Unless and until a new ideology can be developed that sacralizes the administration of, and service in, formally "religious" institutions, they will continue to be unattractive to coming generations of religious virtuosi. As a recent author has commented:

> Few models officially sanctified by the Church show work in the world as a spiritual path—and fewer still reveal this path for women. In reality, women saints have been leaders, managers, preachers, teachers, and innovators. They have begun religious orders, built hospitals, resisted powerful critics, negotiated with popes and politicians. Yet their saintliness seldom is linked predominantly with their work or leadership.[6]

This lacuna has encouraged active, inner-worldly religious virtuosi to compartmentalize their working lives from their faith, a compartmentalization which weakened its transformative potential. As one of the sisters in the preliminary interviews put it:

> We have, and [Catholic religious orders] across the country have, created a dichotomy between the sacred and the profane in ministry. We have declared [some fields] profane and less acceptable. Suppose you had a stockbroker who wanted to enter the Sisters of X. The novice director would feel she had seven years to change this woman's mind and steer her into pastoral ministry before she made final vows. What would happen if we were really *open* to all areas of ministry? Subconsciously, we are setting ourselves up not to attract people from these professions (Individual Sister Interview: Former health care system CEO).

Similarly, nine of the 27 deaconesses' and sisters' focus groups commented on the difficulty of reconciling their institutional involvement with a virtuoso call:

> The word struggle, I think, should be one of the most prominent things we should talk about. Because, it seems to me, we're constantly struggling now, against culture, against the mores of the world and in health care, to maintain our humanity and mercy and compassion in the face of economic constraints. That is really very difficult. It's like knowing what the ideal is, but you have the reality to work with, and how do you do it? It's very difficult to keep feeling positive about it when it seems the whole world is fighting against what we stand for (Focus Group 2.1: Active sisters).

In the absence of a coherent virtuoso spirituality of institutional service, ten of the sixteen focus groups of active[7] sisters and deaconesses, and three of the nine mission society focus groups, expressed a preference for one-on-one personal activities rather than organizational occupations as a way of expressing their spiritual call:

I felt really frustrated in the classroom after a while, because I felt like I really wasn't making a difference in these kids' lives. Because I wasn't getting to their parents. And I read about a family literacy program and I thought, "This is where I want to be. I want to be in a program that strengthens families and helps parents with their literacy skills as well as their children (Focus Group 4.3: Active deaconesses).

I think there is that sense out there of people wanting to be more engaged with things that are religious, at least in some aspect, some direct aspect, not just sort of part of an institution, but you never touch it yourself and you're always dealing with the staff or whatever (Focus Group 2.3: Present and former leaders).

This preference was reflected again when the sisters and deaconesses were asked to list the aspects of their ministries which they found the most satisfying or fulfilling. The most common sources of satisfaction were *personally* meeting an important need, serving people, and being a spiritual or emotional presence to others—whether this occurred in or outside an institutional setting:

It's very rewarding because the people that we visit have nobody, sometimes, to visit them, so it's great to uplift them and to know that somebody cares or that somebody's interested in them. And it's very—I hate to say self-satisfying, because that's not the purpose—but I just enjoy watching these people and how they blossom out when we visit them and they say, "Please don't go, stay a little longer," and "Please come back," and "We're so happy that you have come to see us." So I find it very rewarding in that way. They give us so much, because I have seen so much faith and so much love in these people, that they give us probably more than we give them (Focus Group 1.5: Active sisters).

I love what I'm doing, too. I love listening to people and being there to listen to them and I feel like I'm the link between the older people and the parish and I feel like even going to nursing homes, we have people in nursing homes all over the city, and even people with Alzheimer's. I start talking about the parish and the community and the people they know, and their faces just light up. And just saying an Our Father or a Hail Mary with them, they chime in and it's just so special to be there for them (Focus Group 3.7: Active sisters).

Note that these examples refer to personal, one-on-one service. Far more sisters' and deaconesses' focus groups cited *personal* forms of service or presence as a source of fulfillment or satisfaction than the number of groups that mentioned receiving satisfaction from the *institutions'* service or presence:

What gives me life is the knowledge that we are in the center city, so we serve a broad range of people, but what gives me life is the fact that I know we are serving people who are underserved. And what also gives me great energy is that we are providing employment for a large number of people who are at the lower economic level, but who have not only a place to work, but also have health care benefits, etc. So meeting those people every day is enlivening for me (Focus

Group 2.6: Active sisters).

However, comments such as this last speaker's were rare.

Individual Virtuoso Ideologies

In the absence of a coherent virtuoso ideology that valued institutional administration and service, the sisters' and deaconesses' sense of their vocational distinctiveness declined.[8] Numerous studies have noted a lack of "role clarity" among Catholic sisters that began in the mid-1960s. The distinctions between deaconesses, home missionaries, and lay workers were also blurring among Protestants.[9] One history of Methodist deaconesses noted that:

> On January 6, 1967, Richard H. Bauer, commission member and Executive Secretary of the Interboard Committee on Christian Vocations, responded in a letter criticizing the working paper for getting "lost in a lot of generalities." Having read the statement "several times," Bauer, who was coordinator of the lay worker study, "returned again and again to the conviction" that it could apply to any committed laywoman. He told [the head of the Methodist deaconesses], "If it is necessary to 'justify' the office, then we may be in worse condition than I think we are."[10]

As the specifically religious roles of the sisters and deaconesses became less distinct, some observers feared that their professional identities would begin to eclipse their identities as religious virtuosi. One nationwide study of Catholic religious orders in the United States discovered that:

> Interestingly, the more highly educated individuals among the population experienced lower role clarity as members of religious orders. Considered by field of study, members of religious orders in the more applied disciplines, such as the business, education, or health professions indicated that they were less clear about their role as members of religious orders in the church when compared to those whose training was in the more theoretical disciplines, such as theology, the humanities, and the social sciences. *The role demands of health care provision and education may present pressures that replace or compete with, rather than complement, the current role of members of religious orders in the church. It may well be that other roles take precedence over the religious identity.*[11]

"Boundary-spanning" ties among the most professionalized sisters and deaconesses —their membership in secular professional associations and their employment in increasingly bureaucratized organizational settings—may spark invidious comparisons that place their religious order in an inferior position. "Such situations are likely to create salient identity threats for members."[12] In the face of such competing role demands from professional and bureaucratic sources, religious orders may lose any influence over their members, whose personal identities and roles have become "engulfed" by the larger social structure.

The Catholic sisters interviewed for this study rarely cited their institutional ministries as the key factor distinguishing their order from other religious orders or themselves from lay church workers. Some no longer saw any difference at all between one order and another. Those respondents who did see a difference tended to cite a non-institutional basis for it: their community was friendlier or more down-to-earth than some other order they had once considered entering. Such qualities, of course, are less specific to any given religious order than operating a set of institutions had been, and may not be strong enough to ground the order's identity:

> If you try to get at our identity, I think most [of us] are very comfortable about being just kind of common, ordinary, hardworking, faith-filled [people]. That's about it. Now does that make a religious [sister]? It's not much different than any other person. But I guess my point is that, when there's a group that kind of fits and melds together with that kind of identity, then that's the core of who we are all about. And I can't name it in a word; I know we've tried to come up with a little statement or whatever and we always find it very hard to do that (Individual Sister Interview: Provincial superior).

In addition to having difficulty defining the difference between their own order and another one, many sisters and deaconesses were also unable to articulate how their own service as a social worker, teacher, or nurse differed from being a lay woman in a similar occupation:

> [Interviewer:] How is being a sister-teacher different?
> I don't think there is any difference today. And the children, they don't seem to distinguish between the two (Individual Sister Interview: Retired high school principal).

> - You can serve as a Christian in anything without becoming a deaconess.
> [Several voices] Right.
> - But she wanted a way to express the commitment that she felt to service (Focus Group 4.2: Retired deaconesses).

> I guess, whereas before, I found myself identified personally more by what I did, and when I worked in a Sister of X sponsored institution that identification was easier. Now, more and more, I'm thinking that being a Sister of X really is very different than where I work. This might not be clear. Well, it's not very clear in my own head. . . . Maybe being a sister has more to do with living a religious life and bringing that "who you are" to your job, regardless of what you're doing, because we might be doing a whole raft of things. This is not clear. Maybe someone else can add to what I am saying? (Focus Group 2.5: Active sisters)

This confusion has led, at times, to a profound theological anomie. Timothy Radcliffe, the international head of the male Dominican order, has compared religious orders to "blacksmiths in a world of cars, wandering around looking for a new role."[13] Some of the sisters in the focus groups agreed:

> I don't know. Seems like we were formed to be one kind of person then, and now we're wandering between two worlds, one dead and the other powerless to be born. But that's probably the way it's always been for people (Focus Group 2.1: Active sisters).

In the vacuum left by the dissolution of institutionally-based religious virtuosity, variant virtuoso forms might be imported from the larger environment: from other denominations, for example, or from American society as a whole. This is similar to borrowings noted in the cultures of other kinds of organizations: "For reasons of legitimacy as well as for the reason of adapting a cognitive view of the social world as ordered and comprehensible, people in organizations are sensitive to the meanings, ideas, and definitions" current in similar groups.[14] Many of the religious orders and societies thus engaged in mimetic isomorphism, borrowing each other's attempts to articulate new virtuoso spiritualities based on ecological consciousness, Christian or Eastern mysticism, Native American spiritual forms, or even New Age concepts.[15] Organic farms, ecological centers, hermitages, labyrinths, and religious art studios have sprouted at the motherhouses of various religious orders across the country, often with little reasoned connection to each other or to the order's original spiritual focus.[16]

In the absence of an internally-coherent group spirituality, individual sisters, deaconesses, and mission society members might also forge their own personal spiritualities in an attempt to link together their work and their religious vocations. Some saw their work as a form of moral selving: "the work of creating oneself as a more virtuous, and often more spiritual, person. Moral selving may be understood as one type of deeply emotional self work. It involves a concern for transforming the experience of an underlying moral self, in contrast to a situated identity."[17]

Table 12.1 shows some of the ways that the active sisters and deaconesses, and the mission society members, related their work to their religious vocation (or, in the case of the mission society, to their calling as Christians). Several cited some form of moral selving: eleven of the sixteen[18] active focus groups of sisters and deaconesses, for example, mentioned that their ministries afforded them some sort of personal or spiritual growth:

> All along the way, I've enjoyed the changes and challenges. I guess "strength-ened" is the way to put it. I guess, with it all, I have a sense of personal growth and spiritual growth to be faithful to what we all knew and learned to do together and then to translate that in terms of your own growth and your own variety of situations (Focus Group 1.6: Active and retired sisters).

> I feel like I grow a little bit more because I spend so much time with scripture and [teaching] people who come into the Church, and moving along in their faith, and

Table 12.1. "How Does Your Present Work Relate to Your Religious Vocation/ Your Christian Calling?"
(Asked of 16 Non-retired Focus Groups of Sisters and Deaconesses and All 9 Focus Groups of Mission Society Members*)

Connection Mentioned:	# Focus Groups
Provides opportunity to engage in direct service	13
Provides opportunity for personal fulfillment/spiritual growth	11
This work is God's will for me	9
It is a way to witness or represent God	9
My vocation is a source of strength in ministry	9
Each complements the other	8
Helps continue the work of the founder	7
My vocation/call has catalyzed my involvement in Church service	7
My vocation/call has catalyzed my involvement in social justice activities	4
My present work is less important	13
than my connection with other members of the order/society	7
than my call from God	4
than my personal spiritual growth	3
My present work harms or hinders my vocation	13
by reducing the time spent with other members	9
by reducing the time available for prayer	4

* Mission society members and deaconesses were asked how their activities related to their calling as a Christian; Catholic sisters were asked how their work related to their religious vocation.

faith sharing (Focus Group 3.12: Active and retired sisters).

> Even though I'm retired, I'm a companion at [order's skilled nursing home for elderly sisters], and I find that is a very valuable experience because it helps me to come to grips with my own mortality. To see sisters [dying] and to hear the doctor say, "I can't do anything more for you"—that's a big learning experience for me, so that's neat (Focus Group 3.6: Former leaders and staff).

Respondents in nine of the active sisters' and deaconesses' focus groups found additional spiritual inspiration in those they served or in their lay co-workers:

> I'm always astounded at people in their suffering, and how faith-filled some are. And instead of my giving them ministry, I find they minister to me. Because they are just beautiful. One particular story to give you an example. I was to visit this patient who had no legs, she had only one arm, she was totally blind and I don't even know what her internal problems were, and I'm saying to myself as I'm going to her room, "God, what can I say to bring comfort to her?" And when I went in and identified who I was, she reached for my hand and she said, "Oh, sister, I thank God every day for my blessings." So that's the kind of faith that just absolutely moves you, and you're so glad to be there in that given moment (Focus Group 1.3: Active sisters).

Three of the nine mission society focus groups also mentioned that their society's activities afforded them opportunities for personal spiritual growth:

> I just wanted to go [to the mission society events] and have fun, but the side benefit was that I feel like I've grown in my spirituality more having come, and I am in awe of so many people that are members of this group who I feel are so much more deeply spiritual than I ever have felt like I was and, uh, I, I'm just in awe of them and I so admire their dedication. And they're fun, too [laughter] (Focus Group 5.3: Mission society).

> It's a wonderful place to have in your life. The spiritual nourishment and you get a sense of direction. The involvement with the rest of the world, missions are important and the ideas of the church are important, even though sometimes you don't agree with them (Focus Group 5.5: Mission society).

For all of these respondents, therefore, their activities served in one way or another to strengthen their religious calling or spiritual growth. However, sisters and deaconesses in nine of the sixteen active groups also mentioned the reverse: that their religious calling was a source of strength that enabled them to perform what would otherwise be impossibly draining tasks:

> So now, like when the patients' files and charts are piling up and you just want to slam your head on the table because you've got to get out, I mean, there's that constant reminder to say, among ourselves, "This is what we are about," you know, "We are not a business." You know, we help each other to stay focused on

our mission of mercy and charity so it's much easier where I am now because we
are all sisters [working in this medical clinic] (Focus Group 1.4: Active sisters).[19]

I think, without the faith and the grace of vocation, the struggle would outweigh
what I believe to be the goodness of our presence, even in small numbers. I think
my vocation has become more valuable to me as I minister than I might have
thought about it fifteen or twenty years ago (Focus Group 2.1: Active sisters).

On the other hand, thirteen of the focus groups of sisters and deaconesses also
noted that the demands and stresses of their ministries could have a *detrimental*
impact on their spiritual life, by reducing their opportunities either for prayer or for
interaction with the others in their order:

I do think that there is an element of structured prayer life that we had when we
started out, and in some ways that is missing now. Like, Sister Mary and I—we
pray in the morning as many times as we can, unless we're running late or
something, and certain nights we can pray at 6:15 or 6:10, but if it gets to 6:30
and I have [evening catechism] classes, I can't [pray with her] because I have to
open up doors and classrooms and check them. But we try to establish a prayer
time (Focus Group 3.10: Active sisters).

While the focus group respondents did not minimize the negative impact that their
occupational "busyness" could have on their religious call, they were equally likely
to note the spiritual *benefits* attached to direct service—which implies some
remaining, perhaps unarticulated, assumption that such service is still a legitimate
form of virtuoso spirituality. On the other hand, some respondents in thirteen of the
focus groups also stated that whatever particular service they performed was *less*
important than their personal connection to other sisters, deaconesses, and mission
society members, than their own spiritual growth, or than their internalized sense
of God's personal call.[20] Still others were unable to separate service and call,
stating simply that their ministry was God's will for them, or that each comple-
mented the other.

Toward a Common Definition of Virtuoso Spirituality

Recent work by organizational culture theorists has noted the important role of
"sagas," or commonly shared stories that shape an organization's definition of itself
among its members.[21] In her study of two religious groups aiding the homeless—a
local Salvation Army group and a Catholic Worker house—Allahyari notes how
the volunteers in each setting reinforced their commitment to the sponsoring
group's distinctive ideology through their socializing and camaraderie as they
worked.[22] For the Catholic Worker volunteers, the homeless were Christ in
disguise; for the Salvation Army volunteers, they were individual souls to be pried
from the grasp of Satan and converted to Christ. The volunteers in each group

reinforced the spiritual grounding of their work through their mutual interaction as they prepared and served the daily meal to their "clients" (Salvation Army) or "guests" (Catholic Worker).[23] In like manner, the development of a new group definition of virtuoso spirituality is needed to validate the institutional activities of the sisters, deaconesses, and missionary societies today as truly religious work.

Especially among today's active deaconesses, there was evidence that the women were developing a similar repertoire of sagas or stories to re-shape and re-define the spiritual dimension of their call. Each of the participants in the focus group of active deaconesses recounted lengthy and often emotional tales of how they had come to join the diaconal order. With startling similarity, the stories included the teller's extended search for a form of church service she was not even sure how to describe, her experience of being discouraged from joining the deaconesses (or even being told that deaconesses no longer existed), her sudden feeling of "belonging" upon actually discovering the denomination's deaconesses, and a providential string of "divine coincidences" that led her to her current ministry:

> I've always known, I think, a kind of call to service since I was a child, wanting to work with people, wanting to help others. Not knowing how, but just wanting to do that. And I got involved in a lot of service organizations. . . .There was something missing, something I needed to do, needed to further my education so that I could find that one job or something that would meet this call that I felt. But there was always something missing. . . . Then, last March, my mother and [name of deaconess] were talking and she said to my mother, "Have you ever talked to your daughter?" [general laughter] . . . So I got in touch with [name of deaconess] and actually met her. And the moment I met her, I knew, "This is the right thing."

> In high school, I fell in love with [western state] and said, "I'm going to live and work there one day." Seven years ago at a convocation, there was a minister from [that state] speaking about the need, the invitation from the tribal council to start a church presence, and the [state] conference was looking for an ordained minister to go there. And some others I was sitting with were saying, "You don't really have to be an ordained minister to start what you want to start there." And I turned to [name of deaconess] and said, "That's my job, one day I'm going to do that job." Two years after that, I was teaching in [denomination's] college and wanted something different to do, and I called [head of the deaconesses] and said, "What was the name of that place in [state]?" And she said, "I think you would be great, call them." And I did, knowing all along that's what I'm supposed to do. And it took a year to work out the details . . . I had to go to a new village to get to know the people there to see if they would invite me back. And it was "Yeah, we want you to come but we have to have at least $25,000 to do this." OK. Three months later they had the $25,000. You know, no problem, all along this is where God wants me to be.

> I said, "If I could do anything I want, I would teach English in Colombia." And she said, "Oh, we've been thinking about sending somebody international. And I think the deaconesses have, too." So the next September, I was in Colombia

teaching, and I have first graders through fifth graders in a school that's in a very poor barrio, and I teach English at night to some parents and anybody else who happens to drop in. It's all very informal. But everything just fell into place.

I figured that God wanted these poor kids in [rural southern county] fed, and He just kept fishing until He found somebody that would do it. [laughter] . . . It took a whole year and I did a lot of talking over the year. Then, last spring, we got it going. Had the funniest budget, because every time we thought we had something going, we found out we needed to shift the budget around and so we needed more donations, and every time we did—plump!—in came the donations. It was just an amazing experience. . . . We had volunteers pop up at the right time. . . . (Focus Group 4.3: Active deaconesses).

Over 120 lines of the transcription of the active deaconesses' focus group (13 percent of the total) was devoted to recounting such stories, far more than the percentage for any of the focus groups of sisters or the missionary society. Since the office of deaconess in this particular denomination had undergone a major re-organization in the late 1950s and 1960s, being removed from participation in the denomination's institutions and also admitting married women for the first time, such stories are serving a profoundly useful purpose by articulating a new version of virtuoso spirituality that links the deaconesses' individual occupations—which are often *not* denominationally-sponsored—with their sense of call and church service.

Developing an Institutionally-Based Virtuoso Spirituality

Even if an order or mission society is able to develop anew a common virtuoso identity, however, such an identity may not be based on corporate institutional service. In fact, given the suspicion of all institutions in today's culture, an institution-based corporate identity may be strongly resisted.[24] In one of the active sisters' focus groups, for example, the participants had been discussing whether it was necessary to maintain a "core mass" of sisters working in a hospital or a school in order for it to retain its identity as a "Sister of X" institution. The following exchange then occurred, initiated by the focus group leader:

[Interviewer: Could I turn that on its head—is there a similar "critical mass" of activity in any one field or common area that the Sisters of X need, in order to keep themselves together and get a group identity that is as strong and as motivating as what the Legionaries have?][25]
– I know I've resisted that, and I'm trying to figure out why, exactly. We've had a number of efforts about [the order's charism], and what it is and how we live it, and I do resist that.
[Interviewer: Then you've got what I'm trying to articulate.]
– [The Sister of X charism] is resistency. [general laughter]
– When we talk about our Sister of X philosophy at orientation [of our hospital

employees] and the values within that philosophy, I always bring out that "You probably have those same values, this isn't anything new to you. What makes it different here, in this institutions, is that it's lived out and you're supported in living it out. You're surrounded by people that believe the same thing and, when you have that support, it helps you." That's different than imposing something different on somebody. Like "This is the Sister of X philosophy and everybody has to believe it." Instead we say, "You already bring this to us and you strengthen what we already have" (Focus Group 2.6: Active and retired sisters).

Note, first of all, the resistence to the question of whether their order needed to keep a "core mass" or fixed percentage of its sisters working in its own institutions in order to keep the order's own "apostolic" identity, and how quickly the conversation returned to the safer topic of how to safeguard the religious identity of the institutions. As Chapter 6 has noted, the sisters have made at least some attempts to address the effects of their diminished presence on the religious identity of their institutions, although the jury is still out on how effective these efforts have been. Many religious hospitals, colleges, and other institutions have created special "mission effectiveness" positions to do this. The person filling this role—often the last remaining member of the sponsoring order still in full-time ministry there—has typically been responsible for activities such as the following:[26]

- Orienting new staff and administrators to the philosophy or ethos of the sponsoring order (Jesuit scholarship, Vincentian caring, the spirit of Mercy, etc.),
- Organizing periodic retreats and seminars for long-standing staff and administrators to revive and strengthen their spiritual commitment,
- Conducting various ongoing spiritual activities such as leading daily prayers over the public address system, organizing prayer services, providing short reflective prayers before meetings, disseminating newsletters or daily bulletins, erecting and maintaining religious iconography, etc.,
- Creating psychic and physical spaces where staff and administrators feel encouraged to share their spiritual journeys,
- Establishing rewards for the staff and administrators who most typify the philosophy of the sponsoring order, and publicizing the winners of these awards,
- Writing, updating, and promulgating the mission statement,
- Raising issues of mission and ethics at meetings of the board of trustees, and at other instances when key decisions are made,
- Acting as liaison between the institution and the sponsoring order, to help define the order's expectations of the institution as a result of its sponsorship, and
- Serving as the religious-identity spokesperson to the media, and overseeing public relations activities connected to the institution's religious identity.[27]

A similarly formalized role, however, does not exist within the orders or mission societies themselves to safeguard and enhance their own corporate identity as service-oriented religious virtuosi. Few, if any, Catholic religious orders, for example, have established an office or appointed an individual to be responsible within the order for activities such as the following:[28]

- Orienting new members of the order to its institutional tradition as part of their novitiate training,
- Organizing periodic retreats and seminars for older members, in which theologians and other speakers would begin to develop and teach the theological underpinnings of a new, institutionally-based or service-oriented religious virtuosity,
- Conducting ongoing activities to raise the institutional consciousness of the members, such as providing articles on the sponsored institutions for the order's newsletter, circulating specifically-written prayers for the institutions, organizing the collection of money and goods, erecting and maintaining displays focused on the institutions at the order's motherhouse or central offices, initiating letter-writing campaigns to public officials on issues affecting the institutions, etc.
- Creating psychic and physical spaces where members of the order would be encouraged to share the insights, joys, and sorrows they have derived from their current ministry in the order's institutions, and to explore how this relates to their religious call.
- Establishing awards or other forms of recognition for individual members who have given especially devoted or long-lasting service in the institutions,
- Giving input on institutional concerns during the revising of the order's mission statement,
- Raising issues of the order's institutions at meetings of the order's executive council,
- Initiating a reflection process to define exactly what the "sponsor" relationship requires of the order, not just of the institution,[29]
- Serving as the spokesperson for the order's institutional role to the media.

It is not only religious colleges, hospitals, and social agencies, therefore, that are subject to isomorphic pressures from the larger society. The orders and societies themselves are vulnerable, especially to mimetic isomorphism with other religious groups both within and outside their denomination. As the post-millennial, institutionally-based templates for religious virtuosity inherited from the nineteenth century continue to wane, the orders' and societies' mimetic isomorphism thus exposes their members to other templates for religious virtuosity—templates that, for the most part, give primacy to one's personal spiritual quest.[30] These individualized spiritual foci commonly fill the void left by the loss of the order's institutions. Some orders of sisters and deaconesses have thus become more like faith-sharing groups: their members live apart from each other, minister in various locations and professions, pray privately every day, and meet regularly as a group for shared prayer and/or socializing.[31] Other Catholic orders have formed intentional communities that more closely approximate the monastic model: the members still live together and pray communally, but leave for separate ministries during the day. In either case, the order or society may begin to draw its identity more and more from the common spiritual activities of its members, and less and less from any common institutionally-based activities. New entrants are attracted by the spirituality of the group rather than by its distinctive institutional activities—if, in fact, any of the latter still remain. The group's basic identity may revert to a religious virtuosity based on the more traditional model of the individual spiritual quest, rather than the service-oriented virtuosity that flourished uniquely in Western

Christianity between 1600 and the late twentieth century.[32] Where once the order's institutions had been essential to its virtuoso spirituality, they are now seen as peripheral, or even detrimental, to it.

It remains to be seen whether the orders can survive such a profound shift. As one recent critic, himself a member of an order of brothers, has noted, "Whenever we chose to classify spirituality as a private concern, work as an individual project, and the personal growth of our membership as more important than the valid needs of the group, we helped compromise any possible future that our [orders] might have."[33] This does *not* mean, of course, that all organized religious virtuosity will disappear from Western Christianity. According to Weber, no religious tradition is exempt from the attraction of virtuoso spirituality for at least some fraction of its adherents. What it *does* mean, however, is that Western Christian religious virtuosity may increasingly return to the monastic or eremitic forms still common in other faith traditions.[34]

Implications for the Larger Denominations

While the loosening of ties between the orders or mission societies and their sponsored institutions has affected these groups, it has also affected—profoundly— the denominations themselves. This final section will briefly outline two such impacts: redefining a denomination's identity and reducing its involvement in society.

Denominational Identity

To the extent that ties between educational or health care institutions and their sponsoring denominations are reduced or eliminated, the denominations, too, will experience changes in their identities. As Methodist F. Thomas Trotter put it, "If the church divests itself of all institutional forms expressing its mission, its own sense of mission will be profoundly altered."[35] Without concrete institutions to represent and define a denomination to outsiders, it may be harder to describe exactly what distinguishes one denomination from another. A type of doctrinal isomorphism may occur: one Mennonite official worried that, in the absence of a strong influence by Mennonite colleges on that denomination's local congregations, a number of Mennonites were borrowing theologies and beliefs from American Fundamentalism (e.g., Biblical inerrancy or support for the war in Iraq) that are foreign to their tradition.[36] Similarly, the Association of Presbyterian Colleges and Universities drafted a statement in 1990 noting that "insistence on an intelligible understanding of the faith is one of the most precious contributions we have made as Presbyterians to the church catholic," and worried that the distinctively Presbyterian emphasis on education was in danger of being lost.[37]

Indeed, the Presbyterian Church in America, a splinter offshoot from the mainline Presbyterian Church, "has decided to have neither its own colleges or seminaries. Several of their clergy indicated . . . that there are numerous Evangelical colleges from which to choose, and some local congregations may choose to recommend them or support them."[38] As this process of ideological isomorphism with other Evangelicals occurs, the PCA may become less and less distinctive as Presbyterians, to the point that it will lose the tradition's unique emphasis on learning.

Critics argue that the increasing separation between denominations and their educational institutions has had deleterious effects for both sides:

> It was bad for the colleges, which became thereby increasingly rootless, and it was bad for the churches, which lost, in the divorce, the benefit of the sharp self-criticism which comes from disciplined intelligence.[39]

Or, as one Mennonite educator put it, all church organizations are called to be both prophetic and conservative within the larger church, preserving the best of its tradition and, at the same time, adapting that tradition in light of new societal challenges.[40] No other aspect of a denomination is able to fulfill this role as effectively as its institutions.

One result of the loss of their educational institutions, therefore, is an increasingly anti-intellectual climate in Christian churches, in which religion and morality have become divorced from serious intellectual content. Instead, primary emphasis is given to "mutual witness . . . face-to-face bonding and physical-emotional contact. Intellectual religion in the form of doctrine and theology is at a minimum and found to be objectionable."[41] Without the theological and doctrinal rigor developed through its educational institutions, denominations or denominational subgroups may increasingly become viewed as spiritual "self-help" associations. Religion may be seen as merely a personal option, a psychologically beneficial state for an individual to cultivate, as denominations shift from an outward to an inward focus.[42]

This trend can be seen in the operation of today's Evangelical mega-churches: instead of creating free-standing educational or health care institutions, these churches tend to establish programs that focus on personal or familial spiritual development within the congregation's internal structure. The following quotation from Robert Schuller is illustrative:

> It will be a thrill to look across America in the year 2000 and see tremendous institutions in every significant city carrying out fantastic programs to heal human hearts, to fill human needs; enormous centers of human inspiration where people rally by the thousands and tens of thousands on Sundays—and gather seven days a week for spiritual and personal growth. These tremendous spiritual-growth centers; these dynamic inspiration-generating centers; these great family-development centers will be proof positive of a renewed, revitalized and resurrected institutional church.[43]

Schuller's "institutions" are essentially adjuncts to the individual congregation, and may last no longer than that congregation itself—and not some larger denomination —does.[44] Critics have questioned whether, in the absence of long-lasting denominational institutions, the Evangelical movement can maintain a stable identity:

> The result is that fewer evangelicals than a generation ago stand in a religious tradition that can provide ballast and long-term orientation. . . . Devaluing the church enfeebles Christians in two respects: it cuts us off from the past, and it relieves us of accountability. . . . Evangelicals have difficulty seeing themselves as responsible and accountable to the church. . . . The very structures of Evangelical life are attuned to the intense individualism of American culture.[45]

Declining ties to a denomination's educational institutions will also impact its identity through the type of training available to local and denominational leaders. Precisely to the extent that a denomination enshrines individual conscience and preference as the primary source of member commitment, its ability to create and sustain a "line of believers" is lost. "Only concrete, community-type religious forms can provide the immediacy of match between religious sentiment and community of faith," through the "collective validation for religious meanings."[46] Common college experiences, the solidarity engendered by participating in the activities of a local mission society chapter—these mechanisms are less available to church members after the loss of their institutions. Several Presbyterian and Methodist critics attribute their denomination's membership decline to the severing or loosening of its ties to their former colleges: "It makes a tremendous difference in the quality and quantity of church life when a stream of church college graduates no longer graduate into pastoral and lay church leadership in the congregations of the church."[47] Declining percentages of the denomination's top leaders are being educated in Presbyterian colleges—73 percent prior to 1959, 56 percent between 1959 and 1973, 20 percent between 1973 and 1983. Similarly, fewer Methodist bishops are chosen from the ranks of seminary faculties or agency service.[48] A national study of Catholics found that those who had graduated from Catholic colleges and universities were more doctrinally orthodox, more observant, and more involved in their local parishes than those who had been schooled elsewhere.[49] But a smaller percentage of Catholic college students attend Catholic colleges today.

Denominational Influence

In addition to its impacts on a denomination's identity, attenuated or severed ties to its institutions will also profoundly affect the type of influence it can exert in the larger society. Religious non-profits, O'Neill notes, "provide a forum for countervailing definitions of reality and morality" that challenge the prevailing assumptions in the larger society about what is good public policy. "To quiet the voice of charitable nonprofits," he asserts, "is to lose a major part of the conscience of the nation."[50] Modern Western history has witnessed the progressive removal of one societal segment after another (the economy, the state, education, law, journalism, science) from the religious sphere, to the point that these sectors "no longer need or are interested in maintaining a sacred cosmos or a public religious world view."[51] Recently, even medical bioethics has developed as a largely secular professional field, eschewing religious input.[52]

In the face of such extensive and powerful secularizing pressures, religious educational, health care, and social service institutions alone have been able to stand as a countervailing force. It is more difficult for a denomination to lobby government officials on public issues without institutional weight to back it up, assuming that its governing officials would even wish to do so without the prodding of the institutions and their sponsors.[53] Cahill notes that Catholic bioethics has traditionally had a strong voice in civil society through the Church's health care institutions, which often partnered with other denominational organizations to lobby for changing state and federal policies. Through institutions such as Catholic Charities and Caritas International, the church also had "an international and transnational presence" in social service policies.[54] Similarly, unless denominations are significantly involved in education via their colleges and universities they will risk marginality in today's learning society. To retain their influence in these spheres, however, denominations and their sponsored institutions must resist both the isomorphizing pressures that render the latter indistinguishable from their secular counterparts, and also the spiritual privatization that has lured many individual church members from the public square.[55] Since such resistance is difficult, therefore, although religious schools, hospitals, and social service agencies may still be essential to the continuing presence and influence of sponsoring denominations and denominational groups, their leaders and members may not be willing or able to use them for this purpose.[56] Without the spur of their institutional sponsorship to involve themselves in public policy debates, church voices may be totally lost.

Denominations, of course, may still be involved in societally-focused activities.[57] Increasingly, however, this involvement may take place in ecumenical or parachurch organizations such as Habitat for Humanity or the Interfaith Hospitality Network.[58] It remains to be seen whether a denomination's members will feel the same sense of ownership over these shared endeavors that they once had over their own hospitals and colleges. It is also likely that multiply-sponsored organizations will stress a more generic Christianity over the specific tenets of one particular faith.[59] Ecumenical efforts are also vulnerable to the same isomorphic and secularizing pressures that have afflicted denominationally-sponsored ones— if not more so.[60] With no one denomination exercising ownership over such institutions, their movement to secularization may be even more rapid than that experienced by institutions with a single sponsor.

The implications of institutional loss for denominations are outside the scope of this book, and only a few potential trends may be noted from parallels to the women's groups studied here. To what extent is the connection between institutional loss and identity loss similar across mainline and evangelical denominations? Between Catholicism and Protestantism? Do the rank and file of a denomination's members view continued connection with these institutions as an essential component of denominational identity? If not, how *do* they define this identity? Can Catholics or mainline Protestants exercise influence in the public square without their educational, health care, and social service institutions? What lessons, if any, can they draw from parachurch organizations which eschew such involvement and yet currently wield even greater influence than the mainline churches? What lessons, if any, can Evangelical groups contemplating participation in either federal or state "Faith-Based Initiatives" programs draw from the previous institutional experiences of mainline Protestants and Catholics?

Conclusions and Recommendations

The above findings only begin to explore the many and varied ways in which the institutional ministries of churchwomen's groups have shaped and influenced them in the past, and how losing—or simply changing—their former relationship with their institutions has influenced them today. The findings do show, however, the immense importance of changing institutional relationships for their religious sponsors. It is curious that denominations and denominational groups have not examined their own institutional identity with anything like the urgency their former institutions have expended to examine their religious identity. I thus offer some tentative suggestions of preliminary action steps that religious orders, deaconesses, or missionary societies—or entire denominations—could take.

1. Consciousness of the issue needs to be raised, perhaps by a series of articles in the newsletters or publications of the denominations or sponsoring denominational groups. Such articles might encourage members to focus on the following questions:
— What common bonds tie us together, now that we no longer all minister in the same places? When and how are these ties renewed?
— Has our pool of available leadership expanded or contracted as a result of our lessened ties to our institutions?
— How has the background of our leaders changed? What strengths and weaknesses do these different backgrounds imply?
— What attracts new members to us, and what are their expectations?

2. New ways of implementing policy and personnel decisions may have to be devised, and new structures established to further this implementation:
— As many hospitals and colleges have established a position for a Director of Mission Identity to keep alive the religious dimension of the institutions, the various orders, societies, or denominations may wish to establish a position charged with keeping the service-oriented virtuoso identity of the group salient in

the eyes of its members. Some of the possible activities of such a position have been outlined above (page 272).

— Some religiously-affiliated colleges, both Catholic and Protestant, have debated whether there needs to be a "critical mass" of students and faculty from that denomination present on campus in order to preserve the college's distinctive religious identity. The denominations or denominational groups might wish similarly to debate whether a "critical mass" of members—or a critical mass of the members' time—needs to be involved in their sponsored institutions in order to preserve their own distinctive, ministry-focused identity—and what form (part-time, volunteer, full-time, short-term, long-term) this involvement might take.

— Catholic religious orders apply the term "sponsorship" to three very different relationships: a) their continued, if diminished, relationship with their traditional colleges and hospitals, b) their financial support of, but minimal or non-existent presence in, a set of separate institutions, and c) their support of individual sisters in specific personal ministries. Similarly, institutions may be "related" to Protestant denominations through outright ownership, historical ties, campus ministries, or financial support.[61] This terminology needs to be clarified and the implications of each type of relationship for the sponsoring order need to be explored.

— If they are not already doing so, discussions on sponsorship need to focus specifically on what behaviors the sponsorship relationship requires on the part of the sponsor's leaders and members. By sponsoring a college, hospital, or social service agency, is a denomination, an order, or a mission society merely committing itself to support the organization financially and to retain certain residual alienation powers? Or to provide a certain number or percentage of the personnel? What implications do these commitments have for the sponsor? For the individual members?

3. Whether a denomination, a religious order, or a missionary society has retained its institutions or has dissolved its ties with them, it is no longer possible simply to place underqualified members into administrative positions there, and then mentor or educate them afterward. This implies that:

— The administrative and board needs of sponsored institutions need to be anticipated years ahead of time and members encouraged to undertake the extensive training necessary to meet them. However,

— Without a more compelling theology of institutional operation—or even *with* such a theology—it may be impossible to persuade younger members to support the institutions. Theologians within each denomination might be encouraged to develop such a theology. Special seminars could be held to present the theologians' work and to encourage discussion, expansion, and application.

4. Of course, it will not be enough for the orders to train members of the sponsoring group or denomination to staff institutional positions. The institutions themselves may strongly resist the sponsor's attempts to assert priority for its members in administrative or staff searches. Religious orders or denominational societies desiring to maintain an active institutional presence may wish to consult with each other on the best ways to do so. Groups that have made a decision to retain an active role in their sponsored institutions could, for example, engage in regular workshops or conferences to network and share ideas. Summaries of the

deliberations at these conferences should be made available to the denomination at large.

According to one historian of Catholic religious orders in the United States, the distinctive charism of these orders did not arise full-blown from the vision of a founder or foundress.[62] Instead of "charism," Thompson suggests using the anthropological concept of "deep story," which she defines as "the continuous and cumulative process of a community's identity formation—its spiritual nature, its history—which, of course, in sacred time and space, encompasses the present and future as much as the past." As religious orders and denominational societies have moved away from a religious virtuosity based on institutional service, they have each written new chapters in their own "deep stories." It is time for them to read these chapters, to assess the story they have told, and to choose, insofar as they can, the story of their future. It is my hope that this book will help them to do so.

Notes

1. Soher (2003:5). See also Gallin (1996:4) and Moran (2004).

2. See, for example, Marsden (1997:15) for Protestant colleges; Geiger (2003a:200, 213) for Catholic colleges.

3. See Radcliffe (2005:29), Dunstan (2003:345-6), Moran (2004:308-309), and Sammon (2002:86, 147), who all make this point.

4. A point made by Meyer and Rowan (1977), Jackall (1988), Fulton (1997:121), O'Neill (1989:40), and Alvesson (2002:136-138). As was noted in chapter 5, this has led religious institutions to adopt the same practices as secular institutions, even if this violates church tenets. Sengers (2003:536) notes, for example, that a questionnaire in the mid-1980s found that most Dutch Catholic hospitals had a license to perform abortions and fought vigorously to keep it, despite the bishops' objections to this practice.

5. Meyer (1997:411).

6. Wolfteich (2002:143-4). Wolfteich (2002:144) also makes the point in the following sentence.

7. The retired sisters and deaconesses were not asked this question.

8. In his study of organizational culture in general, Alvesson (2002:176) labels this decline "cultural drifting," and considers it to be a negative result of organizational change.

9. Dougherty (1997:222) makes this point about Methodist deaconesses; Nygren and Ukeritis (1993:147) and Sammon (2001:217-218; 2002:56, 60) make the same point about Catholic religious orders.

10. Dougherty (1997:245).

11. Nygren and Ukeritis (1993:199). Emphasis added. See Nygren and Ukeritis (1993:191-192) also for the inverse relationship between education and role clarity. Gallin (2000:125) expresses a similar concern. And a study of French nursing sisters showed that religious working in congregational hospitals "see clear difference when compared to their lay colleagues," whereas those who work in state health systems "are relatively close to their lay colleagues. 'A lay colleague is not very different from a religious colleague.'" (Talin 2000:144, author's translation).

12. Bartel (2001:380). See Scott (2003:190) for a discussion of role engulfment.

13. Quoted in Sammon (2002:58).

14. Alvesson (2002:155).

15. Note that this also crossed denominational boundaries—the gatherings of deaconesses and mission society members that I attended included many of the same topics as gatherings of sisters did. The Methodist liturgies at the missionary society meetings which I attended were quite similar to parts of the Catholic Mass (or, conversely, the post-Vatican II Catholic Mass is more similar to the Methodist service). At a morning devotional, I heard a woman reading a book excerpt that commented favorably on the practice of liturgical chanting and incense. At least one prayer service also referred to God as "she." A pamphlet advertising lay educational programs at a denominational center included "Ecological Responsibility" and "Ecumenical Commitment" as aspects of its program.

16. McFarland-Taylor (2001) chronicles the wave of ecological centers currently being constructed by various orders of Catholic sisters.

17. Allahyari (2000:4).

18. Note that this is not the same as the groups in Table 11.1 that had listed self-fulfillment/personal growth when asked what they found *satisfying* about their current ministries; the question discussed here concerns how the focus groups *linked their work and their religious identity.*

19. This respondent was employed outside of her order's traditionally-sponsored hospitals in a rural clinic staffed entirely by several different orders of nuns.

20. These numbers in this paragraph do not correspond with Table 12.2 because some groups gave more than one answer.

21. Jackall (1988), Boje (1991), and Alvesson (2002:146-147). See also Morey (1995:165) for a similar point regarding cultures in Catholic colleges and universities.

22. Allahyari (2000:125-126). See also Faver (2000:73).

23. Allahyari (2000:4, 80, 125). See also Faver (2000:67-68).

24. A point made by Moran (2004:311).

25. Reference to the Legionaries of Christ, a new conservative order of Catholic priests that is receiving large numbers of recruits.

26. The material in this section is drawn largely from Wittberg (2002).

27. This is ideal, of course. Many, if not most, mission effectiveness directors do only one or two of these activities. Other mission effectiveness directors may be marginalized, lacking any real input into the direction of the institution.

28. The items in this list are ordered deliberately to parallel the items in the preceding list.

29. See Holtschneider and Morey (2000a:25), who make this point.

30. See Wuthnow (1994:36-40) and Wuthnow (1998).

31. See Wuthnow (1994). The mission societies, of course, have never lived communally but, increasingly, as Chapter 8 has documented, what unites them are prayer and socializing activities rather than commitment to a set of institutions.

32. This is ironic, because Eastern religious virtuosi—monastics in Eastern Orthodoxy, Theravedan and Zen Buddhism, and Coptic Christianity—are turning to the service-oriented version even as the Western orders are abandoning it. See Bartholomeusz (1994), Van Doorn-Harder (1995), Arai (1999), Lozada (2001:40-41), Stebbing (2001), Gutschow (2004), and Leung and Wittberg (2004).

33. Sammon (2002:31).

34. It is interesting to observe that a disproportionate percentage of new Catholic religious orders, both in North America and in Europe, are contemplative rather than

apostolic in focus. See, for example, the work of the Center for Applied Research in the Apostolate (1999).

35. Trotter (1987:133).

36. Albert Meyer, personal interview.

37. Quoted in Stoltzfus (1992:64).

38. Stoltzfus (1992:45).

39. Trueblood (1959:16-17).

40. Meyer (1997:417-418).

41. Fulton (1997:123). See also Burtchaell, (1991), Johnson (1992:557), O'Brien (1994:73), and Smith (2003), who make similar criticisms.

42. A point made by Trotter (1987:133, 136), Wuthnow (1988), Marty (1994), Warner (1994),and Davidson and Koch (1998:302) .

43. Schuller (1974:1-2).

44. Smith (2004) notes that the megachurches like Schuller's are currently facing their first leadership turnover, wherein the largely Baby-Boomer founding pastors relinquish their roles, and she questions whether Generation X and Millennial congregants will choose to worship in the same settings.

45. Hatch and Hamilton (1992:29).

46. Fulton (1997:123). See Shepherd and Shepherd (1998) for an example.

47. Stoltzfus (1992:109). This (1997:4, 16) makes a similar point.

48. See Reifsnyder (1992:272) for the Presbyterians, This (1997:4,6) for the Methodists. Chaves (1991) found a similar separation between the leaders of a denomination's institutions and the leadership of the denominations themselves.

49. Davidson et al.(1997:102-106).

50. O'Neill (1989:15, 121).

51. Casanova (1994:37). See also Smith (2003).

52. See Evans (2003).

53. At least one observer has commented that her denomination never really knew or cared much about the Woman's Society projects: "In general, men, and especially clergy, were not that interested in projects serving women and children, and especially so if that was to mean money" (Barbara Campbell, personal communication).

54. Cahill (2004:13). See Stoltzfus (1992:64) for the argument about religious educational institutions in the following sentence.

55. Of course, a reverse "deprivatization" is also occurring (Casanova 1994), but it is not based on the same sort of institutional presence. See the next paragraph.

56. Cleary (2001:128) quotes one CEO of an Australian Catholic hospital: "The Church is not interested in Catholic health. The Church is doing all it can to be interested in Catholic education."

57. Indeed, with the rise of Charitable Choice and Faith Based Initiatives, some denominations may even increase their involvement (Chaves 2004:45-93).

58. And, of course, parachurch organizations such as Focus on the Family are the primary way Fundamentalist Evangelical churches exercise their influence over public policy. See the following paragraph.

59. Smith and Sosin (1999:16). See also Baggett (2001:198-205).

60. Baggett (2001:239-243) charts this for one such group, Habitat for Humanity.

61. Harris (1974:15-19).

62. Thompson (1999:245-246).

Appendix A

Research Methodology

Most organizational research, Martin[1] notes, takes an "etic" stance: the researcher studies the target group as an outsider to it. While some studies of organizational culture do attempt to "get inside" the minds of the "natives"—to take an "emic" view of the organization—most even of these researchers are not members of the organizations they study. My research is, to some extent, an exception, since I am a member of one of the three religious orders who comprised the focus groups. In contrast, since I am not a member of the denomination to which the deaconesses and mission society members belong, my perspective on these groups is unavoidably more that of an outsider, although I endeavored, as much as possible, to consult with these women and to solicit their input on earlier drafts of this manuscript. In actuality, of course, the two perspectives merge in any study, and it is difficult to find a balance between the two. By the mere fact of studying a group, one becomes somewhat of an outsider to it: it is hard to maintain an emic position uncontaminated by etic distancing[2] while etic research without at least some emic empathy risks "being so enamored of counting and measuring . . . that the texture of life in a culture is lost."[3] I cannot claim to have been successful in striking this balance. Especially with the deaconess and mission society members, my analysis may be less insightful. I can only claim to have made a good faith effort, both to understand the mindset of those in the interviews, and also to analyze this mindset with as much objectivity as possible.

My initial research on the impact of institutional loss on religious sponsors was derived from 30 individual interviews conducted between 1995 and 1997 with Catholic sisters who were or had been administrators either of their order's institutions or of their order itself. Most (25) of these first interviews were conducted with sisters in the Midwestern U.S. provinces of two international religious orders. These two orders were selected on the basis of the type of relationship which they had attempted to maintain with their sponsored institutions. One order ("Order A") was attempting to sustain a strong administrative presence

283

in its institutions. The second ("Order B") had withdrawn from most of the institutions it had once sponsored, although it continued to maintain a presence on the boards of its college and hospital system (both of which were run by lay administrators).[4] In other ways, however, the two orders were similar. Both had traditionally staffed and administered grade and high schools, hospitals, orphanages, settlement houses, and day care centers throughout the North Central and Southern United States, and both had owned and operated a small college. I also interviewed three deaconesses and two former officers of the woman's missionary society. Between 1999 and 2002, I attended both a state and a district conference of the missionary society, several of its annual educational conferences on mission issues, a national denominational conference of deaconesses, and an international, ecumenical gathering of deaconesses from several different denominations.[5]

Table A.1 lists the professional background, administrative experience, and current occupation of the respondents in the individual interviews. The pool was evenly divided between retired and active sisters and deaconesses, and included a significant percentage of the present and former leaders of these groups. The professional backgrounds of the respondents were also evenly spread between health care, education, and social work. Most had had at least some administrative experience.

Many of the preliminary interviews were not as successful as I had hoped. It quickly became evident that few of the respondents had ever thought about the impact of institutional loss on their own order or society. Without persistent, directive questions on my part, which risked compromising the validity of the data, they continued to shift the topic back to the more familiar one of the order's difficulties in keeping *its institutions'* religious spirit alive.

Accordingly, I decided to explore the question further by using focus groups. Such groups are particularly useful for enabling participants to construct and express their own ideas and questions around a given topic as they interact with each other. "The hallmark of focus groups is the explicit use of group interaction to produce data and insights that would be less accessible without the interaction found in a group."[6] People are, in fact, more likely to share experiences around a topic in a group setting than they are in individual interviews.

During the fall of 1999 and the first half of 2000, therefore, I conducted 36 focus groups: 24 with three orders of Catholic sisters, three with members of a Protestant order of deaconesses, and nine with members of a Protestant missionary society. None of the three orders of Catholic sisters had participated in the preliminary interviews: Order #1 was headquartered in a burgeoning urban area of the southern United States where Catholics had been a small minority; Order #2 was based in a large East Coast city with a traditionally strong Catholic subculture, although it, too, had members stationed in the South; and Order #3 was located in a medium-sized Midwestern city with members stationed primarily in the Midwest and Mountain states. Two of the three focus groups of deaconesses were conducted at the order's retirement home; the third was assembled during an annual denomi-

Table A.1. Background of Respondents in Preliminary Interviews

	Professional Field	Administrative Experience	Current Position
Sisters in Order A:			
	Health Care	Hospital CEO	Retired
	Health Care	Hospital CEO	Retired
	Health Care	Hospital CEO	Retired
	Health Care	Hospital CEO*	Patient Advocate/Retired
	Social Work	Social Service Administrator*	Retired
	Social Work	Social Service Administrator	Retired
	Social Work	Social Service Administrator*	Member, Order's Council
	Education	H.S. Principal*	Retired
	Educ./Social Work	College President*	Retired
	Social Work	Social Service Administrator*	Member, Order's Council
	Social Work	Social Service Administrator	Adm. Day Care Center
	Education	H.S. Principal*	Treasurer of Order A
	Social Work	Social Service Administrator	Nursing Home Adm.
	Health Care	Hospital CEO	Order's Liaison with its Health Care System
Other Interviews:			
(Deaconesses)	Social Services	Former Denominational Officer	Retired
	Social Services	Administrator, Social Service Agency	
	Social Services	Staff, Social Service Agency	
(Mission Society)		Former President	Retired
		Former District Officer	Retired

Continued on next page

Table A.1. Continued

	Professional Field	Administrative Experience	Current Position
Sisters in Order B:			
	Health Care	Superintendent of Nurses	Retired
	Education	Elementary School Principal	Retired
	Health Care	Hospital CEO	Retired
	Social Work	Social Service Administrator*	Retired
	Education	Superintendent of Schools*	Retired
	Social Work	None	Retired
	Education	Adm. Adult Literacy Program	Dir. of Communications
	Education	Superintendent of Schools*	Provincial Superior
	Education	None*	Member, Order's Council
	Health Care	Emergency Room Supervisor	Member, Order's Council
	Education	Elementary School Principal/ Treasurer of Order B	Member, Order's Council
Sisters in Other Religious Orders:			
	Health Care	CEO, Health Care System*	Member, Gov. Council
	Health Care	CEO, Health Care System	CEO Health Care
	Health Care	Former Member, Hospital Board	University Faculty
	Social Services	None	Development Director, Social Service Agency

* Indicates additional past or current administrative experience on the governing council of the religious order.

national conference of active and retired deaconesses. The nine focus groups of mission society members were conducted in rural, urban, and suburban churches in one Midwestern state.

Table A.2 lists the composition of each focus group. For each order or society, whenever possible, I conducted several focus groups with the oldest members and several others with more recent recruits. Within the Catholic religious orders, I also stratified the non-retired groups by whether or not the sisters were still working in their order's own institutions or whether they were working elsewhere. For each of the Catholic orders, I also conducted a focus group of present and former leaders. Two of the nine mission society focus groups also contained present and former district-level leaders.

The interview question format varied somewhat, according to the age and background of each focus group (See Appendix B). However, every group was asked how (or if) the order or society had changed since loosening its ties to its institutions, how the members' past or present service related to their identity within the larger Church, and what the basic goal or purpose of the group was at the present time. The leaders' focus groups were also asked to share the insights they had received during their terms of office.

Each of the interviews was transcribed in its entirety, and coded using the NUD*ist software system for qualitative data. This program has proven especially useful for developing classification schemas through an iterative process of interaction with the data.[7] Table A.3 lists the principal coding categories developed through several successive iterations. Once the codes were developed, the transcripts were then given to between one and three additional coders to test for the reliability of the categories. The number of coders for each category and overall inter-coder agreement for these items are given in Table A.3. The subcategories were surfaced by the focus group participants themselves during the focus group sessions. Inter-coder agreement for these subcategories was never less than 90%.

Table A.2. Composition of Focus Groups

Order #1:

Focus Group 1.1	Retired Sisters
Focus Group 1.2	Present and Former Leaders
Focus Group 1.3	Non-Retired Sisters Active Outside Their Order's Traditional Institutions
Focus Group 1.4	Non-Retired Sisters Active Outside Their Order's Traditional Institutions
Focus Group 1.5	Non-Retired Sisters Active In Their Order's Traditional Institutions
Focus Group 1.6	Non-Retired Sisters, Mixed Work Settings

Order #2:

Focus Group 2.1	Non-Retired Sisters Active In Their Order's Traditional Institutions
Focus Group 2.2	Retired Sisters
Focus Group 2.3	Present and Former Leaders
Focus Group 2.4	Retired Sisters
Focus Group 2.5	Non-Retired Sisters Active Outside Their Order's Traditional Institutions
Focus Group 2.6	Non-Retired Sisters, Mixed Work Settings

Order #3:

Focus Group 3.1	Retired Sisters
Focus Group 3.2	Retired Sisters
Focus Group 3.3	Retired Sisters
Focus Group 3.4	Retired Sisters
Focus Group 3.5	Non-Retired Sisters Active In Their Order's Traditional Institutions
Focus Group 3.6	Present and Former Leaders and Staff
Focus Group 3.7	Non-Retired Sisters Active Outside Their Order's Traditional Institutions
Focus Group 3.8	Retired Sisters
Focus Group 3.9	Retired Sisters

Continued on next page

Table A.2. Continued

Focus Group 3.10	Non-Retired Sisters Active In Their Order's Traditional Institutions
Focus Group 3.11	Sisters Who Recently Entered the Order
Focus Group 3.12	Non-Retired Sisters, Mixed Work Settings

Deaconess Focus Groups:

Focus Group 4.1	Retired Deaconesses
Focus Group 4.2	Retired Deaconesses
Focus Group 4.3	Active Deaconesses

Mission Society Focus Groups:

Focus Group 5.1	Small Town/ Suburban Area, White Congregation
Focus Group 5.2	Small Town, White Congregation
Focus Group 5.3	Suburban Area, White Congregation
Focus Group 5.4	Suburban Area, White Congregation
Focus Group 5.5	Inner Suburban Area, White Congregation
Focus Group 5.6	Small Town, White Congregation
Focus Group 5.7	Urban Area, White Congregation*
Focus Group 5.8	Urban Area, Black Congregation
Focus Group 5.9	Inner Suburban Area, Black Congregation

*This group was *not* officially a chapter of the mission society, but rather a "Book Discussion Club" that had formed precisely because the congregation's mission society chapter was seen as "too stodgy."

Table A.3. Main Coding Categories and Subcategories

Category	Number of Coders	Inter-coder Agreement
3. Positive Past Experiences	3	97.5%
3.1 In local living situation*		
3.2 In the work/ministry situation		
3.3 Good friends		
3.5 Shared hardships		
3.7 Freedom		
3.8 Mutual support		
3.9 Inspired by the people served		
4. Negative Past Experiences	3	95.6%
4.1 Difficult working situations		
4.2 Difficult living situations*		
4.4. Isolation**		
5. Relations with the Larger Church	2	94.3%
5.1 Relations with Clergy		
5.2 Relations with the Local Church		
5.3 Church Bureaucracy		
5.4 Does the Church really want us?		
5.5 Impact of denominational reorganization***		
7. Sources of Fulfillment in Current Position	3	97.5%
7.1 There is always something new		
7.2 Meeting needs		
7.3 Being a presence		
7.4 Serving people		
7.5 Self-fulfillment		
7.6 Inspired by the people one serves		
7.7 Opportunities to foster the institutional charism		
7.8 Institutional board work is fulfilling		
7.9 The ability to catalyze change		
7.10 Gaining knowledge about the order/society		
7.11 Facilitating projects		
7.12 Feeling appreciated		
7.13 Preaching the Gospel/Evangelization		
7.14 Ecumenical aspects		
7.16 Friends/ Socializing		

Continued on next page

* Sisters and Deaconesses only.   ** Sisters only   *** Deaconesses and Mission Society only

Table A.3. Continued

8. Sources of Frustration	3	97.6%

    8.1 Lack of money
    8.2 Church rules
    8.3 Lack of personnel
    8.4 Lack of time
    8.5 Loss of influence
    8.6 Diversity, fragmentation
    8.7 Parish/ local congregation difficulties
    8.9 Frustrations with the population served
    8.10 Paperwork
    8.11 Lack of contacts with people
    8.12 Lack of appreciation
    8.13 Necessity of living alone
    8.14 Institutional concerns
    8.15 Too much socializing

10. How the Order/Society has Changed	3	96.6%

    10.2 We have more responsibility now
    10.3 Changes in cohesion
    10.4 Changes in support from order, church
    10.5 Less mentoring
    10.6 Fewer memories
    10.7 We have more freedom now
    10.8.Less dedication to a place or institution now
    10.10 More collaboration now
    10.11 Loss of our institutions has affected us
    10.12 Changes in flexibility
    10.13 Changes in isolation
    10.14 Less relationship with parishes or local congregations
    10.15 Changes in power
    10.16 Changes in visibility
    10.17 We have grown through our difficulties
    10.18 Membership changes
    10.19 More focus on self-development now

14. Link: Work–Religious Call (Past)	4	97.7%

    14.1 Through the Institution
    14.2 My work facilitated my personal growth
    14.5 My work inhibited my vocation
    14.6 The two were linked through service of others
    14.10 It was God's will for me
    14.14 My call led to my work

Continued on next page
Table A.3. Continued

14.16 One enriched the other
14.18 My call came through the witness of other members
14.20 I liked/benefitted from whatever I did
14.21 I gave no thought to it.

15. Link: Work–Religious Call (Past)   4   97.0%
    15.1 Through the spirit of the institution
    15.2 Continues the work of the founders
    15.3 Facilitates personal growth
    15.4 Linking the two is harder today
    15.5 My work inhibits my vocation
    15.6 The two are linked through service of others
    15.7 Lay stereotypes affect the link
    15.8 My work is less important than my call
    15.10. It is God's will for me
    15.11 The religious call is a source of strength in my work
    15.12 What we do is no different than what any lay Christian does.
    15.13 I witness God's/ Christ's presence in my work
    15.14 My religious call catalyzes my involvement
        15.14.1 in social justice activities
        15.14.2 in my present ministry
        15.14.3 with others
        15.14.4 with the Church
    15.16 Each complements the other

19. Basic Purpose of the Order/Society Today   3   97.8%
    19.1 Service
    19.2 To be the presence of Christ/God
    19.3 To carry on the work of our founder
    19.4 Personal spiritual growth
    19.5 To empower the laity
    19.7 Repeats the official mission statement
    19.8 We are too diverse to have one purpose/goal
    19.10 Don't know/can't say
    19.11 To act together
    19.12 To work for systemic change
    19.14 To help the Church
    19.16 The goal has stayed constant through all changes
    19.17 To support the missions
    19.18 Socializing
    19.19 To support each other

Continued on next page

Table A.3. Continued

---

22. What attracted you to join the group?   3   97.4%
    22.1 Through their institutions
    22.2 Through the personal witness of group members
    22.3 Through learning about the life of the founder
    22.6 I wanted to do the group's works.
    22.7 God's will/felt a call
    22.8 Life commitment; wanted to do something significant
    22.9 Had a relative in the group
    22.10 The common life, the fellowship of the members
    22.11 Preferred them to another group
    22.12 Pension plan, financial help attractive
    22.13 Invited by friends, other members
    22.14 Had free time after some life change
    22.15 Wanted to become more involved with the Church
    22.17 Had been involved as a child
    22.18 Flexible time to meet
    22.19 Likes the diversity of the membership
    22.20 Opportunity for spiritual growth

Notes

1. Martin (2002:36).
2. For example, nuns in my order and others have frequently objected to my "bracketing" of religious explanations such as "the power of the Holy Spirit" or "the Providence of God" and basing my research solely on social scientific explanations.
3. Martin (2002:238).
4. Community A had closed its college in 1974.
5. Community A had closed its college in 1974.
6. Morgan (1988:12). See also Kitzinger and Barbour (1999:5) and Farquhar and Das (1999:46).
7. *User's Guide for QSR NUD*IST,* revision 3 (1996). Qualitative Solutions and Research Pty, Ltd., Page 3.

Appendix B

Focus Group Formats

For Retired Sisters

Good morning/evening. I want to thank you all for participating in this focus group. For some time now, I've been interested in what happens to religious orders when they loosen their ties with their sponsored ministries, such as [name examples], as well as those which they traditionally staffed, like [name examples]. Most previous research has looked at the effects on the institution, but few have looked at the effect on the institution's sponsor. Focus groups are a good technique to explore all the different ways in which running schools, hospitals, and social service agencies has affected religious communities in the past.

1.) Let's start with introductions. [Introduce self.] Could each of you give us your name, and also the first place you were on mission, what years that was, and what you did there?

2.) Can you describe a particularly happy, or good memory you have from those days?

3.) Can you describe a particularly unhappy or unpleasant memory you have from those days?

4.) If you could retain or revive one thing from those early days now, what would it be?

5.) What is one thing you were glad changed?

6.) Thinking back to those days, how did your ministry relate to your vocation as a sister? Did you feel it enriched it, detracted from it, or what?

7.) Did you ever work in places that were not sponsored or traditionally staffed by [name of order]? What was the difference, if any, between working in a Sister of X place and a ministry situation that was not?

8.) How is religious life in the Sisters of X different today, now that everyone doesn't all work in the same institutions? What has been gained? What has been lost?

9.) If someone were to ask you what the basic goal or purpose of the Sisters of X is today, what would you say?

10.) Are there any other questions I should have asked?

For Sisters Currently Working
Outside of Their Order's Institutions

[Introduction as above]

1.) Let's start with introductions. [Introduce self.] Could each of you give us your name, and also tell us what your current ministry is—where you serve, what you do, and how long you have been there?

2.) Could some of you share something you find particularly fulfilling or valuable about working in your current ministry? [particularly frustrating or difficult]

3.) Have you ever worked in a position in a Sister of X-sponsored ministry? Where was this?

4.) What differences—if any—are there between working in a Sister of X-sponsored institution, as compared to one that is not connected with the Sisters of X?

5.) How do you feel working in your current ministry relates to your sense of vocation? Does it enrich your vocation, hinder it, or what?

6.) Have any of you ever served as administrators on mission—as principals, hospital administrators, etc.? How were you chosen for this role? Did you have any training or mentoring to help you learn the ropes? [If time—what were the differences, if any, between administering a Sister of X institution and one that did not belong to the Sisters of X?]

7.) How is religious life in the Sisters of X different today, now that everyone doesn't all work in the same institutions? What has been gained? What has been lost?

8.) [If visibility is not mentioned, ask] Has the public image of the Sisters of X changed in any way? Are there ways it has not changed?

9.) What are your plans for after your current ministry? [Probe for leadership of the order.]

10.) If someone were to ask you what the basic goal or purpose of the Sisters of X is today, what would you say to them?

11.) Are there any other questions I should have asked?

For Sisters Still Working
in Their Order's Traditional Institutions

[Introduction as above]

1.) Let's start with introductions. [Introduce self.] Could each of you give us your name, and also tell us what your current ministry is—where you serve, what you do, and how long you have been there?

2.) Could you also tell us the first place you were on mission, what years that was, and what you did there?

3.) What differences, if any, are there between that first place and today?

4.) Could some of you share something you find particularly fulfilling or valuable about working in your current ministry?

5.) Could some of you share something you find particularly frustrating or difficult about working in your current ministry?

6.) Have any of you ever served as administrators on mission—as principals, hospital administrators, etc.? How were you chosen for this role? Did you have any training or mentoring to help you learn the ropes? [If time—what were the differences, if any, between administering a Sister of X institution and one that did not belong to the Sisters of X?]

7.) How is religious life in the Sisters of X different today, now that everyone doesn't all work in the same institutions? What has been gained? What has been lost?

8.) [If visibility is not mentioned, ask] Has the public image of the Sisters of X changed in any way? Are there ways it has not changed?

9.) What are your plans for after your current ministry? [Probe for leadership of the order.]

10.) If someone were to ask you what the basic goal or purpose of the Sisters of X is today, what would you say to them?

11.) Are there any other questions I should have asked?

For Sisters in Leadership Positions in Their Order

[Introduction as above]

1.) Let's start with introductions. [Introduce self.] Could each of you give us your name, and also tell us what your current position is?

2.) Could some of you share something you find particularly fulfilling or valuable about working in your current ministry?

3.) Could some of you share something you find particularly frustrating or difficult about working in your current ministry?

4.) Have there been any specific insights or outlooks you have gotten after being in leadership? What are they?

5.) Some of you have been in leadership before. On the basis of your experience, has leadership changed any between the 1970s and 1980s and today?

6.) Again, based on your experience, how has the role ministry plays in the lives of the Sisters of X changed? Or is there no difference between now and before?

7.) Prior to being chosen for leadership, did any of you ever serve as administrators on mission—as principals, hospital administrators, etc.? How were you chosen for this role? Did you have any training or mentoring to help you learn the ropes? [If time—what were the differences, if any, between administering a Sister of X institution and one that did not belong to the Sisters of X?]

8.) How is religious life in the Sisters of X different today, now that everyone doesn't all work in the same institutions? What has been gained? What has been lost?

9.) [If visibility is not mentioned, ask] Has the public image of the Sisters of X changed in any way? Are there ways it has not changed?

10.) If someone were to ask you what the basic goal or purpose of the Sisters of X was, what would you say?

11.) Are there any other questions I should have asked?

For Retired Deaconesses

Good morning/evening. I want to thank you all for participating in this focus group. For some time now, I've been interested in what happens to religious sponsors when they loosen their ties with their sponsored ministries, such as [name examples]. Most previous research has looked at the effects on the institution, but few have looked at the effect on the institution's sponsor. Focus groups are a good technique to explore all the different ways in which running schools, hospitals, and social service agencies has affected religious communities in the past.

1.) Let's start with introductions. [Introduce self.] Could each of you give us your name, and also the first place you served as a deaconess—where it was, when it was, what you did there?

2.) Can you describe a particularly happy, or good memory you have from those days? [unhappy memory...]

3.) If you could retain or revive one thing from those early days, what would it be? What is one thing you are glad that it changed?

4.) What attracted you to becoming a deaconess?

5.) How did the work you did as a deaconess relate to your life as a Christian woman, and as a [member of the denomination]—did it strengthen your Christian/[denominational] identity, or did it open you more ecumenically, or did it make no difference?

6.) How has the deaconess program changed since you became a deaconess?

7.) You have all served in positions that were explicitly connected with the [denomination] in some way. How many of you have also served in positions that were not connected with the denomination? What was the difference between working in a denominational position and one that was not?

8.) Back when you first became a deaconess, if someone had asked you what the purpose of the deaconesses, as a group, was—what would you have said?

9.) If someone were to ask you now what the basic goal and purpose of the deaconesses as a group is today, what would you say?

10.) Has anyone held office in the larger [denomination] on a conference or district level, or in the [denominational mission society]? How were you prepared for this?

11.) Are there any other questions I should have asked?

For Active Deaconesses

[Introduction as for retired deaconesses, above.]

1.) Let's start with introductions. [Introduce self.] Could each of you give us your name, and also how you got involved in becoming a deaconess and when was that?

2.) How does the work you do as a deaconess relate to your sense of call and your life as a Christian woman, and as a [member of the denomination]—does it strengthen your Christian/[denominational] identity, or does it open you more ecumenically, or does it make no difference?

3.) How has the deaconess program changed since the early days?

4.) If someone were to ask you now what the basic goal and purpose of the deaconesses as a group is today, what would you say?

5.) Has anyone held office in the larger [denomination] on a conference or district level, or in the [denominational mission society]? How were you prepared for this?

6.) You have all served in positions that were explicitly connected with the [denomination] in some way. How many of you have also served in positions that were not connected with the denomination? What was the difference between working in a denominational position and one that was not?

7.) If the denominational leadership were to ask you what the church could do for the deaconess program, what would it be?

8.) What are your dreams/plans for the future?

9.) Are there any other questions I should have asked?

For the Mission Society

[Introduction as for retired deaconesses, above.]

1.) Let's start with introductions. [Introduce self.] Could each of you give us your first name, and also tell us how you first got involved the [mission society]? [Probe: When was that? What did you do?]

2.) What are some of the kinds of activities that the [mission society] did when you first joined?

3.) What attracted you to the [mission society]? What keeps you in the [mission society] now? What attracts new members today? What turns women off or discourages them from joining the [mission society]?

4.) What do you see as the primary goal/function/purpose of the [mission society] today? How has this changed from when you first joined?

5.) Does your local chapter have a special institution/work that you have especially supported? What is/was it? What did you do? Has your chapter's relationship to _____ changed over the years? In what way?

6.) Have you ever been in a leadership position in your church or in [mission society]? How were you prepared for this? Can you tell some of the things you learned from the experience?

7.) What are the main issues facing the [mission society] today?

8.) What has been the relationship between the [mission society] and the rest of the local church —either here at _____ or in the larger conference? What aspects of this relationship work particularly well? Are there points of tension or confusion? What things contribute to the tensions?

10.) What are your dreams for the future of the [mission society]?

11.) Are there any other questions I should have asked?

Bibliography

Abzug, Rikki, and Joseph Galaskiewicz. 2001. "Nonprofit Boards: Crucibles of Expertise or Symbols of Local Identities?" *Nonprofit and Voluntary Sector Quarterly* 30:51-73.

Albert, Stuart, and David A. Whetten.1985. "Organizational Identity." *Research in Organizational Behavior* 7:263-295.

Aldrich, Howard E., and Jeffrey Pfeffer.1976. "Environments of Organizations." *Annual Review of Sociology* 2:79-105.

Allahyari, Rebecca Anne. 2000. *Visions of Charity: Volunteer Workers and Moral Community*. Berkeley: University of California Press.

Alvesson, Mats. 2002. *Understanding Organizational Culture*. Thousand Oaks, CA: Sage.

Ammerman, Nancy Tatom. 1990. *Baptist Battles*. New Brunswick, NJ: Rutgers University Press.

Amos, John R., Melanie DiPietro, Jordan Hite, and Francis Morrissey. 1993. *The Search for Identity: Canonical Sponsorship of Catholic Healthcare*. The Catholic Health Association of the United States. St. Louis, MO.

Annarelli, J. J. 1987. *Academic Freedom and Catholic Higher Education*. New York: Greenwood.

Anderson, M. Christine. 2000. "Catholic Nuns and the Invention of Social Work." *Journal of Women's History* 121:60-87.

Anthony, Geraldine, SC. 1997. *A Vision of Service: Celebrating the Sisters of Charity*. Kansas City: Sheed and Ward.

Arai, Paula Kane Robinson. 1999. *Women Living Zen: Japanese Soto Buddhist Nuns*. New York: Oxford University Press.

Arbuckle, Gerald A. 1996. "It's Time to Refound Healthcare Ministry." *Human Development* 172:24-30.

Arrizabalaga, Jon. 1999. "Poor Relief in Counter-Reformation Castile: An Overview." Pp. 151-176 in *Health Care and Poor Relief in Counter-Reformation Europe*, edited by Ole Peter Grell, Andrew Cunningham, and Jon Arrizabalaga. New York: Routledge.

Baggett, Jerome P. 2001. *Habitat for Humanity: Building Private Homes, Building Public Religion*. Philadelphia: Temple University Press.

Barr, Pat. 1972. *To China With Love; The Lives and Times of Protestant Missionaries in China, 1860-1900*. London: Seeker and Warburg.

Bartel, Caroline A. 2001. "Social Comparisons in Boundary-Spanning Work: Effects of Community Outreach on Members' Organizational Identity and Identification." *Administrative Science Quarterly* 46:379-413.

Bartholomeusz, Tessa J. 1994. *Women Under the Bo Tree: Buddhist Nuns in Sri Lanka.* New York: Cambridge University Press.

Bartunek, J. 1984. "Changing Interpretive Schemes and Organizational Restructuring: The Example of a Religious Order." *Administrative Science Quarterly* 29:355-372.

Beane, Marjorie N. 1993. *From Framework to Freedom: A History of the Sister Formation Conference.* Lanham, MD: University Press of America.

Beaty, Michael D. 2002. "Baptist Models: Past, Present, and Future." Pp. 116-140 in *The Future of Religious Colleges*, edited by Paul J. Dovre. Grand Rapids, MI: Eerdmans.

Beaver, Robert Pierce. 1968. *All Loves Excelling: Protestant Women in World Mission.* Grand Rapids, MI: Eerdmans.

Beck, Robert Holmes. 1965. *A Social History of Education.* Englewood Cliffs, NJ: Prentice Hall.

Bender, Harold S. 1944. "The Anabaptist Vision." *Mennonite Quarterly Review* 182:3-33.

Bendroth, Margaret L. 1993. *Fundamentalism and Gender: 1875 to the Present.* New Haven: Yale University Press.

Benne, Robert. 2002. "The Glass is Half Full, Say the President and the Professor." Pp.95-99 in *The Future of Religious Colleges*, edited by Paul J. Dovre. Grand Rapids, MI: Eerdmans.

————. 2003. "Integrity and Fragmentation: Can the Lutheran Center Hold?" Pp. 206-221 in *Lutherans Today: A Lutheran Identity in the Twenty-First Century*, edited by Richard Cimino. Grand Rapids, MI: Eerdmans.

Berger, Helen A. 1999. *A Community of Witches.* Columbia, SC: University of South Carolina Press.

Bernardin, Cardinal Joseph. 1995. "Making the Case for Not-For-Profit Healthcare." Speech before the Harvard Business School Club of Chicago, January 12, 1995.

Bertrand, Catherine. 1998. "Common Threads: Are We Weaving or Unraveling?" *Horizon* 233:9-17.

Beyerlein, Kraig. 2003. "Educational Elites and the Movement to Secularize Public Education." Pp. 160-196 in *The Secular Revolution: Power, Interests, and Conflict in the Secularization of Public Life*, edited by Christian Smith. Berkeley: University of California Press.

Bielefeld, Wolfgang, Laura Littlepage, and Rachel Thelin. 2002. "The Role of Faith-Based Providers in a Social Service Delivery System." Paper presented at the 2002 annual meeting of the Association for Research on Nonprofit Organizations and Voluntary Action, Montreal, November 2002.

Bogucka, Maria. 1997. "Health Care and Poor Relief in Danzig." Pp. 167-203 in *Health Care and Poor Relief in Protestant Europe, 1500-1700*, edited by Ole Peter Grell and Andrew Cunningham. New York: Routledge.

Boje, D. 1991. "The Story-telling Organization: A Study of Story Performance in an Office-Supply Firm." *Administrative Science Quarterly* 36:106-126.

Bole, William, 1995. "Mercy Sisters Pack Board to Settle Six-Month Strike." *National Catholic Reporter* 31(20):6-7.

Bontrager, Herman. 1997. "Church-Related Organizations: Mission, Image, and Promotion." *The Mennonite Quarterly Review* 71(3): 327-343.

Boyd, Lois A., and R. Douglas Brackenridge. 1983. *Presbyterian Women in America: Two Centuries of a Quest for Status.* Westport, CT: Greenwood.

Brasher, Brenda E. 1998. *Godly Women: Fundamentalism and Female Power.* New Brunswick: Rutgers University Press.

Brereton, Virginia Lieson. 1981. "Preparing women for the Lord's Work." Pp. 178-189 in *Women in New Worlds: Historical Perspectives on the Wesleyan Tradition,* edited by Hilah F. Thomas and Rosemary Skinner. Nashville, TN: Abingdon.

Brereton, Virginia Lieson, and Christa R. Klein. 1979. "American Women in Ministry: A History of Protestant Beginning Points," Pp. 302-332 in *Women of Spirit: Female Leadership in the Jewish and Christian Traditions,* edited by Rosemary Ruether and Eleanor McLaughlin. New York: Simon and Schuster.

Brewer, E. M. 1987. *Nuns and the Education of American Catholic Women, 1860-1920.* Chicago: Loyola University Press.

Brinkman, Marie. 2005. "Invisible—Even to Ourselves?" *Review for Religious* 64(3):259-268.

Brown, Dorothy M., and Elizabeth McKeown. 1997. *The Poor Belong to Us: Catholic Charities and American Welfare.* Cambridge: Harvard University Press.

Brown, M. B. 1949. *History of the Sisters of Providence of St. Mary of the Woods,* vol.1. New York: Benziger.

Bryk, Anthony, Valerie E. Lee, and Peter A. Holland. 1993. *Catholic Schools and the Common Good.* Cambridge, MA: Harvard University Press.

Bukowczyk, John J. 1988. "Mary the Messiah: Polish Immigrant heresy and the Malleable Ideology of the Roman Catholic Church." Pp. 21-48 in *Urban American Catholicism,* edited by Timothy J. Meagher. New York: Garland.

Burtchaell, James Tunstead. 1998. *The Dying of the Light: The Disengagement of Colleges and Universities From their Christian Churches.* Grand Rapids, MI: Eerdmans.

———. 1991. "The Decline and Fall of the Christian College, II." *First Things* 13:30-38.

Byrne, Patricia. 1986. "Sisters of St. Joseph: The Americanization of a French Tradition." *U.S. Catholic History* 5(3-4):241-272.

Cada, Lawrence, et al. 1979. *Shaping the Coming Age of Religious Life.* New York: Seabury Press.

Cahill, Lisa Sowle. 2004. "Realigning Catholic Priorities: Bioethics and the Common Good." *America,* September 13, 2004, Pp. 1-13.

Campbell, Barbara E. 1975. *United Methodist Women: In the Middle of Tomorrow.* Women's Division, General Board of Global Ministries, United Methodist Church, New York.

Campbell, David. 2002. "Beyond Charitable Choice: The Diverse Service Delivery Approaches of Local Faith-Related Organizations." *Nonprofit and Voluntary Sector Quarterly* 31 (2):207-230.

Campion, E. 1987. *Australian Catholics—the Contribution of Catholicism to the Development of Australian Society.* Victoria: Viking.

Carey, Patrick W. 1999. "Changing Conceptions of Catholic Theology/Religious Studies." Pp.65-83 in *Trying Times: Essays on Catholic Higher Education in the Twentieth Century,* edited by William M. Shea, and Daniel Van Slyke. Atlanta: Scholars' Press.

Caronna, Carol A. 1999. "Organizational Identity in Changing Contexts: the Case of Kaiser Permanente and the U. S. Healthcare Field." Paper presented at the annual meeting of the American Sociological Association, Chicago, Ill, August 1999

Carpenter, Joel A. 2002. "The Perils of Prosperity: Neo-Calvinism and the Future of Religious Colleges." Pp. 185-207 in *The Future of Religious Colleges,* edited by Paul J. Dovre. Grand Rapids, MI: Eerdmans.

Carr, Deborah. 2000. "The Entrepreneurial Alternative." Pp.208-225 in *Women at Work: Leadership for the Next Century*, edited by Dayle M. Smith. Saddle River, NJ: Prentice Hall.

Carroll, Jackson W., Barbara Hargrove, and Adair T. Lummis. 1983. *Women of the Cloth*. New York: Harper and Row.

Casanova, Jose 1994. *Public Religions in the Modern World*. Chicago: University of Chicago Press.

Cayton, Horace, and Setsuko Matsunaga Nishi. 1955. *The Changing Scene: Current Trends and Issues, Churches and Social Welfare*, volume II. New York: National Council of Churches of Christ in the U. S. A.

Center for Applied Research in the Apostolate 1999. Emerging Religious Communities in the United States. Washington DC: Georgetown University. CARA@gunet.georgetown.edu.

Cernera, Anthony J. 2000. "Relationship Revisited: A Reflection From a President of a Lay-Led University." *Current Issues in Catholic Higher Education* 21(1):40-42.

Chambliss, Daniel F. 1996. *Beyond Caring: Hospitals, Nurses, and the Social Organization of Ethics*. Chicago: University of Chicago Press.

Chang, Patricia M.Y. 1997. "In Search of a Pulpit: Sex Differences in the Transition from Seminary Training to the First Parish Job." *Journal for the Scientific Study of Religion* 364:614-627.

Charlton, Joy. 1997. "Clergywomen of the Pioneer Generation: A Longitudinal Study." *Journal for the Scientific Study of Religion* 364:599-613.

Chaves, Mark. 1991. "Segmentation in a Religious Labor Market." *Sociological Analysis* 522:143-158.

———. 1994. "Secularization as Declining Religious Authority." *Social Forces* 72:749-774.

———. 1997. *Ordaining Women: Culture and Conflict in Religious Organizations*. Cambridge, MA: Harvard University Press.

———. 1999. "Religious Congregations and Welfare Reform: Who Will Take Advantage of 'Charitable Choice'?" *American Sociological Review* 64:836-846.

———. 2004 *Congregations in America*. Cambridge, MA: Harvard University Press.

Chaves, Mark, and James Cavendish. 1997. "Recent Changes in Women's Ordination Conflicts: The Effect of a Social Movement on Intraorganizational Controversy." *Journal for the Scientific Study of Religion* 364:574-584.

Cherry, Conrad. 1995. *Hurrying Toward Zion: Universities, Divinity Schools, and American Protestantism*. Bloomington, IN: Indiana University Press.

Cieslak, Michael. 2005. "The Lack of Consensus Among Catholics for Establishing New Elementary Schools." *Review of Religious Research* 47:175-89.

Clarissa, M. Mary, OSF, and S. Mary Olivia, OSF. 1948. *With the Poverello: A History of the Sisters of St. Francis*. New York: P.J. Kenedy and Sons.

Clark, J., and G. Anderson. 1990. "A Study of Women in Ministry: God Calls, Man Chooses." Pp. 271-278 in *Yearbook of American and Canadian Churches*, edited by Constant Jacquet. Nashville, TN: Abingdon.

Clarke, Lee, and Carroll L. Estes. 1992. "Sociological and Economic Theories of Markets and Nonprofits: Evidence From Home Health Organizations." *American Journal of Sociology* 97:945-969.

Clear, Caitriona. 1987. *Nuns in Nineteenth Century Ireland*. Dublin: Gill and MacMillan Ltd.

Cleary, Maureen. 2001. "The Management Dilemmas in Catholic Human Service

Organizations Health, Welfare, and Education in Australia." Ph.D. Dissertation, School of Management, University of Technology, Sydney, Australia.

Cnaan, Ram A., with Robert J. Wineburg and Stephanie C. Boddie. 1999. *The Newer Deal: Social Work and Religion in Partnership*. New York: Columbia University Press.

Coburn, Carol K. 2004. "An Overview of the Historiography of Women Religious: A 25 Year Retrospective." *U.S. Catholic Historian* 22(1):1-26.

Coburn, Carol K., and Martha Smith. 1999. *Spirited Lives: How Nuns Shaped Catholic Culture and American Life, 1836-1920*. Chapel Hill, NC: University of North Carolina Press.

Cohn, Robert L. 1987. "Sainthood on the Periphery: The Case of Judaism." Pp.87-108 in *Saints and Virtues*, edited by John Stratton Hawley. Berkeley: University of California Press.

Coleman, John A. 2001. "American Catholicism, Catholic Charities, USA, and Welfare Reform," *Journal of Policy History* 13(1)51-67.

————. 2000. "Religious Authority Structure, Religious Agency, and External Environment: the Case Study of Catholic Charities, USA." Paper presented at the annual meeting of the Association for the Sociology of Religion, Chicago, IL August, 2000.

————. 1987. "Conclusion: After Sainthood?" Pp.205-225 in John Stratton Hawley, ed. *Saints and Virtues*. Berkeley: University of California Press.

————. 1990. "A Company of Critics: Jesuits and the Intellectual Life." *Studies in the Spirituality of the Jesuits* 22:11-12,29.

Conroy, M.C. 1989. "The Transition Years." Pp. 144-163 in *Pioneer Healers: The History of Women Religious in American Health Care*, edited by Ursula Stepsis and Dolores Liptak. New York: Crossroad.

Contosta, David R. 2002. "The Philadelphia Story: Life at Immaculata, Rosemont and Chestnut Hill." Pp.123-160 in *Catholic Women's Colleges in America*, edited by Tracy Schier and Cynthia Russett. Baltimore: Johns Hopkins University Press.

————. 1995. *Villanova University, 1842-1992: American, Catholic, Augustinian*. University Park, PA: Penn State University Press.

Conway, Jill Kerr. 2002. "Faith, Knowledge and Gender." Pp.11-24 in *Catholic Women's Colleges in America*, edited by Tracy Schier and Cynthia Russett. Baltimore: Johns Hopkins University Press.

Cook, Samuel Dubois. 2002. "The United Methodist Church and Its Predominantly Black Colleges: An Enduring Partnership in the Intellectual Love of God." Pp. 246-263 in *The Future of Religious Colleges*, edited by Paul J. Dovre. Grand Rapids, MI: Eerdmans.

Cooke, Marie M., and Mary Chinery. 1995. "Doctoral Degrees Earned by United States Women Religious, 1907-1992." Pp. 31-41 in *Women Religious and the Intellectual Life: The North American Achievement*, edited by Bridget Puzon, OSU. San Francisco: Catholic Scholars Press.

Coser, Lewis. 1974. *Greedy Institutions*. New York: Free Press.

Coughlin, B.J. 1965. *Church and State in Social Welfare*. New York: Columbia University Press.

Crowther, Anne. 2002. "Health Care and Poor Relief in Provincial England." Pp. 203-219 in *Health Care and Poor Relief in Eighteenth and Nineteenth Century Northern Europe*, edited by Ole Peter Grell, Andrew Cunningham, and Robert Jutte. Burlington, VT: Ashgate Publishing.

Cumberland, William H. 1986. "The Jehovah's Witness Tradition." Pp. 447-467 in *Caring and Curing: Health and Medicine in the Western Religious Traditions*, edited by

Ronald L. Numbers and Darrell W. Amundsen. New York: Macmillan.
———— . 1978. "Varieties of Church-Relatedness in Higher Education." Pp. 17-27 in *Church-Related Higher Education*, edited by Robert Rue Parsonage. Valley Forge, PA: Judson Press.

Cuninggim, Merrimon. 1994. *Uneasy Partners: The College and the Church*. Nashville: Abingdon Press.
———— . 1978. "Varieties of Church-Relatedness in Higher Education," Pp. 17-27 in *Church-Related Higher Education,* edited by Robert Rue Parsonage. Valley Forge, PA: Judson Press.

Daigler, Mary Jeremy, RSM. 2000. *Through the Windows: A History of the Work of Higher Education Among the Sisters of Mercy of the Americas.* Scranton: University of Scranton Press.

Davidson, James D., and J.R. Koch. 1988. "Beyond Mutual and Public Benefits." Pp.292-306 in *Sacred Companies*, edited by N.J. Demerath, P.D. Hall, T. Schmitt, and R. H. Williams. New York: Oxford University Press.

Davidson, James D., Andrea S. Williams, Richard A. Lammana, Jan Stenftenagel, Kathleen Maas Weigert, W. J. Whalen, and Patricia Wittberg. 1997. *The Search for Common Ground: What Unites and Divides Catholic Americans*. Huntington, IN: Our Sunday Visitor Press.

Deacon, Florence Jean. 1989. *Handmaids or Autonomous Women: The Charitable Activities, Institution-Building, and Communal Relationships of Catholic Sisters in Nineteenth Century Wisconsin*. Ph.D. Dissertation, History Department, University of Wisconsin.

DeBare, Ilana. 2004. *Where Girls Come First: The Rise, Fall, and Surprising Revival of Girls' Schools.* New York: Tarcher/Penguin.

Deedy, John. 1984. "The Catechism Crisis: Can Catholics Pass Religion 101?" *U.S. Catholic* (August 1984), Pp.20-24.

Demerath, N. J., Peter Dobkin Hall, Terry Schmitt, and Rhys H. Williams, eds. 1998. *Sacred Companies: Organizational Aspects of Religion and Religious Aspects of Organizations.* New York: Oxford University Press.

Denault, Bernard. 1975. "Sociographie generale des communautes religieuses au Quebec, 1837-1970." Pp.17-117 in *Elements pour une sociologie des communautes religieuses au Quebec*, edited by Bernard Denault and Benoit Levesque. Montreal: Les Presses de L'Universite de Montreal.

DeThomasis, Louis. 2002. *Imagination: A Future for Religious Life*. Winona, MN: The Metanoia Group.

Diebolt, Evelyne. 2001. "Women and Philanthropy in France: From the Sixteenth to the Twentieth Centuries." Pp.29-63 in *Women, Philanthropy, and Civil Society*, edited by Kathleen D. McCarthy. Bloomington, IN: Indiana University Press.

DiMaggio, Paul J., and Walter W. Powell. 1983. "The Iron Cage Revisited: Institutional Isomorphism and Collective Rationality in Organizational Fields." *American Sociological Review* 48:147-160.

Diner, Hasia R. 1983. *Erin's Daughters in America: Irish Immigrant Women in the Nineteenth Century*. Baltimore: Johns Hopkins University Press.

Dinges, Martin. 1999. "Health Care and Poor Relief in Regional Southern France." Pp. 240-279 in *Health Care and Poor Relief in Counter-Reformation Europe,* edited by Ole Peter Grell, Andrew Cunningham, and Jon Arrizabalaga. New York:Routledge.

Dobbelaere, Karel. 1982. "Contradictions Between Expressive and Strategic Language in Policy Documents of Catholic Hospitals and Welfare Organizations: Trials Instead of

Liturgies as a Means of Social Control." *Annual Review of the Social Sciences of Religion* 6:107-131.

Doeringer, Peter B., and Michael J. Piore. 1971. *Internal Labor Markets and Manpower Analysis*. Lexington, MA: D.C. Heath.

Dolan, Jay P. 1998. "Social Catholicism" Pp.189-202 in *Making the Nonprofit Sector in the United States: A Reader*, edited by David C. Hammack. Bloomington, IN: Indiana University Press.

———. 1985. *The American Catholic Experience: A History From Colonial Times to the Present*. New York: Doubleday.

Dorff, Elliot N. 1986. "The Jewish Tradition," Pp. 5-39 in *Caring and Curing: Health and Medicine in the Western Religious Traditions*, edited by Ronald L. Numbers and Darrell W. Amundsen. New York: Macmillan.

Dougherty, Mary Agnes. 1981. "The Social Gospel According to Phoebe." Pp. 200-216 in *Women in New Worlds: Historical Perspectives on the Wesleyan Tradition*, edited by Hilah F. Thomas and Rosemary Skinner. Nashville, TN: Abingdon.

———. 1997. *My Calling to Fulfill: Deaconesses in the United Methodist Tradition*. Women's Division, General Board of Global Ministries, United Methodist Church.

Dovre, Paul J., ed. 2002. *The Future of Religious Colleges*. Grand Rapids, MI: Eerdmans.

Dross, Fitz. 2002. "Health Care Provision and Poor Relief in Enlightenment and Nineteenth Century Prussia." Pp. 69-111 in *Health Care and Poor Relief in Eighteenth and Nineteenth Century Northern Europe*, edited by Ole Peter Grell, Andrew Cunningham, and Robert Jutte. Burlington, VT: Ashgate Publishing.

Dudine, Mary Frederica, OSB. 1967. *The Castle on the Hill*. Milwaukee: Bruce Publishing Co.

Duffy, Kathleen. 2004 ."The Spiritual Power of Matter: Teilhard and the Exercises." *Review for Religious* 63(2):192-203.

Dunstan, Peta. 2003. "Anglican Religious Life: Evolving Identity." *Religious Life Review* 42(6):335-352.

Durnbaugh, Donald F. 1997. "Sustainers or Seducers? The Rise and Meaning of Church-Related Institutions." *The Mennonite Quarterly Review* 71(3):345-364.

Dwyer, Judith A. and Charles Zech. 1998. "American Catholic Higher Education: An ACCU Study on Mission and Identity, Faculty Development, and Curricular Review." *Current Issues in Catholic Higher Education* 19(1):11-13,19.

Ebaugh, Helen Rose Fuchs. 1993. *Women in the Vanishing Cloister: Organizational Decline in Catholic Religious Orders in the United States*. New Brunswick, NJ: Rutgers University Press.

Eby, John W. 1997. "Mission Community: A New Image for Church-Related Institutions." *The Mennonite Quarterly Review* 71(3):395-409.

Eby, Judy, RSM. 2000. *"A Little Squabble Among Nuns?" The Sister Formation Crisis and the Patterns of Authority and Obedience Among American Women Religious, 1954-1971*. Ph.D. Dissertation, History Department, St. Louis University.

Edwards, R.A.R. 2003. "Jane Addams, Walter Rauschenbusch, and Dorothy Day: A Comparative Study of Settlement Theology." Pp. 150-166 in *Gender and the Social Gospel*, edited by Wendy J. Deichmann Edwards and Carolyn de Swarte Gifford. Urbana, IL: University of Illinois Press.

Edwards, Wendy J. Deichmann. 2003. "Women and Social Betterment in the Social Gospel Work of Josiah Strong." Pp. 33-52 in *Gender and the Social Gospel*, edited by Wendy J. Deichmann Edwards and Carolyn de Swarte Gifford. Urbana, IL: University of Illinois Press.

Edwards, Wendy J. Deichmann, and Carolyn de Swarte Gifford, eds. 2003. *Gender and the Social Gospel.* Urbana, IL: University of Illinois Press.

———. 2003. "Introduction: Restoring Women and Reclaiming Gender in Social Gospel Studies," Pp. 1-17 in *Gender and the Social Gospel,* edited by Wendy J. Deichmann Edwards and Carolyn de Swarte Gifford. Urbana, IL: University of Illinois Press.

Elliott, T. Michael, Diane Dillard, Renee G. Loeffler, and Kent M. Weeks. 1976. *To Give the Key of Knowledge: United Methodists and Education, 1784-1976.* Nashville, TN: National Commission on United Methodist Higher Education.

Ellor, J.W., F. E. Netting, and J. M. Thibault. 1999. *Understanding Religious and Spiritual Aspects of Human Service Practice.* Columbia, SC: University of South Carolina Press.

Ehrenhalt, A. 1995. *The Lost City: The Forgotten Virtues of Community in America.* New York: Basic Books.

Evans, John H. 2003. "After the Fall: Attempts to Establish an Explicitly Theological Voice in Debates Over Science and Medicine After 1976." Pp. 434-46 in *The Secular Revolution: Power, Interests, and Conflict in the Secularization of Public Life,* edited by Christian Smith. Berkeley: University of California Press.

Ewens, Mary. 1981. "The Leadership of Nuns in Immigrant Catholicism." Pp.101-149 in *Women and Religion in America* vol.1., edited by Rosemary Ruether and Rosemary S. Keller. New York: Harper and Row.

———. 1989a. "The Vocation Decline of Women Religious: Some Historical Perspectives." Pp. 165-180 in *The Crisis in Religious Vocations,* edited by Laurie Felknor. New York: Paulist Press.

———. 1989b. "Women in the Convent." Pp.17-47 in *American Catholic Women: A Historical Exploration,* edited by Karen Kennelly. New York: Macmillan.

Fairbank, John K., ed. 1974. *The Missionary Enterprise in China and America.* Cambridge: Harvard University Press.

Farquhar, Clare, and Rita Das. 1999. "Are Focus Groups Suitable for 'Sensitive' Topics?" Pp.46-63 in *Developing Focus Group Research: Politics, Theory and Practice,* edited by Rosaline S. Barbour and Jenny Kitzinger. London: Sage.

Farren, Suzy. 1996. *A Call to Care: The Women Who Built Catholic Health Care in America.* St. Louis: Catholic Health Association of the U.S.

Faure, Olivier. 2002. "Health Care Provision and Poor Relief in Nineteenth Century Provincial France." Pp. 309-324 in *Health Care and Poor Relief in Eighteenth and Nineteenth Century Northern Europe,* edited by Ole Peter Grell, Andrew Cunningham, and Robert Jutte. Burlington, VT: Ashgate Publishing.

Faver, Catherine A. 2000. "To Run and Not Be Weary: Spirituality and Women's Activism." *Review of Religious Research,* 42(1):61-78.

Feeney, Suzanne. 1997. "Shifting the Prism: Case Explications of Institutional Analysis in Nonprofit Organizations." *Nonprofit and Voluntary Sector Quarterly* 26(2):489-508.

Feldman, Martha S. 1991. "The Meanings of Ambiguity: Learning from Stories and Metaphors." Pp. 145-156 in *Reframing Organizational Culture,* edited by Peter J. Frost et al. Newbury Park, CA: Sage.

Fennell, Mary L. and Jeffrey A. Alexander. 1993. "Perspectives on Organizational Change in the U. S. Medical Care Sector." *Annual Review of Sociology* 19:89-112.

Field, James A., Jr. 1974. "Near East Notes and Far East Queries." Pp. 23-55 in *The Missionary Enterprise in China and America,* edited by John K. Fairbank. Cambridge, MA: Harvard University Press.

Finke, Roger 2004. "Innovative Returns to Tradition: Using Core Teaching as the

Foundation for Innovative Accommodation." *Journal for the Scientific Study of Religion* 43(1):19-34.

Finke, Roger, and Rodney Stark. 1992. *The Churching of America, 1776-1990.* New Brunswick, NJ: Rutgers University Press.

————. 2001. "The New Holy Clubs: Testing Church to Sect Propositions." *Sociology of Religion* 62(2):175-189.

Finke, Roger, and Patricia Wittberg. 2000. "Organizational Revival From Within: Explaining Revivalism and Reform in the Roman Catholic Church." *Journal for the Scientific Study of Religion* 392:154-170.

Fisher, B.C. 1989. *The Idea of A Christian University in Today's World.* Macon, GA: Mercer University Press.

Fitzgerald, Paul A., SJ. 1984. *The Governance of Jesuit Colleges in the United States, 1920-70.* Notre Dame, IN: University of Notre Dame Press.

Flanagan, Bernadette. 2005. "World Congress on Consecrated Life." *Religious Life Review* 44(1):53-63.

Fligstein, Neil. 1987. "The Intraorganizational Power Struggle: The Rise of Finance Personnel to Top Leadership in Large Corporations." *American Sociological Review* 52(1):44-58

————. 1990. *The Transformation of Corporate Control.* Cambridge, MA: Harvard University Press.

Flory, Richard W. 2002. "Intentional Change and the Maintenance of Mission: The Impact of Adult Education Programs on School Mission at Two Evangelical Colleges." *Review of Religious Research* 43(4):349-368.

Friedman, Jean E. 1985. *The Enclosed Garden: Women and Community in the Evangelical South, 1830-1900.* Chapel Hill, NC: University of North Carolina Press.

Frost, Peter J., Larry F. Moore, Meryl Reis Louis, Craig C. Lundberg, and Joanne Martin, eds. 1991. *Reframing Organizational Culture.* Newbury Park, CA: Sage.

Fulton, J. 1997. "Modernity and Religious Change in Western Roman Catholicism: Two Contrasting Paradigms." *Social Compass* 44(1):115-129.

Gallagher, John A. 1996. "The Ecclesiology of the U.S. Bishops' 1994 Health Care Directives." *Review for Religious* 55(3): 230-248.

Gallin, Alice, OSU. 1996. *Independence and a New Partnership in Catholic Higher Education.* Notre Dame, IN: University of Notre Dame Press.

————. 1999. "American Catholic Higher Education: An Experience of Inculturation." Pp. 99-119 in *Trying Times: Essays on Catholic Higher Education in the Twentieth Century,* edited by William M. Shea and Daniel Van Slyke. Atlanta: Scholars' Press.

————. 2000. *Negotiating Identity: Catholic Higher Education Since 1960.* Notre Dame, IN: University of Notre Dame Press.

Garland, Diana B. 1994. *Church Agencies: Caring for Children and Families in Crisis.* Washington, DC: Child Welfare League of America.

————. 1992. *Church Social Work.* Philadelphia: North American Association of Christians in Social Work.

Garroutte, Eva Marie. 2003. "The Positivist Attack on Baconian Science and Religious Knowledge." Pp. 197-215 in *The Secular Revolution: Power, Interests, and Conflict in the Secularization of Public Life,* edited by Christian Smith. Berkeley: University of California Press.

Geier, Woodrow A. 1974. *Church Colleges Today: Perspectives of a Church Agency on their Problems and Possibilities.* Nashville, TN: United Methodist Board of Higher Education and Ministry.

Geiger, John. 2003a. "Faculty." Pp. 199-216 in *A Handbook of Research on Catholic Higher Education*, edited by Thomas C. Hunt, Ronald J. Nuzzi, Ellis A. Joseph, and John D. Geiger. Greenwich, CT: Information Age Publications.

————. 2003b. "Governance of Catholic Higher Education." Pp. 117-136 in *A Handbook of Research on Catholic Higher Education*, edited by Thomas C. Hunt, Ronald J. Nuzzi, Ellis A. Joseph, and John D. Geiger. Greenwich, CT: Information Age Publications.

Gentilcore, David. 1999. "'Cradle of Saints and Useful Institutions': Health Care and Poor Relief in the Kingdom of Naples." Pp. 132-150 in *Health Care and Poor Relief in Counter-Reformation Europe*, edited by Ole Peter Grell, Andrew Cunningham, and Jon Arrizabalaga. New York:Routledge.

Gifford, Carolyn de Swarte. 2003. "'The Woman's Cause is Man's'? Frances Willard and the Social Gospel." Pp. 21-34 in *Gender and the Social Gospel*, edited by Wendy J. Deichmann Edwards and Carolyn de Swarte Gifford. Urbana, IL: University of Illinois Press.

Gijswijt-Hofstra, Marijke. 2002. "Dutch Approaches to Problems of Illness and Poverty Between the Golden Age and the *Fin de Siecle*." Pp. 132-150 in *Health Care and Poor Relief in Eighteenth and Nineteenth Century Northern Europe*, edited by Ole Peter Grell, Andrew Cunningham, and Robert Jutte. Burlington, VT: Ashgate Publishing.

Ginzberg, Lori D. 1990. *Women and the Work of Benevolence: Morality, Politics and Class in the Nineteenth Century United States*. New Haven: Yale University Press.

Gleason, Philip. 1967. "American Catholic Higher Education: A Historical Perspective." Pp.15-53 in *The Shape of Catholic Higher Education*, edited by Robert Hassenger. Chicago: University of Chicago Press.

————. 1993. "The American Background of *Ex Corde Ecclesiae*: A Historical Perspective." Pp.1-31 in *Catholic Universities in Church and Society: A Dialog on Ex Corde Ecclesiae*, edited by John P. Langan, SJ. Washington, DC: Georgetown University Press.

————. 1995. *Contending With Modernity: Catholic Higher Education in the Twentieth Century*. New York: Oxford University Press.

————. 1997. "The American Background of *Ex Corde Ecclesiae:* A Historical Perspective." Pp.79-97 in *Catholic Education at the Turn of the New Century,* edited by Joseph M. O'Keefe, SJ. New York: Garland.

————. 2001. "A Half-century of Change in Catholic Higher Education." *U.S. Catholic Historian* 19(1):1-20.

————. 2003. "A Bibliographic Essay on the History of Catholic Higher Education." Pp.95-113 in *A Handbook of Research on Catholic Higher Education*, edited by Thomas C. Hunt, Ronald J. Nuzzi, Ellis A. Joseph, and John D. Geiger. Greenwich, CT: Information Age Publications.

Goffman, Erving. 1961. *Asylums.* Garden City, NY: Doubleday Anchor.

Goia, Dennis A., and James B. Thomas. 1996. "Identity, Image and Issue Interpretation: Sensemaking During Strategic Change in Academia." *Administrative Science Quarterly* 41(3):370-403.

Golden-Biddle, Karen, and Hayagreeva Rao. 1997. "Breaches in the Boardroom: Organizational Identity and Conflicts of Commitment in a Nonprofit Organization." *Organization Science* 8(6):593-611.

Golder, C. 1903. *History of the Deaconess Movement in the Christian Church.* Cincinnati: Jennings and Pye.

Goren, Arthur A. 1998. "The Jewish Tradition of Community." Pp.203-220 in *Making the*

Nonprofit Sector in the United States: A Reader, edited by David C. Hammack. Bloomington, IN: Indiana University Press.

Gottemoeller, Doris, RSM. 1991. "Institutions Without Sisters." *Review For Religious* 50:564-571.

————. 1995. "Higher Education and the 'Enduring Concerns' of the Sisters of Mercy." *The MAST Journal: The Journal of the Mercy Association in Scripture and Theology* 6(1):33-36.

————. 1997. "The Priesthood: Implications in Consecrated Life for Women." Pp.127-138 in *A Concert of Charisms: Ordained Ministry in Religious Life,* edited by Paul K. Hennessy. New York: Paulist Press.

————. 2005. "Living in Community: Continuing the Conversation." *Review for Religious* 64(3):269-2880.

Graber Miller, Keith. 2000. "Transformative Education." Pp.1-14 in *Teaching to Transform: Perspectives on Mennonite Higher Education,* edited by Keith Graber Miller. Goshen, IN: Pinchpenny Press.

Grant, Mary Kathryn. 2003. "Exercising Sponsorship: Five Essential Tasks." *Current Issues in Catholic Higher Education* 23(2):61-66.

Granquist, Mark. 2003. "Word Alone and the Future of Lutheran Denominationalism." Pp.62-80 in *Lutherans Today: American Lutheran Identity in the Twenty-first Century,* edited by Richard Cimino. Grand Rapids, MI: Eerdmans.

Grell, Ole Peter. 1997. "The Protestant Imperative of Christian Care and Neighborly Love." Pp. 43-65 in *Health Care and Poor Relief in Protestant Europe, 1500-1700,* edited by Ole Peter Grell and Andrew Cunningham. New York: Routledge.

Grell, Ole Peter, and Andrew Cunningham, eds. 1997. *Health Care and Poor Relief in Protestant Europe, 1500-1700.* New York: Routledge.

Grell, Ole Peter, and Andrew Cunningham. 1999. "The Counter-Reformation and Welfare Provision in Southern Europe." Pp. 1-17 in *Health Care and Poor Relief in Counter-Reformation Europe,* edited by Ole Peter Grell, Andrew Cunningham, and Jon Arrizabalaga. New York:Routledge.

————. 1997. "The Reformation and Changes in Welfare Provision in Early Modern Northern Europe." Pp. 1-42 in *Health Care and Poor Relief in Protestant Europe, 1500-1700,* edited by Ole Peter Grell and Andrew Cunningham. New York: Routledge.

Grell, Ole Peter, Andrew Cunningham, and Jon Arrizabalaga, eds. 2002. *Health Care and Poor Relief in Eighteenth and Nineteenth Century Northern Europe.* Burlington, VT: Ashgate Publishing.

Griffith, R. Marie. 1997. *God's Daughters: Evangelical Women and the Power of Submission.* Berkeley: University of California Press.

Gutschow, Kim. 2004. *Being a Buddhist Nun: The Struggle for Enlightenment in the Himalayas.* Cambridge, MA: Harvard University Press.

Hall, S. Jeremy, OSB. 1997. "The Character of Benedictine Higher Education." Pp.98-115 in *Catholic Education at the Turn of the New Century,* edited by Joseph M. O'Keefe, SJ. New York: Garland.

Hammack, David C., ed. 1998. *Making the Nonprofit Sector in the United States: A Reader.* Bloomington, IN: Indiana University Press.

Harder, James M. 1997. " Church-Related Institutions: Driven by Member Commitment or by Economic Forces?" *The Mennonite Quarterly Review* 71(3):377-394.

Harrell, David Edwin, Jr. 1986. "The Disciples of Christ-Church of Christ Tradition." Pp. 376-397 in *Caring and Curing: Health and Medicine in the Western Religious*

   Traditions, edited by Ronald L. Numbers and Darrell W. Amundsen. New York:
   Macmillan.
Harris, Fred E. 1974. "Church-College Relationships and Challenges." Pp. 15-23 in *Church*
   Colleges Today: Perspectives of a Church Agency on their Problems and Possibili-
   ties, edited by Woodrow A. Geier. Nashville, TN: United Methodist Board of Higher
   Education and Ministry.
Harris, Joseph Claude. 1996. *The Cost of Catholic Parishes and Schools.* Kansas City:
   Sheed and Ward.
Harris, Margaret. 1998. *Organizing God's Work: Challenges for Churches and Synagogues*
   New York: St. Martin's Press.
Harrison, Paul. 1959. *Authority and Power in the Free Church Tradition.* Princeton, NJ:
   Princeton University Press.
Harrison, V. V. 1988. *Changing Habits: A Memoir of the Society of the Sacred Heart.* New
   York: Doubleday.
Hassenger, Robert, ed. 1967. *The Shape of Catholic Higher Education.* Chicago: University
   of Chicago Press.
Hatch, Nathan, and M. Hamilton. 1992. "Can Evangelicalism Survive its Success?"
   Christianity Today 36(1):2-34.
Haughey, John C. 1999. "Research and Catholic Identity: In Search of a Concinnity."
   Unpublished talk given at St. Joseph University, Philadelphia PA, June 27, 1999.
Hayes, Alice Bourke. 2000. "Comments on 'Relationship Revisited.'" *Current Issues in*
   Catholic Higher Education 21(1):42-5.
Heft, James L. 2003. "Identity and Mission: Catholic Higher Education." Pp.35-57 in *A*
   Handbook of Research on Catholic Higher Education, edited by Thomas C. Hunt,
   Ronald J. Nuzzi, Ellis A. Joseph, and John D. Geiger. Greenwich, CT: Information
   Age Publications.
Hehir, Bryan J. 1995. "Identity and Institutions." *Health Progress* (Nov.-Dec. 1995):1-7.
Hellwig, Monika K. 2002. "Emerging Patterns Among Roman Catholic Colleges and
   Universities." Pp. 103-115 in *The Future of Religious Colleges,* edited by Paul J.
   Dovre. Grand Rapids, MI: Eerdmans.
———. 2000. "Alternative Plans." *Current Issues in Catholic Higher Education* 21(1):45-
   47.
Henderson, John. 1994. *Piety and Charity in Late Medieval Florence.* Oxford: Clarendon
   Press.
———. 1999. "Charity and Welfare in Early Modern Tuscany." Pp. 56-86 in *Health Care*
   and Poor Relief in Counter-Reformation Europe, edited by Ole Peter Grell, Andrew
   Cunningham, and Jon Arrizabalaga. New York:Routledge.
Hickey, Daniel. 1997. *Local Hospitals in Ancien Regime France: Rationalization,*
   Resistence, Renewal, 1530-1789. Montreal: McGill-Queens University Press.
Higgenbotham, Evelyn Brooks. 1993. *Righteous Discontent: The Women's Movement in the*
   Black Baptist Church, 1880-1920. Cambridge, MA: Harvard University Press.
Hill, Michael. 1973. *The Religious Order: A Study of Virtuoso Religion and Its Legitima-*
   tion in Nineteenth Century England. London: Heinemann Educational Books.
Hill, Patricia R. 1985. *The World their Household: The American Women's Foreign*
   Mission Movement and Cultural Transformation, 1870-1920. Ann Arbor: University
   of Michigan Press.
Himes, Michael. 2000. "Returning to Our Ancestral Lands." *Review for Religious* 59(1):6-
   25.
Hogan, William F. 1996 "Canonical Room for Charisms." Pp.144-149 in *The Church and*

Consecrated Life, edited by David Fleming, SJ, and Elizabeth McDonough, OP. Series: *The Best of the Review,* vol.5. St. Louis, MO: *Review for Religious.*

Hollingsworth, Rogers, and Ellen Jane Hollingsworth. 1986. "A Comparison of Nonprofit, For-Profit, and Public Hospitals in the United States, 1935 to the Present." PONPO Working Paper #113, Program on Non-profit Organizations, Yale University.

Holtschneider, Dennis H., and Melanie M. Morey. 2000a. "Relationship Revisited: Changing Relationships Between U.S. Catholic Colleges and Universities and Founding Religious Congregations." *Current Issues In Catholic Higher Education* 211:3-39.

———. 2000b. "Relationship Revisited: Changing Relationships Between U.S. Catholic Colleges and Universities and Founding Religious Congregations." Occasional paper no.47, Association of Governing Boards of Universities and Colleges, One Dupont Circle, Suite 400, Washington, DC 20036.

———. 2003. "Leadership and the Age of the Laity: Emerging Patterns in Catholic Higher Education." Paper presented at the Lay Leadership Conference, Sacred Heart University, June 14, 2003.

Huehls, Frances. 2004. "Teaching as Philanthropy: Catharine Beecher and the Hartford Female Seminary." Pp. 36-59 in *Women and Philanthropy in Education,* edited by Andrea Walton. Bloomington, IN: Indiana University Press.

Hughes, Richard T. 1999. "Protestant Colleges: 1960-90." Pp.85-98 in *Trying Times: Essays on Catholic Higher Education in the Twentieth Century,* edited by William M. Shea and Daniel Van Slyke. Atlanta: Scholars' Press.

Hughes, Richard T., and William B. Adrian, eds. 1997. *Models for Christian Higher Education: Strategies for Success in the Twenty-first Century.* Grand Rapids, MI: Eerdmans.

Isham, Mary. 1936. *Valorous Ventures: A Record of Sixty and Six Years of the Women's Foreign Mission Society of the Methodist Episcopal Church.* Women's Foreign Mission Society.

Jackall, Robert. 1988. *Moral Mazes: The World of Corporate Managers.* New York: Oxford University Press.

James, Estelle. 1998. "Communication Among Nonprofits: Objectives, Opportunities, and Constraints." Pp. 271-298 in *To Profit or Not to Profit: The Commercial Transformation of the Nonprofit Sector,* edited by Burton A. Weisbrod. New York: Cambridge University Press.

Jeavons, Thomas H. 1994. *When the Bottom Line is Faithfulness: Management of Christian Service Organizations.* Bloomington, IN: Indiana University Press.

———. 1998. "Identifying Characteristics of 'Religious' Organizations: An Exploratory Proposal." Pp. 79-95 in *Sacred Companies: Organizational Aspects of Religion and Religious Aspects of Organizations,* edited by N.J.Demerath III, Peter Dobkin Hall, Terry Schmitt, and Rhys H. Williams. New York: Oxford University Press.

Jiobu, Robert M. 1989. "Ethnic Hegemony and the Japanese of California." *American Sociological Review* 53:353-67.

Johnson, H.C. 1992. "'Down from the Mountain': Secularization and Higher Learning in America." *Review of Politics* 54(4):551-588.

Jones, Arthur. 1995. "Huge Nonprofit System Feels Pressure To Cut Costs, Merge, and Get Bigger." *National Catholic Reporter* 31(2), June 16, 1995, 11-14.

———. 2003. "Catholic Aim: Aid Poor, Survive." *National Catholic Reporter* 39(31), June 6, 2003, p. 3-4.

Jones, Colin. 1999. "Perspectives on Poor Relief, Health Care, and the Counter-Reformation in France." Pp. 215-239 in *Health Care and Poor Relief in Counter-Reformation Europe*, edited by Ole Peter Grell, Andrew Cunningham, and Jon Arrizabalaga. New York:Routledge.

Jutte, Robert. 1997. "Health Care Provision and Poor Relief in Early Modern Hanseatic Towns." Pp. 108-128 in *Health Care and Poor Relief in Protestant Europe, 1500-1700*, edited by Ole Peter Grell and Andrew Cunningham. New York: Routledge.

Kanter, Rosabeth M. 1977. *Men and Women of the Corporation*. New York: Basic Books.

Kauffman, Christopher. 1995. *Ministry and Meaning: A Religious History of Catholic Health Care in the United States*. New York: Crossroad.

Keim, Paul A. 2002. "The Ethos of Anabaptist-Mennonite Colleges." Pp. 264-280 in *The Future of Religious Colleges*, edited by Paul J. Dovre. Grand Rapids, MI: Eerdmans.

Keller, Rosemary Skinner. 1981. "Creating a Sphere for Women." Pp. 246-260 in Hilah F. Thomas and Rosemary Skinner, eds. *Women in New Worlds: Historical Perspectives on the Wesleyan Tradition*. Nashville, TN: Abingdon.

Kelly, Margaret J. 1989. "Toward the Twenty-First Century." Pp. 168-200 in *Pioneer Healers: The History of Women Religious in American Health Care*, edited by Ursula Stepsis and Dolores Liptak. New York: Crossroad.

Kemeny, P. C. 2003. "Power, Ridicule, and the Destruction of Religious Moral Reform Politics in the 1920s." Pp.216-268 in *The Secular Revolution: Power, Interests, and Conflict in the Secularization of Public Life*, edited by Christian Smith. Berkeley: University of California Press.

Kenneally, James J. 1990. *The History of American Catholic Women*. New York:Crossroad.

Kennelly, Karen, CSJ. 1996. "Women Religious, the Intellectual Life, and Anti-Intellectualism," Pp.43-71 in *Women Religious and the Intellectual Life: The North American Achievement*, edited by Bridget Puzon, OSU. San Francisco: International Scholars' Publications.

Kepel, Gilles. 1994. *The Revenge of God: The Resurgence of Islam, Christianity, and Judaism in the Modern World.* University Park, PA: Pennsylvania State University Press.

Kim, Ilsoo. 1981. *The New Urban Immigrants: The Korean Community in New York.* Princeton, NJ: Princeton University Press.

Kitzinger, Jenny, and Rosaline Barbour. 1999. "Introduction: The Challenge and Promise of Focus Groups" Pp. 3-20 in *Developing Focus Group Research: Politics, Theory and Practice*, edited by Rosaline S. Barbour and Jenny Kitzinger. London: Sage.

Klaassen, Walter. 1986. "The Anabaptist Tradition," Pp. 271-287 in *Caring and Curing: Health and Medicine in the Western Religious Traditions*, edited by Ronald L. Numbers and Darrell W. Amundsen. New York: Macmillan.

Kleber, Albert, OSB. 1954. *History of St. Meinrad Archabbey*. St. Meinrad, IN.

Knittel, Margaret M. 1995. "Corporate Sponsorship: The 1990s and the Fruits of our Labor." *Review for Religious* 54:499-507.

Kolmer, Elizabeth, ASC. 1984. *Religious Women in the United States: A Survey of the Influential Literature from 1950 to 1983*. Wilmington, DE: Michael Glazier.

Koontz, Ted. 1997. "Church-Related Institutions: Signs of God's Reign." *The Mennonite Quarterly Review* 713:421-438.

Kouri, E. I. 1997. "Health Care and Poor Relief in Sweden and Finland, 1500-1700." Pp. 167-203 in *Health Care and Poor Relief in Protestant Europe, 1500-1700*, edited by Ole Peter Grell and Andrew Cunningham. New York: Routledge.

Kraatz, Matthew S., and Edward J. Zajac. 1996. "Exploring the Limits of the New Institutionalism: The Causes and Consequences of Illegitimate Organizational

Change." *American Sociological Review* 615:812-836.

Kramer, Ralph M. 1987. "Voluntary Agencies and the Personal Social Services." Pp. 240-257 in *The Nonprofit Sector: A Resource Handbook*, edited by Walter W. Powell. New Haven: Yale University Press.

Kunkel, N. 1988. "Christian Free Schools: A Nineteenth Century Plan." Pp. 67-76 in *Enlightening the Next Generation: Catholics and Their Schools, 1830-1980*, edited by F. M. Perko. New York: Garland.

Lambert, Jerry D., Al Truesdale, and Michael W. Vail. 2002. "Emerging Models in the Church of the Nazarene." Pp. 141-159 in *The Future of Religious Colleges*, edited by Paul J. Dovre. Grand Rapids, MI: Eerdmans.

Landim, Leilah. 2001. Women and Philanthropy in Brazil: An Overview." Pp.65-107 in *Women, Philanthropy, and Civil Society*, edited by Kathleen D. McCarthy. Bloomigton, IN: Indiana University Press.

Langan, John P., ed.1993. *Catholic Universities in Church and Society: A Dialog on Ex Corde Ecclesiae*. Washington, DC: Georgetown University Press.

Langley, Monica. 1997. "Really Operating: Nonprofit Hospitals Sometimes Are That In Little But Name." *Wall Street Journal* 100(9), July 14, 1997.

Langlois, Claude. 1984. *Le catholicisme au feminin*. Paris: Editions du Cerf.

Lawson, Ronald, and Maren Lockwood Carden. 1983. "Ghettoization and the Erosion of a Distinct Way of Life: The Seventh Day Adventist Experience." Paper presented at the annual meeting of the Society for the Scientific Study of Religion, Knoxville, Tenn, November 1983.

Leahy, William P. 1991. *Adapting to America: Jesuits and Higher Education in the Twentieth Century*. Washington, DC: Georgetown University Press.

———— . 1997. "Catholics and Educational Expansion after 1945." Pp.47-78 in *Catholic Education at the Turn of the New Century*, edited by Joseph M. O'Keefe, SJ. New York: Garland.

Lebsock, Suzanne. 1998. "Women Together: Organizations," Pp.225-247 in *Making the Nonprofit Sector in the United States: A Reader*, edited by David C. Hammack. Bloomington, IN: Indiana University Press.

Ledoux, Michael W. 2002. "The Decline of Religious Life: A Success Story." *Review for Religious* 61(2):183-190.

Lehman, Edward C. 1993. *Gender and Work: The Case of the Clergy*. Albany, NY: SUNY Press.

1985. *Women Clergy: Breaking Through Gender Barriers*. New Brunswick, NJ: Transaction.

Leighninger, Leslie. 1999 ."The Service Trap: Social Work and Public Welfare Policy in the 1960s." Pp.63-88 in *The Professionalization of Poverty: Social Work and the Poor in the Twentieth Century*, edited by Gary R. Lowe and P. Nelson Reid. New York: Aldine De Gruyter.

Leonard, B. 1997. "What Can the Baptist Tradition Contribute to Christian Higher Education? In *Models for Christian Higher Education: Strategies for survival and Success in the Twenty-first Century*, edited by Richard T. Hughes and W. B. Adrian. Grand Rapids, MI: Eerdmans.

Leung, Beatrice, and Patricia Wittberg. 2004. "Catholic Religious Orders of Women in China: Adaptation and Power." *Journal for the Scientific Study of Religion* 43(1):67-82.

Light, Ivan. 1972. *Ethnic Enterprise in America: Business and Welfare Among Chinese, Japanese, and Blacks*. Berkeley, CA: University of California Press.

Light, Ivan, and Edna Bonacich. 1988. *Immigrant Entrepreneurs: Koreans in Los Angeles, 1965-1982.* Berkeley:University of California Press.

Lindberg, Carter. 1986. "The Lutheran Tradition." Pp.173-203 in *Caring and Curing: Health and Medicine in the Western Religious Traditions,* edited by Ronald L. Numbers and Darrell W. Amundsen. New York: Macmillan.

Logan, Eugenia. 1978. History of the Sisters of Providence of St. Mary of the Woods, vol.II. Terre Haute, IN: Moore Langren Printing Company.

Longfield, Bradley J. and George M. Marsden. 1992. "Presbyterian Colleges in Twentieth Century America." Pp. 99-125 in *The Pluralistic Vision: Presbyterians and Mainstream Protestant Vision and Leadership,* edited by Milton J. Coalter, John Mulder, and Louis B. Weeks. Louisville: Westminster/John Knox Press.

Lowe, Gary R. and P. Nelson Reid. 1999. "Poverty, Public Welfare, and Professionalism," Pp.89-103 in *The Professionalization of Poverty: Social Work and the Poor in the Twentieth Century,* edited by Gary R. Lowe and P. Nelson Reid. New York: Aldine De Gruyter.

Lozada, Eriberto P., Jr. 2001. *God Aboveground: Catholic Church, Postsocialist State, and Transnational Processes in a Chinese Village.* Stanford, CA: Stanford University Press.

Luddy, Maria. 2001. "Women and Philanthropy in Nineteenth Century Ireland." Pp. 9-28 in *Women, Philanthropy, and Civil Society,* edited by Kathleen D. McCarthy. Bloomington, IN: Indiana University Press.

Lyon, Larry, Michael Beaty, and Stephanie Mixon. 2002. "Making Sense of a 'Religious' University: Faculty Adaptations and Opinions at Brigham Young, Baylor, Notre Dame, and Boston College." *Review of Religious Research* 43(4):326-348.

MacDonald, Heidi. 2001. "Not Mere Victims of Circumstance: The Sisters of St. Martha of Prince Edward Island Encounter the 1960s, 70s, and 80s." Paper presented at the triennial meeting of the History of Women Religious, Milwaukee,WI, June 2001.

Mackin, Kevin E. 2000. "A Response to 'Relationship Revisited.'" *Current Issues in Catholic Higher Education* 21(1):48-51.

Madden, S. M. Roger. 1991. *The Path Marked Out: History of the Sisters of Providence of Saint Mary of the Woods.* St. Mary of the Woods, IN.

Maher, Sister Mary Denis. 1989. *To Bind Up the Wounds: Catholic Sister Nurses in the U.S. Civil War.* Baton Rouge: Louisiana State University Press.

Mahoney, Kathleen A. 2002. "American Catholic Colleges for Women: Historical Origins." pp.25-54 in *Catholic Women's Colleges in America,* edited by Tracy Schier and Cynthia Russett. Baltimore: Johns Hopkins University Press.

March, James G., and Herbert Simon. 1958. *Organizations.* New York:John Wiley and Sons.

Marmor, Theodore R. et al. 1987. "Nonprofit Organizations and Health Care." Pp. 221-239 in *The Nonprofit Sector: A Resource Handbook,* edited by Walter Powell. New Haven: Yale University Press.

Marsden, George M. 1997. *The Outrageous Idea of Christian Scholarship.* New York: Oxford University Press

———. 1994. *The Soul of the American University: From Protestant Establishment to Established Nonbelief.* New York: Oxford University Press.

Martin, David. 1969. *The Religious and the Secular.* London: Routledge and Kegan Paul.

Martin, Joanne. 1992. *Cultures in Organizations: Three Perspectives.* New York: Oxford University Press.

———. 2002. *Organizational Culture: Mapping the Terrain.* Thousand Oaks, CA: Sage.

Martin, Joanne, and Debra Meyerson. 1988. "Organizational Cultures and the Denial, Channeling and Acknowledgment of Ambiguity." Pp.93-125 in *Managing Ambiguity and Change*, edited by Louis R. Pondry et al. New York: John Wiley and Sons.

Marty, Martin E. 1994. "Public and Private: Congregation as Meeting Place." In *American Congregations, vol.2: New Perspectives in the Study of Congregations*, edited by J.P. Wind and J.W. Lewis. Chicago: University of Chicago Press.

Matthes, Kristin. 2003. "Forming Our Identities." *Giving Voice* 5(1):6-7.

McCaskey, Michael B. 1988. "The Challenge of Managing Ambiguity and Change," Pp. 1-30 in *Managing Ambiguity and Change*, edited by Louis R. Pondry et al. New York: John Wiley and Sons.

McCormick, Richard A. 1998. "The End of Catholic Hospitals?" *America* vol. 179(1):5-10. July 4-11, 1998.

McDonough, Peter. 1992. *Men Astutely Trained: A History of the Jesuits in the American Century*. New York: Macmillan

McDonough, Peter, and Eugene Bianchi. 2002. *Passionate Uncertainty: The Transformation of the Jesuits*. Berkeley: University of California Press.

McDowell, John Patrick. 1982. *The Social Gospel in the South: The Women's Home Mission Movement in the Methodist Episcopal Church, 1886-1939*. Baton Rouge, LA: Louisiana University Press.

McDuff, Elaine M., and Charles W. Mueller. 1999. "Social Support and Compensating Differentials in the Ministry: Gender Differences in Two Protestant Denominations." *Review of Religious Research* 40:307-330.

McFarland-Taylor, Sarah. 2001. "Green Nuns and Land: Cultivating New Varieties of Religion and Culture." Paper presented at the annual meeting of the Association for the Sociology of Religion, Anaheim, CA, August 2001.

McGrath, M. S. 1998. *These Women? Women Religious in the History of Australia—the Sisters of Mercy Parramatta, 1888-1988.* Kensington: NSW University Press.

McNamara, Jo Ann Kay. 1996. *Sisters in Arms: Catholic Nuns Through Two Millennia*. Cambridge: Harvard University Press.

Meeker, Ruth Esther. 1969. *Six Decades of Service, 1880-1940: A History of the Women's Home Missionary Society of the Methodist Episcopal Church*. Cincinnati: Steinhauser, Inc.

Meyer, Albert J. Forthcoming. *Realizing Our Intentions: Churches and Distinctive Higher Education in the Twenty-first Century*. Unpublished manuscript provided by author.

———. 2000. "Education With a Difference." Pp. 78-94 in *Teaching to Transform: Perspectives on Mennonite Higher Education*, edited by Keith Graber Miller. Goshen, IN: Pinchpenny Press.

———. 1997. "Toward an Anabaptist Theology of Institutions." *The Mennonite Quarterly Review* 71(3):411-420.

———. 1974. "Peoplehood Education." *Mennonite Educator* 11:1-4.

Meyer, John W., and Brian T. Rowan. 1977. "Institutionalized Organizations: Formal Structure as Myth and Ceremony." *American Journal of Sociology* 83:340-363.

Meyerson, Debra. 1991. "'Normal' Ambiguity? A Glimpse of an Occupational Culture." Pp. 131-144 in *Reframing Organizational Culture*, edited by Peter J. Frost, et al. Newbury Park, CA: Sage.

Miller, Page Putnam. 1985. *A Claim to New Roles*. American Theological Library Association Monograph Series #22. Meteuchen, NJ: The Scarecrow Press, Inc.

Mitchison, Rosalind. 2002. "Poor Relief and Health Care in Nineteenth Century Scotland." Pp. 220-245 in *Health Care and Poor Relief in Eighteenth and Nineteenth Century*

Northern Europe, edited by Ole Peter Grell, Andrew Cunningham, and Robert Jutte. Burlington, VT: Ashgate Publishing.

Mobley, Kendal P. 2003. "The Ecumenical Woman's Missionary Movement: Helen Barrett Montgomery and *The Baptist,* 1920-1930," Pp. 167-181 in *Gender and the Social Gospel,* edited by Wendy J. Deichmann Edwards and Carolyn de Swarte Gifford. Urbana, IL: University of Illinois Press.

Mohan, Mary Leslie. 1993. *Organizational Communication and Cultural Vision.* Albany, NY:SUNY Press.

Moloney, Deirdre M. 2002. "Divisions of Labor: The Role of American Catholic Lay Women, Lay Men and Women Religious in Charity Provision." *U.S. Catholic Historian* 20(1):41-55.

Monsma, Stephen V. 1996. *When Sacred and Secular Mix: Religious Nonprofit Organizations and Public Money.* Oxford: Rowman and Littlefield.

Moore, Dorothy Perrin. 1999. "Women Entrepreneurs: Approaching a New Millennium." Pp. 371-389 in *Handbook of Gender and Work,* edited by Gary N. Powell. Thousand Oaks, CA: Sage.

Moran, Frances M. 2004. "To Be a Religious: Identity and History." *Religious Life Review* 43(5):301-312.

Morey, Melanie Morin. 1995. *Leadership and Legacy: Is There a Future for the Past? A Study of Eight Colleges Founded by Catholic Women's Religious Congregations.* Ph.D. Dissertation, School of Education, Harvard University.

Morgan, D.L. 1988. *Focus Groups as Qualitative Research.* London: Sage.

Moylan, Prudence. 1993. *Hearts Inflamed: The Wheaton Franciscan Sisters.* Privately Printed, Wheaton Franciscans, 26 West Roosevelt, P.O. Box 667, Wheaton, IL. 60189.

Mudd, John O. 2005. "From CEO to Mission Leader." America 193(2): 4-16.

Mulhern, James. 1959. *A History of Education,* 2nd ed. New York: The Roland Press Co.

Muller, Detlef K. 1987. "The Process of Systematization: The Case of German Secondary Education." Pp. 15-52 in *The Rise of the Modern Educational System: Structural Change and Social Reproduction,* edited by Detlef Muller, Fritz Ringer, and Brian Simon. New York: Cambridge University Press.

Murphy, John F. 1988. "Professional Preparation of Catholic Teachers in the 1900's," Pp . 243-255 in *Enlightening the Next Generation: Catholics and their Schools, 1830-1980,* edited by F. Michael Perko, SJ. New York: Garland.

Nason-Clark, Nancy. 1987. "Are Women changing the Image of Ministry? A Comparison of British and American Realities." *Review of Religious Research* 284:330-340.

National Center for Education Statistics. 1996. "How Similar? How Different? Comparing Organizational Qualities of American Public and Private Secondary Schools." http://nces.ed.gov/pubsearch/pubsinfo.asp?pubid=96322. Retrieved Nov. 23, 2005.

Neal, Marie Augusta, SNDdeN. 1984. *Catholic Sisters in Transition: From the 1960s to the 1980s.* Wilmington, DE: Michael Glazier, Inc.

Nelson, Sioban. 2001. *"Say Little, Do Much": Nurses, Nuns and Hospitals in the Nineteenth Century.* Philadelphia: University of Pennsylvania Press.

Nesbitt, Paula D. 1997a. "Clergy Feminization: Controlled Labor or Transformative Change?" *Journal for the Scientific Study of Religion* 36:585-598.

————. 1997b. *The Feminization of Clergy in America: Occupational and Organizational Perspectives.* New York: Oxford University Press.

Nolan, Janet A. 1989. *Ourselves Alone: Women's Immigration from Ireland, 1885-1920.* Lexington, KY: University Press of Kentucky.

Noll, Mark A. 2002. "The Future of the Religious College." Pp. 73-94 in *The Future of*

Religious Colleges, edited by Paul J. Dovre. Grand Rapids, MI: Eerdmans.

Noll, William T. 1981. "Laity Rights and Leadership." Pp. 219-232 in *Women in New Worlds: Historical Perspectives on the Wesleyan Tradition*, edited by Hilah F. Thomas and Rosemary Skinner. Nashville, TN: Abingdon.

Noonan, Paschala, OP. 1997. *Signadou: History of the Kentucky Dominican Sisters*. Manhasset, NY: Brookville Books.

Numbers, Ronald L., and Darrell W. Amundsen, eds. 1986. *Caring and Curing: Health and Medicine in the Western Religious Traditions*. New York: Macmillan.

Numbers, Ronald L., and David R. Larson. 1986. "The Adventist Tradition." Pp.447-467 in *Caring and Curing: Health and Medicine in the Western Religious Traditions*, edited by Ronald L. Numbers and Darrell W. Amundsen. New York: Macmillan.

Nygren, David, CM, and Miriam Ukeritis, CSJ. 1993. *The Future of Religious Orders in the United States: Transformation and Commitment*. Westport, CT: Praeger.

Oates, Mary J. 1980. "Organized Voluntarism: The Catholic Sisters in Massachusetts, 1870-1940." Pp. 141-169 in *Women in American Religions*, edited by Janet Wilson James. University of Pennsylvania Press

————. 1985. "The Good Sisters: The Work and Position of Catholic Churchwomen in Boston, 1870-1940." in *Catholic Boston: Studies in Religion and Community*, edited by Robert E. Sullivan and James M. O'Toole. Boston: Archdiocese of Boston.

————.1987. *Higher Education for Catholic Women: A Historical Anthology*. New York: Garland.

————. 1994. "Mother Mary Regis Casserly." Pp. 95-102 in *Women Educators in the U.S.*, edited by Maxine Schwartz. Westport, CT: Greenwood.

————. 1995. *The Catholic Philanthropic Tradition in America*. Bloomington: Indiana University Press.

————. 1999. *Catholic Philanthropy in America*. Curriculum Guide #4. CUNY Center for the Study of Philanthropy.

————. 2002. "Sisterhoods and Catholic Higher Education, 1890-1960." Pp.161-194 in *Catholic Women's Colleges in America*, edited by Tracy Schier and Cynthia Russett. Baltimore: Johns Hopkins University Press.

O'Brien, David J. 1994. *From the Heart of the American Church: Catholic Higher Education and American Culture*. Maryknoll, NY: Orbis Books.

O'Brien, Kathleen. 1987. *Journeys: A Pre-Amalgamation History of the Sisters of Mercy, Omaha Province*. Privately Printed, Omaha Sisters of Mercy.

O'Connell, David M. 2002. "Staying the Course: Imperative and Influence Within the Religious College." Pp. 63-72 in *The Future of Religious Colleges*, edited by Paul J. Dovre. Grand Rapids, MI: Eerdmans.

O'Connell, Marvin R. 1986. "The Roman Catholic Tradition Since 1548." Pp.108-145 in *Caring and Curing: Health and Medicine in the Western Religious Traditions*, edited by Ronald L. Numbers and Darrell W. Amundsen. New York: Macmillan.

O'Connor, Thomas P., Dean R. Hoge, and Estrelda Alexander. 2003. "The Relative Influence of Youth and Adult Experiences on Personal Spirituality and Church Involvement." *Journal for the Scientific Study of Religion* 41(4):723-732.

O'Donnell, Harold J. 1988. "The Lay Teacher in Catholic Education." Pp. 254-266 in *Enlightening the Next Generation: Catholics and their Schools, 1830-1980*, edited by F. Michael Perko. New York: Garland.

O'Hare, Joseph A. 2000. "Response to 'Relationship Revisited.'" *Current Issues in Catholic Higher Education* 211:51-53.

O'Keefe, Joseph M., ed. 1997. *Catholic Education at the Turn of the New Century*. New

York: Garland.

O'Malley, John W., SJ. 1997. "One Priesthood: Two Traditions." Pp. 9-24 in *A Concert of Charisms: Ordained Ministry in Religious Life,* edited by Paul K. Hennessy. New York: Paulist Press.

O'Neill, Michael 1989. *The Third America: The Emergence of the Nonprofit Sector in the United States.* San Francisco: Jossey Bass.

Olsen, J. P. 1976. "Choice in an Organized Anarchy." Pp. 82-139 in *Ambiguity and Choice in Organizations,* edited by J.G. March and J. Polsen. Bergen, Norway: Universitets Forlagets.

Palmer, Richard. 1999. "'Ad Una Sancta Perfettione: Health Care and Poor Relief in the Republic of Venice in the Era of the Counter-Reformation." Pp. 87-101 in *Health Care and Poor Relief in Counter-Reformation Europe,* edited by Ole Peter Grell, Andrew Cunningham, and Jon Arrizabalaga. New York:Routledge.

Palmer, Susan J. 2000. *Moon Sisters, Krishna Mothers, Rajneesh Lovers: Women's Bodies in New Religions.* Syracuse, NY: Syracuse University Press.

Parker, Rusty. n.d. "Assessing Secularization in Religious Higher Education: Faculty Attitudes on Faith and Learning, Academic Freedom, and Faculty Hiring." unpublished paper.

Pattillo, Manning, and Don MacKenzie. 1966. *The Church, the University, and Social Policy.* Danforth Study of Campus Ministries, Wesleyan University Press.

Parsonage, Robert Rue. 1978. *Church Related Higher Education.* Valley Forge, PA: Judson Press.

Pearson, Michael. 1990. *Millennial Dreams and Moral Dilemmas: Seventh-Day Adventism and Contemporary Ethics.* Cambridge: Cambridge University Press.

Pettit, Joseph. 2004. Enrollment in Catholic Higher Education in the United States: 1981-2000. Pettit@georgetown.edu. Retrieved Nov. 11, 2005.

Pfau, R. S. 1934. "History of Catholic Secondary Education in the Diocese of Indianapolis, 1834-1934." Unpublished Masters Thesis, School of Education, Fordham University.

Pfeffer, Jeffrey, and Gerald R. Salancik. 1978. *The External Control of Organizations.* New York: Harper and Row.

Phillips, Clifton J. 1974. "The Student Volunteer Movement and its Role in China Missions, 1886-1920." Pp. 91-109 in *The Missionary Enterprise in China and America,* edited by John K. Fairbank. Cambridge: Harvard University Press.

Piore, Michael J. 1972. *Notes for a Theory of Labor Market Stratification.* Working Paper 95, Department of Economics, Massachusetts Institute of Technology.

Pipes, Paula R., and Helen Rose Ebaugh. 2002. "Faith-Based Coalitions, Social Services, and Government Funding." *Sociology of Religion* 63(1):49-68.

Popple, Philip, and P. Nelson Reid. 1999. "A Profession for the Poor? A History of Social Work in the United States." Pp. 9-28 in *The Professionalization of Poverty: Social Work and the Poor in the Twentieth Century,* edited by Gary R. Lowe and P. Nelson Reid. New York: Aldine De Gruyter.

Porter, Dorothy. 2002. "Health Care and the Construction of Citizenship in Civil Societies in the Era of the Enlightenment and Industrialization." Pp. 15-31 in *Health Care and Poor Relief in Eighteenth and Nineteenth Century Northern Europe,* edited by Ole Peter Grell, Andrew Cunningham, and Robert Jutte. Burlington, VT: Ashgate Publishing.

Porterfield, Amanda. 1996. "A Sister to Oneida: The Missionary Community at Mount Holyoke." *Communal Societies* 16:1-13.

Portes, Alejandro, and Leif Jensen. 1989. "The Enclave and the Entrants: Patterns of Ethnic

Enterprise in Miami Before and After Mariel." *American Sociological Review* 54:929-949.

Powell, Gary N. 1999. "Reflections on the Glass Ceiling: Recent Trends and Future Prospects." Pp. 325-345 in *Handbook of Gender and Work*, edited by Gary N. Powell. Thousand Oaks, CA: Sage.

Prelinger, Catherine M. 1986a."The Female Diaconate in the Anglican Church: What Kind of Ministry for Women." Pp. 161-192 in *Religion in the Lives of English Women, 1760-1930*, edited by Gail Malmgreen. Bloomington, IN: Indiana University Press.

———. 1986b."The Nineteenth Century Deaconessate in Germany: The Efficacy of a Family Model." Pp.215-230 in *German Women In the Eighteenth and Nineteenth Centuries: A Social and Literary History*, edited by Ruth Ellan B. Joeres and Mary Jo Maynes. Bloomington, IN: Indiana University Press.

Price, Matthew J. 2000. "Place, Race, and History: The Social Mission of Downtown Churches." Pp.57-81 in *Public Religion and Urban Transformation: Faith in the City*, edited by Lowell W. Livezey. New York: New York University Press.

Pullan, Brian. 1999. "The Counter-Reformation, Medical Care, and Poor Relief." Pp. 18-39 in *Health Care and Poor Relief in Counter-Reformation Europe*, edited by Ole Peter Grell, Andrew Cunningham, and Jon Arrizabalaga. New York:Routledge.

Putnam, Robert. 2000. *Bowling Alone: The Collapse and Revival of American Community*. New York: Simon and Schuster.

Puzon, Bridget, OSU, ed. 1996a. *Women Religious and the Intellectual Life: The North American Achievement*. San Francisco: International Scholars' Publications.

———. 1996b. "On the Intellectual Life of Women Religious in Contemporary American Society: an Overview." Pp. 1-8 in *Women Religious and the Intellectual Life: The North American Achievement*, edited by Bridget Puzon, OSU. San Francisco: International Scholars' Publications.

Quartararo, Anne T. 1995. *Women Teachers and Popular Education in Nineteenth Century France*. Newark: University of Delaware Press.

Quinonez, Lora Ann, CDP, and Mary Daniel Turner, SNDdeN. 1992. *The Transformation of American Catholic Sisters*. Philadelphia: Temple University Press.

Rabe, Valentin H. 1974. "Evangelical Logistics: Mission Support and Resources to 1920." Pp.52-90 in *The Missionary Enterprise in China and America*, edited by John K. Fairbank. Cambridge: Harvard University Press.

Radcliffe, Timothy, OP. 2005. "Journey Into the Future." *Horizon* 30(2):29.

Ramirez, Johnny, and Brian Brock. 1996. "The Coherent Institutional Philosophy: Myth or Mandate?" *Journal of Research on Christian Education* 5(1):3-32.

Ramsey, Matthew. 2002. "Poor Relief and Medical Assistance in Eighteenth and Nineteenth Century Paris." Pp. 279-308 in *Health Care and Poor Relief in Eighteenth and Nineteenth Century Northern Europe*, edited by Ole Peter Grell, Andrew Cunningham, and Robert Jutte. Burlington, VT: Ashgate Publishing.

Ranft, Patricia. 1998. *Women and the Religious Life in Premodern Europe*. New York: St. Martin's Press.

Rapley, Elizabeth. 1990. *The Devotes: Women and Church in Seventeenth Century France*. Montreal: McGill-Queens University Press.

———. 2001. *A Social History of the Cloister: Daily Life in the Teaching Monasteries of the Old Regime*. Montreal: McGill Queens University Press.

Rebore, Ronald W. 2003. "Research Concerning Ethical Issues in Catholic Higher Education." Pp. 59-79 in *A Handbook of Research on Catholic Higher Education*, edited by Thomas C. Hunt, Ronald J. Nuzzi, Ellis A. Joseph, and John D. Geiger.

Greenwich, CT: Information Age Publications.

Regnerus, Mark D., and Christian Smith 1998. "Selective Deprivatization Among American Religious Traditions: The Reversal of the Great Reversal." *Social Forces* 76:1347-1372.

Reifsnyder, Richard W. 1992. "Transformation in Administrative Leadership in the United Presbyterian Church in the U.S.A., 1920-1983." Pp. 252-275 in *The Pluralistic Vision: Presbyterians and Mainstream Protestant Vision and Leadership*, edited by Milton J. Coalter, John Mulder, and Louis B. Weeks. Louisville: Westminster/John Knox Press.

Reinhart, Dietrich. 2000. "One Visit, as Good as It Might Be, Calls for Others." *Current Issues in Catholic Higher Education* 21(1):54-59.

Reuben, Julie A. 1996. *The Making of the Modern University: Intellectual Transformation and Marginalization of Morality*. Chicago: University of Chicago Press.

Riis, Thomas. 1997. "Poor Relief and Health Care Provision in Sixteenth Century Denmark." Pp. 129-146 in *Health Care and Poor Relief in Protestant Europe, 1500-1700,* edited by Ole Peter Grell and Andrew Cunningham. New York: Routledge.

Riley, Patricia. 1991. "Cornerville as Narration," Pp.215-223 in Frost, Peter J. et al, eds. *Reframing Organizational Culture*. Newbury Park, CA: Sage.

Risse, Guenter. 1999. *Mending Bodies, Saving Souls: A History of Hospitals*. New York: Oxford University Press.

Roberts, Jon H., and James Turner. 2000. *The Sacred and the Secular University*. Princeton, NJ: Princeton University Press.

Rosenberg, Carroll Smith. 1971. *Religion and the Rise of the American City: The New York City Mission Movement, 1812-1870*. Ithaca: Cornell University Press.

Rosner, David. 1998. "Business at the Bedside: Hospital Care in Brooklyn, 1890-1915," Pp.309-319 in *Making the Nonprofit Sector in the United States: A Reader,* edited by David C. Hammack. Bloomington, IN: Indiana University Press.

Royle, Marjorie H. 1982. "Women Pastors: What Happens After Placement?" *Review of Religious Research* 284:341-350.

Rudolph, Frederick. 1962. *The American College and University: A History.* New York: Knopf.

Ruggie, Mary. 1992. "The Paradox of Liberal Intervention: Health Policy and the American Welfare State." *American Journal of Sociology* 97(4):919-944.

Ryan, Mary Perkins. 1964. *Are Parochial Schools the Answer? Catholic Education in Light of the Council.* New York: Holt, Rinehart and Winston.

Sackman, Sonja. 1992. "Culture and Subcultures: An Analysis of Organizational Knowledge." *Administrative Science Quarterly* 37:140-161.

———. 1991. *Cultural Knowledge in Organizations*. Thousand Oaks, CA: Sage.

Salaman, Graeme. 1981. *Work Organization and Class Structure*. New York: M.E. Sharpe.

Salamon, Lester M. 2003. *The Resilient Sector: The State of Nonprofit America*. Washington, DC: Brookings Institution Press.

Sammon, Sean D. 2001. "By Their Fruits You Shall Know Them: The Challenge of Renewal Among Men Religious in the USA Today." *Social Compass* 48:209-228.

———. 2002. *Religious Life in America: A New Day Dawning*. New York: Alba House.

Sanders, Susan M. RSM. 1988."The Response of Religious-Sponsored Systems and Congregations to the Changing Context of Catholic Health Care: A Study of Realities and Attitudes." Privately printed, Consolidated Catholic Health Care.

Sawatsky, Rodney J. 1997a. "Leadership, Authority and Power." *The Mennonite Quarterly Review* 713:439-451.

———. 1997b. "What Can the Mennonite Tradition Contribute to Christian Higher

Education?" Pp. 187-199 in *Models for Christian Higher Education: Strategies for Success in the Twenty-first Century*, edited by Richard T. Hughes and William B. Adrian. Grand Rapids, MI: Eerdmans.

Schaeffer, Pamela. 1997a. "Notre Dame Disputes May Signal a Shift." *National Catholic Reporter* 34(13).

————. 1997b. "St. Louis Showdown Could Draw Vatican." *National Catholic Reporter* 34(2):5.

Scheiber, Matt. 1984. "Mass Confusion on a Catholic Campus." *U.S. Catholic*, August 1984, pp. 25-27.

Schein, Edgar H. 1991a. "The Role of the Founder in the Creation of Organizational Culture." Pp.14-25 in *Reframing Organizational Culture*, edited by Peter J. Frost et al. Newbury Park, CA: Sage.

————. 1991b. "What is Culture?" Pp.243-254 in *Reframing Organizational Culture*, edited by Peter J. Frost et al. Newbury Park, CA: Sage.

Schier, Tracy and Cynthia Russett, eds. 2002. *Catholic Women's Colleges in America*. Baltimore MD: Johns Hopkins University Press.

Schlabach, Theron F. 2000. "Goshen College and Its Church Relations: History and Reflections." Pp.15-40 in Keith Graber Miller, ed. *Teaching to Transform: Perspectives on Mennonite Higher Education*. Goshen, IN: Pinchpenny Press.

Schmidt, Alvin J. 2003. "Multiculturalism and the Dilution of Lutheran Identity." Pp. 187-205 in *Lutherans Today: American Lutheran Identity in the Twenty-First Century*, edited by Richard Cimino. Grand Rapids, MI: Eerdmans.

Schmidt, Frederick W. 1996. *A Still, Small Voice: Women, Ordination, and the Church*. Syracuse: Syracuse University Press.

Schneider, Mary L. 1986. "The Transformation of American Women Religious: The Sister Formation Conference as a Catalyst for Change, 1951-1964." Cushwa Center Working Paper Series, Series 17, no.1. University of Notre Dame.

————. 1988. "American Sisters and the Roots of Change: the 1950s." *U.S. Catholic Historian* 7(1):55-72.

Schneiders, Sandra M. 2001. *Selling All: Commitment, Consecrated Celibacy, and Community in Catholic Religious Life*. Mahwah, NJ: Paulist Press.

Schubert, Frank D. 1990. *A Sociological Study of Secularization Trends in the American Catholic University: Decatholicizing the Catholic Religious Curriculum*. Studies in Religion and Society, vol. 25. Lewiston, NY: The Edwin Mellen Press.

Schuller, Robert H. 1974. *Your Church Has Real Possibilities*. Glendale, CA: G/L Regal Books.

Schuth, Katarina, OSF. 1996. "The Intellectual Life as a Value for Women Religious in the United States." Pp.9-27 in Bridget Puzon, OSU, *Women Religious and the Intellectual Life: The North American Achievement*. San Francisco: Catholic Scholars Press.

Schwartz, Joel. 2000. *Fighting Poverty with Virtue: Moral Reform and America's Urban Poor*. Bloomington, IN: Indiana University Press.

Schwehn, Mark R. 2002. "Lutheran Higher Education in the Twenty-first Century." Pp. 208-223 in *The Future of Religious Colleges*, edited by Paul J. Dovre. Grand Rapids, MI: Eerdmans.

Scott, W. Richard. 2003. *Organizations: Rational, Natural, and Open Systems*, 5th ed. Upper Saddle River, NJ: Prentice Hall.

Sengers, Erik. 2003. "You Don't Have to be a Saint or a Practicing Catholic... Higher Tension and Lower Attachment in the Dutch Catholic Church Since 1970." *Antonianum* 78:529-545.

Shadron, Virginia. 1981. "The Laity Rights Movement, 1906-1918." Pp. 261-272 in
    Women in New Worlds: Historical Perspectives on the Wesleyan Tradition, edited by
    Hilah F. Thomas and Rosemary Skinner. Nashville, TN: Abingdon.
Sharot, Stephen. 2001. *A Comparative Sociology of World Religions.* New York: New York
    University Press.
Shea, William M. 1999. "Jesuits and Scholarship." Pp.195-218 in *Trying Times: Essays on
    Catholic Higher Education in the Twentieth Century,* edited by William M. Shea and
    Daniel Van Slyke. Atlanta: Scholars' Press.
Shea, William M., and Daniel Van Slyke, eds. 1999. *Trying Times: Essays on Catholic
    Higher Education in the Twentieth Century.* Atlanta: Scholars' Press.
Shepherd, Gary, and Gordon Shepherd. 1998. *Mormon Passage: A Missionary Chronicle.*
    Urbana: University of Illinois Press.
Shortell, Stephen M., et al. 1990. *Strategic Choices for America's Hospitals: Managing
    Change in Turbulent Times.* San Francisco: Jossey Bass.
Shurden, W. 1981. "The Baptist Synthesis: Is It Cracking?" Carver Barnes Lectures,
    Southwestern Baptist Theological Seminary, Fort Worth, TX.
Silber, Ilana Friedrich. 1995. *Virtuosity, Charisma and Social Order: A Comparative
    Sociological Study of Monasticism in Theravada Buddhism and Medieval Catholicism.*
    New York: Cambridge University Press.
Sills, David L. 1998. "The March of Dimes: Origins and Principles." Pp 373-400 in *Making
    the Nonprofit Sector in the United States: A Reader,* edited by David C. Hammack.
    Bloomington, IN: Indiana University Press.
Sloan, Douglas. 1994. *Faith and Knowledge: Mainline Protestantism and Higher
    Education.* Louisville, KY: Westminster John Knox Press.
————. 2002. "Faith and Knowledge: Religion and the Modern University." Pp. 3-34 in
    The Future of Religious Colleges, edited by Paul J. Dovre. Grand Rapids, MI:
    Eerdmans.
Sloan, Frank A. 1998. "Commercialism in Nonprofit Hospitals." Pp. 151-168 in *To Profit
    or Not to Profit: The Commercial Transformation of the Nonprofit Sector,* edited by
    Burton A. Weisbrod. New York: Cambridge University Press.
Smith, Christian, ed. 2003. *The Secular Revolution: Power, Interests, and Conflict in the
    Secularization of American Public Life.* Berkeley: University of California Press.
Smith, Dayle M. 2000. "The Glass Ceiling." Pp. 7-23 in *Women at Work:Leadership for
    the Next Century,* edited by Dayle M. Smith. Saddle River, NJ: Prentice Hall.
Smith, John T. 1998. *Methodism and Education, 1849-1902.* Oxford: Clarendon Press.
Smith, Sheila Strobel. 2004 ."Mega Churches: The Complexities of Leadership Transition."
    Paper presented at the annual meeting of the Society for the Scientific Study of
    Religion, Kansas City, MO, October 2004.
Smith, Steven Rathgeb, and Michael Lipsky. 1998. "The Political Economy or Nonprofit
    Revenues." Pp.454-473 in *Making the Nonprofit Sector in the United States: A Reader,*
    edited by David C. Hammack. Bloomington, IN: Indiana University Press.
Smith, Stephen Rathgeb, and M. R. Sosin. 1999. "The Varieties of Faith-Related Agencies."
    Monagraph, Daniel J. Evans School of Public Affairs, University of Washington,
    Seattle, WA.
Smylie, James H. 1986. "The Reformed Tradition." Pp. 204-239 in *Caring and Curing:
    Health and Medicine in the Western Religious Traditions,* edited by Ronald L.
    Numbers and Darrell W. Amundsen. New York: Macmillan.
Soher, Mary. 2003. "Why Institutions." *Giving Voice* 51:5.
Soly, Hugo. 1997. "Continuity and Change: Attitudes Toward Poor Relief and Health Care

in Early Modern Antwerp." Pp. 85-107 in *Health Care and Poor Relief in Protestant Europe, 1500-1700*, edited by Ole Peter Grell and Andrew Cunningham. New York: Routledge.

Specht, H., and M. Courtney. 1994. *Unfaithful Angels: How Social Work Has Abandoned its Mission*. New York: Free Press.

Stadum, Beverly. 1999. "The Uneasy Marriage of Professional Social Work and Public Relief, 1870-1940." Pp. 29-49 in *The Professionalization of Poverty: Social Work and the Poor in the Twentieth Century*, edited by Gary R. Lowe and P. Nelson Reid. New York: Aldine De Gruyter.

Stark, Rodney, and Roger Finke. 2000. *Acts of Faith: Explaining the Human Side of Religion*. Berkeley: University of California Press.

Starr, Paul. 1982. *The Social Transformation of American Medicine*. New York: Basic.

Stebbing, Nicolas, CR. 2001. "Orthodox Romanian Monastic Life." *Religious Life Review*, 404:221-31.

Stebner, Eleanor J. 2003. "More than Maternal Feminists and Good Samaritans: Women and the Social Gospel in Canada." Pp. 53-67 in *Gender and the Social Gospel*, edited by Wendy J. Deichmann Edwards and Carolyn de Swarte Gifford. Urbana, IL: University of Illinois Press.

Steinfels, Peter. 1997. "Catholic Identity: Emerging Concerns." Pp.199-203 in Joseph M. O'Keefe, SJ, ed. *Catholic Education at the Turn of the New Century*. New York: Garland.

Stevens, Thelma. 1978. *Legacy for the Future: the History of Christian Social Relations in the Women's Division of Christian Service, 1940-1968*. Cincinnati, OH: Women's Division of the United Methodist Church Board of Global Ministries.

Stewart, George C. 1994. *Marvels of Charity: A History of American Sisters and Nuns*. Huntington, IN:Our Sunday Visitor Press.

Stolberg, Michael. 2002. "Health Care Provision and Poor Relief in the Electorate and Kingdom of Bavaria." Pp. 112-135 in *Health Care and Poor Relief in Eighteenth and Nineteenth Century Northern Europe*, edited by Ole Peter Grell, Andrew Cunningham, and Robert Jutte. Burlington, VT: Ashgate Publishing

Stoltzfus, V. 1992. *Church-Affiliated Higher Education*. Goshen, IN: Pinchpenny Press.

Stout, H. S., and D. S. Cormode. 1998. "Institutions and the Story of American Religions." Pp. 62-78 in *Sacred Companies: Organizational Aspects of Religion and Religious Aspects of Organizations*, edited by N. J. Demerath, Peter D. Hall, T. Schmitt, and Rhys Williams. New York: Oxford University Press.

Stuart, Paul H. 1999. "'In a World Gone Industrial': Specialization and the Search for Social Work Practice Above the Poverty Line." Pp. 51-61 in *The Professionalization of Poverty: Social Work and the Poor in the Twentieth Century*, edited by Gary R. Lowe and P. Nelson Reid. New York: Aldine De Gruyter.

Sundar, Pushpa 2001. "Women and Philanthropy in India." Pp. 271-286 in *Women, Philanthropy, and Civil Society*, edited by Kathleen D. McCarthy. Bloomington, IN: Indiana University Press.

Swartz, David. 1994. "Secularization, Religion, and Isomorphism: A Study of Large Nonprofit Hospital Trustees." PONPO Working Paper #210, Program on Nonprofit Organizations, Yale University.

———— . 1998. "Secularization, Religion, and Isomorphism: A Study of Large Nonprofit Hospital Trustees." Pp. 323-339 in *Sacred Companies: Organizational Aspects of Religion and Religious Aspects of Organizations*, edited by N.J.Demerath III, Peter Dobkin Hall, Terry Schmitt, and Rhys H. Williams. New York: Oxford University

Press.

Swidler, Ann. 1986. "Culture in Action: Symbols and Strategies." *American Sociological Review* 51:273-286.

Talin, Kristoff. 2000. "Objets ou sujets? Les religieuses dans la france laicisee entre acceptation et contestation du pouvoir politique." *Claretianum* 40:123-150.

Tatum, Noreen Dunn 1960. *A Crown of Service: A Story of Women's Work in the Methodist Episcopal Church, South, from 1878-1940.* Nashville: Parthenon Press.

Terrada, Maria Lopez. 1999. "Health Care and Poor Relief in the Crown of Aragon." Pp. 177-200 in *Health Care and Poor Relief in Counter-Reformation Europe*, edited by Ole Peter Grell, Andrew Cunningham, and Jon Arrizabalaga. New York:Routledge.

This, Craig. 1997. "Who Gets Elected Bishop in the United Methodist Church?" Paper presented at the annual meeting of the Religious Research Association, San Diego, CA, October,1997.

Thomas, George M., Lisa R. Peck, and Channin G. De Haan. 2003. "Reforming Education, Transforming Religion, 1876-1931." Pp. 355-394 in *The Secular Revolution: Power, Interests, and Conflict in the Secularization of Public Life*, edited by Christian Smith. Berkeley: University of California Press.

Thompson, Margaret S. 1999. "Charism or Deep Story? Towards Understanding Better the Nineteenth Century Origins of American Women's Congregations." *Review for Religious* 58(3):230-250.

———. 1996. "Forward" in Suzy Farren, *A Call to Care: The Women Who Built Catholic Health Care in America.* St. Louis: Catholic Health Association of the U.S.

———. 1991. "Women, Feminism, and the New Religious History: Catholic Sisters as a Case Study." Pp. 136-163 in *Belief and Behavior: Essays in the New Religious History*, edited by Philip R. Vandemeer and Robert P. Swierenga. New Brunswick, NJ: Rutgers University Press.

———. 1989. "Sisterhood and Power: Class, Culture and Ethnicity in the American Convent." *Colby Library Quarterly* (Fall, 1989):149-175.

Toews, P. 1996. *Mennonites in American Society, 1930-1970.* Scottsdale, PA: Herald Press.

Trice, Harrison M., and Janice M. Beyer. 1993. *The Cultures of Work Organizations.* Englewood Cliffs, NJ: Prentice Hall.

———. 1984. "Studying Organizational Cultures Through Rites and Ceremonials." *Academy of Management Review* 9(4):653-669.

Tripole, Martin R. 2000. "*Ex Corde Ecclesiae*: A History from Land O' Lakes to Now." *Review for Religious* 61(5):454-470.

———. 2004. "Secularism, Justice, and Jesuit Higher Education: Are They the Same?" *Review for Religious* 63(1):6-20.

Trotter, F. T. 1987. *Loving God With One's Mind.* Nashville, TN: Board of Higher Education Ministry of the United Methodist Church.

Trueblood, Elton. 1959. *The Idea of a College.* New York: Harper and Brothers.

Tuckman, Harold P. 1998. "Competition, Commercialization, and the Evolution of Nonprofit Organizational Structures." Pp. 25-45 in *To Profit or Not to Profit: The Commercial Transformation of the Nonprofit Sector*, edited by Burton A. Weisbrod. New York: Cambridge University Press.

Turner, Bryan S. 1991. *Religion and Social Theory*, 2nd ed. Newbury Park, CA: Sage

Ukeritis, Miriam D., CSJ, and David J. Nygren, CM. 1997. "Voices of Religious Priests: Data from the FORUS Study." Pp.169-183 in *A Concert of Charisms: Ordained Ministry in Religious Life*, edited by Paul K. Hennessy. New York: Paulist Press.

Vale, Carol Jean. 2000. "Response to 'Relationship Revisited.'" *Current Issues in Catholic*

Higher Education 21(1):59-61.

Vance, Laura L. 1999. *Seventh Day Adventism in Crisis: Gender and Sectarian Change in an Emerging Religion.* Urbana, IL: University of Illinois Press.

Vanderpool, Harold Y. 1986. "The Wesleyan-Methodist Tradition." Pp. 317-353 in *Caring and Curing: Health and Medicine in the Western Religious Traditions,* edited by Ronald L. Numbers and Darrell W. Amundsen. New York: Macmillan.

Vanderwoerd, James R. 2004. "How Faith-Based Social Service Organizations Manage Secular Pressures Associated With Government Funding." *Nonprofit Management and Leadership* 143:239-262.

Van Doorn-Harder, Pieternella. 1995. *Contemporary Coptic Nuns.* Columbia, SC: University of South Carolina.

Van Liere, Carma 1991. *Hallowed Fire: Faith Motivation of Early Women Activists.* Valley Forge, PA: Judson Press.

Ververka, F. B. 1988. *For God and Country: Catholic Schooling In the 1920s.* New York: Garland.

Walch, T. 1995. "Big City Schools." *U. S. Catholic Historian* 13(9):1-18.

———. 1996. *Parish School: American Catholic Parochial Education From Colonial Times to the Present.* New York: Crossroad.

Waldinger, Roger, et al. 1990. *Ethnic Entrepreneurs: Immigrant Business in Industrial Societies.* Thousand Oaks, CA: Sage.

Wall, Barbara Mann. 2002. "'We Might as Well Burn It': Catholic Sister-Nurses and Hospital Control, 1865-1930." *U. S. Catholic Historian* 20(1):21-39.

Wallace, Ruth. 1992. *They Call Her Pastor: A New Role for Catholic Women.* Albany, NY: SUNY Press.

Walsh, Barbara M. 2004 ."Convent Expansion Unveiled." *Religious Life Review* 43(2):106-114.

———. 2002. *Roman Catholic Nuns in England and Wales, 1800-1937.* Dublin: Irish Academic Press.

Warner, R.S. 1994. "The Place of the Congregation in the Contemporary American Religious Configuration." In *American Congregations, vol.2: New Perspectives in the Study of Congregations,* edited by J.P. Wind and J.W. Lewis. Chicago: University of Chicago Press.

Waring, Richard W. 1985. "A Study of the Fiscal and Personnel Resources of Catholic Colleges Founded by Women Religious." Ph.D. Dissertation, University of Toronto.

Weber, Francis J. 2003. *A Legacy of Healing: The Story of Catholic Health Care in Los Angeles.* Mission Hills, CA: St. Francis Historical Society.

Weber, Max. 1958. "Social Psychology of the World Religions." Pp.267-301 in *From Max Weber: Essays in Sociology,* edited by H. H. Gerth and C. Wright Mills. New York: Oxford University Press.

———. 1978a. "Protestant Asceticism and the Spirit of Capitalism." Pp.138-173 in *Max Weber: Selections in Translation,* edited by W. G. Runciman. Translated by E. Matthews. New York: Cambridge University Press.

———. 1978b. "The Religions of Asia." Pp.192-205 in *Max Weber: Selections in Translation,* edited by W. G. Runciman. Translated by E. Matthews. New York: Cambridge University Press.

Weber, Timothy P. 1986. "The Baptist Tradition." Pp.288-316 in *Caring and Curing: Health and Medicine in the Western Religious Traditions,* edited by Ronald L. Numbers and Darrell W. Amundsen. New York: Macmillan.

Wedam, Elfriede. 2000a. "Catholic Spirituality in a New Urban Church." Pp.213-237 in

Public Religion and Urban Transformation: Faith in the City, edited by Lowell W. Livezey. New York: New York University Press.

——— . 2000b. "God Doesn't Ask What Language I Pray In." Pp.107-131 in *Public Religion and Urban Transformation: Faith in the City,* edited by Lowell W. Livezey. New York: New York University Press.

Weick, Karl. 1995. *Sensemaking in Organizations.* Foundations for Organizational Science Series, David Whetten, series editor. Thousand Oaks, CA: Sage.

Weisbrod, Burton A. 1998a."Conclusions and Public Policy Issues: Commercialism and the Road Ahead." Pp. 287-305 in *To Profit or Not to Profit: The Commercial Transformation of the Nonprofit Sector,* edited by Burton A. Weisbrod. New York: Cambridge University Press.

——— . 1998b. "Modeling the Nonprofit Organization as a Multiproduct Firm: A. Framework for Choice." Pp. 47-64 in *To Profit or Not to Profit: The Commercial Transformation of the Nonprofit Sector,* edited by Burton A. Weisbrod. New York: Cambridge University Press.

West, Maxine. 1991. "How to Attract Young Members." *Response* October 1991, p. 6-9.

Williams, Rhys H. 1998. "Organizational Change in Theological Schools: Dilemmas of Ideology and Resources." Pp.208-225 in *Sacred Companies: Organizational Aspects of Religion and Religious Aspects of Organizations.,* edited by N. J. Demerath III, Peter Dobkin Hall, Terry Schmitt, and Rhys H. Williams. New York: Oxford University Press.

——— . 1999. "Visions of the Good Society and the Religious Roots of American Political Culture. *Sociology of Religion* 60(1):1-34.

Wittberg, Patricia. 2003. "Religious Orders and Higher Education." Pp.263-289 in *Handbook of Research on Catholic Higher Education,* edited by Thomas Hunt et al. Greenwich, CT: Information Age Publishing.

——— . 2002. "Reciprocal Identities: Apostolic Life and Consecrated Life." *Review for Religious* 61(4):341-351.

——— . 2000a. "Called to Service: The Changing Institutional Identities of American Denominations." *Nonprofit and Voluntary Sector Quarterly* 29(3):357-376.

——— . 2000b. "Declining Institutional Sponsorship and Religious Orders: A Study of Reverse Impacts." *Sociology of Religion* 61(3):315-324.

——— . 1994. *The Rise and Fall of Catholic Religious Orders: A Social Movement Perspective.* Albany, NY: SUNY Press.

——— . 1996. *Pathways to Refounding Religious Communities.* New York: Paulist Press.

Wolfteich, Claire E. 2002. *Navigating New Terrain: Work and Women's Spiritual Lives.* Mahwah, NJ: Paulist Press.

Wuthnow, Robert. 1998. *After Heaven: Spirituality in America Since the 1950s.* Berkeley: University of California Press.

——— . 1994. *Sharing the Journey: Support Groups and America's New Quest for Community.* New York: Free Press.

——— . 1988. *The Restructuring of American Religion.* Princeton, NJ: Princeton University Press.

Yamane, David. 1997. "Secularization on Trial: In Defense of a Neosecularization Paradigm." *Journal for the Scientific Study of Religion* 36(1): 104-122.

Young, Dennis R. 1998. "Commercialism in Nonprofit Social Service Associations: Its Character, Significance, and Rationale." Pp. 195-216 in *To Profit or Not to Profit: The Commercial Transformation of the Nonprofit Sector,* edited by Burton A. Weisbrod. New York: Cambridge University Press.

Zech, Charles. 1999. "The Faculty and Catholic Institutional Identity." *America* 180(18):11-15.

Zhou, Min, and John R. Logan. 1989. "Returns on Human Capital in Ethnic Enclaves: New York City's Chinatown." *American Sociological Review* 54:809-820.

Zikmund, Barbara, Adair Lummis, and Patricia Chang. 1998. *Clergywomen: An Uphill Calling.* Louisville, KY: Westminster/John Knox Press.

Zucker, Lynne G. 1987. "Institutional Theories of Organization." *Annual Review of Sociology* 13:443-464.

————. 1988. "Where Do Institutional Patterns Come From? Organizations as Actors in Social Systems." Pp. 23-41 in *Institutional Patterns and Organizations: Culture and Environment,* edited by Lynne Zucker. Cambridge, MA: Ballinger.

Index

Academies: Catholic, 9, 26-27, 29, 38,
    91; Protestant, 10, 26, 29, 38
Alexian Brothers, 49n30
Anglican churches, 19n13; and
    schools, 25
Anti-intellectualism, 239; in Catholic
    religious orders, 227-230; in
    Christian denominations, 274-75;
    among deaconesses, 228-30
Asbury, Francis, 26
Association of Jesuit Colleges and
    Universities, 120
Atlanta Baptist Female Seminary, 28,
    48n8. *See also* Spelman College
Ave Maria College, 125

Baptist churches: colleges of, 29-31,
    38, 70, 156-57; deaconesses in, 9;
    hospitals, 43; institutional identity
    of, 70; schools, 28; settlement
    houses, 34; women's missionary
    societies in, 7-8, 20n32, 94
Baptist Hospital, Nashville, 131
Baylor University, 70, 83, 156-57
Bender, Harold, 70
Bennett College for Women, 27-28,

49n16
Bessie Tift College, 87n11
Bethune-Cookman College, 49n16
Bob Jones University, 125
Brewster Hospital, 53n121
Buddhism: and religious virtuosity, 4,
    9, 18n7; 21n41, 280n32

Calvin College, 38
Calvin, John, 36
Capital University, 141n11
Caritas International, 276
Carroll, John, 52n89, 75
Catholic Charities, USA, 103, 135,
    137, 251, 276
Catholic Hospital Association, 42, 126,
    133
Charitable Choice, 18n1, 281n57
Charity Organization Society
    Movement, 34, 35
Christendom College, 125
Claflin College 49n16
Clarke Atlanta University, 49n16
Class divisions; in denominations, 105-
    6, 107-8; in religious orders, 104-
    5

ABOUT THE AUTHOR

Patricia Wittberg is a professor of Sociology at Indiana University-Purdue University, Indianapolis, and also a member of the Sisters of Charity of Cincinnati. She is the author of numerous books and articles on Roman Catholic religious orders and has lectured at meetings and conferences in North America, China, and Australia. She is an active member of the Society for the Scientific Study of Religion and the Association for the Sociology of Religion, and edits the *Review of Religious Research* for the Religious Research Association. Together with the Center for Applied Research in the Apostolate, she is currently compiling the second edition of a directory of new Roman Catholic religious communities in the United States.